# Political Communication In America

# Political Communication In America

## Robert E. Denton, Jr.
## Gary C. Woodward

PRAEGER SPECIAL STUDIES • PRAEGER SCIENTIFIC

New York • Philadelphia • Eastbourne, UK
Toronto • Hong Kong • Tokyo • Sydney

**Library of Congress Cataloging in Publication Data**

Denton, Robert E., Jr.
  Political communication in America.

  Includes index.
  1. Communication—Political aspects—United States.
  2. United States—Politics and government.
  I. Woodward, Gary C.   II. Title.
  JK271.D46   1985        306′.2′0973        85-3599
  ISBN 0-03-071326-9 (alk. paper)
  ISBN 0-03-071324-2 (pbk. : alk. paper)

Published in 1985 by Praeger Publishers
CBS Educational and Professional Publishing, a Division of CBS Inc.
521 Fifth Avenue, New York, NY 10175 USA

© 1985 by Praeger Publishers

Printed in the United States of America on acid-free paper

## INTERNATIONAL OFFICES

Orders from outside the United States should be sent to the appropriate address listed below. Orders from areas not listed below should be placed through CBS International Publishing, 383 Madison Ave., New York, NY 10175 USA

**Australia, New Zealand**
Holt Saunders, Pty, Ltd., 9 Waltham St., Artarmon, N.S.W. 2064, Sydney, Australia

**Canada**
Holt, Rinehart & Winston of Canada, 55 Horner Ave., Toronto, Ontario, Canada M8Z 4X6

**Europe, the Middle East, & Africa**
Holt Saunders, Ltd., 1 St. Anne's Road, Eastbourne, East Sussex, England BN21 3UN

**Japan**
Holt Saunders, Ltd., Ichibancho Central Building, 22-1 Ichibancho, 3rd Floor, Chiyodaku, Tokyo, Japan

**Hong Kong, Southeast Asia**
Holt Saunders Asia, Ltd., 10 Fl, Intercontinental Plaza, 94 Granville Road, Tsim Sha Tsui East, Kowloon, Hong Kong

Manuscript submissions should be sent to the Editorial Director, Praeger Publishers, 521 Fifth Avenue, New York, NY 10175 USA

*We dedicate this book to our families:*
*Paula and Bobby;*
*Rebecca, Trevor, and Hilary.*

# Preface

Humans are, according to Aristotle's *Politics*, "political beings" and "he who is without a polis, by reason of his own nature and not of some accident, is either a poor sort of being [a beast] or a being higher than man [a god]."[1] And because nature makes nothing in vain, Aristotle continues, a human, "alone of the animals is furnished with the faculty of language."[2] Thus, it was recognized over fifteen hundred years ago that politics and communication go hand in hand because they are essential parts of human nature. Both fields claim the subject matter of other fields as part of their own content. Nearly every topic that is fit for comment by someone contains the seeds for political and communication analysis. Neither field can claim an entire subject matter that is exclusively its own. Each necessarily crosses the boundaries and invades the terrain of fields with more neatly defined borders. Advances in medical technology, for example, can be praised or blamed by how they are described. And such descriptions usually have a significant impact on the discussions of the proper role of the state in the control of new technologies. The communication analyst is always a guest (if not an intruder) on someone else's turf. But communication is prior to all other fields of inquiry. What we know about "events" is always revealed first through the communicator's skill and art.

The focus of this study is on the roles and functions of communication in U.S. politics and not on the "politics of communication." In describing the processes common to "political communication," the priorities of the writers would be better reflected if the two terms were reversed. This book is first about the possibilities and problems inherent to public discussion in an advanced industrial society. It is to a lesser extent about political institutions, and controversial issues. Although the frameworks for our analysis utilize conventional categories of political activity—for example, activity in the Congress, the mass media, and the presidency—the essential points of our analysis hinge on what we consider to be pivotal communication processes.

We posit that the essence of politics is "talk" or human interaction. Such interaction is formal and informal, verbal and nonverbal, public and private—but always persuasive in nature causing us to interpret, to evaluate, and to act. Communication provides the basis of social cohesion, issue discussion, and legislative enactment.

As perhaps befits a work on politics, our approach has been eclectic. The point of view developed in these pages is consistently centered on the ideas common to the interactionist and dramatistic perspectives. Both now represent an important tradition in descriptive studies within the social sciences. But we are also indebted to the substantial body of survey research on political attitudes that has enriched our knowledge about the polity. Combined with these two broad academic traditions, we have built our case with a variety of firsthand sources, including private memoranda, memoirs, speeches, and journalistic accounts.

The first part of the book focuses on the variables of political communication. The chapters attempt to define political communication; to present a systematic, theoretical description of communication's role in society and politics; to investigate the use of the political consultant industry to include the activities, functions, and services they provide in the modern campaign; to identify communication activities in political campaigns; and, to explore some of the relevant perspectives, problems, and strategies unique to the communication of administrative control. The second part of the book focuses on communication within the institutions of the presidency, the Congress, and the mass media. Finally, we conclude with a discussion of communication, politics, and the public trust.

The book reflects a reality that we did not wish to gloss over in deference to the heuristic device of a "single theme." Because the subject matter of this study is necessarily broad, the work as a whole is more "horizontal" than "vertical." While the first two chapters lay useful groundwork for the latter ones, the reader can successfully read the chapters separately as well as in the sequence they are published. We made no special effort to weave an artificial thread of continuity in what is a naturally complex and variegated range of subjects.

We also resisted the temptation to give our observations and conclusions an air of finality. The reader may be surprised to see that points are argued as much as they are asserted. Many studies of political activity work from a framework of actual (or grammatically induced) certainty. Such certainty is often unjustified. We think the book speaks to a basic reality about politics that needs to be constantly acknowledged, namely, that political communication is about people making choices of indeterminate quality that will produce indeterminate effects. Of this much we are certain: no subject is more worthy of study than the communication processes which can nurture or starve a nation's civil life.

## NOTES

1. Aristotle, *The Politics of Aristotle*, trans. Ernest Barker (New York: Oxford University Press, 1970), p. 5.
2. Ibid., p. 6.

# Acknowledgments

The authors would like to thank many individuals who made them look hard at their own assumptions about the nature of political communication. Among colleagues who made our thinking over the years more precise than it would have been, we are indebted to Charles Stewart, Roderick Hart, Don Burks, Richard Crable, Trevor Melia, Harold Hogstrom, and Lloyd Bitzer.

An incalculable number of communication and political writers have also influenced our own thinking. Among those to whom we owe the greatest are Kenneth Burke, Murray Edelman, Dan Nimmo, James Combs, Richard Sennett, Todd Gitlin, Hugh Dalziel Duncan, Harry McPherson, and Doris Graber. We have borrowed and adapted material from all of them—we hope with some degree of success. But, of course, any shortcomings in our work are our own.

Although truly a joint effort, each author received help and support from individuals and institutions that deserve special recognition. Robert Denton wishes to thank Jon Powell, chairperson of the Department of Communication Studies at Northern Illinois University for his personal encouragement and departmental support in completing this project. Writing a book is a process—so is life. And in the course of writing this volume Robert's wife got pregnant. Thus, as he was attempting to give birth to this book, his wife gave birth to a son. They shared equally in both labors of love and joy.

Gary Woodward is indebted to the generous support of the Faculty and Research and Sabbatical Committee at Trenton State College for time to explore at the LBJ and JFK Libraries the subject of ghostwriting, and for a summer research stipend. He also acknowledges the help of the patient staff of the West Library at Trenton State College, and the National Endowment for the Humanities for a Summer Study Fellowship at the University of Wisconsin.

# Contents

# I

# The Variables of
# Political Communication

# 1

# Political Communication Defined

Within the life of the generation now in control of affairs, persuasion has become a self-conscious art and a regular organ of popular government. None of us begins to understand the consequences, but it is no daring prophecy to say that the knowledge of how to create consent will alter every political calculation and modify every political premise.[1]

## WIN: A CASE OF FAILED POLITICAL COMMUNICATION

Gerald Ford assumed the presidency in 1973 under well-known and extraordinary circumstances. The taint of political corruption pervaded Washington. Richard Nixon had abdicated the office in disgrace. The nation had witnessed evidence that indicated a White House cover-up was executed to protect the burglars at the Democratic Party headquarters at Watergate. What began as a half-hearted attempt to purloin Democratic Party files had snowballed into a scandal that eventually destroyed a carefully constructed political empire.

Watergate added to widespread public discontent that had actually begun two years earlier with the resignation of Vice-President Spiro Agnew. For a time Agnew presented himself as the enactment of the American dream. He was the progeny of industrious immigrants, and a symbol of the success that can come to an aggressive and honest civil servant. Unfortunately Nixon's choice was apparently more hardworking than honest. Although Agnew had made something of a career as a stump orator who wanted to get tough on lawbreakers, he was charged with accepting illegal kickbacks from contractors while gov-

3

ernor of Maryland. He resigned the vice-presidency after pleading "no contest" to charges of public misconduct.

Against this backdrop of high-level malfeasance, the task facing Nixon's second choice was enormous and obvious. He had to restore faith in the integrity of the presidency, and faith in the ability of the chief executive to place the interests of the nation higher than the urge for self-preservation.

The turmoil of the last months of the Nixon administration created other problems as well. The most pressing need was for federal action to stem the rate of inflation. Economic planning came to a virtual standstill while the Nixon administration unraveled in continuous preoccupation with its own survival. In 1974 prices and wages were increasing at an annual rate of nearly 17 percent. This increase was far too high to produce stable growth, creating uncertainties and pressures on wages and prices. Ford had to do something. Acting in response to vocal expressions of concern from the Congress, and from the members of an economic summit called with the blessing of the White House, he decided to engage in a major campaign to awaken the nation to the dangers represented by rising prices. It was important for the White House to not allow others to seize the initiative, particularly on an issue that had been traditionally at the heart of the Republican political agenda.

The campaign was to end in failure a few short months later.

Ford initially decided to go on the rhetorical offensive by using several well-publicized speeches. His goal was to urge action to control inflation, and to assert his own authority as the newest (and unelected) president. His first major effort was before a joint session of the Congress. It was a nationally televised speech making the case that "we must whip inflation now."[2] It was followed a week later with a second televised address detailing the ways the average American might help reduce inflation. Even an advertising agency, Benton and Bowles from New York, had been enlisted to contribute to the effort: the predictable result of the wary marriage between politics and the merchandizers of the advertising world.[3] The highly publicized plans called for a voluntary grass roots mobilization against inflation. Its symbol was the acronym for "whip inflation now." WIN buttons and banners were produced and readied for mass distribution. Industries were enlisted to help publicize the still unformed program.

The first speech initiating the campaign was an attempt at national mobilization. Urging more private-sector jobs, cuts in wasteful government programs, less federal regulation of business, more productivity, and less dependence on foreign oil, Ford requested a broad range of actions from Congress. The bigger thrust of the program, however, was to be based in the voluntary compliance from the American people. The program's urgency was to be generated not by executive acts, but in a rhetorical campaign that was to be initiated by the president, and then carried to the grass roots by labor and business groups. In his televised address to Congress Ford noted:

> There will be no big Federal bureaucracy set up for this crash program. Through the courtesy of such volunteers from the communication and media fields, a very simple enlistment form will appear in many of tomorrow's newspapers along with the symbol of this new mobilization, which I am wearing on my lapel. It bears the single word WIN. I think that tells it all.

And then Ford added, with perhaps more candor than he intended:

> Many Presidents have come here many times to solicit, to scold, to flatter, to exhort the Congress to support them in their leadership. Once in a great while, Presidents have stood here and truly inspired the most skeptical and the most sophisticated audience of their co-equal partnership in government. Perhaps once or twice in a generation is there such a joint session. I don't expect this one to be.
>
> But I say to you with all sincerity that our inflation, our public enemy number one, will, unless whipped, destroy our country, our homes, our liberties, our property, and finally our national pride, as surely as any well-armed wartime enemy.[4]

With echoes back to the various war mobilization efforts under Franklin Roosevelt, Ford promised that his next speech would specify "how volunteer inflation fighters and energy savers can further mobilize their total efforts."[5]

That second address was to come on October 15, before an audience of 13,000 people attending a convention meeting of the Future Farmers of America. As with the first speech, the White House requested full network television coverage. But the broadcasting giants initially declined, sensing that there was little news value in yet another recital of the familiar problems that come with high inflation. Only insistent pressure from the Ford staff forced the three networks to relent into a second clearance of time.[6] After the Nixon years, network executives were beginning to resent demands to replace the lucrative prime-time schedule with presidential addresses. Most felt that presidential requests for television coverage were based in objectives that were more cosmetic than substantive.

This address became known among insiders who worked on it as the "lick your plate clean" speech.[7] It proved to be the beginning of the end for the voluntary inflation campaign. "It may not have been news," journalist Richard Reeves recalls, "but it certainly was entertaining."[8] The message turned out to be a litany of what can only be described as corny and painfully simplistic suggestions on how to cut waste on the job and in the household. Whatever entertainment value it had for hardened Washington journalists was unintentional. With a WIN button firmly implanted in his lapel, the president enthusiastically suggested remedies for an economy caught in both a recession and incessant wage and price increases:

> The American people, I can report tonight, have responded magnificently. A great citizen's mobilization has begun and is beginning to roll. It is already evident here in this eager, up-beat convention of Future Farmers of America, and I thank you from the bottom of my heart.[9]

After citing some of the recommendations sent to the Congress, Ford plunged into a lengthy and broad recital of written suggestions that had ostensibly come from ordinary citizens around the country:

> Robert Steward writes from Waverly, Tennessee, that he has a heart condition, unfortunately, and draws a pension of only $251.28 a month. This allows him just two meals a day. "But thank God we are not on welfare," says Mr. Steward. He asks me, and again I quote: cut our government spending except for national defense. Again, I think his example is a good one for all of us to observe.[10]

These few homespun suggestions were only the start. As he worked his way through them Ford visibly warmed to the task of "whipping inflation" by passing along hints for running a thrifty household:

> From Hillsboro, Oregon, the Stevens family writes they are fixing up their bikes to do the family errands. They are also using fewer electrical appliances, turning the thermostat down, and the lights off. Bob Cantrell, a 14-year-old in Pasadena California gave up his stereo to save energy. Bob urges the initiation of high school courses that teach students how to conserve energy. He adds, and I quote: if a kid nags his parents to conserve energy long enough it will help.[11]

To successful "energy efficient" and "inflation fighting" communities the president promised WIN flags. Local municipalities were urged to set up WIN committees. No recommendation was too small for a presidential endorsement:

One friend told me we could probably whip—just understand this—whip inflation with the contents of our trash cans. In your own home, let me make a simple suggestion. Just take one hour to make a trash inventory.[12]

Obviously, something was missing in these statements. Suggestions for better management of life's little domestic problems are not representative of the kinds of utterances that inspire the building of presidential legends. The nation's political cartoonists had a field day sketching the leader of the Western world as a penny-pinching miser. Ford's concerns, however sincere, were measured against the normally majestic presidential ethos. In his best moments Lincoln had reshaped the political landscape of the entire nation, setting up a true federal republic. Theodore Roosevelt had staked out a philosophy for an "American Century" that would affect most of the world's populations. Ford, in contrast, seemed to describe big problems while at the same time offering small solutions. On this particular initiative his indiscriminate enthusiasm contributed to the doomed effort. How ever well intentioned his attempt, it was widely perceived as hopelessly inadequate in the face of long-term economic changes. He had saddled himself with the presidential equivalent of a Mr. Goodwrench, offering abundant reassurance, but very little substance. He became the victim of a transparent public relations hype that ultimately made him seem weaker for not exercising the full extent of his presidential authority. If Richard Nixon exploited and misused the considerable powers of the presidency, Ford appeared to underutilize them.

The final blow to the effort came less than three months later, when the whole project was suddenly abandoned. White House advisers recommended new remedies based on different information about the economy's weaknesses. It turned out that the existence of a serious recession made economic stimulation rather than control the primary economic objective. In simple terms, the WIN campaign was based on the need to save rather than the need to spend. As Ford recalls it, "Instead of asking Congress for a tax increase, as I had on October 8, I would have to plead for a tax cut. The WIN portion of the program would also have to be scrapped. I didn't mind abandoning the symbol, which was probably too gimmicky."[13]

He was equally candid in recalling the press criticisms that followed the two inflation speeches:

The *Wall Street Journal* called my proposals "neither surprising nor bold." The *New York Times*, in a series of editorials, was even more critical. "The overall impact of Mr. Ford's speech was weak, flaccid and disappointing. While some of his measures are good and some are questionable, they in no sense add up to a program for an emergency."[14]

A deeper problem, however, was recognized by Ford speechwriter Robert Hartmann. By demanding national television time for speeches with too many ideas, and by allowing himself to assert more than he could personally deliver, he "made WIN a conspicuous symbol of his leadership."[15] To even the most casual observer the whole effort appeared to represent the degeneration of presidential politics, rather than the exercise of decisive leadership. The much publicized "war" on inflation seemed to be fought with the rhetorical equivalent of a toy pistol. As one critic concluded:

> If the situation was as serious as Ford proclaimed, why was not more risked? If the situation was as serious as Ford's metaphor proclaimed, then the metaphor, the instrument of definition, was inaccurate and inappropriate to the economic reality, causing one to wonder what reality it did describe. . . . [W]hen he chose the war metaphor the substance of the figure demanded much substantive action.[16]

## GENERAL CHARACTERISTICS OF POLITICAL COMMUNICATION

Even though its failure was painfully conspicuous, the WIN campaign remains as a useful representation of several fundamental traits of political address. In a number of basic ways it shares the same elements found in messages delivered on the floors of state assemblies, from the hustings in a mayoral campaign, in the comments of countless state or federal political lieutenants, and in the posturing that precedes an election or a key legislative vote. To be sure, the elements we discuss in this book are not exclusive to political messages, but are frequent companions to them.

### Short-term Goals

Perhaps the most common feature of political address is the existence of set and limited time frames. Messages are typically planned, prepared, and delivered with an eye on short-term goals and deadlines. They must enter the continuous flow of public discussion within a period that is beneficial to the communicator, and timely for the mass media and the audiences that must be reached. Gerald Ford seized the topic of inflation when public concern created a naturally receptive environment. He was in danger of being upstaged by his own White House task force. Most political communication benefits from a "window of opportunity" that can pass as quickly as it appears. Waiting any longer might have risked the impression that he lacked a decisive will to act, or that he was insensitive to the economic dislocations created by an overheated economy.

## Communication Based on Objectives

What such communication is typically not about is talk for its own sake. Behind virtually every political message is at least one specific goal, an intention to use discussion as an instrument for power or leadership. Political behavior is almost always directed to some specific end, even when it seems to take on the appearance of predictable ritual. For example, what is overlooked in the common complaint that political talk is a meaningless substitute for political action is the important fact that it often intended to increase the prospects of the talker, the agent for the ideas. As in the WIN campaign, if the appearance was of a rhetorical patch up of a serious economic problem, the benefits of such an effort were still surely tangible to the White House. The sheer act of talking about inflation and its remedies had its advantages. Concern had to be expressed by the president when it was clear that public awareness for the problem demanded an administration response.

## Importance of the Mass Media

The mass media are basic to the study of politics. No claim about the conduct of modern political life seems more self-evident. Speeches, press conferences, pleas for support, justifications of controversial decisions all imply the presence of constituencies—audiences for those acts. Those audiences are frequently only reached by the extended coverage provided by public media. Political reporting is dedicated—in philosophy if not always in practice—to a watchdog role over those public officials who are clearly within their own sphere of influence. In the familiar terms of this philosophy, the free press performs an adversary function that provides a check, a fourth branch of government, to keep a wary eye on the other three. "The only security of all," said Jefferson, "is in a free press."[1][7] This role is an obvious and largely undisputed objective of the political press in America. And yet for all of its familiarity, the norm of a constitutionally protected independent press is perhaps the greatest single contribution America has made to the lore of democracy. Many other nations honor similar ideals, but few have so successfully acted upon them.

But the mass media function in an important second way, a way that reverses the familiar reporter-subject relationship. In forms that are detailed more fully elsewhere in these pages (see, for example, Chapters 6 and 9), the political press controls as well as reports. Given the protected status of the press, which evolved particularly in the 1900s, journalists were able to grasp considerable power to lead rather than just follow the course of an unfolding political story. In ways an Eastern European or Soviet politician perhaps could not grasp, modern American politics requires the ability to respond to an agenda of issues and events created in America's newsrooms. The newsmaker initiates many stories, but their control and management is clearly shared. The public's perception of politics is a result of a complex sequence of interactions between political professionals on one hand, and the demands made by the news media to attract and hold audiences.

When Theodore Roosevelt denounced the "muckracking press" just after the turn of the century, he was not paying a compliment to the new investigative muscle of the Randolph Hearsts or Ida Tarbells. He was making what has since become a familiar complaint based on the realization that the public media placed their own demands on those engaged in political discourse. Like nearly all politicians before and since, he savored the attentions of the press, but not their explicit demands for greater public accountability. In exchange for the importance conferred by the reporting of political news, the mass media are now frequently more insistent in demanding accountability than the constituencies that supposedly produced an electoral mandate. Gerald Ford's lament over the way the *New York Times* and *Wall Street Journal* described his WIN program is recognition of the fact that highly visible politicians are at best only co-equals as shapers of American public opinion.

### Short-term Orientation

All of this readily points to another key fact about modern political communication; namely, that it is almost always concerned with transitory and short-term phenomena. Because they involve discussions of decisions that touch the day-to-day lives of ordinary people, political messages are obviously not the kind of cultural artifacts that talk to the ages. Political communicators seek practical and immediate effects. Like Ford's quick reversal on WIN, when mere days required a new approach, there may be little sense that an important rhetorical legacy has been abandoned. If the fast-paced world of instantaneous communication and overnight crises tells us anything, it is that one must be prepared to accept political rhetoric that must change to serve altered realities.

Most casual observers note that the rhetorical grace of Lincoln, Wilson, or Kennedy seems unduplicated in the modern presidential speeches of Gerald Ford or Ronald Reagan. To be sure, nothing appears as mundane and as limited in vision as Ford's hints-from-Heloise approach to reducing inflation, or Jimmy Carter's similar dramatic but unsustained campaign on energy conservation in 1977. Even Abraham Lincoln's speeches from the Senate campaign of 1858 will appear to the reader as dated: intended for a different age with vastly different values and needs.

But it is largely uninstructive to expect that political communication will display the enduring qualities we expect from other facets of communication, such as the film or the novel. Indeed, this perspective puts the modern public figure in what is sometimes an impossible dilemma. The politician who seems rigid in the face of new realities often seems too ideological. On the other hand, the public figure caught in a shift to new ground is often criticized for rudderless and hypocritical beliefs. The more appropriate attitude toward political communication requires a willingness to reconstruct the immediate political context—the relevant climate of opinion—that the political communicator felt duty-bound to honor. While it may be the case that serious novels with aesthetic pretenses may permit measurement against timeless standards, serious attempts to shape opinion on public policy rarely profit from the same firm types of critical certainty. Indeed, the effectiveness of most political discourse hinges on the degree to which the planning that goes into it takes into account the transient nature of public opinion and the fleeting attention of the mass media.

## The Importance of Considering Audiences

As a common activity, political discourse is thus distinctly audience-centered. We assume that the verbal behavior of politicians and other political actors is propelled by the desire to gain the identification and support of specific constituencies. The arts of compromise, creative adaptation, emphasis, de-emphasis, and simplification are all very much a part of the process. Rather than lamenting the avenues for blatant manipulation that are implicit in such a point of view, we prefer to think of an audience-centered activity as wholly natural and often democratic. There can be no doubt that politics offers the potential for pandering to the lowest of human impulses. But the price we pay for an open political system is the risk that there will be excesses. At their best, democratic societies are strengthened by exchanges between those in a position of authority, and by citizens and the press with countervailing rights to revoke it. The audience-centered approach properly forces the analyst to think in the terms of the processes that govern the search for a consensus, or to its unmaking. We think the danger lies not in the manipulation of audience allegiances to political ideas, but in the society that lessens the prospects for the articulation of such ideas, or gives only lip service to the rhetorical rights of the politically active.

Generally, then, we conceive of political communication as a practical, process-centered, decision-oriented activity. Because it is dependent on the approval of specific audiences, its utility is strongly restricted by time, and by the willingness of the political media to make its messages accessible. We have necessarily cast our net quite broadly. It includes speeches and addresses, whether heard first hand or reported in highly edited segments. It also includes many other forms of public discussion: reports, public letters, defenses of administrative action or inaction, hearings, mediated accounts of events from the press, and even ostensibly nonpolitical messages such as films and entertainment-oriented television. Ultimately, a crucial factor that makes communication political is not the source of a message, but its content and purpose.

## POLITICAL COMMUNICATION DEFINED

### The Mistaken Use of Scientific Accuracy as a Goal for Political Communication

There is something inescapably seductive about describing political communication so that it is nearly synonymous with obfuscation. Normally astute and thoughtful writers are frequently tempted to characterize it in terms of the abuse it gives to some set notion of the Truth. This tendency is based in part on what we think is the mistaken assumption that political address is primarily about discovering "the right" answer. If an observer believes that one side in a debate has the correct answer, the only possible way to explain the other side is in terms of their obfuscating of ideas. George Orwell's widely admired description of political address is evidence of this tendency:

In our time, political speech and writing are largely the defense of the indefensible. Things like the continuance of British rule in India, the Russian purges and deportations, the dropping of the atom bombs on Japan, can indeed, be defended, but only by arguments which are too brutal for most people to face, and which do not square with the professed aims of political parties. Thus political language has to consist largely of euphemism, question-begging and sheer cloudy vagueness.[18]

In a recent study devoted to *Political Language and Rhetoric* Paul Corcoran provides a similar expression of dissolutionment that functions implicitly as a kind of operational definition:

Contemporary political language . . . has assumed a peculiar and in some sense an inverted social function as a technique of linguistic expression. This is borne out in the uses to which political language is often put: not to convey information, but to conceal or distort it; not to draw public attention, but to divert or suppress it. In short, contemporary political language may play precisely the reverse role from that classically conceived for political rhetoric. Instead of a rhetorical "method" to inform, persuade and enlighten, contemporary political language aims at an etiolated monologue which has no content, which placates, and which bears no relationship to the organization, coherency and clarification of information and ideas.[19]

These descriptions render political communications deficient by definition. The only task that remains for the analyst is to point out the irrationality and imprecise nature of such discourse. And that is a much easier task than pointing out how it works: how audiences are affected, converts are made, and opponents are treated. The counterpart definition for another subject—architecture, for example—might be to label it as the "design and building of what are largely inadequate and deficient structures by people intent on profiting at the expense of others." To be sure, architects can and do build structures poorly, and for the wrong reasons. But the essence of architecture, like the essence of political communication, involves more.

The problem, of course, is that negative definitions masquerade judgments as descriptions, indicting general processes by inviting consideration of examples intended to stand for the whole. If one dislikes a policy, the easiest way to attack it is to dismiss the general category of communication used to defend it. Most of us are wary of the capricious and ever-shifting grounds of political discourse. It is easier to dismiss its alien and varied forms than to understand it.

This debate over the nature of practical persuasion is far from new. Aristotle's own seminal discussion of the topic in *The Rhetoric* was a rejection of low priority to which his own teacher, Plato, had relegated it. Plato craved certainty and exactitude from human institutions. Science and rationality might permit such closed systems, but audience-centered politics could not. Aristotle noted that the arts of rhetoric were like many other skills that can be used for evil or beneficial purposes: "A man can confer the greatest benefits by a right use of these, and inflict the greatest of injuries by using them wrongly."[20]

The fundamental problem with most efforts to come to terms with the nature of political communication is that we often impose inappropriate scientific and rationalistic models on it. But discussions of social policy are not primarily scientific. They cannot be. Their essence is not to be found in truth-telling, but in consensus-seeking. Most policy discussions are more about values and shared attitudes than about facts. Even so insightful a political analyst as Walter Lippmann at times succumbed to the temptation to find a scientific basis for a "public philosophy." Like Plato, it was his belief that discourse devoid of self-interest could produce a kind of total agreement on many political questions. He wrote—overoptimistically, we think—that "All issues could be settled by scientific investigation and by free debate if—but only if—all the investigators and debaters adhered to the public philosophy; if, that is to say, they used the same criteria and rules of reason for arriving at the truth and for distinguishing good and evil."[21]

Lippmann's conditions are too stringent. It is probably unrealistic to base an understanding of political debate on the *hope* that there can be a kind of universal standard from which to measure its validity. On most political questions (for example, questions involving choices with competing advantages to different constituencies) the Truth is not easily located. Political conflict typically concerns itself with decisions implying priorities or preferences rather than determinations of fact. Policy debates, for example, are rarely settled with appeals to the facts, even though there may indeed be relevant facts that will or should inform the debate. The bulk of most political discourse is centered on the engineering of consensus: a process that involves rationality and fact-finding, but frequently denies a superior point of view. It is primarily a process that works by using existing beliefs and attitudes to build agreements.

As long as policy lies at the heart of politics, values will have to be discussed rather than precisely reckoned. Values admit to no one standard for judgment. As Lloyd Bitzer has written:

The fact that human valuation interacts with contingent subject matter helps explain why political rhetoric must ever remain unscientific—that is, why it will refuse to be held to statements of the true-false variety. Values and interests will exert such force that persons contending in the same context and about the same subject will disagree in what they perceive and say, a political speaker will be inconsistent from one situation to another, and the perceived truth of political discourse will vary markedly across contexts.[22]

We share what seems to be the enlightened distinction made by Chaim Perelman between arguments of all forms that "demonstrate" and those that "argue." The former tend to be analytic, arbitrary, and a priori: as in the synthetic formulas of physics and mathematics where the same conclusions are generated by a wide diversity of individuals. A true demonstration provides no reasonable intellectual basis for dissent. On the other hand arguments—the ever-present products of what may be legitimate differences of opinion—exist in the realm of preferences.[23] Political conflict is legitimate when it originates in the innate pluralism of thought. A position in a political dispute is necessarily a combination of the individual's own intellectual and social history, and the history of the group that he or she seeks to influence. There clearly are moral, logical, and evidentiary bases for arbitrating disputes. Facts, evidence, sources with high or low credibility, should encourage some conclusions and discourage others. But to start from the premise that political address is a form of obfuscation because it fails to tally with some a priori standard is to force a subject into alien territory. Such a perspective carries a reassuring certainty, but it fails to provide the tools that are necessary to discover the processes of public decision making.

## The Three Concerns of Political Communication

At base, democratic politics is concerned with the power to decide. Everyday political acts function to influence decisions or defend them. The public communication that accompanies most forms of political activity serves to alter, justify, or clarify the range of choices that are in dispute in the public arena. The more open the society and the more active the political press, the better the chances that rhetorical disputes will be productive vehicles for governance.

In concise terms we define political communication as *public discussion about the allocation of public resources (money), official authority (who decides), and official sanctions (what is to be rewarded or punished*). Such discourse makes its way into the life of the nation, state, or community when there is conflict between competing interests about what the official position of the state shall be, and when such conflict finds a public voice. At best, the language of political communication is a valuable mediating agent that replaces sheer violent conflict, and makes orderly change possible. It serves to prepare the way for eventual compromise and acceptance by making arguments, facts, and opinions a part of the public record on an issue. But it is also the language of the faction, of the "friend" and the "foe."[24] It may sharpen differences beyond the point of repair, or it may dull them. It can be a vehicle to mask what should be highlighted, or it may actually repair what has been deeply divisive. One can express optimism for its ability to transform the society for the better; but one can also despair for its widespread abuse. It may be therapeutic, divisive, alienating, inspiring, or informational. And it may be all of these at once to various opposed factions.

### Revenue

Discussions on the allocation of scarce resources are common. The funding of social programs, assignment or removal of administrative staffs, whether to build a local baseball field or repair decaying roads, whether to permit federal funding of abortions for poor women, or the leasing of federal lands to oil speculators, all only hint at the broad range of resource-based debates that reach Americans daily. The much vaunted cliché that politics is about the exercise and control of power finds its best examples in discourse involving the power to spend. Not all questions require the use of public funds, but the exceptions are rare. What is more certain is that the spending of money will produce organized advocacy and opposition. As every city mayor knows, the demands placed on political institutions will almost automatically exceed available revenues.

### Control

The question of who decides is the focus of the political campaign. In all levels of government public officials are given the power to act as trustees of the public interest. The heart of the myth of republican democracy resides in the assignment of power based upon the consent of the governed. Direct democracy predicated on direct popular decision making remains as more of an ideal than a reality. The much romanticized town meeting and periodic bursts of publicity about state or local direct referenda should not obscure how thoroughly professionalized American politics has become in the last quarter century. Fewer public servants are elected. Increasingly, complex bureaucracies and civil service systems have replaced the citizen-politician. Decreasing numbers of employees in the public sector are accountable through the electoral process. Even so, the chain of responsibility ends most dramatically with the elected leader. He or she is at least nominally accountable for the massive professional government that itself can never be voted in or out of office.

## Sanctions

A final class of political discussion is concerned with the ongoing debate that accompanies administrative decisions and controversial legislative issues. These disputes typically involve the assignment of sanctions: public expressions of approval or disapproval for a course of action, and for its advocates. These discussions are not necessarily in the control of politicians. Many are, but many also originate among members of the small minority that makes up the interested public on any one question. Whether to punish an errant foreign regime, whether to close a local school, and countless other policies with large or small consequences become subjects of public debate. And in such debates there is often a concerted effort to assign blame or honor to those who are felt to be responsible. The importance of single-issue interest groups—churches, academics, business leaders, and even Hollywood celebrities—cannot be overlooked as potential contributors. A discussion may be on the deployment of new deadly weapons systems in a foreign locale, or only on the possible reclassification of a protected bird sanctuary. The agenda is set in accordance with how well the political establishment responsible for official approval of the decision can justify its acts, and how public opinion is orchestrated by opposing factions—press, interest groups, opposing political leaders. Such rhetoric, then, is concerned with the focusing of interest on the wisdom or failures of a public policy, and frequently on the wisdom of its advocates and detractors as well. On occasion it may also be the stuff of high political drama, because deep conflict about how the state and its resources are aligned involves the highest of stakes.

## The Manifest and Latent Functions of Political Discourse

Modern studies of communication fall generally into two broad approaches. The older and broader tradition is to examine and judge messages largely in light of their publicly stated purposes. These purposes involve the formal and official functions of communication. Our definition of political communication cited above fits into this general pattern. To use the pivotal terms provided by sociologist Robert Merton,[25] the manifest functions of communication are objectives that are intended to achieve clearly understood ends. Individuals publicly express their intentions to exert influence, to promote understanding, to educate, and to reinforce. Political communication promotes understanding about pending questions. Studies of national figures written by rhetorical critics and political journalists largely operate at this level, though the best are not naive about the subtle latent purposes to which an artful political defense can be put.

The newer tradition owes its origins to the social sciences, and to the strong analytical motive to discount public actions in favor of private or unconscious motives. This pattern did not originate with Sigmund Freud, but it perhaps received its most forceful perspective in the Freudian notion that human expression is a product of the mediation between an instilled sense of public duty and ego-defensive impulses.[26] What we say is a combination of divergent impulses. We speak to serve ideas, and honorable civic goals. But it is also now an unshakable article of faith that we seek to nurture a public regard for our fragile inner selves.

The edifice of the modern behavioral sciences is built upon this premise. Human behavior with apparently simple motivations signifies infinitely more complex latent objectives: based in the psyche and its inner logic—a *psycho-logic* —rather than on the idealized rhetorical logic of the public forum.[27] For example, Harold Lasswell's *Power and Personality* starts with the hypothesis that an individual's psychology governs his fundamental political choices. The "power seeker," he notes, "pursues power as a means of compensation against deprivation. Power is expected to overcome low estimates of the self. ..."[28]

The explanation that follows may be not intended to excuse the political actor from responsibility for the choices that are made. But when the analyst is primed for the discovery of latent causes and effects, he may refuse to entertain the possibility that a public figure engaged in the process of seeking consensus is able to rise above personal inadequacies. One such case may be Freud's and William Bullitt's excessively psychoanalytic study of Woodrow Wilson, which has the effect of reducing the former president to a one-dimensional caricature whose every decision was apparently the product of earlier discontents.[29]

To say that most accounts of political communication today focus on latent functions and subtle effects is to restate the obvious. Political language naturally invites consideration of the private investments, the personal and group needs, that are served under the benign symbolism of the public interest. Some of the most penetrating analyses in recent years have explored relationships between personal motives and public rhetoric, or between groups separated and protected by hierarchical distinctions.[30] To a great extent, the study of public rhetoric has been revolutionized in the last two decades by the search for ideological motives underpinning justifications that present themselves as something quite different. Following the lead of Karl Marx, Kenneth Burke especially influenced a wide range of political communication scholars in the search for doctrinal "investments" in all sorts of public discourse.[31]

Our position, however, cannot be reduced to only one approach. Political communication demands analysis and criticism in terms of its own widely accepted goals. But to go no further, not to look beyond the contents of specific messages taken at face value, denies valuable insights about the complex social and psychological processes that contribute to political discourse. We therefore reject a focus that is exclusively technique-centered, focused only on calculations and manipulations leading to a political decision. And we equally reject a purely product-centered view that overlooks personal and institutional influences. It is both a challenge and a source of frustration that even so simple an act of communication as a campaign speech cannot be reduced to a single invariant system of analysis. We believe that the eclecticism that exists in a well-rounded study of political communication has an important role. It should fill the enormous gaps of knowledge left between the time journalists have finished their immediate assessments, and history has had its final say.

Our perspective thus suggests that a good deal more could be asked about the WIN campaign than was perhaps initially apparent. For example, why was such a visible rhetorical campaign developed around a policy that was still in a great deal of flux? Why was the president so indifferent to the risk of subjecting the considerable prestige of the presidency to so ephemeral an effort? Does the campaign itself offer insights into the way Gerald Ford perceived his public role? Was the decision to accept the contrived solutions of an advertising agency well advised? These questions all seek to explore the dimensions of the decision to seize the initiative for a voluntary program for the control of inflation. Many others could be considered from the point of view of the intended audiences. For instance, do the expectations that Americans carry about presidents include a receptivity to old-fashioned advice-giving? Is moderately high inflation an issue that can be made salient for a significant percentage of Americans? And, if so, which groups within the society are best able to control the news agenda and thereby shape public opinion on topics as complex as economic policies?

All of these questions center on the subject matter of this book. Our goal in these pages is to consider a wide range of concerns, including the ever-shifting relationships that exist between political agents and their inherited roles, their strategists, and their publics. Our pragmatism leads us to measure political messages and media against the honored goals assigned to that of debate and discussion in an open society. But it also encourages us to consider the many subtle social functions that political communication performs in the public life of a nation.

## NOTES

1. Walter Lippmann, *Public Opinion* (New York: Macmillan, 1930), p. 248.

2. Gerald Ford, Address to a Joint Session of the Congress on the Economy, October 8, 1974, in *Public Papers of the Presidents, 1974*, August 9 to December 31, 1974 (Washington: U.S. Printing Office, 1975), p. 229.

3. Richard Reeves, *A Ford, Not a Lincoln* (New York: Harcourt Brace Jovanovich, 1975), pp. 159-64.

4. Ford, Address to Congress, October 8, p. 238.

5. Ibid.

6. Ron Nessen, *It Sure Looks Different From the Inside* (Chicago: Playboy Press, 1978), pp. 75-76.

7. Gerald R. Ford, *A Time to Heal* (New York: Harper and Row and Reader's Digest, 1979), p. 195.

8. Reeves, *A Ford, Not a Lincoln*, p. 161.

9. Gerald Ford, Remarks to the Annual Convention of the Future Farmers of America, Kansas City, Missouri, October 15, 1974, in *Public Papers of the Presidents*, August 9 to December 31, 1974, (Washington: U.S. Printing Office, 1975), p. 304.

10. Ibid., p. 307.

11. Ibid., p. 308.

12. Ibid., p. 310.

13. Ford, *A Time to Heal*, p. 204.

14. Ibid., p. 195.

15. Robert T. Hartmann, *Palace Politics: An Inside Account of the Ford Years* (New York: McGraw-Hill, 1980), p. 300.

16. Hermann G. Stelzner, "Ford's War on Inflation: A Metaphor That Did Not Cross," *Communication Monographs* 44 (November 1977): 296.

17. Quoted in Douglass Cater, *The Fourth Branch of Government* (New York: Vintage, 1959), p. 75.

18. George Orwell, "Politics and the English Language," in *The Orwell Reader* (New York: Harcourt, Brace, 1949), p. 363.

19. Paul E. Corcoran, *Political Language and Rhetoric* (Austin, Texas: University of Texas, 1979), p. xv.

20. Aristotle, *The Rhetoric*, Bk. I, 1355b.

21. Walter Lippmann, *The Public Philosophy* (Boston: Little, Brown, 1955), p. 134.

22. Lloyd Bitzer, "Political Rhetoric," in *Handbook of Political Communication*, ed. Dan D. Nimmo and Keith R. Sanders (Beverly Hills, Calif.: Sage, 1981), p. 233. The same point has also been made by John Bunzel in *Anti-Politics in America* (New York: Vintage, 1970). He notes that the "essence of the political . . . situation is that someone is trying to do something about which there is no agreement. He is trying to use some form of government as a means to advance and protect his interest. In other words, politics arises out of disagreement. For politics to exist there must be disagreement over what to do about the particular problem. Where there is perfect agreement, there is no politics." (p. 7)

23. Chaim Perelman and L. Olbrechts-Tyteca, *The New Rhetoric*, trans. John Wilkinson and Purcell Weaver (Notre Dame: University of Notre Dame Press, 1969), pp. 509-14.

24. Carl Schmitt, *The Concept of the Political*, trans. George Schwab (New Brunswick, N.J.: Rutgers University, 1976), p. 37.

25. The terms were used in a similar sense by Freud. Merton, however, gave them a sociological context. See Robert Merton, *Social Theory and Social Structure*, 1968 enlarged ed. (New York: Free Press, 1968), pp. 73-138.

26. See, for example, Sigmund Freud, *A General Introduction to Psychoanalysis*, trans. Joan Riviere (Garden City, N.Y.: Garden City Publishing, 1938), pp. 102-50.

27. For a critique of the "discounting" of manifest content in favor of latent content see Benjamin De Mott, "The Little Red Discount House" in *Critical Responses to Kenneth Burke*, ed. William H. Rueckert (Minneapolis, Minn.: University of Minnesota, 1969), pp. 349-57.

28. Harold D. Lasswell, *Power and Personality* (New York: Viking, 1962), p. 39.

29. Sigmund Freud and William C. Bullitt, *Thomas Woodrow Wilson* (Boston: Houghton Mifflin, 1967).

30. Many are cited throughout this book, including Murray Edelman, *The Symbolic Uses of Politics* (Urbana, Ill.: University of Illinois, 1967); Claus Mueller, *The Politics of Communication* (New York: Oxford University, 1973); Hugh Dalziel Duncan, *Communication and Social Order* (New York: Oxford University, 1962); Dan Nimmo and James E. Combs, *Mediated Political Realities* (New York: Longman, 1983); and David L. Patetz and Robert M. Entman, *Media Power Politics* (New York: Free Press, 1981).

31. Perhaps Burke's most influential book in this area has been *A Rhetoric of Motives* (New York: Prentice-Hall, 1953), Part II.

# 2

# Politics, Communication, and Society

And however important to us is the tiny sliver of reality each of us has experienced firsthand, the whole overall "picture" is but a construct of our symbol systems.[1]

Is government a set of laws, people, institutions, or specific functions? Is government the White House, Capitol Hill, Supreme Court, or local town halls? Is politics a social activity, a method of power, a process of government, or a hobby of the idle rich? These questions illuminate the abstract and pervasive nature of the concepts of government and politics. But most books on government and politics focus on specific institutions and functions. Yet government and politics are more than any building, statute, individual, or campaign. Rather, they involve many elements of a process that influences the beliefs, attitudes, values, and behavior of people. Macroscopic analyses are needed which focus on the interrelationship between society and government. From this perspective the concepts of government and politics encompass more than the end products or outputs of a system. Rather, the acts of government and politics are reciprocal, processual, dramatic, purposeful, and pervasive in nature.

"Politics," according to Dan Nimmo, "extends to any activity that regulates human conduct sufficiently to ensure that other, nonpolitical activities continue."[2] For him, the purpose of political talk is to "preserve other talk" and thus "the words of politics consist of far more than those listed in any dictionary."[3] Likewise, the functions of any government, democratic or otherwise, encompass more than regulating behavior through the formulation of laws. Gabriel Almond asserts that the main functions of government include: political social-ization and recruitment, interest articulation, the aggregation of in-terests, political communication, role-making, rule application, and rule adjudication.[4] These functions are of a quality nature and demon-strate that specific laws are of lesser importance than trust and confi-dence in the viability of a system of government.

## SOCIETY AS SYMBOLIC INTERACTION

### The Concept of Interaction

At the heart of this perspective of government and politics is the notion of interaction. Interaction is not so much a concept as an orientation for viewing human behavior and, ultimately, society. Through interaction, people are continually undergoing change and consequently, society is also continually changing through interaction. Interaction is a process involving acting, perceiving, interpreting, and acting again. This interaction among people gives rise to reality which is largely symbolic. Thus, it is through symbolic interaction with others that meaning is given to the world and creates the reality toward which persons act.

Interaction, as a concept, is not limited to spoken and written language. Objects may exist in physical form but they are identified, isolated, catalogued, interpreted, and given meaning through social interaction. Thus, artifacts and objects should be viewed as social objects. For the peasant, a rake is a gardening tool as well as a weapon for revolution. Such a transformation results from social interaction. Objects take on meaning for individuals as they interact with others.

Interaction, as a concept, is also not limited to the notion of self-development. Interaction is the very fabric of society. Human society should be viewed as consisting of people in interaction. Robert Lauer and Warren Handel observe that "when two people interact, each influences the behavior of the other, and each directs one's own be-havior on the basis of the other's behavior towards oneself."[5] Be-havior, then, is created by interaction rather than simply occurring during interaction. Human behavior is as much a function of interac-tion as a consequence of qualities individuals bring into an interaction.

Individuals, of course, interact within larger networks of other individuals and groups. Although many of society's networks are far removed from individuals, the impact of such networks may be con-siderable. Social networks, formal or informal, provide a framework within which social action takes place. Thus, the networks are not determinants of action. Even structural aspects of society, such as social roles or class, should be viewed as setting conditions for behavior and interaction rather than as causing specific behavior or interaction.

Interaction, therefore, is at the core of human existence. The self arises in interaction; symbols and language are defined in interaction; social networks and societies are formed through interaction; world views arise in interaction; and social objects are defined in interaction.

## Symbols

It is impossible to talk of human interaction without addressing the symbolic nature of man. Distinctively human behavior and interaction are carried on through the medium of symbols and their attached meanings. The human being is a symbolic creature. Despite the growing research with primates, sympathy exists for the view that what distinguishes humans from lower animals is their ability to function in a symbolic environment. Man alone can create, manipulate, and use symbols to control his own behavior as well as the behavior of others. All animals communicate. However, humans are uniquely symbolic.

"An object," according to Herbert Blumer, "is anything that can be indicated, anything that is pointed to or referred to."[6] There are three general categories of objects: physical, social, and abstract. Physical objects refer to concrete objects such as tables, chairs, desks, trees, houses, etc. Social objects are generally people or positions occupied by people. This category includes students, teachers, parents, mayor, president, etc. Abstract objects are moral principles, ideas, or philosophical doctrines such as love, justice, freedom, or democracy. Each of these categories of objects has a symbolic dimension or may become a symbol. What an object is depends upon the meaning it has for an individual. The meaning will dictate how the individual sees the object, acts toward the object, and talks about the object. The Democrat or Republican Party will be addressed differently depending upon whether the person favors one party or the other and the degree of involvement with a political party. Common objects result from a process of mutual indications or being seen in the same manner by a given set of people. For Blumer, "human group life is a process in which objects are being created, affirmed, transformed, and cast aside. The life and action of people necessarily change in line with the changes taking place in their world of objects."[7]

George Herbert Mead defined symbols in terms of meaning. A system of symbols "is the means whereby individuals can indicate to one another what their responses to objects will be and hence what the meanings of objects are."[8] The human, as a cognitive creature, functions in a context of shared meanings which are communicated through language (which is itself a group of shared meanings or symbols). Symbols, therefore, are more than a part of a language system. Joel Charon defines a symbol as "any object, mode of conduct, or word toward which we act as if it were something else. Whatever the symbol stands for constitutes its meanings."[9] This definition by Charon has important implications for individual action as well as for the nature of society.

We posit that nearly all human action is symbolic. Human action in all its forms, represents something more than what is immediately perceived. Symbols form the very basis of our overt behavior. Human action is the by-product of the stimulus of symbols. Before a response to any situation can be formulated, the situation must be defined and interpreted to ensure an appropriate response to the situation. Symbols, then, are the foundation of social life as well as of human civilization. Meanings for symbols derive from interaction in rather specific social contexts. New interaction experiences may result in new symbols or new meanings for old symbols which may, consequently, change one's understanding or perception of the world. Our view of the world alters and changes as our symbol system is modified through interaction. This process suggests that our reality is made up of symbolic systems.

## Social Reality

Simply stated, reality is a social product arising from interaction or communication. Reality for everyone, therefore, is limited, specific, and circumscribed. Of course, communication can be used to extend or limit "realities." To discover our own reality or that of someone else, we must first understand the symbol system and then the meanings the symbols have for all concerned. Mutual understanding and subsequent action is accomplished through communication or interaction.

Reality for people has three dimensions: "the outside world (for example, knowledge), an inner private world, and a shared symbolic world of beliefs, experiences, and meanings generated and maintained through communication."[10] Reality, then, results from the sharing of experiences with others through symbol systems. It is very important to recognize that the construction of reality is indeed an active process. It involves recognition, isolation, definition, interpretation, action, and validation through interaction. Communication becomes the vehicle for the creation of society, culture, rules, regulations, behavior, etc. From such a change of actions grows a complex and constantly changing matrix of rather specific and varied individual as well as societal expectations.

The capacity to learn culture (or the process of socialization) enables people to understand one another and at the same time creates behavioral expectations. Consequently, we are in a continual state of orienting our behavior to that of others.

### Society

Historically, there have been two dominant approaches to the study of society. These approaches, however, are too deterministic for our purposes. The sociological approach emphasizes structure. Behavior results from factors such as status position, cultural prescriptions, norms, values, social sanctions, role demands, and general system requirements. These factors are viewed as causation for behavior while ignoring social interaction which influences the factors. Similarly, the psychological approach emphasizes such factors as motives, attitudes, hidden complexes, and general psychological processes. These factors also attempt to account for behavior while ignoring the effects of social interaction. Thus, rather than focusing on causative factors, the psychological approach focuses on the behavior such factors produce.

As we have already noted, social interaction is of vital importance. Social interaction, as viewed by Blumer, "is a process that forms human conduct instead of being merely a means or a setting for the expression or release of human conduct."[11] Therefore, we emphasize the dynamic, changing nature of society. Individuals are constantly interacting, developing, and shaping society. People exist in action and consequently must be viewed in terms of action. To analyze human society, the starting point must be an analysis of human beings who are engaging in action. Society, then, may be defined as individuals in interaction, individuals acting in relation to each other, individuals engaging in cooperative action, and people communicating with self and others. From this definition we may succinctly state that people "make" society and society "makes" people.

This position rejects the notion that human society is simply an expression of preestablished forms of joint action. New situations are constantly arising requiring modification or reinforcement of existing rules of society. Even "old" joint action arises out of a background of previous actions of the participants. Participants of any action bring unique "worlds of objects," "sets of meanings," and "schemes of interpretation." In this way all joint action is "new" resulting from interaction although, indeed, from a familiar pattern of action.

Mead identified two levels of social interaction in human society.[12] The most simple level of social interaction he called "the conversation of gestures." This form is nonsymbolic interaction which occurs when one responds directly to the action of another without any interpretation of the action. The use of significant symbols, however, involves the interpretation of an action. Nonsymbolic interaction, then, is really reflex responses whereas symbolic interaction demands, in addition to some response, recognition and interpretation. To demonstrate how subtle these may be Blumer illustrates by discussing the responses of a boxer.[13] When a boxer automatically raises his arms to counter a blow from an opponent, the boxer is engaged in nonsymbolic interaction. If, however, the boxer identifies and interprets the blow from his opponent as a feint to trap him, symbolic interaction has occurred.

This distinction has several implications for viewing the nature of society. Society is people acting toward one another and engaging in social interaction. The interaction is largely on the symbolic level. Group life involves defining what others do, interpreting such definitions, and, consequently, fitting one's activities to those of others.

As already noted, self-control is inseparable from social control. The notion of free will is restricted and limited by the culture of an individual. The interrelationship between social control and self-control is the result of commitment to various groups that produce a self-fulfillment, self-expression, and self-identity. Lindsmith, Strauss, and Denzin argue that there are three forms of group commitment.[14] Instrumental commitment emphasizes material benefits. One's occupational membership is an example. An emotional commitment emphasizes the personal attachment among group members. Such a commitment is best illustrated as that between a husband and a wife. Finally, a moral commitment results from identification of self to the values or principles of a specific group. Social control is not, therefore, a matter of formal government agencies, laws, rules, and regulations. Rather, social control is a direct result of citizens identifying and internalizing the values of a group so that the values become essential to their own self-esteem and thus act so as to support the social order. Adherence to the rules of society becomes a fair price to pay for membership in the society.

Dan Faules and Dennis Alexander define regulation as "symbolic processes that induce change or maintain stability in self and others.[15] Of course language provides the major framework dictating ways of thinking and seeing society. Language is certainly more than the vehicle of thought. Rather, language is the thought. There are, however, many types or forms of symbols. Symbols may regulate behavior by: creating expectations, producing negative bias, or by subordinating other considerations by allowing a norm or value to supercede other symbols.[16] In addition to creating expectations of behavior, symbols create social sanctions (i.e., war as God's will) or function as master symbols (i.e., to die for freedom).

Social organization is merely a frame within which identifiable units develop their actions. Structural features of society set conditions for action but in no way determine action.

## CREATION OF POLITICAL REALITY IN SOCIETY

When considering politics, it becomes necessary to link the functions and characteristics of government to the general nature of society. Richard Rose identifies four criteria that gauge the impact of governmental actions upon the fabric of society.[17] The first criterion to consider is the scope of a government activity. How many individuals of the population are affected by the action? The second criterion is the intensity of the impact of the government's action. How much importance is attached to the action by the general public? Third, the frequency of impact of governmental decisions is important. Here, the key question becomes how often or how long are people affected by the governmental action? Finally, probability is the last criterion. How likely is it that a person will be affected by a governmental policy or action? These criteria gauge the magnitude of influence of government over society.

Mass support for any individual, institution, or system of government is not automatic. Societal support is a long, continual, and active process. The greatest task confronting any government, collectively defined, is to generate enough support for governmental authority and action to meet the needs of all segments of society. David Easton defines political legitimacy as "the conviction on the part of the [citizen] that is *right* and *proper* for him to accept and obey the authorities and to abide by the requirements of the regime."[18] Legitimacy, according to Easton, is a two-way proposition. It is desirable for citizens because it sustains political order, stability, and consequently minimizes stressful changes and surprises. A sense of legitimacy is advantageous for authorities because it becomes the most significant device for regulating the flow of diffuse support.[19]

The remainder of this chapter focuses on the interaction of politics broadly defined and society. Such interaction clearly influences societal behavior. And behavior is grounded in the process of examination and deliberation of a situation. An individual's response in any particular situation is really a function of how they define the situation rather than how the situation is objectively presented.[20] Thus, by understanding the creation of reality (or meaning) of a situation for individuals we may better understand the behavior of individuals in a situation or society. We are especially interested in ways politics affects behavior by defining and controlling societal situations and social settings. One can view political influences upon societal behavior by noticing the manipulation of campaign settings, leadership impressions, political symbols, and the resulting manifestation of social order.

## Political Settings

A political setting, as defined by Murray Edelman, is "whatever is background and remains over a period of time, limiting perception and response. It is more than land, buildings, and physical props. It includes any assumptions about basic causation or motivation that are generally accepted."[21] The setting, then, creates the perspective from which mass audiences will analyze a situation, define their response, and establish the emotional context of the act that enfolds. Political actors must carefully assess the situation, calculate the appropriate action, and identify the proper roles to assume. Settings, therefore, condition political acts.

Implicit in the discussion is the need for government or leaders to create appropriate political settings which legitimize a set of values. The assumption is that control over the behavior of others is primarily achieved by influencing the definition of the situation. In a democracy, the secret is to act in such a way that creates an image of the actor or scene that stimulates others to act voluntarily as desired. As early as 1928, W. I. Thomas wrote, "If men define situations as real, they are real in their consequences."[22] Getting others to share one's reality is the first step toward getting others to act in a prescribed manner. This is best achieved by creating or defining reality for others. In turn, the use of potent symbols, rituals, and myths is useful in creating commonalities in the midst of national diversity. The interrelationship of these factors is succinctly described by Nimmo:

> By inducing people to respond in certain ways, to play specific roles toward government, and to change their thoughts, feelings, and expectations, significant political symbols facilitate the formation of public opinion. As significant symbols of political talk, the words, pictures, and acts of political communicators are tipoffs to people that they can expect fellow citizens to respond to symbols in certain anticipated ways.[23]

The entire process, however, yields more than desired behavior. Soon, the process becomes a commitment and total belief in the institutions and system of government.

If settings and situations are created, the next question becomes, How are settings constructed? In properly answering this question, one must consider the role of language, symbols, myths, and rituals. Such considerations are necessary in understanding how the impact of government transcends individual influence to societal influence. Although political symbols, myths, rituals, and talk are all rather commonplace, their implications upon behavior are significant although subtle.

## The Role of Language

Socialization depends upon language and is key in the process of creating a political system's claim in legitimacy. Language, as the means of passing cultural and political values, provides a group or individual a means of identification with a specific culture, values, or political entity. As people assess their environment, language is created which structures, transforms, or destroys the environment. Words are the molds for concepts and thoughts and become symbols reflecting beliefs and values. Thus, the creation of language, or symbol systems, is required before societies can develop as well as political cultures. Language serves as the agent of social integration; as the means of cultural socialization; as the vehicle for social interaction; as the channel for the transmission of values; and as the glue that bonds men, ideas, and society together.

Language, therefore, is a very active and creative process which does not reflect an objective reality but creates a reality by organizing meaningful perceptions abstracted from a complex world. Language becomes a mediating force that actively shapes one's interpretation of the environment. "Metaphorically, language and the words embedded in it," according to Claus Mueller, "are posed between the individual and his environment and serve as an invisible filter. The individual attains a certain degree of understanding through the classification made possible by concepts that screen and structure perception."[24]

## Political Language

Political consciousness is dependent upon language, for language can determine the way in which people relate to their environment.[25] At the very least, language should be viewed as the medium for the generation and perpetuation of politically significant symbols. Political consciousness, therefore, results from a largely symbolic interpretation of sociopolitical experience. To control, manipulate, or structure the interpretation is a primary goal of politics in general. The language of government, in many ways, is the dissemination of illusion and ambiguity.[26] A successful politician will use rather specific linguistic devices that reinforce popular beliefs, attitudes, and values. Politically manipulated language can, therefore, promote and reinforce the existing political regime or order.

From this brief discussion, it is clear that what makes language political is not the particular vocabulary or linguistic form but the substance of the information the language conveys, the setting in which the interaction occurs, and the explicit or implicit functions the language performs. As Doris Graber observes, "When political actors, in and out of government communicate about political matters, for political purposes, they are using political language."[27]

Graber identifies five major functions of political language: information dissemination, agenda-setting, interpretation and linkage, projection for the future and the past, and action stimulation.[28] It is useful to briefly discuss each of these functions. However, several aspects of these functions are discussed in greater detail in other chapters.

There are many ways information is shared with the public in political messages. The most obvious, of course, is the sharing of explicit information about the state of the policy. Such dissemination of information is vital to the public's understanding and support of the political system. This is especially true in democratic nations where the public expects open access to the instruments and decision making of government officials. But the public, being sensitized to uses of language, can obtain information by what *is not* stated, *how* something is stated, or *when* something is stated. Often times, especially in messages between nations, the public must read between the lines of official statements to ascertain proper meanings and significance of statements. Such inferences are useful in gauging security, flexibility, and sincerity. Sometimes the connotations of the words used communicate more truth than the actual statements. Are our relations with the Soviet Union open, guarded, or friendly? There are times, especially in tragedy, that the very act of speaking by an official can communicate support, sympathy, or strength. Thus, the act of speaking rather than the words spoken conveys the meaning of the rhetorical event.

The very topics chosen by politicians to discuss channels the public's attention and focuses issues to be discussed. The agenda-setting function of political language primarily occurs in two ways. First, before "something" can become an issue, some prominent politician must articulate a problem and hence bring the issue to public attention. The issue can be rather obvious (poverty), in need of highlighting (status of American education), or created (the Great Society). A major way political language establishes the national agenda is by controlling the information disseminated to the general public. Within this realm there is always a great deal of competition. There are a limited number of issues that can effectively maintain public interest and attention. While certain self-serving topics are favored by a person, party, faction, or group, the same topics may be perceived as meaningless or even harmful to other factions, persons, or groups. While President Nixon wanted to limit discussion and public attention to the Watergate break-ins and tapes, rival groups wanted public debates and revelations to continue.

The very act of calling the public's attention to a certain issue defines, interprets, and manipulates the public's perception of an issue. Causal explanations are often freely given. Such explanations may be suspect. Control over the definitions of a situation is essential in creating and preserving political realities. Participants in election primaries, for example, all proclaim victory regardless of the number of votes received. The top vote-getter becomes the *front runner*. The second-place winner becomes *the underdog* candidate in an *up-hill battle*. The third-place candidate becomes a *credible* candidate and alternative for those *frustrated* or *dissatisfied* with the *same old party favorites*. Political language defines and interprets reality as well as provides a rationale for future collective action.

A great deal of political rhetoric and language deals with predicting the future and reflecting upon the past. Candidates present idealized futures under their leadership and predictions of success if their policies are followed. Some predictions and projections are formalized as party platforms or major addresses as inaugurals or state of the unions. Nearly all such statements involve promises—promises of a brighter future if followed or Armageddon if rejected. Past memories and associations are evoked to stimulate a sense of security, better times, and romantic longings. An important function of political language, therefore, is to link us to past glories and reveal the future in order to reduce uncertainty in a world of ever-increasing complexity and doubt.

Finally, and perhaps most importantly, political language must function to mobilize society and stimulate social action. Language serves as the stimulus, means, or rationale for social action. Words can evoke, persuade, implore, command, label, praise, and condemn. Political language is similar to other uses of language. But it also articulates, shapes, and stimulates public discussion and behavior about the allocation of public resources, authority, and sanctions.

Before discussing specific aspects of language usage, it is useful to identify Edelman's four distinctive governmental language styles.[29] They include: hortatory, legal, administrative, and bargaining styles. Hortatory language is the style most directed toward the mass public. It is employed by individuals and contains the most overt appeals for candidate and policy support. Consequently, the most sacred of national symbols and values are evoked. Legal language encompasses laws, constitutions, treaties, statutes, contracts, etc. Legal language is very formal. For most citizens, such language is often confusing and intimidating. Because of the ambiguity of the language style, lawyers and judges have a political as well as social function. Legal language compels argument and interpretation. Administrative language is certainly related to legal language. The style usually encourages suspicion and ridicule by the public. Interestingly, administrative language, in its attempts to be clear and concise, is often as confusing to the public as legal language. Bargaining language style "offers a deal, not an appeal" and is acknowledged as the real catalyst of policy formation. Yet, public reaction or response politically is avoided. Once a bargain is created, the rationalization of the bargain often assumes the hortatory language style.

It is important to note that these language styles are content-free. In addition, the styles are not limited to certain individuals or government agencies. For example, a president must utilize the linguistic devices in the bargaining style to win congressional approval of favorite legislation; the legal style to draft special legislation; administrative style for enforcing or providing the mechanics for operationalizing the legislation; and the hortatory style in attempting to gain public support for a measure. Each style creates a different reality and subsequent behavior. The realities of crisis, confidence, patriotism, and action may all be created to achieve the final goal. For the basic assumption, according to Edelman, is that the public "responds to currently conspicuous political symbols; not to 'facts', and not to moral codes embedded in the character or soul, but to the gestures and speeches that make up the drama of the states."[30] The task remains to investigate the types of political symbols and their impact upon societal behavior.

## Political Symbols

We have already argued that humans live in a symbolic environment. Our "significant symbols" arise through the process of social interaction. A significant symbol, defined by Mead, is one that leads to the same response in another person that it calls forth in the thinker. Thus, significant symbols are those with a shared, common meaning by a group. Consequently, a political vocabulary of significant symbols may evolve which provides common understandings among individuals. Significant symbols are socially constructed and provide common references for people to engage in more interaction to help solve the problems of the group life.

As a group, there are three ways an individual may respond or relate to a significant symbol. First, there is a content or informational dimension. The content dimension, although debatable, is rather easy to pinpoint and define. Facts can, of course, be manipulated but are rather readily recognizable. There is, second, an affective or emotional dimension to a symbol. Such responses are less predictable and result from years of cultural socialization. Politically, the trick is to use symbols where the affective responses are rather predictable. Finally, there is an evaluative dimension reflecting the importance of the symbol. Each of these dimensions is defined through interaction and hence becomes a rather potent motivator for action.

There is a large number of significant political symbols in society. They have evolved, according to Dan Nimmo, in five ways.[31] From "authority talk" arise laws, constitutions, treaties, etc., which often sanction specific political orientations. "Power talk" usually creates symbols dealing with international politics. Detente, cold war, or national self-determination are such significant symbols. In contrast, "influence talk" provides the domestic creation of significant symbols arising from such sources as party platforms, slogans, speeches, or newspaper editorials. Often, "complex issues," when condensed into a single term or phrase, become a powerful political symbol. Such symbols include: busing, gun control, abortion, capital punishment, law and order, or civil rights. Finally, significant symbols arise from the "types of objects symbolized" such as democracy or Old Glory. This characterization emphasizes the dynamic, evolving, and emerging nature of significant, natural political symbols. Their origins are from many sources but through interaction they become recognized and significant.

Roger Cobb and Charles Elder provide a hierarchical typology of political symbols which is also most useful.[32] They identify four types of stimulus objects as the universe of political symbols. At the top of the hierarchy are symbols of the political community comprising the community's core values. Old Glory, democracy, equality, liberty, and justice fall within this category. The next type of political symbols is regime symbols or those relating to political norms of the society. These include such concepts as due process, equal opportunity, or free enterprise. Third in the typology are symbols associated with formal political roles and institutions such as the president, Congress, or FBI. The last type, situational symbols, is comprised of three components. These components include: governmental authorities (Reagan, Burger, etc.), nongovernmental authorities (Ralph Nader, Common Cause, etc.), and political issues (inflation, gun control, etc.). Those symbols high in the typology are the most abstract and general, whereas those in the lower divisions are more specific in nature. Thus, the abstract political symbols are more encompassing, applicable, salient, and less temporally specific. Although the typology is clear, the response to the symbols may not be as clear cut. On the informational level, the same information may be gleaned from the more specific symbols but certainly debatable for those higher in the typology. The affective nature of all the symbol types depends upon the rather unique experiences, culture, and socialization of an individual or group. The same is true for the evaluative dimension. The point is, hopefully, obvious. The classification of a symbol without the appreciation of the social construction and interaction aspects of symbol making is limited in utility.

The next logical consideration is how are symbols used to structure reality and thus to motivate behavior? For Nimmo, governmental groups and individuals use political symbols to "assure people that problems are solved even if current policies actually achieve relatively little" and to "arouse and mobilize support for action."[33] The use of euphemism, puffery, and metaphor are vital in creating a sense of assurance. During the Ford administration, the word *detente* was avoided because it had become associated with a controversial policy. Carter consistently referred to the Iranian students as *terrorists* in their takeover of the American embassy and Reagan called the Soviet pilot who shot down a Korean airliner a *murderer*. Such uses define the situation and communicate aspects of the informational, affective, and evaluative dimensions of an event. Puffery attempts to exaggerate or to overstate matters of subjective experience. Especially in election years, every issue is of the "gravest importance to the future of our country." Metaphor, as a language device, is useful for explaining the unfamiliar by associating it with something more immediate, clear, or known. A "war on poverty" or a "war on crime" reveals a degree of seriousness, priority, and intensity. Simply labeling a problem a "crisis" often mobilizes support. Appeals to the "national good" and "self-sacrifice" induce cooperation and support which may restrain free choice. Myth and ritual, which will be viewed later, are potent language forms in arousing public action. Each of these uses of symbols influences individual and group behavior. These influences are conveyed through interaction, molded in language, and are more pervasive than any legal power granted in the Constitution.

How do political symbols work? It is their abstract semantic hollowness that makes symbols so powerful. Although political symbols function as objects of common identification, they simultaneously allow for idiosyncratic meanings to be attacked. Two individuals may disfavor abortion but do so based upon religious or constitutional arguments. The same individuals may disagree about abortion for rape victims but clearly support congressional or presidential action disavowing the practice of abortion. Political symbols are powerful not because of the broad commonalities of shared meaning but because of the intense sentiments created and attached to them resulting in the perception that the symbols are vital to the system. As elements of the political culture, political symbols serve as stimuli for political action. They serve as a link between mass political behavior and individual political behavior. Political symbols, then, are vital to the functioning of both the individual and society.

## THE POTENCY OF POLITICAL SYMBOLS

There are three aspects of political language and symbols that endow them with emphasis and power.[34] The content or subject matter of political discourse deals with issues and concerns of the general public. Whether the issue is local in nature or national in scope, the subject matter of political discourse affects large numbers of people. There is no such thing as a neutral political issue. The second consideration is that the communicators involved in political discourse are often perceived of as powerful and important individuals. This fact impacts in two ways. First, as highly visible actors, the arguments and messages will gain public attention. Because of their role and status, their credibility may not be questioned and facts are accepted as truth. Second, most political officials have easy access to the means of mass communication. In addition, they have access to privileged information. Thus, political actors have resources that aid in evoking and stimulating national debate and issue considerations. Somewhat related to the preceding point, the impact of political discourse is enhanced by the means of dissemination. Use of mass media possesses unique attributes that can increase impact and influence.

There are aspects, however, unique to symbols that endow them with power whether political or not. Myth, ritual, and ideology are three such symbolic forms. They are especially valuable in arousing public action.

### Myth

Myth bridges the old and the new. Myth is composed of images from the past that help us cope and understand the present. Myth functions to reduce the complexity of the world identifying causes that are simple and remedies that are apparent. "In place of a complicated empirical world," Edelman observes, "men hold to a relatively few, simple, archetypal myths, of which the conspiratorial enemy and omnicompetent here-savior are the central ones."[35] Virtually all of our political behavior lies in the realm of myth. For James Barber, myth is the essence of human politics. Barber writes:

> The pulse of politics is a mythic pulse. Political life shares in the national mythology, grows in the wider culture, draws its strength from the human passion for discovering, in our short span of life on this peripheral planet, the drama of human significance. Ours is a story-making civilization; we are a race of incorrigible narrators. The hunger to transform experience into meaning through story spurs the political imagination.[36]

Politics, then, relies upon a multitude of images constructed over time comprised of various values, prejudices, facts, and fiction.

Nimmo and Combs provide four views or orientations to social myths.[37] Each view shares insight into the social construction of myths. The "common sense" view of myths perceives them as simple distorted beliefs based more upon emotion than fact. Myths are dangerous, therefore, because of their falsification of truth. The "timeless truth" view of myths, in contrast, argues that what is important is the fact that people believe the myths. Thus, the issue of accuracy is not important. Myths must be dealt with as true because they are believed to be true by the general public. The "hidden meanings" view of myths is a compromise of the other two. Here, all myths are believed to contain some element of truth of moral principle. Consequently, all myths are grounded in truth. Finally, the "symbolic" view of myths defines myths as "collective representations" of society's beliefs, values, ideologies, cultures, and doctrines. "Myths symbolize codes of approved beliefs, values, and behavior and thus function to legitimize authority."[38] Each of these approaches to myths emphasizes the dynamic and utility aspects of myths. They are constructed through social interpretations of the past and become predictions of the future.

The word *myth* comes from the Greek word *mythos* meaning "a tale uttered by the mouth" and was generally associated with religious ceremony.[39] Even from the earliest usage of the word, myth had a dramatic quality. Today, however, most people associate myth with illusion and refuse to acknowledge the social utility of myths. We prefer Nimmo and Combs' definition of myth as

> a credible, dramatic, socially constructed representation of perceived realities that people accept as permanent, fixed knowledge of reality while forgetting (if they were even aware of it) its tentative, imaginative, created, and perhaps fictional qualities.[40]

This definition satisfies our concerns and acknowledges the dramatic nature of myths.

There are several different types of political myths.[41] One type of political myth, master myths, is national in scope and encompass the collective consciousness of a society. These myths are usually utopian in nature. One such prevailing myth in America is the myth of the American dream. We believe that if we work hard, there is no limit to our capacity for success. Such a myth serves to motivate individuals and reinforce societal values. Another prevalent form of political myth in America is myths of "us and them." These myths focus on social structures or collectivities. Specific groups, movements, and governmental institutions encourage myth development in order to generate credibility, to enlist support, and to sustain existence. The myth of American democracy and free enterprise reduces the complexity of our systems of government and economy to rather abstract notions. We all know that our government is a form of democracy and our economy is a variation of free enterprise. Nevertheless, the myths serve to legitimize the governmental institutions. Definitional myths are useful in another way as well. In addition to defining what is preferred, good, and proper, myths can also define what is bad, unjust, and evil. The notions of communism and socialism are fraught with criticism while most of Europe has been more socialistic than democratic for many years. In defining, myths sanction and reinforce societal values. In contrast to "us and them" myths, "heroic" myths focus on individuals. Humans need heroes for motivation and emulation. To state that George Washington, our founding father, never told a lie not only adds esteem for the individual but also espouses the virtue of honesty for the citizenry. Finally, an increasing category of political myths are pseudo myths. They are myths in the making. Most politicians, especially during elections, are attempting to be perceived as "heroic underdogs," the "common man," or the "new maverick." Messages are created and disseminated by the candidate to reinforce desired images. The mass media, which will be investigated in Chapter 6, plays an important role in the development of pseudo myths.

Within the realm of politics, there are four basic uses of myths.[42] First, and perhaps the most obvious function, myths increase public comprehension and understanding of rather complex notions, theories, or structures. Second, myths function to unite a society and to create common bonds among the populace. Myths can reinforce and articulate common elements within a diversity of social mores. The careful construction of political myths can prescribe proper and legitimate public beliefs, attitudes, values, and behavior. Third, political myths offer unique identities for the citizens. They provide the link between the individual and the polity. Although broad in nature, myths become personalized and the views or morals expressed are internalized. Finally, myths are persuasive. Myths can legitimize, stimulate, and motivate behavior. They can sustain commitments to a specific polity. Thus, whether long-term or short-term impact, myths affect behavior and are persuasive in nature.

Political myths, in summary, are socially conceived, created, permeated, and structured entities and are real. Because they are real, political myths are credible and pragmatic. And because they are socially constructed, political myths are dramatic, involving a story, actors, and morals. The importance of this notion will be discussed later.

### Ritual

Ritual, in many ways, functions in the same way as does myth. Ritual may be defined as "a motor activity that involves its participants symbolically in a common enterprise, calling their attention to their relatedness and joint interests in a compelling way."[43] Ritual is the bridge between individuality and society. It functions as a leveler providing instant commonality. By allowing one to become a part of a larger entity, ritual promotes conformity in a rather satisfying way. Rituals, as myths, unite people. Rituals also have special significance or meaning that when performed can evoke and reinforce a certain value, belief, attitude, or desired behavior. Rituals, therefore, are pragmatic, dramatic, and symbolic in nature. They can be manipulated as well as myths. Both are highly symbolic.

### Ideology

Ideology is a "symbolic belief system" that functions to "turn listeners into believers and believers into actors."[44] Richard Brooks defines ideology as "any set of beliefs about appropriate ways of acting toward the political institution which have been saliently incorporated into the individual's view of himself."[45] From this perspective ideology is more than a set of political norms. Rather, ideology is linked to an individual's perception of political reality. Ideologies are socially constructed and are in a continual process of definition and interpretation. For the individual, internalizing an ideology requires a continual assessment of political acts based upon norms or values that become a permanent motivation for political action. America, however, is generally characterized as being less ideological than most nations. Our political system focuses on specific issues and personalities rather than political parties and abstract ideologies. Nevertheless, to accept an ideology implies a commitment toward a specific social reality. On a larger scale, the commitment toward an ideology links one to a community of believers who largely share the same interpretation of the world. Thus, such a commonality of viewing reality provides a strong rationale for specific societal behavior or action.

By briefly discussing myth, ritual, and ideology, aspects of the unique nature of political symbols are well illustrated. First, political reality is socially constructed and created through the use of political symbols. There is a participant dimension to political discourse. Second, political symbols are pragmatic in nature. No matter how abstract the idea or concept, the evoking of political symbols affects behavior. Political discourse is persuasive, pervasive, and influences beliefs, attitudes, and values. Finally, because political discourse and symbols are pragmatic, they are also dramatic. This means that nearly all political discourse seeks to construct a certain reality. Of course, there is usually a great deal of competition in constructing realities. This dramatistic orientation to politics is rather unique and requires further explanation.

## A DRAMATISTIC ORIENTATION TO POLITICS

Dramatism, created and developed by Kenneth Burke, is grounded in the symbolic nature of man. Burke argues that as a symbol-using animal, one must stress symbolism as a motive in any discussion of social behavior. By 1968, dramatism was promoted to equal status with "symbolic interaction" and "social exchange" as being one of three areas of "interaction" discussed in the *International Encyclopedia of the Social Sciences.*[46] In that article, Burke summarizes dramatism as

> a method of analysis and a corresponding critique of terminology designed to show that the most direct route to the study of human relations and human motives is via a methodical inquiry into cycles or clusters of terms and their functions.[47]

He calls his method dramatism ". . . since it invites one to consider the matter of motives in a perspective that, being developed from the analysis of drama, treats language and thought primarily as modes of action."[48]

Thus, at the heart of dramatism is action. For dramatism is a heuristic for the analysis of human action.[49] An "act" is a "terministic center" from which many related influences and considerations derive.[50] Daily actions constitute dramas with created and attached significance. For Burke, drama serves as an analytic model of the social world. As Burke explains:

> Though drama is a mode of "symbolic action" so designed that an audience might be induced to "act symbolically" in sympathy with it, insofar as the drama serves this function it may be studied as a "perfect mechanism" composed of parts moving in perfect adjustment to one another like clockwork.[51]

American politics is not a discrete, identifiable phenomenon. Our political process is one of transformation from societal order (the prevailing hierarchy, beliefs, attitudes, and values); division (redefinition of societal attitudes, values, goals, and cessation of identification with the prevailing hierarchy); action (symbolic behavior of articulating grievances, altering perceptions of society, providing courses of action); drama (symbolic acts, events, episodes); conflict (separation, confrontation, violence, tragedy); victimage (identification of the causes of societal evil, conflict, and violence that must be destroyed); transcendence (the purging and removal of social ills while establishing new levels of social identification, cooperation, and unity); redemption (forgiveness of social sins); and order (hierarchy and societal values accepted, sanctioned, and legitimized). Of course, where one phase ends and another begins is often difficult to isolate.

As already noted, leaders and superiors must create and use symbols that unite and transcend individual and collective differences. "The legitimation of authority," argues Hugh Duncan, "is based on persuasion."[52] Leaders, in their struggle for power and attempts to stay in power, must provide integrative symbols for the masses to transcend the ambiguities and conflicts of heroes and villains; of loyalty and disloyalty; of concern and indifference; of confidence and fear; of obedience and disobedience; of hierarchy and anarchy; of peace and violence. On the side of order are notions of faith and reason. Faith is expressed by accepting the authority of others as legitimate. Reason is expressed by the acceptance of authority based upon the quality of performance and positive impact upon the quality of life. On the side of disorder are the temptations of emotions and prevalence of imagination. Emotions are articulated through dramatic actions, issues, and statements. Imagination creates a new order, governmental system, and social utopia. In simple terms, therefore, when division in society is so great that symbols no longer possess common meanings, people will turn to leaders who will create new symbols. When symbols can no longer transcend differences among people, conflict can only be solved through violence.

Burke states that there are four basic motives arising in human communication: hierarchy, guilt, victimage, and redemption.[53] For him, these motives are revealed in observing human relationships and encompass all human motivation. These terms also very nicely describe the process of birth, maturation, and ending of political campaigns and movements. Hierarchy, as addressed earlier, stems from human desire of order. Rejection of the established hierarchy, however, produces a sense of guilt. This guilt is relieved through victimage or the sacrifice of a scapegoat that epitomizes the evils of society. In primitive societies, purification came from sacrificing animals to a god. In sophisticated and complex societies of today, however, purification comes from endowing a person, government, idea, or practice with social evils that dictate removal. Removal can range from redefinition to murder. Scapegoats become the sacrificial animal upon whose back is ritualistically placed all the real or perceived evils.

Redemption follows victimage. Order is restored. Evil is defeated. Sins are forgiven. Mystification returns promoting social cohesion. Symbol-users transcend the mysteries of class. The world is redefined. New attitudes and values are tested and legitimized primarily in the symbolic realm.

## Sociodramas

Because many aspects of our political process are difficult to isolate, individual episodes or sociodramas can be investigated. Wherever there is action, there is drama. For Duncan, "failure to understand the power of dramatic form in communication means failure in seizing and controlling power over men."[54] It is important to remember that sociodramas are not just symbolic screens or metaphors but they are social reality because they are forms of social interaction and integration.

To analyze a sociodrama one needs to identify some act or action. To focus on dramas of authority one should ask: Under what conditions is the act being presented? What kind of act is it? What roles are the actors assuming? What forms of authority are being communicated? What means of communication are used? What symbols of authority are evoked? How are social functions staged? How are social functions communicated? How are the messages received? What are the responses to authority messages?

The scope of a social drama is prescribed by the investigator. The drama can involve one person or many; a symbolic (rhetorical) event or physical act; one moment or a specific period of time. Sociodramas are the acts and scenes that comprise our lives. Individual photographs capture moments and evoke reflection, memories, analysis, and emotions of joy or sadness. Taken together and shown sequentially the snapshots produce movement, action, and behavior. Although drama can be analyzed frame by frame it is essentially a composite of individual acts.

Politics, in Burkean terms, is a study of drama composed of many acts. They are acts of hierarchy, transformation, transcendence, guilt, victimage, redemption, and salvation. With act as the pivotal concept, Burke suggests that we investigate scenes that encompass and surround the act, for the scene provides the context for an act. Next, he suggests that we consider the agents involved in an act; the actors who mold, shape, create, and sustain movements. Likewise, consideration of the agency or the channels of communication in an act help reveal the impact of rhetorical activities. And consideration of purpose of an act aids in discovering the ultimate motives or meaning of the act.

Drama is part of the communication process where public issues and views are created, shared, and given life. Ernest Bormann calls this process "group fantasy."[55] A relatively small number of people may attach significance to some term or concept such as the notions of justice, freedom, or the American dream. These fantasies are shared and passed on to others. Fantasies are contained in messages that channel through the mass media to the general public. When a fantasy theme has "chained through the general public," there emerges a "rhetorical vision." "A rhetorical vision is a symbolic reality created by a number of fantasy types and it provides a coherent view of some public problem or issue."[56] Slogans or labels that address a cluster of meanings, motives, or emotional responses usually indicate the emergence of a rhetorical vision.

There are several useful implications to the notion of fantasy themes. As a result of creating and sharing fantasies, there is a greater sense of community, cohesiveness, and shared culture. "They have some common heroes and villains; they have sympathized and identified with dramatic characters in suspenseful situations; they have come to share the attitudes implied by the theories."[57] There are, then, common beliefs, attitudes, and values upon which to live and act. And communication is the foundation of it all.

## THE MANAGEMENT OF IMPRESSIONS

Although this chapter is largely theoretical in attempting to describe the nature and importance of communication in political and social life, we must, nevertheless, address the notion of political manipulation of symbolic reality. Can the creation and manipulation of significant political symbols affect beliefs, attitudes, or values? The apparent answer to this question is yes. To argue that political behavior is a product of individual or collective rationality is, according to Edelman, rather simplistic and misleading.

> Adequate explanation must focus on the complex element that intervenes between the environment and the behavior of human beings: creation and change in common meanings through symbolic apprehension in groups of people of interests, pressures, threats, and possibilities.[58]

Thus, the focus becomes one of cognition control and reality.

There is little empirical evidence to support the notion that hard-sell media campaigns significantly alter the attitudes of large numbers of people. Much of the research on political socialization and political cognitions, however, has been short-term studies. Cognition dealing with broad, societal concepts develops over long periods of time. The influence of media and official appeals, therefore, may indeed be greater than current research suggests. In addition, most studies tend to distinguish between attitudes and cognitions.[59] They focus on clearly persuasive messages while ignoring the subtle effects of educational messages upon attitudes. The assumption often is that cognitions can be isolated and measured separately from attitudes. We, however, disagree and concur with Brecker, McCombs, and McLeod denying any real difference among attitudes, values, and opinions.[60] It is much more useful to understand that cognition and persuasion are complex, interdependent processes of which fantasies, myths, rituals, and symbols are all a part. We argue that people interpret messages in such a way that is compatible with long-term commitments, with the beliefs created by events (or drama), and with the current (that is, believable) reality.

Political impression management takes two basic forms. One form is to control the flow and amount of information. Information is power and the control of information is the first step of propaganda. Certainly, the Vietnam War spanning from America's initial involvement to the nation's final withdrawal is a classic case of government controlling information in attempting to create rather specific political impressions (for example, stable regime, protecting democracy, winning, etc.). The second major form of political impression management is the symbolic mobilization of support. Symbolic mobilization of support calls attention to front-stage performances where symbols, verbal and nonverbal, are used to strengthen or maintain the position of political actors.[61] This is the most potent form of impression management in America.

Our position is that public views on issues are mobilized rather than fixed. Issues are largely created, identified, and permeated throughout society. Neither issues nor specific positions on issues exist in a vacuum. Even governmental outputs are results of the creation of political followings and mass support.

Public situations consist of many images and perceptions that are created and evolve from interaction among people, government, and political leaders. Political culture is not transmitted like a telegraph message. Culture is taught in human endeavors which are largely created, staged, and performed by people in the community who have been trained and who are, in turn, training others in cultural presentations. Social action and behavior, according to Blumer, as quoted in Hall, is "the establishment through interpretative interaction of common definitions of the situation. Even though much of joint action is in the form of repetitive, patterned responses to common situations, each instance of it has to be recreated, reconstituted, and reenacted."[62] Political contests are really contests of competing definitions of situations. Winners are those who successfully articulate the definition of situation held by the majority or those who successfully create a potent definition of situation held by the majority of voters. Such a view of society and politics is grounded in dramatistic orientation.

All drama is powerful in the sense that it impacts upon cognitions, perceptions, and hence, behavior. Orin Klapp posits that "the transcending tendency of drama has a creative power to make and break statuses, to give and take prestige, to generate enthusiasm, to involve and mobilize masses in new directions, and to create new identities."[63] Situations provide, then, the boundaries or context, for drama. Situations are not or should not be objectively defined but are created. Such creation affects cognitions, impressions, and perceptions of those involved.

## POLITICS, COMMUNICATION, SOCIETY, AND SOCIAL ORDER

This chapter has indeed drawn a rather large circle. It began with discussing the inherent symbolic nature of humans and concludes with a perspective or orientation to view politics and society. The nature and role of human communication in the realm of politics was the focus of discussion.

Political symbols are the direct link between individuals and the social order. As elements of a political culture, they function as a stimulus for behavior. The use of appropriate symbols results in getting people to accept certain policies, arouse support for various causes, and obey governmental authority. Political symbols are the means to social ends and not ends in themselves.

There is, however, a long process from creation, definition, acceptance, and subsequent behavior. For implicit in our argument is the notion that successful leadership and control is dependent upon successful manipulation of political symbols. On one level, then, is the competition and manipulation of political symbols for support. On a broader level, however, national symbols are perpetuated in order to preserve the prevailing culture, political beliefs, and values. Roger Cobb and Charles Elder believe that "rather than a value consensus, we suspect that the stability of the American polity has long rested on a rather shallow symbolic consensus. This type of consensus," they argue, "rests upon symbols that are commonly viewed as important and are the objects of relatively homogeneous affective attachments but which lack any commonality of substantive meaning across individuals and groups."[64] Social unrest results from poor political communication. For the legitimacy of political order depends upon the articulation of social needs, the staisfaction of social needs, and the transmission of political values that allows for the development of a sense of community among the people. This process, while complex, is primarily one of communication.

## NOTES

1. Kenneth Burke, *Language as Symbolic Action* (California: University of California Press, 1966), p. 5.

2. Dan Nimmo, *Political Communication and Public Opinion in America* (California: Goodyear, 1978), p. 66.

3. Ibid., p. 66.

4. Gabriel Almond and J. Coleman, *The Politics of the Developing Areas* (Princeton, N.J.: Princeton University Press, 1960), see Introduction.

5. Robert Lauer and Warren Handel, *Social Psychology: The Theory and Application of Symbolic Interaction* (Boston: Houghton Mifflin, 1977), p. 41.

6. Herbert Blumer, *Symbolic Interactionism* (Englewood Cliffs, N.J.: Prentice-Hall, 1969), p. 10.

7. Ibid., p. 12.

8. George H. Mead, *Mind, Self, and Society* (Chicago: University of Chicago Press, 1972), p. 122.

9. Joel Charon, *Symbolic Interactionism: An Introduction, An Interpretation, An Integration* (Englewood Cliffs, N.J.: Prentice-Hall, 1979), p. 40.

10. Don Faules and Dennis Alexander, *Communication and Social Behavior*: *A Symbolic Interaction Perspective* (Mass.: Addison-Wesley, 1978), p. 92.

11. Blumer, *Symbolic Interactionism*, p. 8.

12. The discussion of these two levels of social interaction occur throughout Mead, *Mind, Self, and Society* but especially see pp. 13-18, 61-68, 253-60.

13. Blumer, *Symbolic Interactionism*, p. 8.

14. Alfred Lindsmith, Anselm Strauss, and Norman Denzin, *Social Psychology* (Illinois: Dryden Press, 1975), p. 430.

15. Faules and Alexander, *Communication and Social Behavior*, p. 130.

16. Ibid., p. 140.

17. Richard Rose, *People in Politics* New York: Basic Books, 1970), pp. 196-97.

18. David Easton, *A Systems Analysis of Political Life* (New York: John Wiley and Sons, 1965), p. 279.

19. Ibid., p. 249.

20. Lauer and Handel, *Social Psychology*, p. 85.

21. Murray Edelman, *The Symbolic Uses of Politics* (Urbana, Ill.: University of Illinois Press, 1964), pp. 102-3.

22. As quoted in Peter Hall, "A Symbolic Interactionist Analysis of Politics," *Sociological Inquiry* 42: 51.

23. Nimmo, *Political Communication*, p. 69.

24. Claus Mueller, *The Politics of Communication* (New York: Oxford University Press, 1973), p. 16.

25. The strongest statement of this notion is provided by Benjamin Lee Whorf. For him, "If a man thinks in one language, he thinks one way; in another language, another way." The structure of language "is itself the shaper of ideas, the program and guide for the individual's mental activity, for his analysis of impressions, for his synthesis of his mental stock in trade." See John Carroll, ed., *Language, Thought, and Reality: Selected Writings of Benjamin Whorf* (New York: John Wiley and Sons, 1956).

26. Murray Edelman, *Politics as Symbolic Action* (Chicago: Markham Publishing, 1971), p. 83.

27. Doris Graber, "Political Languages," in *Handbook of Political Communication*, ed. Dan Nimmo and Keith Sanders (Beverly Hills, Calif.: Sage Publications, 1981), p. 196.

28. Ibid., pp. 195-224.

29. Edelman, *The Symbolic Uses of Politics*, pp. 133-46.

30. Ibid., p. 172.

31. Nimmo, *Political Communication*, pp. 67-68.

32. Roger Cobb and Charles Elder, "Individual Orientations in the Study of Political Symbolism," *Social Science Quarterly* 53 (June 1972): 82-86.

33. Nimmo, *Political Communication*, pp. 83-86.

34. Graber, "Political Languages," pp. 196-97.

35. Edelman, *Politics as Symbolic Action*, p. 83.

36. James David Barber, *The Pulse of Politics* (New York: Norton, 1980), p. 20.

37. Dan Nimmo and James Combs, *Subliminal Politics* (Englewood Cliffs, N.J.: Spectrum Books, 1980), pp. 9-13.

38. Ibid., p. 13.

39. Lee McDonald, "Myth, Politics, and Political Science," *Western Political Quarterly* 22 (1969): 141.

40. Nimmo and Combs, *Subliminal Politics*, p. 16.

41. Ibid., pp. 26-27.

42. Mainly based upon ibid., pp. 20-23.

43. Edelman, *The Symbolic Uses of Politics*, p. 16.

44. Peter Hall, "A Symbolic Interactionist Analysis of Politics," *Sociological Inquiry* 42 (1972): 59.

45. Richard Brooks, "The Self and Political Role: A Symbolic Interactionist Approach to Political Ideology," *The Sociological Quarterly* 10 (Winter 1969): 23.

46. Kenneth Burke, "Interaction-Dramatism" in the *International Encyclopedia of the Social Sciences* (New York: 1967), pp. 445-52 (hereafter cited as *IESS*).

47. Ibid., p. 445.

48. Kenneth Burke, *A Grammar of Motives* (Berkeley: University of California Press, 1969), p. xxii.

49. Michael Overington, "Kenneth Burke and the Method of Dramatism," *Theory and Society* 4 (Spring 1977): 129-56.

50. Kenneth Burke, "Dramatism" in *Communication Concepts and Perspectives*, ed. Lee Thayer (New Jersey: Hayden, 1967), p. 332.

51. Burke, *IESS*, p. 449.

52. Hugh Duncan, *Symbols in Society* (New York: Oxford University Press, 1968), p. 200.

53. Kenneth Burke, *Permanence and Change* (New York: Bobbs-Merrill, 1965), p. 274.

54. Duncan, *Symbols in Society*, p. 25.

55. For a good and simple explanation of the fantasy process see Ernest Bormann and Nancy Bormann, *Speech Communication: A Comprehensive Approach* (New York: Harper and Row, 1977), pp. 306-17.

56. Ibid., p. 311.

57. Ibid., p. 308.

58. Edelman, *Politics as Symbolic Action*, p. 2.

59. See W. J. McGuire, "The Nature of Attitudes and Attitude Change" in the *Handbook of Social Psychology*, vol. 3, ed. Lindzey and Aronson (Mass.: Addison-Wesley, 1969).

60. Lee Becker, Maxwell McCombs, and Jack McLeod, "The Development of Political Cognitions" in *Political Communication: Issues and Strategies for Research*, ed. Steven Chaffeem et al. (Beverly Hills: Sage Publications, 1975), p. 26.

61. Hall, "A Symbolic Interactionist Analysis," p. 58.

62. Ibid., p. 41.

63. Orin Klapp, *Symbolic Leaders* (Chicago: Aldine, 1964), p. 257.

64. Cobb and Elder, "Individual Orientations," p. 6.

# 3

# The Professionalization of Political Communication

Whoever causes another to become powerful is ruined because he creates such power either with skill or with force; both these factors are viewed with suspicion by the one who has become powerful.[1]

Without doubt, the king makers of contemporary politics are the new breed of political and media consultants. Larry Sabato asserts that "there is no more significant change in the conduct of campaigns than the consultant's recent rise to prominence, if not preeminence, during the election season."[2] They have become the new power in American politics. In the days before consultants, the old party bosses served as the link between electoral politics and campaigns. Their job was to generate support, control conflict, and reinforce party discipline. Today, political consultants have access to the candidate and develop local campaign strategies and tactics from offices miles away. The focus of their attention is primarily on uncommitted and independent voters. "Whereas traditional campaigns concentrated on mobilizing the faithful," according to Sidney Blumenthal, "modern campaigns ignore them."[3]

In this chapter we will investigate the use of the political consultant industry to include the activities, functions, and services it provides in the modern campaign.

## THE PROFESSIONAL POLITICIAN

When the general public speaks of a politician they are usually referring to an elected official or a candidate running for an elected office. Others may also include visible party leaders who serve over a period of time in various administrations. Few, however, consider the new campaigners as professional politicians. The new campaigners include consultants, pollsters, television producers and directors, fund-raisers, speechwriters, and direct marketers—all professionals who shape the true character of modern political campaigning in America.

Sabato defines a political consultant as "a campaign professional who is engaged primarily in the provision of advise and services (such as polling, media creation and production, and direct mail fund raising) to candidates, their campaigns, and other political committees."[4] He identifies two kinds of consultants: a generalist advises candidates on all phases of a campaign as well as serves as coordinator of special technical services provided to the candidate; a specialist concentrates only on a specific activity of the campaign. Because of the sophistication and technological advancement of mass communication and persuasion techniques, the trend is toward segmenting campaign activities into areas of specialization. The professional politician today, then, is more likely to be a specialist focusing on one activity of a campaign endeavor.

The number of firms and individuals who earn a living working on campaigns is increasing. Most firms, however, are rather small, often employing five to seven people. During a campaign the more specialized tasks of polling, advertising, fundraising, etc. are subcontracted to firms specializing in such activities. Most political consulting firms are owned and operated by a well-known successful professional. Being associated with winning campaigns is vital to the professional political consultant. Matt Reese, a well-known consultant, states that the "trinity of necessity" for a political consultant consists of winning (or the reputation of winning), working for people whose names are well known, and winning when you're not supposed to.[5]

Being a professional political consultant can be a profitable venture. Most successful consultants or firms require an upfront, flat fee to secure their services for a campaign which usually ranges from $10,000 to $100,000. Of course, all incurred costs and expenses are paid for by the candidate. In addition, most consultants and firms charge a commission of 15 percent on top of all fixed costs. Sabato reports that about 20 percent of a candidate's campaign budget goes directly toward consulting fees, expenses, and commissions.[6] This equates to several million dollars for presidential elections and hundreds of thousands of dollars for various state electoral contests.

But perhaps what makes today's professional politician most unique is the general lack of commitment to any political party or cause. Peter Hart, Walter Mondale's pollster for the presidential campaign of 1984, conducted surveys for the 1976 Republican senatorial nominee John Heinz. Independent presidential candidate John Anderson, in 1980, received help from David Garth, a noted liberal, and from the liberal Democratic firm of Craver, Mathews, Smith, and Company.[7]

Today's professional politicians are politicians only insofar as they earn their living working for political candidates and campaigns. They are professionals in the sense that they possess unique skills and knowledge relevant to human motivation and mass communication technology. They are experts and specialists first, and political in the traditional use of the word second. One cannot properly consider the functions, tasks, and impact of contemporary political consultants without first considering the growth of mass media in America and the changing nature of political campaigns.

## THE BIRTH OF THE POLITICAL CONSULTING INDUSTRY

The forefathers of our government laid the groundwork for what they believed to be a dignified, rational electoral process. But the first real presidential contest between Jefferson and Adams resulted in a campaign marked by name-calling and heated debate. In newspapers and pamphlets, Jefferson was called an atheist and enemy of the Constitution. Adams was described as a monarchist and aristocrat.[8] "From the country's first contested election," notes Kathleen Jamieson, "strategists have offered voters advertising that venerated their candidate and vilified his opponents."[9]

Dan Nimmo effectively asserts that today's political consulting industry is a direct descendant of the public relations profession that matured during the 1920s.[10] Their task was to "propagandize" the activities of American business. It is not surprising that the skills and techniques of advocacy became the mainstay of American politics.

Edward Bernays, cited in *Time* magazine as "U.S. Publicist Number One," is considered the father of public relations. In the 1920s, Bernays introduced the "engineering of consent," scientific approach to public opinion formation and dynamics. President Calvin Coolidge was the first president to benefit from Bernays's skills. The press of the day portrayed Coolidge as "cold and aloof." To counter this image, Bernays invited Al Jolson and 40 other vaudevillians to a White

House breakfast. The next day the *New York Times* headline read "Actors Eat Cakes With The Coolidges . . . President Nearly Laughs." This act was, according to Blumenthal, the "first overt act initiated by a media advisor for a President."[11] A decade later, Bernays called for the creation of a cabinet position titled secretary of public relations.

The first political consulting firm was created by Clem Whitaker (a newsman and press agent) and Leone Baxter (a public relations specialist) in 1933.[12] In that year the California legislature passed a bill authorizing a flood control and irrigation project. Pacific Gas and Electric Company viewed the project as a direct threat to the company and thus initiated a campaign to reverse the decision. In turn, proponents of the project hired Whitaker and Baxter to develop a campaign that would defeat the electric company's effort. With a budget of $39,000 the team was victorious in stopping the opposition. Soon after the effort, Whitaker and Baxter formed Campaigns, Inc. Between 1933 and 1955 they won 70 out of 75 campaigns they managed. Their last campaign was the congressional race of Shirley Temple Black in 1967. They developed many of the techniques and strategies that are used in political campaigns today.

Whitaker believed that most Americans do not seek information during a campaign and have no desire to work at being a good citizen. Thus, he argued that "there are two ways you can interest [citizens] in a campaign, and only two that we have ever found successful. Most every American loves a contest. He likes a good, hot battle, with no punches pulled. So you can interest him if you put on a fight! Then, too, most every American likes to be entertained. He likes fireworks and parades. So if you can't fight, put on a show."[13]

By 1950, advertising agencies handled national election campaigns. But by 1970, advertising agencies realized that handling campaigns was not as profitable as other products. A political campaign ends in a few months whereas selling soap, cars, or clothes goes on for years. And selling soap is less stressful. The last advertising agency campaign was Nixon's 1968 presidential race, well documented in Joe McGinniss's *The Selling of the Presidency*. He writes of the role advertising played in creating and re-creating a "new Nixon."[14]

Public relations specialists were a permanent part of every campaign effort by 1960. Between 1952 and 1957, about 60 percent of all public relations firms had some kind of political account.[15] Part of John Kennedy's campaign staff was a research group, speech-writing group, and publicity group all comprised of public relations personnel.[16] At first, however, Republicans used public relations specialists in campaigns more than Democrats because of their natural ties to business firms, publicity firms, and available money.

Today, campaigns are run by professional consultants who coordinate the activities of media, advertising, public relations, and publicity. They understand both the new technologies and the unique requirements of campaigning. It is that blend of expertise and experience that makes them a sought-after commodity.

## THE CASE FOR THE USE OF POLITICAL CONSULTANTS

There are several reasons why political officeholders and candidates need the services of campaign specialists. The modern campaign requires the performance of many specialized tasks to include advertising, issue research, strategy development, polling, and fundraising. Each of these tasks is complex, requiring training, experience, and knowledge of the industry. It is unrealistic to expect a candidate for public office to have the technical expertise in each of these areas or to even have the time to manage these activities in addition to campaigning or governing.

Another reason for campaign specialists is the impact of behavioral and social science concepts and theories of human motivation. The scientific approach to opinion formation and dynamics has become an essential element of every campaign. Predicting public attitudes and behavior is key to the development of campaign strategy. The measurement, tracking, and analysis of demographic and psychographic data forms the bases for issue positions and public appeals. Social science has provided the necessary tools and methodologies monitoring public beliefs, attitudes, and values.

The electoral process itself places unique requirements upon candidates and campaigns. Historically, Americans value the notion of candidates meeting the public and discussing issues. But as our society becomes larger, more diverse, and complex, the requirements of campaigning also become more complex. There are neither simple issues nor solutions to problems. Extensive direct voter contact is usually impossible. At the national level, each primary becomes an individualized contest requiring professional help and analysis. American electoral politics is a unique process.

But, of course, the greatest reason for the need of consultants is the role of mass media in our society. Every requirement and characteristic of the mass media impacts upon the nature of political campaigning. To meet the public through the media requires money and 30-second discussions of issues. Actions and statements are carried beyond the immediate audience. Television especially likes drama, a contest, and often favors an underdog. A mistake is recorded forever and subject to instant replay without contextual explanation. The media serve as a source of information, persuasion, and presentation of reality. To use a medium requires knowledge of the medium—its strengths, weaknesses, and nature. The growth and necessity of political consultants and professional politicians are directly related to the growth of the mass media and communication technologies.

The political consultant and professional is needed today because of what Blumenthal calls "the permanent campaign." The permanent campaign, a direct result of the new technology in the age of information, has become "the steady-state reality of American politics. In this new politics, issues, polls and media are not neatly separate categories. They are unified by the strategic imperative . . . the elements of the permanent campaign are tangential to politics: they are the political process itself."[17] The political consultants are permanent, the politicians ephemeral. With the decline of party structure, discipline, and workers, television commercials and media appearances not only serve to mobilize voters but for governing the nation. Governing the nation, then, becomes a perpetual campaign where "the public is constantly roiled and its support continually demanded."[18] Ronald Reagan brought into the White House some of the most sophisticated marketers, pollsters, and media advisers to ever work for a president. Much of his success in opinion formation, information control, and law enactment is a result of Reagan's use of the new technologies. While the "permanent campaign" is a recognizable and dominant aspect of presidential politics, Blumenthal contends that the "permanent campaign will permeate politics down to the most remote legislative district as politicians feel the need to retain consultants to give them the advantage."[19]

## FUNCTIONS OF POLITICAL CONSULTANTS

### Campaign Management

An important function of a political consultant is the management of an entire campaign. Management personnel are involved in the planning and execution of a campaign. First, they must establish the campaign organization consisting of professionals, committed party regulars, and citizen volunteers. Complete campaign management requires the implementation of campaign strategies and the allocation of candidate time, money, and talent.

## Campaign Planning and Strategy

Strategic considerations are an important part of the consultant's duties. In planning a political campaign, the consultant considers the candidate's personality, temperament, experience, strengths, and weaknesses. The basic themes, slogans, issues, and modes of attack are created and the game plan is formulated. The scheduling of campaign appearances and activities is also an important part of the total planning of a campaign. Strategy development, refinement, and execution is a continual process. This function lies at the heart of any campaign. Its success or failure directly impacts upon the reputation of the consultant and future jobs. This function, then, is critical to both the candidate and consultant.

## Campaign Research

Campaign research is a highly specialized function and provides the basis for strategy development and execution. Campaign research includes investigating voting patterns, voter turnout, demographic correlates of voting, voter attitudes, opinions, issues, registration, and election projections. Most campaigns prepare a bible that summarizes the relevant issues of the campaign, profiles "friendly" voters, analyzes opposition strengths, weaknesses, and strategy, and provides local data for campaign stops.[20] Like campaign planning and strategy development, research is a continual process, especially as election day approaches.

## Candidate Image and Personality

A major task of the consultant is to assist in the development of the candidate's public image. Images are the conceptions of qualities people associate with certain objects, products, or individuals.[21] The consultant's job is to design and stimulate favorable associations so that the voters believe the candidate fulfills their wishes, desires, and needs. The candidate's personality is a composite picture presented to the voters of the candidate's political views, roles, and personal characteristics. During the 1980 presidential campaign, Reagan was presented as "tough"—equal to the task of facing the Soviets and believing in a strong defense. Once in office, Reagan was presented as a nice guy, humble, and easy-going unless pushed into a corner.

Candidate image and personality are important features of every campaign. After an extensive investigation of mass media and elections, Thomas Patterson reported that images are easily acquired by the voters and once developed, they are not likely to be altered even with the presentation of new information and efforts.[22] In fact, Patterson found that the impressions acquired during the 1976 presidential campaign between Carter and Ford tended to be more stylistic, focusing on candidate mannerisms and campaign performance than on issue propositions or leadership qualities.[23] Political consultant David Garth is so concerned about image control that he requires candidates to watch their weight and prescribes physical exercise for his clients. He even made Ed Koch lose 15 pounds for his New York mayoral race.[24]

Of course, concerns over image and personality do not end on election day. Elected officials have a continuing need to reinforce the properly defined image. Carter soon discovered that although the public admired the qualities of a populist president, they also wanted their leader to be presidential and to bring back the majesty of the office. Carter soon authorized a return to playing "Ruffles and Flourishes" and "Hail to the Chief" upon his entrance. He also quit wearing jeans in the Oval Office and donned the traditional blue suit and white shirt.

But no president is more aware of the need and value of projecting the proper image than Ronald Reagan in his first term. The sole job of presidential aide Michael Deaver was to present the "right" image of the president. Upon his election, Reagan created the Office of Planning and Evaluation. Staff members from the office realized that it is within the first 100 days that a president establishes the persona and character of the administration. Reagan retained Mark Goode, a media consultant and television producer, who was to make sure that nothing was left to chance and every public appearance was fully orchestrated. The pervasive nature of the news media is simply a fact of political life in America.

## MAIN SERVICES OFFERED BY POLITICAL CONSULTANTS

In executing the functions described above, political consultants provide many services for candidates and elected officials. These countless services, ranging from day-to-day campaign operations to fundraising to image definition depend upon three main services: advertising, public opinion polling, and direct mail. Each of these services is communication-based and has become the bread and butter of the industry.

### Advertising

Political advertising is the most recognized and controversial service provided by consultants. It is also, perhaps, the most important. Each ad is carefully constructed and crafted to fulfill a specified purpose. The media adviser was once primarily a technical adviser not privy to the overall strategy and tactics of the campaign. Today the media consultant is often responsible for a campaign's advertising and communication strategy.[25]

Of course, modern political advertising is a far cry from the distribution of flyers and campaign buttons of the 1800s. As radio and television became the primary means of communicating to a large number of people, it was natural for politicians to seek access to the media. But utilizing the commercial, business format of advertising as a way to gain voter acceptance was an evolutionary process. For Joe McGinniss, the process was also a natural one. He wrote in 1968 that "politics in a sense, has always been a con game. . . . Advertising, in many ways, is a con game too. . . . It is not surprising then, that politicians and advertising men should have discovered one another. And, once they recognized that the citizen did not so much vote for a candidate as make a psychological purchase of him, not surprising that they began to work together."[26]

Although in 1948 only 3 percent of the population owned a television, Harry Truman produced a spot encouraging citizens to vote. It wasn't until 1952 when about 45 percent of the nation owned a television set that political ads became commonplace events.[27] In that presidential contest, the Republicans spent $1.5 million and the Democrats only $77,000. Eisenhower's advisers felt television spots could be more controlled and counter his "stumbling press conference performances."[28]

It was also in that year that Richard Nixon, Eisenhower's vice-presidential running mate, took to the airwaves to deny charges of maintaining a slush fund of $18,000 and to save his spot on the ticket. The advertising agency of Batten, Barton, Durstine, and Osborn purchased 30 minutes of network time for $75,000 for Nixon to answer charges. The presentation was carefully constructed, rehearsed, and successful. The medium was not only a way to communicate to an audience but was also a means to persuade them. This key incident is investigated further in Chapter 6.

The early format of political ads was the candidate speaking directly to the camera. For media specialists, this format was lacking. It did not utilize the full capabilities of the medium and was certainly boring to the general public. Later, in a more creative use of the medium, campaign events were broadcasted live. Live events are, however, difficult to control and staged interactions soon followed. Extended half-hour documentaries and telethons were a popular format from 1960 to 1972 but are much too expensive to broadcast today. In some respects, political advertising has come full circle. David Garth, a noted political consultant, now prefers the candidate speaking directly to the audience.[29] He believes that in this format the candidate can provide a great deal of information that motivates people to view a spot several times. More interestingly, members of Congress are becoming concerned about the costs and nature of contemporary political advertising. Consequently, a bipartisan group of congressmen are suggesting legislation that would limit political ads to a "tombstone" formula where candidates are "talking heads" only.[30]

For consultants, according to Blumenthal, candidates are a "dream problem." "The consultant must stimulate the public's wish fulfillment for the candidate through manipulation of symbols and images, enticing voters to believe that the candidate can satisfy their needs. The relationship of dreams to reality is analogous to the relationship between advertising and politics. Ads are condensed images of wish fulfillment."[31]

There are seven basic functions of political ads: to create interest in the candidate, to build name recognition, to stimulate citizen participation, to provide motivation for candidate support, to identify key issues and frame questions for public debate, to demonstrate the talents of the candidate, and to provide entertainment. The content, approach, and thrust of an ad are based upon several considerations: the strengths and weaknesses of the candidates, the strengths and weaknesses of the opponent, available funds, the nature of news coverage of the candidate, public information and views of the candidate, and the general artistic and aesthetic inclinations of the consultant.[32]

Campaign ads from any election, whether a mayoral race as in Chicago in 1982, a highly contested senatorial race as between Jesse Helms and Jim Hunt of North Carolina in 1984, or the presidential primary and race of any year provides, in capsule form, the basic issues, strategies, and tactics of the campaign. Together they provide the psyche of the public—their likes and dislikes, their concerns and worries, their hopes and dreams. They indeed provide future historians snapshots of American politics. But political advertising is and will continue to be controversial. Even David Ogilvy, co-founder of the advertising agency Ogilvy and Mather, in an interview in 1984 stated that "political advertising ought to be stopped. It's the only really dishonest kind of advertising that's left. It's totally dishonest."[33]

## Public Opinion Polling

The *Harrisburg Pennsylvanian* published in 1824 contained the first political opinion poll in America.[34] It consisted of a survey of presidential preferences of the constituents between Andrew Jackson and John Quincy Adams. Jackson won the straw vote two to one. But scientific polling did not begin until the 1930s. Mrs. Alex Miller was the first candidate to use polling by her son-in-law George Gallup. She became the first female secretary of state in Iowa by utilizing sampling techniques that Gallup developed in his doctoral thesis. He founded the polling industry in 1935. Franklin Roosevelt's use of public opinion polls was to gauge his popularity and not for issue or policy formation. Although Eisenhower's advertising agencies consulted Gallup in the development of themes to use in the 1952 television ads, extensive use of polling did not begin until 1960. John Kennedy used Louis Harris to analyze public opinion in key primary states. Upon Harris's urging, Kennedy entered the West Virginia primary—a heavily Protestant state. Kennedy nearly lost the primary and lost faith in Harris's predictions. Harris was no longer used in strategic campaign decision making.

Patrick Caddell enjoyed the closest relationship with a presidential candidate and subsequent president than any pollster in history. He was a vital member of not only Carter's campaign staff but also a member of the president's inner circle. Consequently, Caddell influenced most decisions of the Carter administration. Caddell did more than simply report results. He developed a world view and a theory of voter motivation. According to Caddell, voters are volatile and feel alienated. He operates from the assumption that politicians generally lack the public's confidence. Voters are primarily motivated by self-interest. He uses polls extensively to note subtle changes in the mood of the electorate. For example, Caddell noted that young mothers were unsure of Carter in terms of "stability"—control and evenhandedness. Caddell instructed Carter to smile more during an upcoming presidential debate and not to get excited.[35] For Caddell, there is little difference between governing and campaigning. "Essentially, it is my thesis that governing with public approval requires a continuing political campaign."[36] Reagan, as already noted, extended Carter's use of media consultants as a vital part of his White House staff.

Today, polling is a $1.5 billion industry.[37] There are literally hundreds of polling organizations. But, for political purposes, there are three major Republican firms (Lance, Tarrance & Associates; Market Opinion Research; and Decision Making Information, Inc.) and three Democratic firms (Caddell's Cambridge Survey Research; William Hamilton and Staff, Inc.; and Peter Hart Research Associates). Some consultants maintain their own polling services. David Garth's research staff works year round and all polling is done in-house. By doing his own polling he controls the interpretation of data.

During elections, political polls play an important role in the electoral process. Many Political Action Committees (PACs) now require a candidate to demonstrate viability in the polls before making a financial contribution to a campaign. Some candidates base their decision whether or not to run for office on their showing in the polls. For example, as a result of reported polls showing him behind in New Hampshire, George Romney withdrew from the 1978 Republican presidential nomination contest.

Political polls are used most often, however, to gauge a candidate's viability, identify issues of most concern to the public, and identify a candidate's strong and weak personality characteristics. Polls don't necessarily cause candidates to change their views on certain issues but may inform them on the topics to discuss or gauge their public impact. Stu Spencer, Ford's consultant in the 1976 presidential campaign, openly admits to attempts of creating issues and getting Reagan to make mistakes.[38] His research revealed that in 1975 Reagan advocated cutting $90 billion from the federal budget. For New Hampshire, a $90 billion cut would eliminate aid to the state. Thus, a fact sheet was prepared and distributed to the press. When Reagan was confronted, he had no answers to the charges that he would end aid to the state and became rather defensive.

Colorado Senator Gary Hart's polling prior to the Alabama, Georgia, and Florida primaries in mid-March 1984 found that Walter Mondale was perceived as tied to special interests. Thus, Hart attacked

Mondale as a "lackey of special interest." It was within hours that Mondale retorted to Hart "Where's the beef?"—a phrase of a popular advertising commercial for Wendy's Hamburgers. Mondale's polling found the retort effective and thus kept hurling the question at Hart at every campaign stop for weeks.

Although polling has become very sophisticated and scientific, it still remains problematic despite its popularity. Critics claim that polls do not distinguish between awareness of an issue and intensity of opinion. There is often no link between an attitude and subsequent behavior. In the closing days of a campaign, public attitudes, desires, and motivations may change too frequently for pollsters to monitor and predict. After all, in October of 1975, Carter had only a 3 percent support rating according to a Gallup poll yet still became president a year later.[39] Polls should not, then, become the basis for decision making. But perhaps most alarming is the fact that despite the current science of opinion polling, they are often wrong. In January of 1984, the *New York Times*'s CBS poll showed Reagan a 16-point favorite over Mondale while at the same time a *Washington Post*/ABC poll reported Reagan only a 3-point favorite.[40] Political opinion polls, unlike public polls of Gallup and Harris, are more tools of persuasion, image control and creation, than reports of information. They are, simply, an important element of a consultant's service arsenal.

### Direct Mail

Of all the services provided by consulting firms, the public is probably less aware of the importance and role direct mail plays in a campaign. As a relatively new industry, direct marketing has rapidly become the cornerstone for mounting a political campaign. And direct mail specifically is a powerful and persuasive communication medium. Sabato refers to direct mail as "the poisoned pen of politics."[41] Its effectiveness lies in the fact that a study conducted by Edward DeBolt revealed that 65 percent of the people surveyed look forward to receiving their daily mail.[42] Direct marketing has become the fastest growing advertising industry and an industry that utilizes the latest technology and theories of social science research.

In terms of politics, it was the 1972 presidential campaign that demonstrated the power and effectiveness of direct mail.[43] George McGovern was generally unknown and had great difficulty obtaining endorsements from party regulars, wealthy supporters, or organized groups. He was forced to use direct mail to generate funds from individual citizen supporters. Even in a difficult campaign, by 1972 direct mail was bringing in over $200,000 a month.

But Republicans have benefited most from direct marketing. In 1974, following Nixon's resignation, Congress enacted legislation that set a $1,000 limit on individual political contributions. The Republicans immediately began developing a sophisticated direct mail program utilizing the latest technology; Republicans consistently raise four or five times more money using direct mail than Democrats.[44]

But the main problem for Democrats, according to Richard Viguerie, a conservative and political direct mail consultant, is that they view direct mail as only a fundraising activity and not as a form of advertising. He further argues that conservatives were forced to use direct mail because of the need to bypass the "liberal mass media." It became, for them, "a way of mobilizing our people, it's a way of communicating with our people; it identifies our people, and it marshals our people. It's self-liquidating and it pays for itself. It's a form of advertising, part of the marketing strategy. It's advertising."[45]

Thus, fundraising is the primary function of direct mail in political campaigns. Candidates use direct mail to supplement federal financing of elections. Fundraising objectives include reaching new contributors as well as continual contact with previous ones. Republicans in 1984 generated nearly $100 million from direct mail solicitation.[46] They compiled a list of 2.2 million donors and the average contribution was $26.00. A letter devoted solely to Reagan's reelection effort produced an average contribution of $55.00. The National Republican Committee utilized two direct mail membership programs. Sustaining membership required a contribution of at least $25.00 and for a contribution of $10.00 a month, one could belong to the Republican Presidential Task Force.[47] The National Committee tests about 600 mailing lists each year and conducts about 18 mailings to the "house list" each year.[48]

Gary Hart's presidential nomination campaign was successful in using direct mail for fundraising. From one mailing in March 1984, Hart generated $1.1 million. Mondale, however, used direct mail indirectly to only contact those attending parties, dinners, and other political functions. Jesse Jackson simply could not afford a major direct mail effort.[49] Although direct mail can generate a great deal of money, it does require a sizable investment for a national effort. Sabato reports that a $200,000 investment can easily produce a $2 million return.[50]

Other uses of direct mail include targeting voters, developing issues, recruiting volunteers, molding opinions, getting out the vote, and laying the groundwork for future campaigns by establishing a list of donors and supporters. Such organizations as the National Conservative Union, Young Americans for Freedom, and the Moral Majority use computerized mailing lists and letters to identify and organize supporters as well as to solicit funds. Democrats in the presidential race of 1984 used direct mail to target voters or groups of voters for special messages. As Reagan was perceived to threaten social security, Democrats formulated a mailing to older Americans focusing on Reagan's position. Thus, direct marketing techniques have strategic implications. Richard Parker notes that "the computer will be central to the 1980s. Without mastery there's no reason to express a coherent position. For this period, direct mail is appropriate technology. It's a qualified way of reaching people. It makes you think strategically. You have to decide which people will respond to which issues. You have to identify constituencies. You have to identify questions of timing and geography."[5] [1]

Direct mail is powerful because the package is carefully constructed. Starting with the envelope, there is some teaser or attention-getting statement that leads the reader to open the correspondence. The letter usually begins with a startling or dramatic statement by the politician or a celebrity. The letter is conversational and personal using a lot of *I*'s and *you*'s. There is an early identification of an enemy which is either the opponent, a group, or an issue position. The situation is described as being critical, desperate, and urgent. Of course, most letters conclude with an appeal for support and financial assistance. In short, the copy must get attention, arouse interest, stimulate desire, and ask for action.

Techniques of emotion and motivation are well known by the professionals. They know that a letter is more likely to generate a response for funds if the letter is very specific as to what the money will be used for. A direct mail piece for gubernatorial candidate William Clements included a list of all the reserved television advertising spots by city, station, and program so that each person could see what they would be "purchasing."[5] [2] Experts know that participation devices stimulate interest and focus concentration upon the issues or action discussed. Many mailings include opinion surveys, boxes required to be checked, or sample ballots to be marked. In terms of fundraising, the amount of contribution will be greater if not only the amount is specified but also if the suggested amounts start with the largest going to the smallest amount (i.e., $500, $250, $100, $50, rather than $50, $100, $250, $500). A two-page letter is more likely to be read than a one-page letter and the signature should be in blue ink and appear to be personally signed. The timing of a mailing is critical to its impact and success. Generally, it is best to mail just before or after an announcement of candidacy, before a primary or general election, and to coincide with a major media blitz. The day Reagan announced his forming of a committee to explore his reelection, 600,000 letters were mailed and generated $3 million in contributions. A massive mailing to 2.2 million people was timed so that the people would receive the letter the Monday after Reagan's Sunday announcement of seeking reelection.[53] And finally, experts know that direct mail donors are more committed to the candidate and issues than single-event donors. Single-event donors are usually one-shot contributors who like being near the candidate or at a party whereas the direct mail donor will be responsive even in tough times. Thus, the list of contributors is a valuable commodity.

There are several advantages to the direct mail medium. There is more complete control not only over the construction of the message but also over who receives the message and where the message will be sent. The message appeals can be tailored and targeted and tell the full story and present a detailed issue position. The message is not limited to 30 seconds. In direct mail there is wider coverage, personalized and guaranteed contact, and the ability to capitalize on current events. It is also less costly and very effective. The importance and impact of direct marketing techniques will continue to be a factor in every campaign endeavor.

## THE PROFESSIONAL POLITICAL CONSULTANT: CONSEQUENCES AND IMPACT

One cannot consider the role of the new politician without also considering the impact upon our political process of new technologies and media consultants. Although Jamieson views media consultants as "persons of good will and human failings and as such are neither as innocent as their mothers believe nor as invidious as their doubters aver"; the fact is that now they are the "king makers" and are at the heart of our electoral process.[54] An industry has developed, according to Nimmo and Combs, to communicate "political celebrities" much like the Hollywood star system and movie gossip magazines.[55] Politicians have become fantasy figures and symbolic leaders because they represent more than politics but also values, lifestyle, visions, and glamor.

There are two factors that have contributed to the development of today's political celebrity. First, historically Americans have believed in democratic politics which dictate that from the masses the best, most qualified individual will rise to lead the people representing their desires and reflecting their values.[56] To succeed, politicians must honor this illusion. The public has a host of expectations relevant to behavior, beliefs, and values for those in public life. Second, what most Americans know about politics comes from the media. Few citizens experience the process of politics through direct experience. Thus, political realities are mediated through group and mass communication activities.[57] As a result of Patterson's study of presidential campaigns, he concludes that "it is no exaggeration to say that, for the large majority of voters, the campaign has little reality apart from its media version."[58] Thus, mediated politics give media consultants a great deal of influence and power. This fact alarms Herbert Schiller, who believes that when media people "deliberately produce messages that do not correspond to the realities of social existence, the media managers become mind managers."[59] The ultimate danger is that by "using myths which explain, justify, and sometimes even glamorize the prevailing conditions of existence, manipulators secure popular support for a social order that is not in the majority's long-term real interest."[60]

But are the dangers that great? Consultants, of course, believe that they are actually making the electoral process more democratic. They claim that they cannot control votes as the old political bosses did through the patronage system. Also, consultants can't enforce voter discipline or the voting behavior of elected officials. There is even no empirical evidence of a direct causal relationship between watching a commercial or series of commercials and voting. Consultants further argue that they make elections more open and provide access for reporters to candidate strategy, views, and campaign information.

At worst, Caddell believes consultants are serving as preselectors of candidates. "We decide who is best able to use the technology, who understands the technology. It's a self-fulfilling prophecy."[61] Of course there is nothing inherently wrong or evil in the new technologies or even the desire of politicians to present their best attributes to the public. But the pressure of winning for both the candidate and the consultant cannot be ignored. Therein lies the potential for abuse. For consultants to get business they must continue to win elections.

They are more likely, then, to accept only sure bets and once in the battle, they may not recognize any limits to winning. The fact is, most candidates are willing participants. They seldom question the advice or strategy of consultants. Candidates are paying a great deal of money for consultant services, seldom understand the new technologies nor have the time to develop the necessary expertise to become a full partner in media decisions. The epitome of consultant manipulation is presented in the movie *The Candidate* which is reported to be based upon the experiences of David Garth.[62] In the film, a consultant takes a good-looking nobody (Robert Redford) and leads the individual to electoral victory. Upon election, the candidate can only ask "What do I do now?" Garth was even offered the role of the consultant but turned it down because it represented "every [deleted] cliche in the book."[63]

In the demise of political parties, consultants have taken their place in generating supporters, motivating voters, and raising money. Consultants rather than parties have become the intermediaries between politicians and the public and the press. The consequences, according to Sabato, are the continuing decline of party organizations; emphasis of images over issues; candidate independence from party ideology; more narrow elections with focus on single issues which can be packaged; dissemination of communication tools and techniques to Political Action Committees or issue groups that greatly influenced the 1980 and 1984 elections; resorting to, during elections, factual inaccuracies, half-truths, and exaggerations; using deceptive and negative advertising resulting in voter distrust and apathy; emphasis on emotional themes over rational discussion of issues, and drastically increasing the cost of elections.[64] Campaigns at all levels have become more costly. Since the arrival of political consultants, costs of congressional campaigns have risen from $175 million in 1972 to $1.2 billion in 1980. Some individual senatorial contests in 1984 surpassed $20 million, such as the North Carolina senatorial race between Jesse Helms and Jim Hunt.[65]

## CONCLUSION

The professional politicians of today are not the political officeholders, for the latter are paid for governing while the former are paid for managing and winning elections. For professional politicians, politics is a permanent, continual campaign and not the process of governing. Political consultants possess the tools, skills, and techniques of mass communication and human motivation. As argued in Chapter 2, the basis of politics is human interaction. Communication is the vehicle for the sharing and creation of human beliefs, values, and goals. Elections are primarily mass communication events carefully orchestrated to produce a desired result. In Marshall McLuhan's phrase, it is impossible to separate the "medium" from the "message" or results from motives. But this chapter has recognized the role of the mass communication specialist in American electoral politics. As communication became more complex, sophisticated and technological, the need for assistance was natural. The functions and services of political consultants, while communication-based have indeed had a profound effect upon our electoral process. Consultants influence more than just *how* we elect officials, but *who* we elect as well.

## NOTES

1. Machiavelli, *The Prince*, trans. and ed., Mark Musa (New York: St. Martin's Press, 1964), p. 25.

2. Larry Sabato, *The Rise of Political Consultants* (New York: Basic Books, 1981), p. 3.

3. Sidney Blumenthal, *The Permanent Campaign*, 2nd ed. (New York: Touchstone Books, 1982), p. 22.

4. Sabato, *The Rise of Political Consultants*, p. 8.

5. As reported in ibid., p. 18.

6. Ibid., p. 52.

7. Ibid., p. 30.

8. Kathleen Jamieson, *Packaging the Presidency* (New York: Oxford University Press, 1984), p. 5.

9. Ibid., p. vii.

10. Dan Nimmo, *The Political Persuaders* (Englewood Cliffs, N.J.: Spectrum Books, 1970), p. 36.

11. Blumenthal, *The Permanent Campaign*, p. 40.

12. See Sabato, *The Rise of Political Consultants*, pp. 11-13; ibid., pp. 161-65; and Nimmo, *The Political Persuaders*, p. 36.

13. As quoted in Blumenthal, *The Permanent Campaign*, p. 164.

14. See Joe McGinniss, *The Selling of the President: 1968* (New York: Trident Press, 1969).

15. Sabato, *The Rise of Political Consultants*, p. 12.

16. See Melvyn Bloom, *Public Relations and Presidential Campaigns: A Crisis in Democracy* (New York: Thomas Crowell, 1973), p. 86.

17. Blumenthal, *The Permanent Campaign*, p. 10.

18. Ibid., p. 311.

19. Ibid., p. 18.

20. Nimmo, pp. 70-71.

21. Ibid., p. 144.

22. Thomas Patterson, *The Mass Media Election* (New York: Praeger, 1980), pp. 135, 142.

23. Ibid., p. 134.

24. As reported in Blumenthal, *The Permanent Campaign*, p. 92.

25. See Jamieson, *Packaging the President*, especially pp. 3-38.

26. McGinniss, *The Selling of the President: 1968*, pp. 26-27.

27. Sabato, *The Rise of Political Consultants*, p. 113.

28. As reported in ibid., p. 113.

29. As reported in ibid., p. 96.

30. "This Idea Deserves a Tombstone," *Advertising Age*, April 16, 1984, p. 16.

31. Blumenthal, *The Permanent Campaign*, p. 21.

32. Jamieson, *Packaging the President*, p. 37.

33. James Forkan, "Political Ads Are Dishonest: Ogilvy," *Advertising Age*, June 7, 1984, p. 3.

34. Sabato, *The Rise of Political Consultants*, p. 69.

35. Blumenthal, *The Permanent Campaign*, p. 55.

36. As reported in ibid., p. 56.

37. "Are Pollsters Getting Out of Hand?" *U.S. News & World Report*, May 7, 1984, p. 30.

38. As reported in Blumenthal, *The Permanent Campaign*, pp. 174-76.

39. Sabato, *The Rise of Political Consultants*, p. 84.

40. *U.S. News & World Report*, p. 30.

41. Sabato, *The Rise of Political Consultants*, p. 220.

42. *Direct Mail in the Political Process* (New York: Direct Marketing Association), p. 1.

43. See Blumenthal, *The Permanent Campaign*, pp. 242-44.

44. Richard Edel, "GOP Leaves Democrats In The Dust," *Advertising Age*, April 16, 1984, pp. 52-53.

45. As quoted in Blumenthal, *The Permanent Campaign*, p. 245.

46. Richard Edel, "Direct Marketing Gets Politician's Vote," *Advertising Age*, April 16, 1984, pp. 52-53.

47. Ibid., p. 53.

48. Ibid.

49. Ibid., p. 51.

50. Sabato, *The Rise of Political Consultants*, p. 227.

51. As quoted in Blumenthal, *The Permanent Campaign*, p. 254.

52. As reported in Sabato, *The Rise of Political Consultants*, p. 238.

53. Edel, "Direct Marketing gets Politician's Vote," p. 52.

54. Jamieson, *Packaging the President*, p. viii.

55. Dan Nimmo and James Combs, *Mediated Political Realities* (New York: Longman, 1983), p. 96.

56. See Robert Denton, *The Symbolic Dimensions of the American Presidency* (Prospect Heights, Ill.: Waveland Press, 1982).

57. For a detailed discussion of "mediated political realities" see Nimmo and Combs, *Mediated Political Realities*.

58. Patterson, *The Mass Media Election*, p. 3.

59. Herbert Schiller, *The Mind Managers* (Boston: Beacon Press, 1973), p. 1.
60. Ibid., p. 1.
61. As quoted in Blumenthal, *The Permanent Campaign*, p. 74.
62. Ibid., p. 111.
63. Ibid.
64. Sabato, *The Rise of Political Consultants*, p. 313.
65. "This Idea Deserves a Tombstone," p. 16.

# 4

# Political Campaigns

Every four years a gong goes off and a new Presidential campaign surges into the national consciousness: new candidates, new issues, a new season of surprises. But underlying the syncopations of change there is a steady, recurrent rhythm from election to election, a pulse of politics, that brings up the same basic themes in order, over and over again.[1]

Much has already been written about political campaigns. The classic "limited effects model" of campaign communication research dominated scholars' views of the impact of campaigns upon voters for nearly 40 years. The model was based upon data from the 1940 elections presented by Lazarsfeld, Berelson, and Gaudet in *The People's Choice*.[2] They found that most voter decisions were based upon attitude predispositions, group identification, and interpersonal communication. Thus, mediated messages would contribute little to the actual conversion of voters favoring one candidate over another.[3]

But today, in terms of voter behavior and campaigns, political outcomes are less predictable than in previous decades. With the decline of political parties, the increase of single issue politics, the prominence of mass media, and the sophistication of social science research the studies of the 1940s and 1950s are no longer apropos to today's electoral campaigns. Scholars are now recognizing the variety of factors that influence voter preferences. The "uses and gratifications model" of campaign effects is increasing in popularity. This model basically argues that campaign effects upon voters depend upon the needs and motivations of the individual voter. Voters may turn

71

to campaign messages for information, issue discussion, or pure entertainment.[4] There are a variety of motives, therefore, for exposure to campaign communication.

## A COMMUNICATION APPROACH TO CAMPAIGN ANALYSIS

Gary Mauser has identified four basic approaches to campaign analysis.[5] The academic perspective is grounded in behavioralism. The goal of most of this research has been to understand individual voting behavior. Within this perspective is a sociological emphasis that attempts to identify the factors that influence *how* people decide to vote and a psychological emphasis that attempts to understand *why* people vote as they do.

The positive approach to campaign analysis based on the rational-choice theory of human behavior, attempts to explain how voters make decisions based upon personal goals of economic and social well-being. From this approach, elections are merely instruments to obtain group and subsequently individual goals.

The pragmatic approach focuses on the day-to-day decisions and choices confronting the politicians. There is a tremendous difference between being a student of politics and a practitioner of politics. Except for aspects of the popular press, there are few systematic analyses from the perspective of campaigners.

A communication approach to campaign analysis, the perspective of this book, takes issue with the basic assumption of the behavioralists that political campaigns really do not play a major role in election results. Communication scholars argue that too much emphasis of campaign research has been focused on voter conversion. Such research tends to ignore the long-term, subtle effects or cumulative effects of politics and political campaigns. As argued in Chapter 2, political reality is created, manipulated, and permeated. Campaigns are exercises in the creation, re-creation, and transmission of significant symbols through communication. Communication activities are the vehicles for action—both real and perceived. It is true, however, as Samuel Becker argues, that "any single communication encounter accounts for only a small portion of the variance in human behavior."[6] He characterizes our communication environment as a "mosaic."[7] The mosaic consists of an infinite number of information "bits" or fragments on an infinite number of topics scattered over time and space. In addition, the "bits" are disorganized, exposure is varied and repetitive. As these "bits" are relevant or address a need, they are attended. Thus, as we attempt to make sense of our environment, our current state of existence, political bits are elements of our voting choice, world view, or legislative desires. As voters, we must arrange these bits into a cognitive pattern that comprises our mosaic of a candidate, issue, or situation. Campaigns, then, are great sources of potential information and contain, however difficult to identify or measure, elements that impact decision making. Information bits can replace other bits to change or modify our world view, attitudes, or opinions.

## FUNCTIONS OF CAMPAIGNS

From a communication perspective, Bruce Gronbeck has constructed a "functional model of campaign research."[8] The model, consistent with the uses and gratifications model, assumes that "receivers are active human beings who are subjecting themselves to communicative messages because certain needs can be satisfied and hence certain gratifications can be gained from exposure to those messages."[9]

In campaigns, there are both instrumental functions and consummatory functions. There are three instrumental functions which serve as means to some secondary end. One such function is behavioral activation. Campaigns serve to not only reinforce voter attitudes or convert voter preference but also to motivate voters to actually vote or help in a campaign. Another instrumental function of campaigns is cognitive adjustments. Campaigns, by discussing issues, may stimulate awareness of issues, reflect upon candidate views, or result in voter position modification. Finally, campaigns function to legitimize both the new leadership and the subsequent rules, laws, and regulations.

Consummatory functions are those embodied in the communication processes that go beyond candidate selection and legislative enactments. They help create the meta-political images and social-psychological associations that provide the glue that holds our political system together.[10] Campaigns provide personal involvement in many forms: direct participation, self-reflection and definition, social interaction and discussion, and aesthetic experiences of public drama and group life. And campaigns provide the legitimation of the electoral process reaffirming commitment to *our* brand of democracy, debate, and political campaigning.

Campaigns, then, communicate and influence, reinforce and convert, increase enthusiasm and inform, and motivate as well as educate. As Gronbeck argues, campaigns "get leaders elected, yes, but ultimately, they also tell us who we as a people are, where we have been and where we are going; in their size and duration they separate our culture from all others, teach us about political life, set our individual and collective priorities, entertain us, and provide bases for social interaction."[1]

## PRESIDENTIAL CAMPAIGNS

There are numerous channels of campaign communication to include: public performances (speeches, rallies); interpersonal (luncheons, meetings with opinion leaders); organizational (party machines, workers); display media (buttons, posters, billboards); print media (campaign literature, ads, newspapers); auditory media (radio, telephone); and television (advertising, news coverage, programs). Campaigns are complex communication activities. In the last chapter we noted the growing influence of communication specialists in every level of political campaigns. Some local campaigns are as complex, long, and expensive as national campaigns. But the American presidential contest is the most unique in the world. Because of the magnitude of the office, every presidential election is historical and impacts upon the rest of the world. It is for this reason that we chose to investigate the overt and subtle role communication plays in the realm of presidential election campaigns. Many of the general notions explicated here are indeed true for all campaigns. To appreciate and understand a presidential contest is to also understand the nature of American electoral politics.

The formal criteria for becoming president as set forth in Article II, Section 1 of the Constitution are threefold: natural born citizen, at least 35 years old, and a resident of the United States for 14 years. But the informal criteria are numerous and include: political experience, personal charisma, fundraising, and audience adaptation. Today, the presidential contest extends beyond the traditional three-month campaign between Labor Day and November every four years. In fact, the contest has become continual and for some participants, a matter of life-long training and maneuvering. A "good man" for the job is not just found but is created, demonstrated, and articulated to the American public. The distinction between being a president and being a presidential candidate has virtually disappeared. Godfrey Hodgson even argues that the presidential election campaign is no longer simply the way a president is chosen but it actually influences the *kind* of person chosen and the priorities they will have as president.[12] Thus, the strategies and tactics presidential candidates use to present themselves and to communicate with the American public are of vital importance and are the focus of this chapter.

## PRE-PRIMARY PERIOD

A run for the presidency has become a long, expensive, and complicated process. The period between elections is vital for the success of any presidential campaign.[13] During elections, voters are bombarded with persuasive appeals. The salience of politics is high and campaign persuasion is aimed primarily at reinforcing the perceptions and commitment of the electorate to a candidate. Therefore, the period between elections is ideal for issue and image development when political awareness is low and partisan appeals are less salient. During this time, potential candidates cultivate contacts in the media, write or have books ghostwritten (Kennedy's *Profiles in Courage*, Nixon's *Six Crises*, Carter's *Why Not the Best?*, Reagan's *Where's the Rest of Me?* or Hart's *A New Democracy*). Candidates also start syndicated radio programs and national news columns. Such activities serve to advance the views of the candidate as well as keep the individual before the public. And the public is more susceptible to the views and the candidate than in periods immediately preceding the election.

In 1976, Reagan believed that there was a large conservative constituency in the nation. By expressing this belief publicly, he was able to identify supporters, demonstrate a continuing interest in politics, and show a commitment to an ideology. Such an approach allowed Reagan to campaign for an idea rather than self thus resulting in greater media success and name recognition.

Late in 1976, Reagan started a radio show to over 100 stations and a newspaper column that was syndicated nationally. This allowed Reagan to keep his views before the public as a "working citizen."

After the 1976 presidential campaign, Reagan had over $1.2 million left over. He used these funds to help "friendly" Republican candidates in the 1978 midterm elections as well as a base for his 1980 presidential contest. In 1977 alone, Reagan visited 75 cities, delivered over 150 speeches, and always avoided any hint of running in 1980. Also, speaking as a "noncandidate," President Carter could not respond to Reagan's numerous attacks. Thus, by 1978, Reagan had nurtured a constituency, enlarged his political base, cemented relations with the media, and collected many political I.O.U.'s. By 1980, of course, Reagan had become the man to beat. His image and issue concerns were firmly established in the minds of the public.

The lesson is rather clear—start early. Only two weeks after Reagan's inauguration in 1981, former Vice-President Walter Mondale formed a Political Action Committee and began raising funds for 1984. By August 1983, six presidential candidates had visited the early primary and caucus states of New Hampshire and Iowa an average of 12 times. Five of the candidates established permanent campaign headquarters in the states.[14] In the first three months of 1983, Mondale raised over $2 million. And in May 1984, months before the presidential election, Tennessee's retiring Senator Howard Baker, a rumored Republican candidate for the 1988 presidential contest, announced he would start writing a newspaper column and doing radio commentary.[15]

Late in the pre-primary period, Judith Trent recognizes the ritualistic and crucial first act of "presidential surfacing."[16] For Trent, presidential surfacing is a series of rather specific, predictable, and planned rhetorical transactions which serve both consummatory and instrumental functions during the pre-primary phase of a presidential campaign. Surfacing activities include: building state organizations, speaking before public groups and formal gatherings, conducting public opinion, attitude and issue research, developing a formal campaign strategy, raising money, and maintaining media contacts for early exposure. Such activities become even more pronounced from the first day of the election year to the New Hampshire primary.

During the surfacing period, many of the activities are symbolic and ritualistic in nature. It provides the candidate an opportunity to appear presidential, confront various groups and issues, and to demonstrate a fitness for the office. Ritualistically, every candidate must call a press conference, make an official public announcement of his intention, and officially embark on the campaign trail to capture the party's nomination. But there are equally important instrumental or pragmatic functions during the surfacing period. The mass media are introduced to the candidate, public expectations are established, campaign issues and themes emerge, and serious contenders are identified.

The pre-primary period has increased in length. Candidates must start their presidential conquest early. In fact, the presidential contest is an ongoing process. To become president takes both time and money. For some scholars, this is not a cause for alarm. An individual who wishes to be president must demonstrate desire, determination, sincerity, and fortitude. But much of the process is false. The issues, image, and person are created in carefully prescribed and predetermined ways. Nevertheless, the pre-primary period is a vital part of the total campaign and seves both symbolic and pragmatic purposes.

## PRIMARY PERIOD

Presidential primaries, in terms of number and importance, are a rather recent phenomenon. In fact, running in too many primaries was considered a sign of weakness rather than strength. In 1952, Democratic Senator Estes Kefauver entered 13 primaries, won 12 of them, but was still denied the nomination. John Kennedy, in 1960, ran in only four primaries to demonstrate that he could draw Protestant voters. And even as recently as 1968, Hubert Humphrey won the Democratic nomination without entering a single primary.

Today, of course, primaries are a vital part of the total presidential campaign. Television more than any other element has increased their significance. In addition, the role of the party has become less important and voters are more independent. The public, in the democratic tradition, expect to see and hear candidates wooing the voters. Primaries, according to Kathleen Kendall, are "rituals of rebellion" which ultimately serve to release conflict and emotions that will result in cohesion and consensus.[17] Each primary is a localized contest with a national audience observing the game. Primaries define issues, identify groups, and test the fabric of the individual candidate. Although there are numerical winners and losers, it is the process of the symbolic battles that defines the candidate and creates public expectations of behavior. From a communication perspective, then, it is not the specific issues or general strategies used to win the localized contests that are most important. Rather, it is how the candidates position themselves in relation to the outcomes of the contest. Are they winners or losers? Front runners or also rans? Gaining momentum or declining in appeal? Achieving upsets or predictable levels of performance?

Thus, there is a rather specified ritual associated with each primary contest. The candidates must confront each other (either rhetorically or face-to-face), meet the public (to press the flesh), predict the outcome of the immediate and ultimate contest, and interpret the results. Each aspect is very important in creating and reinforcing the image of the candidate. The first two elements are obvious in terms of their importance. The importance of the latter two elements is perhaps less obvious.

Predicting the outcome of a primary contest has several functions. It gives the candidate exposure to the press and allows the candidate to reinforce desired image perceptions of winner, presidential material, front runner, etc. It also gives the candidate the opportunity to predict modestly and then to look better than predictions. In short, it allows the candidate the opportunity to shape pre-primary election expectations. Finally, predicting the outcome helps to generate interest in the election and hopefully increase voter turnout.

Dwight Freshley argues that there are three "rhetorical laws" of primaries.[18] First, candidates will play down their chances for winning a primary or their take of the vote so if they receive more than predicted the candidate can claim victory regardless of the results of the primary. The second rhetorical law of primaries is what Freshley calls the "40 percent law." The underdog candidate will be declared a winner if he receives over 40 percent of the vote in a two-man race. Finally, Freshley argues that the post-primary comments will take one of four positions. The rhetorical choices abound for the winner. The specific interpretation of the win depends upon how many primaries won or lost, time of primary season, margin of victory, and number of delegates at stake. A second position a participant can take is to make it appear that the winner fell short of goal and prediction. Another position a candidate can take is to confirm pre-primary predictions and stress that the candidacy is viable, successful, and gaining momentum. Finally, if a candidate comes in third or greater, some explanation of losing must be provided. Usually such an explanation is one of "can't win them all," "expected all along to lose," or complete candor that one did not do well and congratulate the winner.

Post-primary comments and interpretations of results is another way of getting voters involved in the election. By completing the immediate event they also set the stage and tone for the next contest or rematch. Post-primary comments also provide additional media coverage for candidates to make national proclamations.

Of course, the timing of the primary influences the rhetorical stance a candidate takes. The New Hampshire primary, as the first popularity contest, is the most important one. It can serve as the springboard for long-shot candidates such as McGovern in 1972 and Carter in 1976. It can also make candidacies credible as Hart in 1984 or, if a candidate receives more votes than expected, make candidates moral winners as McCarthy in 1968 and McGovern in 1972. Interestingly, however, New Hampshire only provides 19 out of 3,331 convention delegates for the Democrats and 22 out of 1,994 Republican convention delegates. The importance of the New Hampshire primary cannot be overestimated.

For each presidential election there appears to be an increasing number of candidates—especially in the party not in the White House. In 1980 there were four Republican candidates and in 1976 four Democratic candidates. In 1984, there were seven Democratic candidates. Actually, by December of 1983, over 125 candidates had filed with the Federal Election Commission. Nevertheless, such large numbers of candidates require them to differentiate themselves based upon aspects of personal image rather than issues. The simple truth is that there are not enough issues or positions on issues to separate a wide field of candidates. Carter, in 1976, was masterful at projecting a personal image of honesty, goodness, and common man. Even in the 1980 primaries Carter stressed character in his ads as "husband, father, president." Edward Kennedy stressed leadership—not his controversial liberal views on many domestic issues.

Within the primary period, there does exist a unique situation when an incumbent is challenged for the nomination. The incumbent usually emphasizes the fact that he represents the party and to deny him the nomination would indeed divide the party and hence jeopardize the election. The incumbent also usually argues that severe attacks upon the president are, in effect, attacks upon the nation. This is indeed a strong appeal. Not since 1856 when James Buchanan replaced Franklin Pierce has a president who sought renomination failed to receive the approval from his party. The power of the incumbent cannot be overestimated. On the eve of the New Hampshire primary in 1980, Carter had the U.S. Olympic hockey team that defeated the Soviet team visit the White House. Much favorable press resulted. In addition, for example, on the mornings of the Wisconsin and Kansas primaries, Carter made a public announcement of a "positive step" toward the release of the American hostages in Iran—a very hot political problem for Carter.[19]

Challengers to the president will usually claim that the incumbent is not providing the leadership needed by the nation. They will also argue that the president is so weak that all the party candidates will go down in defeat in the November election. Finally, most challengers will also charge that the president did not keep promises made in the last election. In 1980, this charge was consistently made by Kennedy against Carter.

The presidential primaries today are most important. They make or break a campaign. The rhetorical strategies are vast but the structure and stance of the ritualized conflict are predictable and prescribed. Election interpretations and presentations are most important during this period.

## THE CONVENTIONS

Political conventions really serve three functions. They, of course, officially nominate the party's candidate. Conventions also unify the party for both local and national candidates. And, perhaps most importantly, conventions provide a free forum to present the candidate's issues and image to those watching the proceedings on television. With the increase in the number of primaries, the convention is no longer a political party affair but a candidate's bash. The nominee is the star and focus of attention. The entire convention serves as center stage for the nominee and can provide a good beginning for the official campaign. Thus, a deadlocked convention may be a spectator's dream but it is a candidate's nightmare. Division, debate, and controversy may provide excitement but contribute little to unity, loyalty, and the reinforcement of candidate image. Thus, from a communication perspective, the more the eventual nominee of the party can control the agenda, speakers, rallys, etc., the better the convention serves the candidate.

## THE CAMPAIGN

At the microscopic level, each presidential campaign is a unique historical event. Each possesses its own cast of characters, issues, conflicts, and contexts. A presidential campaign, according to James Barber, "is a rousing call to arms. Candidates mobilize their forces for showdowns and shootouts, blasting each other with rhetorical volleys. It is a risky adventure; its driving force is surprise, as the fortunes of combat deliver setbacks and breakthroughs contrary to the going expectation, and the contenders struggle to recover and exploit the sudden changes."[20] Yet, from a macroscopic level, modern presidential campaigns are all very similar. There are a limited number of issues, images, tactics, and strategies available for any campaign. In fact, Barber even argues that "from the turn of the century to present day, three themes have dominated successive campaign years: politics as conflict, politics as conscience, and politics as conciliation. That sequence runs its course over a twelve year period and then starts over again."[21] Thus, there are strong similarities in all presidential campaigns. The role and nature of communication is the structure that provides for the commonalities. In this section we will consider the role of communication in determining candidate campaign strategy and techniques.

## The Role of Marketing

In Chapter 3 the importance and role of the political consultants were discussed in great detail. Suffice to say that presidential politics are big business, complicated and high tech. Politics has changed from an art to a science. Especially with the supreme importance of the mass media, politicians are utilizing marketing techniques and research tools. Gary Mauser argues that candidates and marketers have the same basic problems and goals. They both are competing for the support of a specified, target group under the constraints of time, money, and personnel.[22] It is rather natural, then, for politicians to utilize the techniques of product marketing for election campaigns. This development, according to Jack Honomichl, reached a new high during Ronald Reagan's 1979 presidential campaign.[23] It was, from a marketing standpoint, the most sophisticated and well-funded research program in the history of American politics.

Reagan's 1979 presidential bid was based on a marketing plan developed by Richard Warthlin, president of the firm Decision Making Information (DMI). He developed a 176-page strategy statement that became the bible of the campaign.[24]

In addition to the normal national polling of attitudes, DMI budgeted $1.5 million for four major national studies and continual tracking studies in nine pivotal states.[25] As early as June 1979, a major psychographic study was conducted to help understand the motives underlying people's attitudes and opinions.[26] Until this time, most politicians relied upon simple attitude surveys, voter characteristics, and demographics for voter profiles. The main conclusion of the study was that Reagan voters obtained high scores on the scales for: respect for authority, individualism, authoritarianism, and a low score on egalitarianism. Also, the study revealed that Democrats over age 55 shared the same characteristics and thus are a prime target for conversion. The study also identified three groups of people Reagan should address: employed head-of-household Democrats, 35 years of age, earning less than $15,000 a year; voters who prefer Reagan over Carter and Edward Kennedy; and voters who switched to Edward Kennedy in the Democratic presidential primaries. This last group would, on the surface, appear to be nonsense. Why would anyone who would vote for a self-professed Democratic liberal ultimately vote for a self-professed Republican conservative? Actually, the study revealed that people who vacillated between Carter and Kennedy really did not have strong ideological positions since the two were so different themselves.

Although traditional polling identified a list of pressing national problems, DMI early ascertained that the electorate really wanted a positive view of the future. In order to win, the candidates had to change the electorate's perceptions of the future. Thus, when Carter chose to make Reagan the main issue, he virtually lost the election. This conclusion was based on a study of voter expectations conducted in June prior to the conventions and main campaign period.[27] The study revealed that when voters were asked to name something bad that would happen if Reagan were elected, 72 percent named something but in terms of Carter 83 percent named something. If people, then, simply voted based upon their expectations of the future, Reagan would win the election.

Hopefully the point is rather obvious—perhaps once again. Often it is not concrete issues that win elections but the images, visions, and persona communicated to the electorate. And the use of marketing techniques goes beyond the simple identification of key issues or public concerns. Rather, they help to focus on the subtle likes and dislikes as well as motivations for human behavior in rather quantifiable terms.

## Channels of Communication and Communication Strategy

There are four basic communication channels: the electronic media, the print media, display media (i.e., billboards, etc.), and personal contact. It is a most difficult task to determine the best combination of media to reach the potential audience and that which best communicates the desired theme. In addition, the factors of timing, money, and distribution are also important considerations. Candidates must decide when and where they will concentrate their communication efforts making sure that they do not peak too soon or spend too much in areas of little consequence.

To determine the communication strategy, the target audience must be identified and segmented. This includes both committed loyalist and potential voters. Next, most campaigns attempt to "map" voter perceptions. The goal here is to identify the ways voters classify the candidates and issues viewed as important in the decision process.

A great deal of time is also spent on identifying and characterizing the competition. By mapping voter preferences candidates can better identify specific strengths, weaknesses, and likely patterns of competition. From all this information, various strategies can be identified, discussed, and evaluated. Ultimately, a budget is allocated, a strategy determined, time and content of appeals isolated, and a detailed media and marketing plan established.

But despite all this activity, there is a high degree of homogeneity in the political perceptions of the American people.[28] It is difficult for well-known politicians to radically alter their image once it has become fixed in the minds of the public. There is little advertising can do to drastically change or convert voter perceptions, beliefs, and attitudes. Thus, most strategies seek to reinforce and link campaigns to existing perceptions, beliefs, and attitudes.

There is a standard, well-known marketing and advertising dictum. Products compete best against each other as long as they are perceived as being similar to each other. As Mauser observes, "the patterns of competition for any new product can be predicted from its pattern of perceived similarity with the other products in the markets."[29] Thus, challengers must appear presidential and presidents must act presidential. With this in mind, Mauser argues that the following communication strategies are probably most effective.[30]

1. Stress importance of features that are most attractive to target electorate.

2. Avoid, or state euphemistically, the features that are deemed to be undesirable.

3. Coordinate all information and advertising to reinforce the most important features of the candidate.

4. If possible, attempt to move the candidate along those dimensions that can place him in an advantageous position.

## Campaign Strategies

### Public Statements about Campaign Strategies

There is a rather clear distinction, as Henry Ewbank observes, between campaign strategies and public statements about campaign strategies.[31] Public statements about campaign strategies come from three sources: the candidate, the candidate's spokesperson, or from an opponent. For example, in 1976, Ford claimed Carter was not specific on issue positions and thus revealed that his strategy was to attack issues known; that he could not counter Carter's "pure, wholesome, outsider's" strategy. Often strategy statements result from a direct challenge by an opponent, the media, or a specific voting bloc of citizens. Sometimes, in an effort to gain media attention or redefine the campaign issues, a candidate will provide a statement articulating a position or campaign strategy. Most public strategy statements deal with specific actions to be taken if elected, feelings or emotions relevant to the current state of affairs, and intentions relating to the execution of the campaign. The latter serves to establish appearances of fairness, openmindedness, and honesty. The themes of most public statements about strategy are twofold: consistency and uniqueness. Consistency is related in terms of how the candidate will meet the needs and expectations of the public and uniqueness is related in terms of how the candidate will provide new leadership and new solutions to old problems.

For Ewbank, strategy statements can be classified in five ways according to apparent intent:

1. offering an interpretation of a past great event,
2. offering an explanation of current campaign events,
3. offering a description of the future,
4. soliciting reaction to some aspect of the campaign that may serve as a "trial balloon" for future reference, and
5. constructing a desired perception of an event or issue position that is about to become a visible part of a campaign.

A strategy is a way to achieve an objective or goal. In politics, the goal is to win the election. To do this, of course, requires getting individuals to become committed to one's candidacy, and then, of equal importance, to actually vote in the election. This is indeed a long, complicated process. No single variable, issue, event, or personal characteristic can motivate enough people to become committed and to vote in sufficient numbers to win an election. Likewise, no single strategy can win an election. But we argue that there are a limited number of communication approaches or strategies in which to articulate and motivate voters. Thus, to a large extent, specific issues, candidates, and elections are not of great importance. What is important is whether or not the candidate is an incumbent or challenger.

### Incumbent Strategies

Judith Trent and Robert Friedenberg have identified several incumbent campaign strategies.[32] It is useful to review those strategies.

An incumbent has many more strategy options than challengers. Some of the strategies involve maximizing the symbolic, subtle aspects of the office. Incumbents are certain to surround themselves with the purely symbolic trappings of the office. Such trappings include the use of the presidential podium and seal, "Hail to the Chief," and various official backdrops. Such devices communicate the strength and grandeur of the office. They serve to remind the audience that they are listening to the president of the United States and not just an average citizen. It is not surprising, therefore, that in April of 1984, President Reagan changed the location of his televised press conferences. He stood before an open doorway in the East Room of the White House that reveals a long, elegant corridor. The cameras record a majestic setting and a stately exit that dramatizes the importance of the office. In addition to the physical artifacts that enhance the prestige of the incumbent, the office itself evokes a sense of legitimacy, competency, and charisma to its occupant. Any individual who holds the office is perceived as rational, intelligent, and is granted deference. The pageantry, history, and majesty of the office is transferred to its occupant. In a campaign, such perceptions are worth a great deal.

Presidents have immediate and almost total access to the media. It is very easy for them to create pseudoevents for the purpose of gaining favorable media exposure. Such pseudoevents include making special announcements, appointments, or proclamations that have more political impact than policy impact. When Reagan visited South Korea, his aides ensured that he was surrounded by barbed wire and sandbags. In fact, they had an armored vehicle placed in the background when he spoke to the troops.[33] Although Reagan stayed for just one inning at the opening day of the baseball season in Baltimore, he was seen the next day in the media throwing a ball and eating a hot dog in the dugout.

During the campaign period, presidents make many appointments to jobs and special committees. This is a way to line up supporters early in the campaign, tap talent for the reelection bid, and identify people for key positions after the election. Also reports of special task forces are usually revealed during the campaign period. Task forces are effective ways to address special issues or concerns of the voters without committing resources or personal support. The very act of forming a task force communicates concern about an issue and the promise of future action. Actually, it allows the candidate to postpone taking a stand on controversial issues while at the same time making an appeal to a particular group of voters.

An incumbent president will appropriate billions of dollars to "cooperative" public officials for cities and projects in return for support. By the 1980 election, Carter had given over $80 billion in the form of federal grants.

Without doubt, incumbent presidents will visit world leaders during an election year. Such trips provide great drama and show the president as a world leader respected by other countries. The foreign visits also provide a repertoire of future references that can be worked in debates and discourse to reinforce notions of leadership and experience. How ironic indeed in 1980 when President Reagan, who spent most of his political career opposing the Chinese Communists, not only visited mainland China but offered U.S. economic and technological assistance. But most important, the trip was a television spectacular. Michael Deaver, a presidential aide, spent nine days in China scouting locations for the president to visit.[34] The Republican National Committee sent a special film crew to record footage to be used in political commercials. Even Reagan's itinerary was influenced by the potential of media coverage. A trip down the Yangtze River was canceled because there was no way to get the tapes to the networks for showing.[35]

Incumbent presidents have the opportunity to manipulate domestic issues. This is done in two ways. First, presidents can divert or lessen the impact of news by creating competing pseudoevents. For example, the day unemployment climbed to 10 percent in 1982, Reagan called a press conference to announce the suspension of Poland's status as a most-favored-nation. Another way to manipulate domestic issues is to take short-term actions that will provide at least a temporary impact. This is especially true in the economic realm. Usually, by election time, interest rates and inflation are down. In fact, the stock market has gone down only six times in the 21 years in which presidential elections were held since 1900.[36] The reason is fairly simple. Administrations in the final two years of a term focus on economic expansion to enhance the party's reelection endeavors.

A strategy that is especially useful for incumbent presidents is to obtain the public endorsements of local respected, successful, and well-liked politicians. Here the candidate is trying to link himself with already established leaders.

Presidents can also use surrogates to campaign for them. Popular members from the administration or locals who are part of the administration can have a very positive effect upon a campaign. Simply because of the daily job requirements, nearly all presidents are forced to rely upon the help of others during the campaign season. In 1972, Nixon used over 50 surrogates and in the midterm elections of 1982, the Republican National Committee developed a program called "Surrogate 82" where all cabinet members were required to give 15 days to campaign activities. During the 1980 presidential campaign, Carter was forced to use surrogates because of his statement that he would not campaign while Americans were still held as hostages in Iran. As their length of captivity lengthened, Carter had to rescind his statement. There is a limit to the use of surrogates. The American public expects candidates to travel and press the flesh—up to a point. An incumbent president must not appear to be neglecting the job of running the country. Thus, the use of surrogates best complements the campaigning of an incumbent president rather than replacing it.

Somewhat related, most incumbents try to create the image that they are above the political battle and removed from the day-to-day charges and countercharges of politics. Early presidents, as already noted, seldom actively participated in campaigns or even attended the party conventions. Such participation appeared undignified and unstatesmanlike. In contemporary times, the extreme of such a strategy is called the "Rose Garden" strategy. Very strong candidates can stay at the White House appearing presidential, committed, and serious. Gerald Ford used this strategy in 1976 until it was clear that he faced stiff competition from Jimmy Carter.

Nearly all presidents claim that reelection will communicate to the world a sense of stability. Most incumbents intensify their description of foreign policy problems to create an illusion of crisis to motivate voters to rally around and support the administration. Roosevelt was most successful using this strategy. History has shown that regardless of the crisis, Americans offer support to their leaders rather than condemnation.

Finally, the major strategy of every incumbent president is to emphasize administration accomplishments. They must demonstrate tangible results to promises made or problems solved. If not, they must deny problems are problems or clearly place blame on a single individual or group. Actions often speak louder than results. To propose a constitutional amendment to balance the budget even though such a proposal would never be taken seriously is to at once fulfill a campaign promise and to place blame if not accepted. For every action, there is an official interpretation that must be provided.

Despite the appearance of an almost limitless number of strategy options, Trent and Friedenberg are correct in claiming that there are several major disadvantages of incumbency campaigning.[37] First, as already mentioned, every president must run on his record. All actions or interactions must be explained and justified. Naturally, the challenger will blame the incumbent for all ills and problems of the nation. As the total presidential campaign period lengthens, challengers literally have years to question, second-guess, and negate the efforts of the current president. In the real world and especially in politics, there are seldom complete victories. Most victories are partial and it becomes demoralizing for every effort to be criticized or questioned. Finally, the media create a climate of expectations, conflict, and excitement during a campaign. There is a great deal of pressure associated with being the incumbent. America traditionally favors the underdog and a good fight. Thus, there are more restrictions on behavior and performance pressure associated with the incumbent than with the challengers.

### Challenger Strategies

When campaigning against an incumbent president, challengers must take the offensive position in a campaign. Every action, issue, and stance of the president is questioned, challenged, and sometimes ridiculed. This often goes beyond simply attacking the record of the incumbent. The probing and questioning seldom results in the presenting of concrete solutions. John Kennedy never provided the details to the New Frontier nor Nixon on how he would end the war in Vietnam nor Reagan on how he would end inflation. In fact, being too specific can lead to counter-questions and attacks. For example, in 1972 McGovern provided the details of a tax plan and guaranteed income that caused many problems.

Most of the time, challengers call for a change—a change in direction and leadership. They emphasize optimism for the future and share a vision of future prosperity and peace. Challengers focus their appeals on traditional values as Carter did in 1976 (honesty, self-rule, humility, morality) and Reagan did in 1980 (free enterprise, capitalism, democracy, and moral courage).

Challengers must create constituency groups and will always claim to speak for the forgotten American, the silent majority, and middle America. This transforms into a strategy of articulating the values and feelings of an average American. The philosophical center is the road to follow.

## THE CAMPAIGN PROMISE

A recent feature of American politics is the campaign promise. In theory, an elected official is obligated to fulfill promises made during a campaign as a result of the electoral mandate. Despite jokes about campaign promises, each election generates countless promises from candidates. To demonstrate the seriousness with which they are made, Carter's transition team compiled a 114-page listing of his 1976 campaign promises. But promises are difficult to keep or fulfill. In 1980 Reagan promised to reduce federal spending, to cut federal taxes, to reduce inflation, to balance the federal budget, and to increase defense spending. By 1984, Reagan's federal budget had the highest deficit in American history. Some would argue that the fulfillment of three out of five major campaign promises is not a bad record. Of course, for test purposes that represents a score of 60 percent—a failing mark by most standards. Others would argue that to even promise reduced federal spending and a balanced budget reflects supreme naivete. But keeping campaign promises is a difficult task and their fulfillment depends upon the cooperation of others. Few promises can be met with a simple presidential declaration. From a communication perspective, there are three observations about campaign promises. First, the degree of importance attached to a promise depends upon how much the fulfillment of the promise affects each of us. Thus, of the promises made during a campaign, only those relevant to us as a group or individuals are to be remembered. Second, what constitutes fulfillment of a promise is likely to be an attempted action rather than a complete fulfillment of the promise. To lower inflation by 1 percent is to fulfill the promise of lowering inflation but may be of little real value in real economic terms. The issue of what determines fulfillment of a campaign promise, then, is a matter of interpretation and campaign debate. Finally, there is indeed a rhetoric of campaigning that differs from a rhetoric of governing. One is the rhetoric of hope, promise, and certainty. The other is one of negotiation, persuasion, and compromise.

## THE BASIC CAMPAIGN SPEECH

Local appearances by candidates demand a few appropriate remarks. With the frequency of travel and the nature of national campaigning, candidates develop a set speech that becomes the basis of their remarks for every speaking situation. The basic campaign speech has four purposes.[38] First, the basic speech defines the crucial issues of the campaign. Most issues fall within the areas of policy issues, personal issues, or leadership issues. Issues in campaigns also display similar characteristics. They tend to be very broad, small in number, lack definition, and seldom defined in terms that will arouse controversy. Also, campaign issues are often linked to claims about the personal qualities of the opponent. Finally, some issues are indeed localized as education for the South, unemployment for the Northeast, farming for the Midwest, and environmental protection for the West.

The second purpose of a basic campaign address is to identify and emphasize the failures of the opposition. Here past issue positions, actions, and voting records are used to demonstrate either a lack of ability to lead by the opponent or a lack of proper position on the issues by the opponent. The speech must at least attempt to show why the opponent should not obtain the office. Statements concerning actions, positions, or personal characteristics are offered as evidence of failure.

Another important purpose of the basic campaign speech is to appeal to the audience. This is achieved through style and substance of the address. Stylistically, the candidate hopes to use common words and phrases unique to the area. The goal is to give the appearance of being one of the locals, sharing their concerns and speaking their language. Dress is also a part of this process. When speaking to farmers, candidates often wear jeans and a plaid shirt.

Finally, the basic campaign speech offers a vision of the future. The vision is usually a carefully constructed articulation of the American dream: a world of peace, prosperity, justice, and equality. The vision often involves evoking a sense of duty and obligation to make the future better than the present for the sake of our children and grandchildren. The vision portion of the speech need not be logical but uplifting and inspiring.

The structure of the basic campaign speech also follows a rather fixed pattern or formula. The speech describes, in general terms, "the problem," fixes blame for "the problem," calls for change, and promises that change will indeed improve the future. Thus, each candidate defines the current state of affairs as one of crisis and blames the current situation on the opponent. The candidate calls for change and the change is, of course, the election of the candidate who will provide a glorious future.

The basic stump campaign speech is truly a localized affair. The major issues of the campaign have long been decided. But the candidate meeting the public face-to-face has become an important part of presidential politics. Such events, however, hold little interest for the national newspeople traveling with the candidate. They hear the basic speech hundreds of times. What interests them most are the question and answer exchanges that follow most addresses. Here the candidate may show unexpected emotion, share a new statement or position, or stimulate some newsworthy event. Thus, although the basic speech is given over and over again, the national audience is unlikely to have heard the speech. The campaign event is new and appears spontaneous to those hearing the candidate in person.

## PRESIDENTIAL CAMPAIGN DEBATES

Presidential debates are becoming an expected element of presidential campaigns. Historically, the Lincoln-Douglas debate of 1858 provided the precedence for the debating of political issues. But the Kennedy-Nixon debates of 1960 firmly established the debates as a part of presidential politics. In fact, the 1960 presidential debates attracted the largest television audience (at that point in history) of over 100 million viewers.[39] Incumbent presidents view debating opponents as too risky. Gerald Ford became the first incumbent president to debate his opponent, Jimmy Carter. Four years later, Carter also debated his challenger. In both cases, however, the incumbent lost the election.

Debates have three general benefits for the electorate. They provide an opportunity to compare the personalities and issue positions of the candidates. They can, therefore, be more revealing than simply listening to the basic campaign speeches of the candidates. And finally, political debates can stimulate voter interest in the campaign. But contemporary presidential debates are not as freewheeling or spontaneous as most voters think. They are as planned, rehearsed, and constructed as any other speech, commercial, or public presentation. The candidates place a great deal of importance on the debates. Image definition and confirmation is supreme to issue development and debate.[40]

To get candidates to even debate requires a great deal of negotiation. In the debates of 1976, the issues of lighting, staging, position of cameras, use of reaction shots, camera movement, and the height of the podiums became major points of discussion and negotiation between the candidates prior to agreeing to debate.[41] In the 1980 debates, an issue of discussion was whether or not the candidates would sit or stand. Carter favored sitting while Reagan favored standing. The compromise was to have stools for both candidates such that if seated the candidate would still appear standing. Are such issues, totally irrelevant to running the nation and current problems, really important? Most campaign organizations believe so and there is a growing body of research to support such conclusions.[42] For example, one study of the 1960 presidential debates reports that those listening to the debates on the radio thought neither candidate won the debates but those watching the debates on television thought Kennedy clearly won the debates.[43] Robert Tiemens, in investigating factors of visual communication in the 1976 presidential debates, found that differences in camera framing and composition, camera angle, screen placement, and reaction shots seemingly favored Carter.[44]

The 1980 debates, according to Myles Martel, represents the ultimate in candidate planning and preparing for presidential debates.[45] Reagan's preparation for the debates was much more elaborate than Carter's preparation. As early as August, Reagan developed a Debate Task Force that would perform the following tasks: negotiate the formats, prepare briefing materials, conduct research, develop debate strategies and tactics, and provide professional consultation on presentational aspects of the debates. Reagan spent three intense days prior to the debates practicing before knowledgeable panelists. In addition to strategy, they discussed such things as how he should arrive at the debates (they chose by airplane because it would appear more presidential), whether or not he should shake hands (they decided to shake hands first to give appearance of friendliness), and when to smile.[46] The Reagan campaign even had a Debate Operations Center where 50 researchers carefully monitored the debates to see if Carter committed any errors in statements so they could contact the media immediately.[47]

There are numerous strategies and tactics one can use during debates. Each one must be carefully analyzed to assess the potential gain or loss for the candidate. Many decisions are based upon the perceived image or approach by the opponent. The simple point is, there are many communication variables involved in any presidential debate. The strategies and tactics are carefully planned and rehearsed.[48]

## POST-CAMPAIGN

Ruth Weaver argues that there are rather strong rules that govern victory and concession statements made by candidates on election night.[49] Acknowledgment of victory and defeat have almost become a ritual of American politics. There are three rules that govern post-campaign statements. The loser of the contest must concede before the winner can claim victory. The statements of the candidates are often made in response to each other. The loser reads the congratulatory telegram sent to the winner and the winner re-reads the telegram before supporters. The loser appears before supporters surrounded by family. Thus, the sequence of messages, the reading of loser's telegram, and personal appearances of candidate surrounded by family members provide the contextual expectation associated with victory and defeat statements.

But the content of such statements is also familiar. Losers usually, first of all, offer thanks for family, friends, workers, and supporters during the campaign. They often then provide a statement of support for the newly elected president. Such support, depending upon the margin of defeat, may make reference to the notion of loyal opposition. Weaver observes that the greater the margin of defeat the more prevalent the theme of continual challenging of the opponent becomes in the concession statements.[50] Support statements often contain explicit offers of help and direct assistance to the newly elected president.

Victors also thank their supporters, workers, and family. In addition, they are often laudatory in the comments about their opponents. They acknowledge a good campaign and express respect for their opponent. Next, the winner must make overt appeals for national unity. He is and will be president of all the people regardless of issues or views. Most of these statements are less policy-oriented and more general in nature. The victor, without doubt, expresses humility and offers a pledge to all the citizens that he is dedicated to the principles that make America great. Finally, most winners reassure the public that there will be a continuity in the transition of power or, if an incumbent, a continuation of the administration without an interruption of government.

Election night statements of victory and defeat are only the first elements of the process that ultimately unites the citizens behind the reign of a new president or the continuation of an old one. In the months prior to the inauguration, the media floods the nation with background information about the new president. The person is set within a historical perspective of the office. Anticipation of the members of the new administration mounts. The newly elected leader, when speaking before groups, makes appeals to national unification, support, and rearticulates a vision of the future that inspires hope, confidence, and excitement. By inauguration day a candidate has emerged as president. A tremendous transformation, at least in the eyes of the public, has occurred. The citizens are committed to the democratic process and notion that one of them has been elevated to the position of leader fully deserving a chance of success. In fact, a large majority of citizens will report voting for the new president regardless of the actual size of electoral victory.[51] The inauguration activities and speech culminate the process of acknowledgment and acceptance of the new administration.

## CONCLUSION

Political campaigns are long and expensive. They offer numerous messages about our past, future, and current situations. As primarily communication phenomena, they influence and impact our behavior in both obvious and subtle ways. Their importance transcends the preference of one individual over another.

Although many countries have elections, American presidential elections are most unique. Political campaigns are truly communication events: communication of images, characters, and persona. Presidential campaigns are long, nearly continuous events. The burden is on the candidate to appear presidential, capable, and worthy of trust and confidence.

The pre-primary period is when most of the candidate creation takes place. During this period the public is more susceptible to the ideas and arguments of future candidates. The groundwork for the campaign is carefully planned and constructed during this period.

For most Americans, the political season really begins during the primary period. The period tests the fabric of the candidates, the depth of their views, and the dimensions of their persona. Election interpretations and presentations are most important during this period.

Presidential campaigns follow rather predictable patterns. There are a limited number of issues, images, tactics, and strategies that are available for any campaign. Today, as never before, the tools of marketing and research are the instruments of electoral victory. American presidential politics is not based upon issue development as much as specified images, visions, and persona targeted to identified and segmented audiences.

Most campaign strategies are designed to do more than get votes. They are designed to project a certain image, alter a perception, or counter the opposition. Communication is at the heart of every campaign strategy. Strategies can be grouped based upon whether the candidate is an incumbent or challenger. In terms of American presidential politics, the incumbent has many more strategy options than challengers. From the strategies, the promises, the basic speeches, and even the acceptances of victory and defeat, the rhetorical patterns are predictable in both form and content. In the end a president is elected who must confront new communication challenges.

## NOTES

1. James Barber, *The Pulse of Politics* (New York: W. W. Norton, 1980), p. 3.

2. P. Lazarsfeld, B. Berelson, and H. Gaudet, *The People's Choice* (New York: Columbia University Press, 1984).

3. See also Garrett O'Keefe, "Political Campaigns and Mass Communication Research," in *Political Communication: Issues and Strategies for Research,* ed. Steven Chaffee (Beverly Hills, Calif.: Sage, 1975), pp. 129-64 and Garrett O'Keefe and Edwin Atwood, "Communication and Election Campaigns" in *Handbook of Political Communication,* ed. Dan Nimmo and Keith Sanders (Beverly Hills, Calif.: Sage, 1981), pp. 329-58.

4. For a full explanation of this approach, see R. Sanders and L. Kaid, "An Overview of Political Communication Theory and Research: 1976-1977," in *Communication Yearbook II,* ed. Brent Rubin (New Jersey: Transaction Books, 1978), pp. 375-89.

5. Gary Mauser, *Political Marketing* (New York: Praeger, 1983), pp. 31-50.

6. Samuel Becker, "Rhetorical Studies for the Contemporary World," in *The Prospect of Rhetoric,* ed. Lloyd Bitzer and Edwin Black (Englewood Cliffs, N.J.: Prentice-Hall, 1971), pp. 21-43.

7. Ibid., p. 33.

8. See Bruce Gronbeck, "Functional and Dramaturgical Theories of Presidential Campaigning," *Presidential Studies Quarterly* 14 (Fall 1984):487-98 and "The Functions of Presidential Campaigning," *Communication Monographs* 45 (November 1978):268-80.

9. Gronbeck, "Functional and Dramaturgical Theories," p. 490.

10. Gronbeck, "The Functions of Presidential Campaigning," p. 271.

11. Gronbeck, "Functional and Dramaturgical Theories," p. 496.

12. Godfrey Hodgson, *All Things to All Men* (New York: Touchstone, 1980), p. 211.

13. James Cantrill, "Reaching the People When They Least Expect It: The Role of Inter-Campaign Communication" (Paper presented at the Annual Convention of Eastern Communication Association, Hartford, Connecticut, May 8, 1982). This paper provided a good discussion of this notion.

14. Steven Manning, *1984 Presidential Election Handbook* (New York: Newsweek, 1984), p. 3.

15. "Washington Whispers," *U.S. News and World Report,* May 14, 1984, p. 18.

16. See Judith S. Trent, "Presidential Surfacing: The Ritualistic and Crucial First Act," *Communication Monographs* 45 (November 1978):281-92 and Judith Trent and Robert Friedenberg, *Political Campaign Communication* (New York: Praeger, 1983), pp. 25-35.

17. Kathleen Kendall, "Fission and Fusion: The Primaries and the Conventions" (Paper presented at the Annual Convention of the Central States Speech Association, Chicago, Illinois, April 11, 1981).

18. Dwight Freshley, "Manipulating Public Expectations: Pre- and Post-primary Statements in the '76 Campaign" (Paper presented at the Annual Convention of the Speech Communication Association, Minneapolis, Minnesota, November 4, 1978).

19. As reported in Richard Watson, *The Presidential Contest* (New York: John Wiley & Sons, 1980), p. 34.

20. Barber, *The Pulse of Politics*, p. 3.

21. Ibid.

22. See Mauser, *Political Marketing.*

23. Jack Honomichl, *Marketing/Research People: Their Behind-the-Scenes Stories* (Chicago: Crain Books, 1984), p. 67.

24. Ibid., p. 70.

25. Ibid.

26. Ibid., pp. 69-70.

27. Ibid., p. 74.

28. For a good statement and rationale provided see Mauser, *Political Marketing*, especially pp. 266-68.

29. Ibid., p. 267.

30. Ibid.

31. Henry Ewbank, "Public Statements Concerning Campaign Strategies" (Paper presented at the Annual Central States Speech Association Convention, Lincoln, Nebraska, April 8, 1983).

32. Trent and Friedenberg, *Political Campaign Communication*, pp. 83-105.

33. "It's Show Time for President in China," *U.S. News and World Report*, May 7, 1984, p. 23.

34. Ibid.

35. As reported in ibid.

36. As reported in *U.S. News and World Report*, January 16, 1984, pp. 60-61.

37. Trent and Friedenberg, *Political Campaign Communication*, pp. 104-5.

38. Lenny Reiss and Dan Hahn, "The Dichotomous Substance and Stylistic Appeals in Kennedy's 1980 Basic Speech" (Paper presented at the Annual Convention of Eastern Communication Association, Pittsburgh, Penn., April 24, 1981).

39. Myles Martel, *Political Campaign Debates* (New York: Longman, 1983), p. 1.

40. Ibid., p. 2.

41. Robert R. Tiemens, "Television's Portrayal of the 1976 Presidential Debates: An Analysis of Visual Content," *Communication Monograph* 45 (November 1978):362-70.

42. See Martel, *Political Campaign Debates*; Sidney Kraus, *The Great Debates (Carter vs Ford)* (Bloomington, Ind.: University of Indiana Press, 1976); Sidney Kraus, *The Great Debates (Kennedy vs Nixon, 1960)* (Bloomington, Ind.: Univer-

sity of Indiana Press, 1962); Earl Mayo, *The Great Debates* (Santa Barbara, Calif.: Center for the Study of Democratic Institutions, 1962); *Report of the Commission on Presidential Campaign Debates* (Washington, D.C.: American Political Science Association, 1964).

43. Elihn Katz and Jacob Feldman, "The Debates in the Light of Research: A Survey of Surveys," in *The Great Debates*, ed. Sidney Kraus (Bloomington, Ind.: Indiana University Press, 1962), pp. 173-223.

44. Tiemens, "Television's Portrayal," p. 370.

45. Martel, *Political Campaign Debates*, p. 7.

46. Ibid., pp. 12-76.

47. Ibid., p. 27.

48. For the best identification and description of political debate strategies and tactics, see ibid., pp. 62-76.

49. Ruth Ann Weaver, "Acknowledgement of Victory and Defeat: The Reciprocal Ritual" (Paper presented at the Annual Convention of the Central States Speech Association, Chicago, Ill., April 1980).

50. Ibid., p. 10.

51. William Mullen, *Presidential Power and Politics* (New York: St. Martin's Press, 1976), pp. 2-3.

# 5

# Dimensions of
# Administrative Rhetoric

Political discussion possesses a character fundamentally different from academic discussion. It seeks not only to be in the right, but also to demolish the basis of its opponents' social and intellectual existence.[1]

Knowing how confused and fragmented the system is, how intense the forces are that tend to induce ill-advised decisions, and how fallible the leaders who serve in public office [are], it is almost a miracle how well our nation survives and prospers.[2]

How is it that people accept poverty amid affluence, hopelessness in a land of opportunity, government by unresponsive institutions that are pledged to human service? Why do they not rebel or at least speak out more forcefully against the political and social order?[3]

In this chapter we explore some of the relevant perspectives, problems, and strategies that are unique to the communication of administrative control. We treat the topic broadly, but by no means comprehensively. Our goal is to offer both historical perspectives to administrative communication, and a variety of insights from participants and observers concerned with understanding the dynamics of leadership from the executive side of government. Two general orientations are examined. One is analytic and critical: how the process of ruling affects the rest of the polity for good or ill. The second—which opens and closes the chapter—examines the human and structural constraints that elected executives and their staffs must master. Our concerns are not about the development of an administrative style, but the communication of administrative competence. And, though we dwell on the nature of modern executive-branch departments at various governmental levels, our concern is less for how bureaucracies work, than how they effect the communication options of those who are elected to make them function effectively.

## ADMINISTERING POLICY: DILEMMAS OF COMMUNICATING ADMINISTRATIVE CONTROL

### The "Interests" and the "Bureaucracy"

In a perceptive study of the American presidency, British journalist Godfrey Hodgson puzzles over the question, "Why are the President and his men so powerless when it comes to carrying out their policies, even within their 'own' government?"[4] This query is a perennial one from foreign observers who are puzzled by the limits placed upon executives who, on paper at least, appear to be so strong. It is asked not only about the presidency, but about a wide range of elected executives faced with the task of implementing policy.

Part of the answer, of course, is that the reality of government is much more complex than is first apparent. Official authority in the United States is not evenly or simply vested in three coordinate institutions. Executives must do more than master the hurdles thrown up by the legislators and the courts. Some of the most penetrating studies of the political process have focused on the partially invisible barriers that render traditional organizational charts inadequate as maps to guide the observer through the varied political terrain.[5]

The most formidable barrier is the presence of large bureaucracies that political leaders find indifferent to vulnerable elected executives. It is a first principle of government life that high-level professional managers see their elected or politically appointed superiors as far more transient and vulnerable than themselves. The recognition of that fact makes them far more immune from the pressures and directives from the top than in a comparable private organization. When a bill becomes law—the official policy of the state or municipality—its administration typically passes to an agency under nominal supervision of the mayor, governor, or president. But in actual fact the law is essentially in the hands of civil servants who are removed from the political process. To politicians these careerists are frequently unresponsive and conservative—out of touch with public sentiment and unmoved by the political pressures that perhaps guided a program down the rough road to enactment. The elected official is perforce a communicator, guiding opinion while at the same time attempting to adapt to it. All but the very top officials of most agencies are comparatively immune to the ebb and flow of public opinion. In a study of the State Department, for example, Smith Simpson points with some disdain to the vastly differing objectives that separate a president from the bureaucracy that is supposed to serve him:

> The politician keeps one eye on the next election, which the Department ignores. The politician keeps tab on votes in Congress, not only on foreign issues but on the whole range of his program, while the Department assumes the high ground of what is best for the country. The politician is also sometimes involved in situations which make him appear to act the clown with redskin headgear . . . while the other, too far from domestic politics to view such spectacles with understanding, only shudders to think how such tomfoolery will appear abroad.[6]

Differences in constituencies also create natural tensions. Executives must be more or less continuously available to the members of the mass media that offer access to the polity they are trying to serve. Ostensibly representing the whole, their appeals must be inherently universal rather than specific, designed to serve at least some vague sense of the public interest rather than the more specialized needs served by specific state or federal agencies. A president or governor cannot seem to have clients who receive favored treatment at the expense of other constituents. But most agencies clearly do have special attentive constituencies that have strong vested interests in their actions. Some of the clients to a state Department of Education are the powerful teachers' unions, state school boards, and teacher training colleges. The clients to the Federal Communications Commission are broadcasters, cable television operators, the major networks, and a comparatively small number of consumer action groups. Such agencies have special interests, and are frequently staffed by people fundamentally sympathetic to fostering the growth of the institutions they regulate, sometimes with very little critical oversight. In addition, they are frequently involved in major struggles for power with competing agencies, creating a partially submerged level of bureaucratic politics that even a president may find difficult to handle.

The battle over the Carter administration's position on smoking and health is just one recent example. Then Health, Education and Welfare Secretary Joseph Califano wanted a much tougher administration stand on smoking, in line with the disturbing findings of the surgeon general, and of other research organizations. However, his counterpart in the Department of Agriculture had a different constituency to consider. Tobacco is a major cash crop for thousands of

American farmers. A serious offensive against smoking, from Agriculture's perspective, could weaken the administration's avowed commitment to strengthen American farming. To further complicate matters on what first seemed an uncomplicated objective, Califano was reminded that the president's own state of Georgia was built on an economy that depended heavily on the tobacco industry.[7] He went ahead with at least part of his HEW campaign, but with an awareness that even the improvement of the health of Americans carried a multitude of concealed political liabilities. "The permanent bureaucracies," notes Morton Halperin, "tend to define issues in terms of the organizational interests of the career group to which they belong. They easily come to believe that the well-being of their group is a necessary precondition for the prosperity and security of the country as a whole."[8] As a result, they may delay and temporize when asked to carry out an administrative order. And some may simply ignore all but the most direct of presidential orders.

Because of the continued existence of constraints like these, Franklin Roosevelt and Harry Truman became keen students of the limits of their own power. Roosevelt's summation of ingrained bureaucratic inertia of several executive departments is widely recalled:

> The Treasury is so large and far-flung and ingrained in its practices that I find it is almost impossible to get the action and results I want. . . . But the Treasury is not to be compared with the State Department. You should go through the experience of trying to get any changes in the thinking, policy and action of the career diplomats and then you'd know what a real problem was. But the Treasury and the State Department put together are nothing compared with the Na-a-vy. The admirals are really something to cope with, and I should know. To change anything in the Na-a-vy is like punching a feather bed.[9]

New York Mayor Edward Koch likes to tell similar stories about the organizational labyrinths that exist between a decision and its enactment. When the city decided to build fences around its heavily vandalized subway yards, for example, the mayor encountered endless red tape from the Metropolitan Transportation Authority, a fact that he was only too happy to relay to a receptive audience. With a New Yorker's fine-tuned sense of the daily compromises required of the urban dweller, his demonstration of the MTA's largesse made a salient political point about the limits of his own power:

> We are building the fence. But with the MTA, do you know what they have to do *before* they build the fence? They have to have an R.F.P.—Request for Proposal. Any place else you go out and buy a fence. Not

in the city of New York. This fence, before it will be built, I will be in my third term.[10]

In the United States, public policy at various levels of civil life is designed, enacted, and implemented by groups with distinctly different objectives and needs. A policy may surface for the first time in a city council, state legislature, or the Congress. Its key supporters may include governors, presidents, businesses, trade associations, or a coalition of legislative leaders. This pattern is familiar to us, and conforms to our sense of what public service is about. But not infrequently a bill-cum-policy will originate from yet a third source: a legislative office of a special interest group, or a politically oriented law firm. Constructed by a powerful group that seeks legislative redress or protection, and then introduced by a sympathetic lawmaker, official policy often starts down the long path toward approval and enforcement well *outside* of government itself. In recent years, for example, consumer protection legislation and antitrust policies have been successfully changed or redrafted in part with the help of a powerful Business Roundtable based in Washington.[11] At the state level the same pattern of interest-group participation in the drafting of initiatives is evident as well.[12]

The process of policy formation thus involves a wide range of interests and needs, many of which are well beyond the control of the elected leader who will be charged with administration and frequently justification of the final legislative product. From the elected executive's view the complexities of administering a government charged with enforcing decisions that have been made both in and out of one's control pose many logistical communication problems. Has the input of other interests—private and political—made the proposal untenable? Will the typically slow process of policy implementation dissipate the carefully orchestrated support that accompanied the introduction and passage of the legislation? Will new circumstances arise that make identification with the policy a political liability? Will an unfriendly bureaucracy—or bad press—sabotage implementation of a plan? And can the plan still work if public concern can no longer be aroused on the problems it was intended to treat?

All of these questions clearly indicate the extent to which policy at various levels of government is in the hands of a plurality of interests, many of which are not directly accountable to public opinion. A rhetoric of administration must therefore take into account the varied and often private audiences that are affected by the necessity to enforce or administer a public policy. In theory, the elected executive may have a clear mandate to carry out what officially designated deliberative bodies have decided: to administer the law to the benefit of the general public. In practice, however, the leader is frequently left with the enforcement of decisions that are, in the end, only partially of his own making.

There is thus an inherent tension that exists between the highly eulogized objectives of the policy-making process on one hand, and the reality of day-to-day governmental processes heavily influenced by the needs of an entrenched bureaucracy or special interests. The interests generally seek economic protection; political reformers and activists seek more efficient and effective performance of the state as a trustee of the public interest. On items such as the minimum wage, corporate income taxes, and environmental policy the lines are usually clearly drawn. The executive and his appointees are at the vortex of these many opposing forces. On issues of "high visibility" the news media encourage the public to look to the offices of the mayor, governor, or president as the agencies that will reconcile politically based decisions with the general public good.

## The Expressive Function of Policy Advocacy

The enforcement of a policy or initiative necessarily carries the obligation to give an acceptable public accounting of governmental decisions in a way that does not bring discredit to the process or the key participants. Such an accounting involves a carefully constructed expression of an action's intent: a summation of the motives behind what are often the obscure elements that go into the literal enforcement of an initiative. This is the expressive (as opposed to the instrumental) function of a policy. Policy discussion symbolizes the motives, intentions, and character of those who intend to enforce it. We may not be able to see a policy at work, but we can witness the visible symbols of its enactment which reassure us of its existence. With regard to regulation of industries in the public interest, for example, Edelman argues that the result is a process of mediation among special interests and is an expressive rhetoric of the "public interest":

> Administrative agencies are to be understood as economic and political instruments of the parties they regulate and benefit, not of a reified "society," "general will," or "public interest." At the same time ... they perform an equally expressive function as well: to create and sustain an impression that induces acquiescence of the public in the face of private

tactics that might otherwise be expected to produce resentment, protest, and resistance.[13]

## Coping With Change

In most democracies, public sentiment is quicker to grasp the expressive elements that accompany change than the specific consequences of the change itself. Although democracies depend upon a very slow and incremental pattern of evolution from the status quo, it is frequently the promise of improvement rather than a measure of actual performance that redeems sagging faith in political institutions. The romance of politics resides in simple evocations of a better life, a more just society, and the enactment of shared ideals.

Thus we may be more attracted to the idea of change than the less certain events it inevitably brings with it. Civilizations are commonly ranked by their abilities to foster stable institutions within a framework that provides for incremental change. But the fire and drama of politics is usually produced by at least the appearance (or a fantasy) of change: social improvements that create hope and at least a sense of progress. For decades, as historian Daniel Boorstin notes, American institutions have justified their worth by their "missions," by the belief in the rewards of individual and collective initiative.[14] The ethic of work and enterprise thrives on the belief in the possibility of improving one's lot in life. Large numbers of Americans see themselves not as members of an exclusive class, but as individuals and groups who are generally responsible for their own successes and failures. "People came to America," Richard Nixon recalled in a State of the Union Address, "because they wanted to determine their own future rather than to live in a country where others determined their future for them."[15] Although this view is not necessarily taken naively, in contrast to most Europeans, Americans largely minimize the constraining effects of class. It is a widespread article of faith to believe in the possibility of political redress of injustices. Belief in the possibility of improvement, in the responsiveness of political institutions, and in the power of executives is still a key American commonplace. The idea of a land of opportunity makes Americans less deterministic about the influences of class than their European counterparts. We therefore bank on the possibility of change (and the problem-solving rhetoric that accompanies it), but change per se rarely occurs in ways that are anticipated or wanted. We honor the idea of reform—of the pending legislative remedy—far more than the specific political manifestations those reforms actually take. This fact is perhaps one reason so many politicians turn out to be better campaigners than administrators. The function of a campaign is almost totally expressive.

## The Problem of Sustaining Attention

The continuing evolution of the information age has also created an additional problem that requires skillful political maneuvering. To put it simply, compared to almost any other era, the amount of time that is devoted to the public discussion of an issue is often too short in relation to the time it takes to produce concrete legislative results. The transient focusing on new initiatives is frequently out of sync with the necessarily delayed and incremental solutions that political institutions are capable of putting in place. Over the years increasingly sophisticated forms of newsgathering and dissemination have combined to give unprecedented exposure to selected issues, but usually in the absence of any sustained attention. Today major forms of national news media rarely allow for an accumulated understanding of a problem. An issue is not allowed to age and develop over time. The fickle nature of the television audience, for example, requires a news-delivery pace that approximates the variety and scattershot approach taken in the remainder of the entertainment schedule. So, while presidents may be encouraged to do something about unemployment, the initiatives that are negotiated and eventually put in place—such as job training or anti-inflation efforts—may be judged a failure by the same media well in advance of a date in which it would be reasonable to look for actual reductions in the unemployed. Implementation of a policy is now often totally out of phase with public consciousness of the policy itself. Expectations rise quickly with the announcement of an initiative, and often turn to cynicism well ahead of the time when a sound judgment could be made. This leaves the political process without the sustained attention it frequently needs to ultimately achieve long-term objectives.[16]

To cite just one instance, few Americans will forget the serious gas shortages that developed in the late 1970s. Many car owners waited in long lines for very limited supplies. As it turned out, every action taken by the government, and every major change in public opinion was seriously behind the initial unfolding events. Jimmy Carter finally secured funds for the development of alternate forms of energy, but only after oil supplies had again become plentiful in 1978. Predictably, public interest had diminished. At the same time the federal government adopted guidelines to encourage American automobile companies to give up the ubiquitous "land cruiser" in favor of lighter, fuel-efficient cars. But these actions took effect after gas prices actually began to drop, and after mass media attention began to wane. So lower prices and a lost sense of urgency allowed consumer interest in larger cars to once again develop. However there was an unanticipated irony in this rapid change of fate. By the time gas prices had again dropped, American automakers had already made irreversible changes in order to produce smaller cars. Moreover, in the belief that Japan's inexpensive "econo-boxes" were going to ruin America's car industry, the automakers and the unions had succeeded in getting government-negotiated quotas placed on Japanese imports. So the market was made unintentionally ripe for the Japanese again. Their response to a policy of strict quotas was to export fewer but more expensively equipped cars: larger automobiles that catered to the American sense of luxury, and allowed profits to be made from extras. They achieved this goal just in time to benefit from the short public memory of gas shortages, and favorable comparison with the unsold stocks of newly designed, American "stripped-down" small cars.

A pessimist might come away from such an episode of missed opportunity with the feeling that the only political certainty the politician can count on resides in the rhetoric of policy enactment, not policies and administrative acts. Public opinion is more clearly created by the former, and often hopelessly out of touch with the latter. In terms of attitude-centered effects, an administrative decision or a statute can often be reduced to what is said rather than what is done. A president's civil rights enforcement record, for example, is popularly measured more by what has been promised—what goals have been set and what passion has been demonstrated—than by the inevitably selective enforcement of various civil rights statutes by the attorney general or the Department of Justice. For this reason there is no consensus from professional historians on the civil rights legacy left by the tragically incomplete presidency of John F. Kennedy. An important part of what the Kennedy administration *did* was what the President *said*. His words were the more accessible representations of his policy than the occasionally erratic civil rights actions of his administration.[17]

## Shifting Fashions in Leadership Styles

Another dilemma inherent to the phase of politics concerned with the defense of day-to-day leadership is what has become a pronounced ambivalence Americans feel toward a strong executive. With regard to the presidency in particular, two attitudes toward executive power have been embraced since the invention of the office.

On one hand, as we note in Chapter 7, we often view the presidency as an imperial office. Its perks and prerogatives seem enormous, and have been dramatized by a wide range of observers.[18] There is almost an irresistible urge to characterize the position as the preeminent seat of power occupied by "great men" performing "great acts."[19] This was the model embraced by Alexander Hamilton, and opposed by Jefferson, when the designers of the Constitution tangled with both the unhappy memories of the English monarchy, and the need for centralized authority.[20] The great man idea leads us to expect a great deal of activism from a leader, and tolerates little approval for narrowly defined limits. The proud and activist Kennedy, for example, seemed genuinely frustrated by the slow pace that the various federal agencies held him to. But the most he would admit was that "it is a much tougher job from the inside than I thought it was from the outside."[21] It was only later that we learned that some of his presidential orders—such as his explicit request that missiles be removed from Turkey—were routinely delayed or ignored.[22]

The second model builds on knowledge of the complex nature of bureaucracies, and presents a sharp contrast to the image of decisive executive power. This view is of a bureaucratized executive whose powers are greatly circumscribed by an inert and apolitical establishment. Politicians make up a decreasing percentage of the public sector. Repeated civil service reforms have had the effect of limiting the role of political appointees in many governmental units, particularly at the local and state levels. Many cities, for example, are virtually run by a professional class of managers who are unelected, and often insulated from political officeholders. The same fact is evident in federal agencies. A president may be unable to locate, let alone replace, a desk officer in the State Department responsible for leaking a memo to the press that casts doubt on administration policy. He may find it equally difficult to determine why a specific order has been delayed, or why an agency continues to perform services seriously at odds with the stated objectives of the administration. The possibilities for delay are almost endless. To seasoned aides and departmental staffers, the president frequently appears as a well-pampered and powerful leader, but hardly the counterpart to even the corporation executive who holds much more decisive control over his own extensive domain. It is only partially true to conclude that a state or federal executive's power comes from the constitutional imperative to administer the government. The executive is also constrained by countless forces who have the ability to render him ineffective: by the occasionally aroused public, opposing party leaders, congressional potentates and their jurisdictional committees, and the mass media, to name only a few.

In the remainder of this chapter our task is to explore both general and specific explanations of how support for existing policy and leadership is maintained. For now we leave our contemporary focus on the constraining characteristics of modern bureaucracies. In the following section the emphasis is primarily on theories and tactics that account for the communication of administrative authority. Although it has been traditional to analyze the process of political *change*—for example, elections and legislative debate over controversial new proposals—it is obvious that politics is more frequently the activity of maintaining stability. No single thread extends so continuously into the history of political thought than explorations into how the political process secures social order, how political systems maintain their credibility as well as their occasional venality. The essence of the political process at all levels of government is in the maintenance of continuity. All governments, even the most authoritarian, seek to maintain a semblance of approval, or at least the creation of a climate of indifferent acceptance.[23]

We therefore begin the next section with a broad review of several major analytic schemes that account for the process of legitimizing political rule. And we conclude in the final section of this chapter with an overview of communication tactics intended to engender public trust and to contain capricious opinion.

The following discussion points to representative stages in the evolution of perspectives on forms of political legitimacy and illegitimacy, starting from the idealizations of Platonic philosophy.

## THREE BASIC DOCTRINES FOR ASSESSING THE ROLE OF ADMINISTRATIVE RHETORIC

It is worthwhile to momentarily divert our attention from modern problems of civil administration to review some of the pivotal ideas from some major early contributors. Three classic representations of the ways administrative rhetoric can be studied are found in Plato's *Republic*, Machiavelli's *The Prince*, published in 1532, and *The German Ideology* written by Karl Marx and Friedrich Engels in 1845. Each thinker wrote from a distinctly different point of view. Plato was generally prescriptive, offering a visionary's summation of how leaders should be trained, and how they should function. Machiavelli was a dramatist. His format for political analysis is now a well-entrenched fixture: he used satire—the characterization of very human and sometimes very raw political impulses—to show how administration could be reduced to a pattern of techniques and calculations. And Marx sought to explain an entire organic system: tying politics to the "fetish" of money, the pattern of selling one's labor as a commodity, and the exploitation of labor. He not only thought he had found some iron political laws, but that he had explained how political power was maintained in the industrial state. As we shall see, his contributions in this latter area, and the contributions of the other two, are still useful reference points.

## Plato and the Idea of Administrative Elites

Plato's thought, echoed intentionally or unintentionally by virtually every critic of political life, emphasizes the moral and rational responsibilities of the leader. *The Republic*,[24] *The Phaedrus*,[25] and other tracts on politics are accounts of an idealized civil life. Plato instructed his students that political agents were to discount for their own interests, and perform in accordance with the good of the state as their only objective. He wanted policy makers to be epistemologists or seekers of true knowledge. The ideal society was a world that was immune from the impulses of the frail ego, imperfect knowledge, and the urge to pander to popular beliefs. In many ways Plato's proposals for the ideal state today look distinctly unpolitical, and clearly undemocratic.[26] His conceptions were not particularly people-centered; nor were they ideological in the modern sense. Instead, his was a world of ideas rather than policies. He expressed contempt for the arts of securing popular approval for civic decisions. Because most public debate was hopelessly inadequate and ill-informed, politics was an obligation for the philosopher: for those specifically trained to be agents in the search for enduring Truth and justice. It was not an enterprise open to endless public participation and speculation. The decisions made by the state were too important to be left to people turning their backs on Truth, and engaged in the demeaning art of brokering conflicting interests. Indeed, the opinions of most were unworthy of any kind of serious consideration. Politics was a duty. The brightest and the best, trained to place their sights higher than the opinions of the crowd, were to serve as trustees of the community.

"Most of the time," Plato noted, the ideal leaders' efforts "must be spent in philosophy, but when their turn comes, they must labour hard yet again in politics; rulers they must be for the city's sake, doing it not as a beautiful thing but as a necessity."[27]

Plato saw himself as a dialectician, not a politician or rhetorician. The leader first had to ascertain what was right—what was True, what was best for the state—and then implement decisions based on "the good" even if the resulting courses of action were unpopular. The ruler was to seek out "the best" rather than the feasible, the "ideal" rather than the acceptable. His vision of government was clearly not to implement the ideal of "the consent of the governed," but to put the polity under the benign control of "guardians" with greater knowledge and wisdom. This contempt for public opinion still haunts contemporary political analyses today, torn as many observers are between the imperative (dismissed by Plato, but accepted by many of his philosophical heirs) to honor the judgments of public opinion, and by the contradictory impulse to assess political courage as something that implies a willingness to rise above the limited understandings of the popular mind. Political life, he felt, was to be dominated by the pursuit of *arete*—excellence in thought, character, and knowledge of what was good for the general population.

Through the ages the major criticisms that have been made of Plato's idealization of political life have not been that it is wrong, but that it is largely irrelevant to the ways in which human institutions work. Many have pointed out that our reasoning is situational rather than absolute: largely determined by contingent and tentative claims rather than eternal "deductive" first principles.[28] Our politics is governed to a great extent by egocentric needs and the attitudes of reference groups, rather than consistent altruism.[29] Plato's starting points may well have placed an impossible burden on real political life. Critics have argued that human institutions cannot be made superhuman, particularly when their subject matter is concerned with the rules that govern the daily interaction of a community. It might be possible to make a logic or a science that contains its own certain rules and procedures. But the governing of people with inherently different priorities and values requires a willingness to start from what is possible—what attitudes will permit—rather than what is perfect.

These conclusions are not new. Plato himself was obsessed by his educational competitors, the so-called Sophists, who provided rigorous and respectable training in the arts of democratic leadership: often emphasizing political skills based on a pluralist outlook that seems to share a great deal with contemporary notions about the variability of perceptions, values, and beliefs.[30] In his dialogue, *The Gorgias*, Plato made the Sophists out to be slow-witted and manipulative, concerned with efficient persuasion over solid rational methods. He thought they were indiscriminate teachers of the political arts (including political persuasion) without a political epistemology—a method to determine what was "proper" to advocate. In actual fact, they were probably far more effective and rigorous than Plato's view of them would suggest. Indeed, the Sophists were centuries ahead of their time in anticipating what are today considered the legitimate situational constraints that govern almost all forms of political action.[31] Protagoras's famous aphorism that "man is the measure of all things" was an explicit affirmation of the importance of human attitudes that was totally at odds with the absolutism of Plato. It was also a profound antecedent of the coming pluralism in modern Western thought. Attitudes, beliefs, and options are now unquestionably a part of fields as varied as politics, religion, art, historiography, and the social sciences.[32] In the tradition of democratic pluralism, the Sophists properly directed attention to political dialogue as debate over judgments rather than unshakable truths. Along with Aristotle, they anticipated the key role of policy debates that hinged less on a simple discovery of the facts, and more on the imperative to cultivate allegiances from citizens with legitimate but differing priorities. W. K. Guthrie describes Protagoras's subjectivism as a position whereby "the standard of truth or falsehood is abandoned, but replaced by the pragmatic standard of better or worse. Some appearances are better than others, though none is truer."[33] Ultimately this was precisely the view that was to dominate the tone of calculation and moral indifference in Machiavelli's *The Prince*.[34]

### The Administrator as Pragmatist

If Plato fought against what he considered to be the corrosive effects of political relativism, the Florentine aristocrat signaled a willingness to *account* for political success from the dispassionate perspective of the careful observer (though the contrived pragmatism was clearly intended to prick the reader's critical sensibilities). In its short space it sets out the unremarkable and sometimes ordinary principles for effective governance of the state. If its flagrant pragmatism offends it is perhaps because readers tend to forget that Machiavelli was a comedian and dramatist. The work was at least partially intended to give local politicians their due. As Kenneth Burke has noted, the lessons in *The Prince* offer a virtual catalogue of communication-based administrative techniques. Burke's own summary is instructive:

> [E]ither treat well or crush; defend weak neighbors and weaken the strong; where you foresee trouble, provoke war; don't make others powerful; be like the prince who appointed a harsh governor to establish order (after this governor had become an object of public hatred in carrying out the prince's wishes, the prince got popular acclaim by putting him to death for his cruelties); do necessary evils at one stroke, pay out benefits little by little; sometimes assure the citizens that the evil days will soon be over, at other times goad them to fear the cruelties of the enemy; be sparing of your own and your subjects' wealth, but be liberal with the wealth of others.[35]

Machiavelli's world was light-years away from Plato's. The Italian's was totally control-oriented. Hugh Dalziel Duncan surmised that he was "concerned with how the ruler can address the people to make them want to do what they ought to do in a republic here on earth, not in heaven. . . . The ruler who would protect his people must admit the need of adapting himself to things as they are."[36]

What changed significantly in Machiavelli's work was his perspective. The emphasis is on the efficient communication of the roles and expectations between the powerful and their constituents. The tone of the study—written in the form of a handbook for the leader set on maintaining his control is (on one level, at least) descriptive rather than evaluative. Compared to Platonic theory, the arrows are reversed. The study takes human nature as a given, rather than a collection of imperfect traits in need of extensive remediation. It requires the leader to choose courses of action in terms of their acceptability and credibility to the public. In short, it remains a classic statement from the fifteenth century on the durable principles for keeping and maintaining political control. One cannot read it without noting how universal many of its recommendations still are, even in the context of its crafty opportunism. The Platonic legacy of judging political decisions for their moral nature eats at our consciousness as we read the accurate but troubling calculations presented to us:

> Thus it is well to seem merciful, faithful, humane, sincere, religious, and also to be so; but you must have a mind so disposed that when it is needful to be otherwise, you may be able to change to the opposite qualities. . . . [The Prince] must have a mind disposed to adapt itself according to the wind, and as the variations of fortune dictate, and, as I said before, not deviate from what is good, if possible, but be able to do evil if constrained.[37]

Machiavelli's tract remains as one of the strongest early statements of the importance of appearances—symbolic political gestures—in the process of governance. The denigration of a political act as "Machiavellian" stems from the awareness that political processes are known more through the outward rituals than more substantive changes. When he educates the reader with the observation that "Everybody sees what you appear to be, few feel what you are, and those few will not dare to oppose themselves to the many,"[38] he makes observations at several important levels. On one hand he recognizes the multiple roles that make the public figure necessarily a "different" individual in private than in public. The public figure has expectations to fulfill, roles to play well or badly, audiences to please. In addition, he gives weight to the truism of democratic life that widespread popular support produces a kind of momentum of its own, a form of general acceptance that may produce acquiescence in the critical minority. Leadership is necessarily the manipulation of support in such a way that outward ritual becomes a process whereby leadership is authorized in a tacit form of approval that is essentially coaxed out of spectators.

The Italian's model is necessarily a rhetorical one: based less on absolute first principles, but more on technique derived from the audience-based analysis. Ironically, his explicit suggestions of the frailities of the audiences to political acts leads many to condemn the opportunistic advice written into every page. But in fact the mock dispassionate style of explaining the world of real politics has the effect of rendering the analysis quite moral as well. When he writes that "the vulgar is always taken by appearances . . . and the world consists only of the vulgar" he has clearly implied that bogus political justifications come from regrettably low levels of political sophistication. And that itself implies a "flaw" in democratic politics that has troubled countless other analysts.[39]

Machiavelli at least pretended to separate description from judgment, leaving an invaluable account of administrative control bereft of the usual layers of Platonic incantations for a nobler style of politics. We are given a description of politics that is also a handbook of administrative justification. We are told that there are conventions for winning the assent of loyal followers, that political authority must be displayed as well as earned, and—most importantly—that politics is an audience-centered activity even when it is clearly coercive and undemocratic. Politics is represented as it is: a very human form of interaction. Raw and unadorned, it involves the securing of power and influence, and ironic combinations of deference and absolute control.

## Marx and the Study of Administrative Manipulation

The uses to which political control could be put received a far more detailed theoretical framework under the evocative analyses of the German writer and scholar, Karl Marx. Marx's contributions can be measured in many ways. He was an essayist, social critic, social theorist, and, obviously, a political theorist.[40] He even served a stint as correspondent for Horace Greeley's *New York Herald Tribune* in the mid-1800s. In reality all of these roles are inseparable, requiring the careful reader to adapt what is useful and discard what is not.

He was also what we would classify today as a futurist. His deterministic predictions about the technology and change, based on what he claimed was the "scientific" doctrine of historical materialism, lead to his now familiar assessment of the inevitability of a workers' revolt as part of the evolution of modern states.

According to Marx, the great driving force behind social change resided in the ownership and control of production. For him, the key mental equation that could never be overlooked was that labor was unjustly treated as just another commodity, just another form of capital—like money. The abuse of labor by those holding vast amounts of capital was bound to unify the exploited proletariat. He tried to see his idealistic determinism as a historical inevitability. The exploited, he thought, would rise up by producing a humane state-sponsored socialism, and eventually evolve into a refined "dictatorship of the proletariat." "History," he pessimistically concluded, "is nothing but the succession of the separate generations, each of which exploits the materials, the forms of capital, the productive forces of capital handed down to it. . . . "[41]

If Marx greatly overestimated the degree to which workers would see their own exploitation (and there is ample evidence to suggest that the workers in many societies see themselves as *among*, not apart from, the holders of vast amounts of capital), his concerns for explaining the maintenance of unjust economic orders provided a wealth of productive sociological insights. Following the lead of Burke, numerous contemporary scholars of politics and communication have pointed out the rich applications of Marx's sociology in describing the relationships between social stratification, and its legitimation.[42] In the milieu of pre-war Europe, Marx acquired a keen sensitivity to the economic and symbolic aspects of class. In the Soviet Union and its clients, Marx's insights have been reduced to the stalest of all forms of rhetoric, that of rigid official dogma. But the impact of his intermediate sociological assumptions is still very much with us, particularly his sensitivity to the ways in which private interests can be represented in a rhetoric of the public good.

Two important concepts are especially relevant to the discussion of political communication intended to argue and justify existing regimes or existing policies. One is the encompassing notion of "ideology," or what Karl Mannheim has called the "collective unconsciousness" of shared and unchallenged cultural assumptions. The second is the description of a theory of social "mystification": a multiform process of rhetorical placation directed to audiences denied political power, from those who actually have it. As we shall see, both concepts are related. And although the discussion of both has drifted well beyond the original observations of Marx, they remain as significant conceptual tools for describing the ways in which the *acceptance* of administrative dicta can be coaxed out of political audiences.

### Ideology and the Notion of Ruling Ideas

Any discussion of ideology is necessarily filled with many intellectual obstacles which are interesting, but have been adequately elaborated elsewhere.[43] The concept itself, as Burke has shown, is open to a wide range of interpretations.[44] Decades of debate have not resolved the question of whether the political and economic ideologies defined by Marxist and non-Marxist alike still govern the content of major forms of political discourse. For their part, most North American analysts (in contrast to many of their counterparts in Europe) today treat the subject of "class" less from the hard realities of nineteenth-century economics, and more from the individual's sense of self-worth. Where the workers cited by Marx were the victims of shameful economic exploitation, the workers studied by many contemporary social theorists are "individualists, concerned with their right to be exempted *personally* from shaming and indignity."[45]

But certain essentials seem indisputable and, collectively considered, provide a valuable frame of reference from which to construct a partial model for administrative control.

At its simplest, an ideology is a set of widely held core beliefs about the ongoing relationships between the state and man. It is not a set of random ideas, but a cluster of basic assertions that represent a complete and orderly perspective about the proper goals of the state, or the inevitable consequences of certain kinds of political action. The conventional tenets evoked in the word *democracy* compose an ideology, in much the same way that *Marxism* itself boldly asserts its own set of invariant conclusions and predictions. Ideologies are ways to order individual and otherwise apparently discrete events into some sort of meaningful whole. Happenings within a nation "fit" into, and are explained through, shared expectations that are attributed to the national character. A governor's dedication of a new city hospital or a president's State of the Union Address provides ample opportunities to demonstrate the common beliefs and principles that bind us to the existing political culture.[46]

The critical point to note here is that political rationalizations proceed from shared commonplaces that are continually expressed and affirmed. They are language-centered: loaded with evocations of the proper role and conduct of the state. As "familiar ways of thinking," they emerge as primary schemata for organizing our perceptions of the world, our consciousness. They give clarity to the confusing array of events that implicitly ask for our understanding. An ideology, notes Joseph LaPalombara, tends

> to specify a set of values that are more or less coherent and that it seeks to link given patterns of action to the achievement or maintenance of a future, or existing, state of affairs. . . . [I] deologies frequently insist that in order to achieve or maintain desired ends, deemed to be morally superior and therefore desirable for the entire collectivity, public authority is expected to intervene.[47]

To cite a few obvious examples, the political process in America is—at an ideological level—about voting and choosing, having a say about who will govern, and making decisions about our and the nation's future. We know our ideological beliefs from the familiar and reassuring words that can be used to bring a sense of continuity to something that—left unexplained—might seem totally discontinuous and unwelcome.

In political terms our ideologies tend to be populist (wisdom resides with the common person), democratic (everyone should be equal under the law), religious (One nation, under God), cautiously liberal (the state has an obligation to provide what people who, through no fault of their own, cannot provide for themselves), libertarian (I'll defend your right to disagree), and conservative (America is a land that preserves individual initiative). For these and other ideological forms one can specify clusters of beliefs that add a point of view to the vagaries of civil life. For the French, the Soviets, the Haitians, or any of hundreds of other cultures differences and similarities could be noted.

Although modern usage of the term tends to emphasize radical ideologies, Marx pointed out that the most pervasive function of ideological rhetoric was in the service of the status quo. He felt that the dominant group in a society will naturally use language in a way that favorably extends and justifies its power. In doing so, elites tend to give favorable and benevolent accounts of themselves which, over time, may become seen as objective justifications of the existing social order. To be sure, his proposal was perhaps too deterministic—giving a diverse collection of people (a class) a unitary objective that defies our awareness that there is a natural pluralism in any group. But the underlying principle of using familiar and comfortable ideological views to ground administrative action is still an important principle in understanding administrative rhetoric:

> The ideas of the ruling class are in every epoch the ruling ideas: i.e. the class, which is the ruling material force of society, is at the same time its ruling intellectual force. The class which has the means of material production at its disposal, has control at the same time over the means of mental production, so that thereby, generally speaking, the ideas of those who lack the means of mental production are subject to it. The ruling ideas are nothing more than the ideal expression of the dominant material relationships, the dominant material relationships grasped as ideas; hence of the relationships that make the one class the ruling one.[48]

Marx felt that "the State is the form in which the individuals of a ruling class assert their common interests."[49] And, of course, he went on to assert that the largest holders of capital were the oppressors of the very people who provided them with their wealth. For him this exploitation was frequently based on planned and calculated deceptions. Elites were clearly discernible centers of power within the society. Starting from the fixed view of a class struggle, it was inevitable to study political life (especially in Germany and England) as the product of economic interests. Today the world seems far more complex. And, while elite theory is still a matter of debate and refinement, it seems that we can be less certain that such a simple label fits easily in more diffuse and pluralistic societies.

Later usage of concepts that were first developed by Marx and Engels frequently separated the political doctrine from the sociological insights. Mannheim, for example, looks at communication dominance from elites with a less suspicious eye, but with Marx's key thesis intact:

The concept "ideology" reflects the one discovery which emerged from political conflict, namely, that ruling groups can in their thinking become so intensively interest-bound to a situation that they are simply no longer able to see certain facts which would undermine their sense of domination. There is implicit in the word "ideology" the insight that in certain situations the collective unconscious of certain groups obscures the real condition of society both to itself and to others and thereby stabilizes it.[50]

The defense of political acts can be expected to routinely proceed with the universal idea that obscures a more divisive reality. Criticism is diluted if a point of identification is established. The widely accepted ideological maxim can be expected to divert attention from a partisan or controversial point, saving both administrator and audience from what may be painful evidence of an irrevocable split between the two. Familiar commonplaces of ideologies provide an ever-present reservoir of bases from which to justify potentially unpopular or threatening decisions. Consent is engineered by a political rhetorician capable of giving self-serving decisions a more acceptable and benign rationale.

An inverted order thus develops. Political discourse that could focus on the hard choices facing the administration of a government with limited means and resources instead becomes a vehicle of placation. The task becomes not to sharpen distinctions, but to deny them by moving to a higher and nondebatable level of ideological universals. Thus, in fighting to maintain administrative control of the Vietnam War in the face of growing congressional hostility, both Lyndon Johnson and Richard Nixon defined the stakes in general ideological terms. Both men were forced by will and circumstance to consider tactical military solutions: whether to bomb North Vietnam and Cambodia, whether to defoliate wide areas of the North, and so on. But their public justifications at home were both political and ideological, and therefore carried a far more appealing level of explanations. We were there to stop the spread of a presumably universal form of communism. We were there as leaders of the free world, honoring necessary treaty commitments. In 1970 the bombing of North Vietnamese supply routes in neutral Cambodia became a way of "winning the just peace we all desire" and producing a "world of peace, freedom and justice."[51] Ideas discussed initially as principles for the determination of a public philosophy were reduced to elements intended to appease an increasingly skeptical and unbelieving public.

In the short run such rhetoric worked.[52] But no extended rational debate could sustain the view that the outcome of a Vietnamese civil war could affect our own freedom and justice, nor that of the beleaguered South Vietnamese. Indeed, given the internal and international unpopularity of our participation in the war after 1967, it was at least as plausible to argue that continued fighting in Vietnam jeopardized both cherished principles. As for the eventual fall of South Vietnam, it produced little change in the political maps of neighboring states, and served to point up tensions within the region that decades of rhetoric about monolithic communism had caused us to overlook.

## Mystery and the Rhetoric of Control

"Mysteries," notes Kenneth Burke, "are a good ground for obedience. . . . [I] f a man in accepting a 'mystery,' accepts someone else's judgment in place of his own, by that same token he becomes subject willingly."[53] In various ways most students of politics have had to come to terms with communication forms that induce greater acceptance than understanding. Ideological rhetoric is one such form, but not the only one. There is a special class of rhetorical appeals that play on the credulity of an audience, with the goal of producing greater reassurance than knowledge. It is a rhetoric that asks for acceptance, or at least tacit approval. But it does so in a way that avoids the need for detailed and thorough argumentation. Political discourse is especially prone to communication that signals more than it really says: a rhetoric of appearances rather than of explanation. And it depends to a large extent on the use of communication within a context of official situations and formal authority. Respect is produced because the persuaded are ignorant, gullible, or trusting.[54]

In response to a rhetoric of mystification a listener adapts to the prevailing definition of the social order by trading status for security. Such language provides verbal evidence that legitimate authority is being exercised. The key difference between this and other forms of communication is that the evidence resides not in the legitimacy of the ideas being communicated, but in the aura of the source and the impressive language it uses. The penniless may be told that their condition is natural (The poor shall always be with us), and that a better life remains after death (The meek shall inherit the earth). At the same time the powerful—in control of the symbols of authority and beneficiaries of the "ruling ideas"—cultivate symbols designed to impress, knowing in some cases that they will provide a basis for continuing the illusion that those at the top of the political hierarchy are there for natural rather than contrived reasons. Agency reports, presidential commissions, white papers, hearings testimony, policy addresses, press conferences, self-study surveys, all provide an aura of competence and governmental activism that extends well beyond what any of these forms can specifically yield in terms of individual comprehension. Like the visitor confronted with the bewildering new technology of a data processing center, one may be unable to assess the competence of those involved, but there is reassurance in the apparent knowledge and order that the computer paraphernalia confers on those who work there. The visit affirms the expertise of others, and just as importantly suggests our own need to defer.

Burke has pointed out the importance of mystery to religion.[55] But virtually every complex institution or body of knowledge has a built-in rhetoric of mystification. Such language is sometimes the last or only link that exists between the outsider and a complex governmental entity—a commission, a federal or state agency—which seeks to justify its existence. Thurmond Arnold's assessment of the impossibly opaque elements of the law points to how the symbols of authority can wear down potential hostility or disrespect. He notes that "the literature of jurisprudence performs its social task most effectively for those who encourage it, praise it, but do not read it. For those who study it today it is nothing but a troubling mass of conflicting ideas."[56] Arnold's point is that the very impenetrability of the language *communicates* an aura of permanence that conceals its fallibility. One of the most productive analysts of verbal mystifications has been Murray Edelman at the University of Wisconsin. In a number of studies he has systematically explored the inexact but vital linkages between administrative rationales and public opinion. Drawing on linguistic theory, Marx, Burke, and modern survey research, Edelman has constructed a valuable picture of a complex society that has taken refuge from the uncertainties of policy in the more reassuring symbols that accompany policy enforcement. He notes that the prime dimensions of public opinion reside in the emotional reactions that the symbols of government produce. If specific proposals and actions are only vaguely understood, there is a clearer sense of threat or reassurance that can be discerned on many issues. "Politics is for most of us a passing parade of abstract symbols, yet a parade which our experience teaches us to be a benevolent or malevolent force. . . . [I]ts processes become easy objects upon which to displace private emotions, especially strong anxieties and hopes."[5] [7] Primed for the necessity to ease concerns about taxes, war, economic exploitation by corporations, restrictive laws, and powerful interest groups, most political establishments seek to defend actions in terms of reassurance. Hard choices are concealed or not seriously considered. Political rituals frequently replace open vigorous debate. Symbolic gestures substitute for rigorous policy enforcement that could alienate the politically powerful in and out of government. For example,

> government measures, ostensibly designed to protect the consumer, have long since been shown to yield more in symbolic reassurance and mystification than in protection. Regulatory agencies and public utility commissions serve largely to place a governmental sanction on rate increases that would otherwise be much more militantly resented and resisted. Antitrust laws similarly sanction mergers and pricing agreements, with occasional token wrist slaps to keep the symbolism pure. Such laws have performed these dubious functions for almost a century, and critics and scholars have exposed the hiatus between promise and performance almost as long.[5] [8]

As we note in the last chapter of this study, mystifications can represent a major form of political deceit.

## ADMINISTERING POLICY: COMMUNICATION STRATEGIES AND TACTICS

Consider the following administrative dilemmas—all based on actual situations—and the appropriate strategic responses that they require:

• The president's cabinet secretary in charge of health and welfare has declared a personal dislike for a policy of abortion on demand, even though the federal government (and, hence, the secretary) is necessarily committed to providing for the health care of thousands of poorer women, many of whom seek federally funded abortions.

• On the recommendation of his education commissioner, the governor of a state has established several specially funded "Governor's schools" at local colleges for high-school students with outstanding abilities in various fields. Only one in 100 applicants will be admitted to the various programs, thus leaving thousands of students and their families angry at the governor for promoting an elitist program with taxpayers' money.

• An outspoken member of the president's administration, who has raised thousands of dollars for his party and is strongly liked by party activists, has made comments at a public gathering that suggest a not so veiled racism. He has never broken himself of the habit of saying in public what others would confine to a private conversation. The cabinet member has become a clear political liability in an election year, but the activists in the president's party have made the president's continuing support of the errant official a measure of his political mettle.

• The vice-president, who has covered the nation making addresses favoring tougher enforcement of local and national criminal statutes, suddenly pleads no contest to a charge of accepting cash from contractors while a state governor, and resigns in disgrace. The much-promoted law-and-order campaign of the administration takes a drubbing in the press, and appears to lack all credibility.

• The Federal Aviation Administration has failed to act on what now appears to be clear evidence that the air worthiness of a large commercial aircraft is uncertain. A recent crash with heavy loss of life focuses attention on what is widely perceived as regulatory carelessness and bureaucratic lethargy.

• The presidential nominee for the sensitive position of director of the CIA is given highly visible support from the administration. But in congressional hearings the nominee is charged with improperly using CIA data as a member of a previous administration. The president is left with a personal declaration of full support, and a director-designate who is not inclined to fight for the appointment.

• A new press secretary has resigned just days after taking office, claiming that he cannot defend or explain a major presidential decision in good conscience. In a public letter of resignation the secretary also indicates that a presidential decision violates a personal commitment that the president has made privately to the secretary.

• An election campaign was based on promises to reduce government spending and to lower a dangerously high federal deficit. Neither action has occurred, and a second campaign is about to begin.

• In a nationally televised debate, the incumbent president has declared that some of the Eastern bloc nations—such as Poland—are not dominated by the Soviet Union. The press asks if the president misspoke, and he says that he meant what he said. Every public appearance after that includes insistent questions asking if the president really believes that the Polish people have the right of self-determination.

• A big city mayor, who was once a policeman, expresses faith in the use of so-called lie detectors: "If they say a man lied, then he lied."

To demonstrate his confidence, he takes a widely publicized lie detector test. He fails it.

Each of these situations carries a common imperative: they require a response, an explanation. The credibility and accountability of the administrator is at stake. Circumstances have arisen that challenge the integrity of the executive, and the effectiveness of his leadership.

This section focuses on some of the practical options available to the administrators faced with the need to shape the public discussion of the actions taken during their tenure. Although our discussion can only be suggestive rather than definitive, its inclusion brings our study full circle. We started with a survey of several broad objectives contained in the administrative response. And we end with a look at the very specific tactical options employed by political leaders and their staffs.

Faced with the need to manage the governmental agencies for which they are responsible, and the need to shore up their political capital for future political wars, what are the tactical communications conventions that guide the public responses of politically elected administrators? Here is a brief survey of some of the approaches that are common to many levels of policy-enforcing offices.

## Controlling and Using the Bureaucracy

The chief problem that an executive faces is how to maintain a semblance of control over the agencies and offices that fall under his jurisdiction. The size of the federal bureaucracy is of legendary proportions: a $600 billion budget used to finance over 1,100 domestic programs. There are over 400 separate agencies employing about two and one-half million civilian employees. And it is estimated that ten times that number in the private sector are indirectly supported by government contracts.[59]

At the local level the numbers can be equally impressive, with some 80,000 local governments and municipalities dispersed throughout the United States.[60] In the state of New Jersey, which is but a fraction of the physical size of most states, there are some 19 executive departments with over 80,000 employees, and a yearly budget that exceeds $5 billion.[61]

When looking at the diffuse nature of most executive branches—local, state, or federal—one marvels not so much at the power of American chief executives, but at the ability of a transient leader to achieve a sustained and consistent policy over time. As some governmental insiders have noted, "the reins of command" seized by even the president are "more a skein of tangled threads that he must somehow weave into a coherent pattern." For all of his supposed power, "he must struggle mightily even to influence the course of events within his administration."[62] Harry Truman could have been speaking for many executives at many levels when he noted:

> The difficulty with many career officials in the government is that they regard themselves as the men who really make policy and run the government. They look upon the elected officials as just temporary occupants. Every President in our history has been faced with this problem: how to prevent career men from circumventing presidential policy.[63]

The difficulty leaders face is how to get the system they are ostensibly in charge of to respond in a way that meets the high expectations that the promise of executive power produces in the popular mind. In contrast to the image of executive might, for example, a president must be concerned about how deputy officials with access to secret departmental data in various agencies can be made sufficiently loyal to avoid leaking to the press information that is at odds with official statements. A governor must be concerned with creating a chain of command that will make certain that the enforcement of an environmental policy (i.e., on strip mining) fits with previous statements, budgetary requests, and the interests of political allies. From an executive's point of view the possibilities for miscommunication and inconsistent action are nearly endless. His protection is partially based on having a staff that can serve as the political equivalent of a rear-view mirror—checking for the consequences that will trail behind a sensitive political maneuver.

The safest and most obvious approach to policy implementation is also perhaps the most widespread. Politically elected administrators must be willing to use surrogates to carry most of the explanation and defense of policy. A public statement of any kind is a legacy that can come back to haunt the speaker. The rhetoric of the surrogate—cabinet official, executive assistant, White House counselor, press aide—has the prime virtue of deniability. Some space or distance can always be placed between the statements of one official, and the views of the executive, if such a statement becomes a liability to an administration. The statement of an intermediary shields the executive. It can be disowned, downplayed, ignored, explained in the proper context, and—on occasion—repudiated. The press will generally be forgiving, knowing what the executive knows: that it would be unreasonable to expect that every official statement carried the authorization of the chief executive. If an announced decision is met with widespread approval the reverse is also possible. If it goes over well, it can be embraced as something that reflects the thinking of the president (or governor, or mayor).

Several specific tactics result from this objective of shielding the top political leader from the fates produced by even the most distant regions of the bureaucracy. One convention of bureaucratic life is the standard procedure of requiring agencies to announce their own bad news, leaving the prerogative of bearing good news to the leader in the State House or the Oval Office. For example, there was no surprise in the fact that the Johnson and Nixon administrations reserved statements of Vietnam troop pull-outs to themselves, and announcements of American casualties to low-level military briefers in Saigon and Washington. The goal was obviously to put as much distance as possible between unhappy information and the politically sensitive White House. A president could not really deny the casualty figures, but he could at least put the burden of explaining their significance to reporters brave enough to query him on them. The effect of assigning negative reports to the bureaucratic backwaters of officialdom serves to subtly deny their importance, and to remove them from direct association with the executive.

Another variation of this pattern occurs when highly controversial proposals are announced by executive agency staffers who are particularly good at taking the heat that is certain to result. Every administration has the rhetorical equivalent of a "lightning rod"—the cabinet official, commissioner, or aide who will divert potential criticism away from the executive. The individual that is going to draw the fire must necessarily be thick skinned. Some have actually relished this role, particularly if they have decided not to seek elective office on their own. Vice-President Spiro Agnew took the strongest anti-media speeches written by presidential speech writer Patrick Buchanan and delivered them with a zeal that increased their impact. President Nixon, who wished to maintain a more statesmanlike image, denied that they reflected administration policy. But he approved the texts, and allowed the first speech to be followed up by a second attack with equal vituperation.[64] Joseph Califano, former secretary of health, education, and welfare under President Carter, gladly voiced his long-held opposition to federally funded abortions, diverting attention from a president who had generally held the same highly controversial view.[65] And former Secretary of the Interior James Watt served the same general purpose for President Reagan: baiting the environmental movement with strong doses of the free-enterprise ethic applied to the unlikely topic of land management policy.

A slightly less flamboyant approach to the introduction of policy with indeterminate public support is the trial balloon. On a "backgrounder" (not for attribution) basis, members of the press are appraised of the administration's thinking on a problem that will be the subject of an initiative. The official giving the briefing is occasionally the executive, but more likely some other high-placed source. The goal is to get the proposed action into general circulation to test public reaction. It is done, however, in a way that preserves the "deniability" of the administration. If reaction from the press, special interests, party leaders, congressional leaders, and the like is negative, or if consequences are raised that an executive overlooked, the proposal can be abandoned before it carries an official endorsement. If reaction is favorable, a formal announcement confirming the administration-induced speculation may go ahead as planned. F. D. R. is known to have used his backgrounder press conferences for just these purposes, planting an idea in the press well in advance of a final decision, in order to prevent a significant failure in reading public opinion.[66] Two members of the Carter administration have promoted the use of the trial balloon to future presidents:

> It will get public opinion and important actors focused on some of the alternatives, which will help you decide which of several paths to follow. It may also help the consultative process with the [congressmen on Capitol] Hill, since they too will be able to gauge public opinion before you make the decision and give more concrete advice.[67]

### Speaking With One Voice

Nothing eats away at the fabric of goodwill between an executive and the bureaucracy as quickly as an executive's feeling that his stature is being weakened by dissent that is coming into public view. Executives new to their jobs can be counted on to resent the leaks that result when unauthorized information reaches the press and public. Almost every president, governor, and mayor talks about conducting an open administration at the start of their winter terms. But usually before the leaves are off the trees by the next autumn efforts are well underway to tighten up public access to staffers and subordinates. Even Jimmy Carter, who seemed particularly willing to conduct an open administration, soon came to resent reading dissenting views from anonymous members of the executive branch in the press. In his words, "After Watergate it seemed that every subordinate functionary in government wanted to be Deep Throat."[68] From his standpoint the problem was one of presenting a misleading view of an administration in disarray:

> During the early days of consideration, when a matter was not likely to have been studied thoroughly within the Oval Office, I was always careful to avoid making any public statement. Sooner or later, though, I would see news reports beginning, "Carter is considering . . . " or, "The President believes. . . . " When told that the source was mistaken, the reporter was likely to respond with another headline, "Administration confused about . . . " or "Carter Reverses Policy on. . . . "[69]

In the jargon of organizational politics, what presidents and executives want from members of their closest appointees are people who are willing to front for the official policy line. They seek staffers who can resist the urge to "go native": that is, to place special or private interests above those of the team and the administration. This need for absolute loyalty is especially vital in an individual who serves in the capacity of press officer or press secretary. Such people must be willing to represent the president's views or the views of a cabinet official or agency they serve with a high degree of accuracy and considerable conviction. The task can be a difficult one, since it is impossible at times to determine what the official view is. That can be a problem in addition to the obvious one of occasionally being asked to defend the indefensible. But they must be prepared to face hard questioning on the potential inconsistencies, vagaries, and general criticisms that may come with the defense of official thinking. Fronting is not a job that is suited to people who place a high value on the rightness of their own individual thoughts. Political columnists who switch to the other side of the adversary relationship, for example, are not likely to make the adjustment easily from opinion-giver to spokesperson. Straight reporters—such as the Ford administration's Ron Nessen and the Eisenhower regime's James Hagerty—have succeeded more ably.

On the Carter administration's position on abortion, for example, HEW spokesperson Eileen Shanahan made it clear to Secretary Califano before she took the job that she could not defend his view. Califano recalls her saying "What you have to know about me is that abortion is one subject I cannot front for you on. I cannot be your public affairs spokesperson on abortion."[70] But he notes that the *New York Times* reporter turned out to be an excellent department representative, largely because "her loyalty once a decision was made was as fierce as her arguments for her views in the course of making the decision."[71]

The scope of this problem cannot be overemphasized. Every capital city is infused not only with the traditional constituent-based politics, but with the organizational politics that come with the built-in insecurities of electoral life. Cabinet figures, major commissioners, and key agency executives have egos and ambitions almost as large as the executives who appointed them. Their careers depend on their outward loyalty to the administration under which they are serving. But because of the tenuous nature of their positions—in with one administration, but usually out with the next—they must also cultivate independent ties to the outside institutions that they work with: businesses, the press, unions, lobbies, foundations, and universities. Organizational loyalty may be total and undivided, as in the devoted service of Harry Hopkins to F. D. R., or Jack Valenti to Lyndon Johnson. Or it may be as tentative and fragile as press secretary Gerald TerHorst's was to President Ford,[72] or John Dean's was to Richard Nixon.

A presidential or cabinet-level assistant who could count on being courted by an interested press and competing congressional or private bureaucracies had to decide how to treat the job. Johnson wanted his aides to have a "passion for anonymity." And some of the best, such as Harry McPherson, approached political jobs with a keen awareness of the necessity for professional loyalty. Of the newly created White House job of special assistant for national security affairs, for example, McPherson saw the sensitive structural problems built into a job. Its duties fell somewhere between the normal cabinet-level lines of responsibility. As an aide who had to deal with ambiguous lines of command, he had to assess his unique place in the hierarchy:

> The debatable questions were (1) to what extent the special assistant should press his independent judgments; (2) whether he should develop private relationships with foreign ambassadors and ministers; (3) whether he should impose his own intelligence and policy requirements on the departments; (4) to what extent he spoke for the President in interdepartmental meetings.[73]

The word most frequently used to describe the process of approving an official administration view is called clearance. In most organizations there are clusters of individuals and separate departments through which press releases, proposals, and statements must be cleared.[74] A statement on a budget request, for example, may need a president's or governor's approval before interested parties are notified, and the press is given a release. The purpose of such a procedure is obviously to unify the outlook and ideas that carry the official administration line. In most cases clearance channels evolve in piecemeal fashion, or end up being delegated somewhat unevenly to various agencies, departments, and executive staff assistants. These are the formal channels through which a speech, press release, clarification, or proposal must pass. In theory at least, the agency or individual with special expertise on a question is involved in the clearance process. In practice, it is a fact of organizational life that access to an executive may become as jealously protected as a football on the two-yard line. No agency or major official wants to be by-passed on a proposal that is even remotely related to their jurisdiction. All want to have a chance at influencing the outcome of the political process. The author of a speech prepared for a president, to cite one kind of clearance discussed more fully in Chapter 8, may deliberately delay its preparation and "staffing out" through appropriate departments in order to preserve the cherished prerogative of writing the words of so prominent a figure.[75] The life history of a specific proposal or major speech is thus frequently a study in intergovernmental intrigue. The spoils go to the aide or high-ranking official who is able to establish open lines of communication that permit direct access to the decision-maker.

## Back Channels and Leaks

From an organizational perspective, public communication is channeled through a series of gatekeepers who scrutinize it for its overall appropriateness. But organizations are also riddled with what are sometimes known as more illicit back channels, which serve as convenient but hidden byways around the normal bureaucratic chain. Some back channels lead to other bureaucrats; others lead to interested parties outside, particularly the press, particularly regulated business and the press. Every bureau or agency chief also seeks to develop at least some back channels to the top of the hierarchy that he hopes to influence. The goal is to by-pass most intermediaries who might obstruct a cherished objective. These channels usually lead to a willing assistant who will convey the information around a bottleneck and to the very top. For example, a department head who is facing a major budget cut from an executive's own budget office may seek the personal intervention of a staffer who regularly has the executive's ear.

The use of back channels has taken on some surprising forms in the recent history of the presidency. F. D. R. enlisted Eleanor Roosevelt as his eyes and ears to assess the concrete effects certain New Deal programs were having on the portions of the country. Roosevelt's paralysis obviously made all but the most essential travel difficult. But beyond that he sought to get information through ways other than the inflated optimistic reports submitted by the heads of his "alphabet agencies." Mrs. Roosevelt, in turn, became a back channel for priorities and views that were slightly different than those of the staff surrounding the president.[76] Seeking the same kind of unfiltered assessment that he realized he was not getting from the Joint Chiefs of Staff, Lyndon Johnson belatedly sent some of his own independent-thinking staffers to Vietnam to assess the course of the war.[77]

The most notorious back channel in recent American political history was "Deep Throat," the name given to a secret administration source who allegedly passed on incriminating clues to the *Washington Post* during the unraveling of the Watergate caper. But perhaps the most unusual back channel developed during the tense days in October 1962, during the Cuban missile crisis. The Soviet Union's new offensive missiles on Cuba forced the Kennedy administration into a dangerous blockade of that island which could have entailed the sinking of Soviet vessels thought to be carrying more arms. One of the first breaks to end the 13-day crisis began with an unlikely restaurant meeting between a high Soviet embassy official and ABC news correspondent John Scali. Scali was surprised to learn that his lunch companion was giving him what appeared to be an official proposal from Moscow for a face-saving compromise: the Soviets wanted guarantees that the United States would not invade Cuba. He was urged to pass it on. For reasons that are still unclear, he became a participant as well as an observer. The information that he carried helped pave the way for an end to the conflict.[78]

Leaks of bureaucratic intelligence represent both a widely used form of communication by members of a government, but also one of the most heavily condemned. As the term implies, a *leak* supposedly represents the unauthorized and unexpected release of information from within an official agency or government office. But political reporters today frequently note that a leak can have the aura of a carefully planted story. Disclosing secret information is now sometimes part of a planned news-management offensive within a governmental office, even the presidency itself.[79] When done with official approval, its purpose is usually to conceal motives: to make information available to the press without having to face questioning on why it came from official sources. In the tradition of the political novel, for example, an incumbent might leak compromising information about his opponent's previous three marriages. As described by Daniel Schorr, who was on the receiving end of many unofficial statements, the leak became

> something consciously done to enhance an official, float a trial balloon, promote a viewpoint or torpedo a contrary viewpoint. The Air Force "leaked" classified information about what was wrong with the Army's missiles; at appropriations time the whole Pentagon leaked classified studies of Soviet armed might; a "senior official" traveling on Secretary Kissinger's shuttle diplomacy plane developed leaking into an art form.[80]

In its most interesting incarnation, however, the leak serves a safety-valve function. Unauthorized information from an insider makes secret information available which serves at least the short-term interests of the press and the interests of the "leaker." The reporter ostensibly gets an exclusive story (though most are wary of this bait). And a range of possible goals is open to the information-giver. Such a person may have personal or organizational motives: the information may embarrass an enemy, point out a blatant contradiction between public statement and private intentions, provide information of use to an agency but at odds with administration policy, or weaken the credibility of agency opponents within the executive branch. At times a leak may compromise security as well, though the veil of national security can be a convenient mystification for a botched policy.[81]

Schorr himself tried his hand at this art form, eventually losing his job at CBS because of the tangle he helped create. As the recipient of a damaging House study of covert and often illegal CIA activities known as the Pike Report, he sought a place to publish it. His network paraphrased from the report, but not as extensively as Schorr felt was warranted. With the House voting to make the report secret, Schorr went ahead with his plans to find another outlet. Eventually he sold the document to the *Village Voice*, but only after an embarrassing episode in which he remained silent while colleagues at CBS were wrongly accused of having being involved.[82] Like the "secret" Pentagon-prepared history of the Vietnam War that was leaked to the *New York Times* by Pentagon analyst Daniel Ellsberg, the Pike Report became a major news story. Both also served to remind a decade of presidents that the Congress and most of the federal bureaucracy cannot be trusted. From their view each remains unresponsive to the need for one voice in the affairs of government. Each is thought to undermine the executive's ability to guide public opinion on administrative objectives down a single path.

## SUMMARY

This chapter has only touched on a few of the possible approaches that could be examined for insights on the tactics and affects of administrative communication. Our plan here has been eclectic: mixing prescriptive and descriptive theory, discussing administrative tactics as well as much broader philosophical questions, and mentioning classical as well as contemporary thought. This topic admits to no one method or point of view. Countless other derivative theorists and analyses could be mentioned as outgrowths of the insights of Machiavelli, Marx, Burke, and Edelman. Indeed, the very presence of so well-established theorists perhaps suggests the need for a new generation of scholars willing to tackle the subjects and problems cited here, but with perhaps new sets of skills, and a willingness to develop a new lexicon. It may well be that the discussion of the public interest, elites, ideologies, ruling ideas, interest groups, and other common terms of description have outlived their utility. It may be the case, as well, that the day-to-day processes of communicating the legitimacy of a regime can only be furthered by development of a critical theory that uses a new and more neutral linguistic vocabulary, rather than the loaded terms used by critics such as Marx with explicitly political objectives in mind. There is perhaps also a need to make clear distinctions between the logistical problems and communication options employed by administrators who function largely outside of the limelight. The presidency, for example, might in fact be an inadequate model from which to generalize to other less observed political offices.

However, there can be no doubt about the need to continue the search for conceptual tools that help us explain the complex psychological and social processes that occur as political institutions continue to exercise their powers over public opinion. A huge spectrum of disciplines—some of which we have sampled here—have useful concepts and information to contribute: ranging from those doing traditional criticism, to those engaged in survey research on political attitudes; from neo-Marxist social scientists who explore the dynamics of concealed investments, to memoirists who remind us of the tactical options weighed and taken by practitioner-politicians faced with the task of husbanding public support.

# NOTES

1. Karl Mannheim, *Ideology and Utopia*, trans. Louis Wirth and Edward Shils (New York: Harvest Books, 1936), p. 38.

2. Jimmy Carter, *Keeping Faith: Memoirs of a President* (New York: Bantam, 1981), p. 89.

3. Murray Edelman, *Political Language: Words that Succeed and Policies that Fail* (New York: Academic Press, 1977), p. xvii.

4. Godfrey Hodgson, *All Things to All Men* (New York: Simon and Schuster, 1980), p. 86.

5. See, for examples, Douglass Cater, *Power in Washington* (New York: Vintage, 1964); Charles Peters, *How Washington Really Works* (Reading, Mass.: Addison-Wesley, 1980); and Kim McQuaid, *Big Business and Presidential Power* (New York: William Morrow, 1982).

6. Smith Simpson, *Anatomy of the State Department* (Boston: Beacon Press, 1967), p. 132.

7. Joseph A. Califano, Jr., *Governing America: An Insider's Report from the White House and the Cabinet* (New York: Simon and Schuster, 1981), pp. 184-87.

8. Morton H. Halperin, "The Presidency and its Interaction with the Culture of Bureaucracy," in *The System: The Five Branches of American Government*, ed. Charles Peters and James Fallows (New York: Praeger, 1967), p. 8.

9. Emmet John Hughes, *The Living Presidency* (New York: Coward, McCann and Geoghegan, 1972), p. 184.

10. "A Mayor for All Seasons," *Time*, June 15, 1981, p. 23.

11. McQuaid, *Big Business*, pp. 293-95.

12. Alan Rosenthal, "The Governor, the Legislature, and State Policy Making," in *Politics in New Jersey*, rev. ed., ed. Richard Lehne and Alan Rosenthal (New Brunswick, N.J.: Eagleton Institute of Politics, 1979), p. 142.

13. Murray Edelman, *The Symbolic Uses of Politics* (Urbana, Ill.: University of Illinois, 1967), p. 56.

14. Daniel J. Boorstin, *The Americans: The Democratic Experience* (New York: Vintage, 1974), pp. 557-58.

15. Richard M. Nixon, "State of the Union Address," January 22, 1971 in *Presidential Rhetoric*, 2nd ed., ed. Theodore Windt (Dubuque, Iowa: Kendall-Hunt, 1980), p. 155.

16. The inability of the American public to "stay the course" was one of Lyndon Johnson's most urgent complaints about his attempts to seek a victory in Vietnam. For his assessment see the chapter, "The Making of a Decision," in his *The Vantage Point: Perspectives on the Presidency* (New York: Holt, Rinehart and Winston, 1971), pp. 365-424.

17. Jim F. Heath, *Decade of Disillusionment: The Kennedy-Johnson Years* (Bloomington, Ind.: Indiana University, 1975), pp. 69-73.

18. The term, "imperial," is Arthur M. Schlesinger, Jr.'s. For studies of the "powerful" presidency see Schlesinger's *The Imperial Presidency* (Boston: Houghton Mifflin, 1973) and George Reedy's, *The Twilight of the Presidency* (New York: World, 1970).

19. A book that takes this general approach is Thomas A. Bailey's *Presidential Greatness* (New York: Appleton-Century, 1966).

20. See especially papers 67-75 of *The Federalist Papers* written by Hamilton, Madison, and Jay. Hamilton especially makes a defense for a strong executive (New York: Mentor, 1961).

21. Kennedy quoted in Sidney Warren, ed., *The American President* (Englewood Cliffs, N.J.: Prentice-Hall, 1967), p. 54.

22. Robert F. Kennedy, *Thirteen Days: A Memoir of the Cuban Missile Crisis* (New York: Signet, 1968), p. 94.

23. Hugh Dalziel Duncan, *Communication and Social Order* (New York: Oxford, 1970), p. 196.

24. See, for example, W. H. D. Rouse, trans., *Great Dialogues of Plato* (New York: Mentor, 1956).

25. *Phaedrus*, trans. by J. Wright, in *Five Dialogues of Plato* (New York: E. P. Dutton, 1947), pp. 215-87.

26. This is one of the general points of view expressed by Karl Popper in *The Open Society and its Enemies* (London: Routledge and Kegan Paul, 1947).

27. *The Republic*, bk. vii, p. 340.

28. Stephen Toulmin, *The Uses of Argument* (Cambridge, Eng.: Cambridge University, 1964), chap. 4.

29. The classic contemporary statement of this view is found in David Riesman's *The Lonely Crowd*, abridged ed. (New Haven, Conn.: Yale University, 1961), especially Part II.

30. W. K. C. Guthrie, *The Sophists* (Cambridge, Eng.: Cambridge University, 1971), pp. 3-13.

31. A selective but interesting representation of the dispute between the Sophists and Plato can be found in the best-selling novel by Robert M. Persig, *Zen and the Art of Motorcycle Maintenance* (New York: William Morrow, 1974).

32. Guthrie, *The Sophists*, pp. 170-71.

33. Ibid., p. 187.

34. See, for example, Niccolo Machiavelli, *The Prince*, trans. Luigi Ricci (New York: Mentor, 1952).

35. Kenneth Burke, *A Rhetoric of Motives* (New York: Prentice-Hall, 1953), p. 158.

36. Duncan, *Communication and Social Order*, p. 216.

37. Machiavelli, *The Prince*, pp. 93-4.

38. Ibid., p. 94.

39. See, for example, Walter Lippmann, *The Public Philosophy* (Boston: Little, Brown, 1955), pp. 16-27.

40. For a brief biography and a partial bibliography on Marx see Neil McInnes, "Karl Marx" in *The Encyclopedia of Philosophy, Volume Five*, ed. Paul Edwards (New York: Macmillan and the Free Press, 1967), pp. 171-73. For a broad application of Marxist concepts to political communication see Claus Mueller, *The Politics of Communication* (New York: Oxford University, 1973).

41. Karl Marx and Freidrich Engels, *The German Ideology, Parts I and III*, ed. R. Pascal (New York: International Publishers, 1946), p. 38.

42. Burke, *A Rhetoric of Motives*, pp. 101-14, and various sections of *Attitudes Toward History* (Boston: Beacon, 1957) are two influential studies. The importance of Burke as an eclectic user of Marx and other innovators is well

documented in the tribute, *Critical Responses to Kenneth Burke*, ed. William Rueckert (Minneapolis: University of Minnesota, 1969).

43. See Chaim I. Waxman, ed., *The End of Ideology Debate* (New York: Funk and Wagnalls, 1968) and Daniel Bell, *The End of Ideology* (New York: The Free Press, 1960).

44. Burke, *Rhetoric of Motives*, p. 104.

45. Richard Sennett and Jonathan Cobb, *The Hidden Injuries of Class* (New York: Knopf, 1973), p. 150.

46. Many examples can be found in W. Lloyd Warner, *The Living and the Dead* (New Haven, Conn.: Yale University, 1959), pp. 258-59, and Dan Nimmo and James E. Combs, *Subliminal Politics: Myths and Mythmakers in America* (Englewood Cliffs, N.J.: Prentice-Hall, 1980), chapters 2 and 3.

47. Joseph LaPalombara, "Decline of Ideology: a Dissent and an Interpretation," in Waxman, *The End of Ideology Debate*, p. 320.

48. Marx and Engels, *The German Ideology*, p. 39.

49. Ibid., p. 60.

50. Mannheim, *Ideology and Utopia*, p. 40.

51. Richard Nixon, "Televised Address to the Nation," April 30, 1970, in Windt, *Presidential Rhetoric*, pp. 139, 141.

52. The continuance of the Vietnam War produced angry clashes on college campuses, and four deaths at Kent State University in Ohio in a protest involving poorly trained National Guardsmen. But the president was always able to reclaim some credibility for the war after each speech. See Richard B. Gregg and Gerald A. Houser, "Richard Nixon's April 30, 1970 Address on Cambodia: The Ceremony of Confrontation," *Speech Monographs* (August 1973) pp. 167-81.

53. Kenneth Burke, *The Rhetoric of Religion: Studies in Logology* (Berkeley, Calif.: University of California, 1970), p. 307.

54. Duncan, *Communication and Social Order*, pp. 190-245, and Burke, *Rhetoric of Motives*, pp. 101-10.

55. Burke, *Rhetoric of Religion*, pp. 307-9.

56. Thurman W. Arnold, *The Symbols of Government* (New York: Harcourt, Brace and World, 1962), p. 70.

57. Edelman, *Symbolic Uses of Politics*, p. 5.

58. Edelman, *Political Language*, p. 148.

59. Peters, *How Washington Really Works*, p. 35.

60. George E. Berkley and Douglas M. Fox, *80,000 Governments: The Politics of Sub-National America* (Boston: Allyn and Bacon, 1978).

61. Charles E. Jacob, "The Governor, the Bureaucracy and State Policy Making" in Rosenthal, *Politics in New Jersey*.

62. Ben W. Heineman, Jr. and Curtis A. Hessler, *Memorandum for the President: A Strategic Approach to Domestic Affairs in the 1980s* (New York: Random House, 1980), p. xiii.

63. Truman quoted in Arthur Bernon Tourtellot, *The Presidents on the Presidency* (New York: Doubleday, 1964), p. 129.

64. William Safire, *Before the Fall* (New York: Doubleday, 1975), pp. 352-53.

65. Califano, *Governing America*, pp. 49-62.

66. Samuel and Dorothy Rosenman, *Presidential Style: Some Giants and a Pygmy in the White House* (New York: Harper and Row, 1976), p. 331.

67. Heineman and Hessler, *Memorandum for the President*, p. 250.

68. Carter, *Keeping Faith*, p. 59.

69. Ibid., p. 59.

70. Califano, *Governing America*, p. 36.

71. Ibid., p. 36.

72. Robert T. Hartmann, *Palace Politics: An Inside Account of the Ford Years* (New York: McGraw-Hill, 1980), pp. 240-46, 265-67.

73. Harry McPherson, *A Political Education* (Boston: Little, Brown, 1972), p. 256.

74. For a discussion of clearance in the presidency see Richard E. Neustadt, "Presidency and Legislation: The Growth of Central Clearance," in *The Presidency*, ed. Aaron Wildavsky (Boston: Little, Brown, 1969), pp. 601-32.

75. Transcript, Robert Hardesty Oral History Interview, August 2, 1971 by Joe B. Frantz, p. 11, LBJ Library, Austin, Texas. See also, Harold L. Wilensky, *Organizational Intelligence* (New York: Basic Books, 1967), pp. 48-57.

76. James MacGregor Burns, *Roosevelt: The Lion and the Fox, 1882-1940* (New York: Harcourt Brace Jovanovich, 1956), pp. 173-74.

77. Townsend Hoopes, *The Limits of Intervention* (New York: David McKay, 1969), pp. 159-85.

78. Robert Kennedy, *Thirteen Days*, p. 91.

79. Richard Halloran, "A Primer on the Fine Art of Leaking Information," *New York Times*, January 14, 1983, p. A16; Tom Wicker, *On Press* (New York: Viking, 1978), p. 101.

80. Daniel Schorr, *Clearing the Air* (New York: Berkley, 1978), p. 182.

81. Wicker, *On Press*, pp. 201-2.

82. For his own account, see Schorr, *Clearing the Air*, pp. 187-225.

# II

# The Presidency, the Congress, and the Mass Media

# 6

# Mass Media and
# Politics

One of the basic troubles with radio and television news is that both instruments have grown up as an incompatible combination of show business, advertising, and news. Each of the three is a rather bizarre and demanding profession. And when you get all three under one roof, the dust never settles.[1]

In 1952 a small footnote to history became something of a big milestone in the evolution of American political campaigns. That year saw a presidential race between Democrat Adlai Stevenson and the venerable Dwight Eisenhower. Eisenhower's running mate was a brash young senator from California named Richard Nixon. Like most vice-presidential contenders, Nixon would have normally passed in and out of public attention with a minimum of public interest. That might have happened. But it did not. It was to be the year that Nixon single-handedly salvaged his political career on the tenuous thread of one 30-minute nationwide television speech.

The speech was a master political move brought on by two problems to which a less adroit politician might have succumbed. The first was the largely baseless charge that he had used campaign funds to establish a private slush fund of $16,000. The second problem grew out of this dilemma. Eisenhower characteristically kept his own counsel. He was reluctant to reassure Nixon and the nation of his continuing support, thereby giving weight to press speculation that indeed the scrappy California senator was in deep political trouble. Hours and days passed until it became evident to Nixon that he had to engineer his own political salvation. As has frequently been noted by nearly every analyst of campaign politics, it was both a masterful and a tawdry apologia. Speaking to the nation from an empty theater in Hollywood, Nixon explained the necessity to seek outside financial support to run for the Senate.

In the speech he dramatically recounted his own modest finances. An audience of perhaps 60 million saw or heard it.[2] Everything seemingly was mentioned to vindicate the charge that he was making a fortune in politics: the paid-off loan on his old car, his mortgage on a modest home, the necessity of buying only a "cloth coat" for "Pat," and, finally, his steadfast refusal to return the gift of a dog named Checkers. The defense was clothed in the rhetoric of honor, but it was by implication a calculated attack on the press and the Democrats. With his roots in the hardworking middle class firmly established, he went on to challenge Stevenson to explain his own finances, and to urge voters to repudiate a campaign of "smears" and innuendos.

Nixon bet on his skill in building the image of a man unfairly wronged. He asked his viewers to decide his fate, making the brief television appearance a referendum on his candidacy. "Wire and write the Republican National Committee," he stated in his closing, "whether you think I should stay on [the ticket] or whether I should get off. And whatever their decision is, I will abide by it."[3] The $75,000 telecast yielded thousands of supporting telegrams and letters. It ignited the campaign, and Eisenhower belatedly embraced his running mate. Even today the impact of the Checkers speech is impressive. It saved the career of a leader who would go on to the presidency, and on to a further (but vain) attempt at rhetorical salvation against charges of covering up evidence. Arguably, 30 minutes of political rhetoric has never had a greater effect on the course of American history.

But was it television that saved Nixon, or was it Nixon? Was this an omen of the new politics? Could so much support aroused in such a short period of time make the political event more important than the long-haul campaign? These questions suggest the need to begin our discussion with some fundamental observations about the elusive ties that link politics to the mass communication machinery that now shapes our perceptions of politicians.

## THE TROUBLING EPISTEMOLOGY OF THE MASS MEDIA

By their very nature, the components of political culture are rarely witnessed in their raw forms. They are, instead, represented to us by intermediaries. Most of life's larger events are out there beyond the realm of the individual's capacity to experience them firsthand. It falls to others to serve as our eyes and ears. Others focus our attention on the speeches, debates, political meetings, and votes which form the mosaic of political impressions that we acquire. There is nothing novel in this. Politics, like theater, and similar to any arena where the discussion of human intentions and motives weighs significantly, invites layers of bureaucracies, writers, and journalists to construct versions of political reality. To those uninitiated in the folkways of politics the witnessing of a debate in state assembly, of hearings on Capitol Hill, or thick reports issued by an executive agency research staff will seem frustratingly inconclusive. It often takes a press report appearing in a morning paper to allow us to make sense of the unintelligible events that are too complex in their raw forms. As Walter Lippmann noted, "The world that we have to deal with politically is out of reach, out of sight, out of mind. It has to be explored, reported, and imagined." Through the mass media, man learns "to see with his mind vast portions of the world that he could never see, touch, smell, hear, or remember. Gradually he makes for himself a trustworthy picture inside his head of the world beyond his reach."[4] What is learned is not firsthand but derivative. It is a world that is not known because we have instructed ourselves. It is more like the sum of impressions that we intuit from the explanations of the vast information sources that incessantly sell, entertain, and inform.

Grounded as it is in words and symbols that sustain an inexact and illusory reality, political communication deals in firm and vivid ways with topics that have a far less than certain epistemology. What we "know" to be the case—that government is taking care of the poor, that there is mismanagement and corruption in a federal agency, that a Latin American government is democratic—may be far less certain than the news summary that sorts it into consumable form. Indeed, full and accurate news stories that really matched the intricate contours of actual events might well be considered unreadable. The presence of news has a way of placing organization over what is inherently disorganized.

Part of the focus of this chapter is on the news in its many forms, but also on other common forms of political intelligence which come to the perceiver through one of the many vehicles for mass communication. Forms of advertising and entertainment are considered, particularly for how they are shaped by pressures from within the media, and those seeking the free publicity that the mass media can supply.

Our intention here is to look at the conventional formats, routine relationships, and subtle effects which stem from the uneasy marriage between politics and the commercial media.

By the mass media we mean the news and entertainment organizations—large and small—who sell their wares to the general public on a routine basis. We include newspapers, films, magazines, radio and television programs, especially newscasts, publishers, and even the music industry. Combined, these mass media represent an enormous and sometimes diverse range of individual outlets: over 10,000 television and radio stations, about 1,700 daily newspapers, perhaps 40 major "opinion" journals, and scores of large and small companies supplying networked or syndicated programs and stories to individual outlets.

We begin with three basic clarifications based on what we believe are several common misunderstandings.

### Media and Pluralism

It is important to remember that the term, *media*, is and should be considered a plural concept, not a singular one. In a trivial sense this is just a grammatical point. But the "singularizing" of media which is common in much writing (i.e., the media ruined his chances for reelection) implies much more. Properly used, *media* is a collective plural noun. It refers to a number of information sources with a wide degree of diversity. Although it has become commonplace to link them together for descriptive purposes, the media collectively represent quite different kinds of entities. There is often little justification for using the term as at the head of a description of common traits. A big city newspaper, for example, and a small town radio station are both part of the media. But their differences are as evident as their similarities. Each will have starkly different objectives and audiences, naturally different means of constructing messages, different types of owners, etc. They may have some key similarities as well; for example, each may use the same wire service or network news sources. But the gulf separating them is too wide to gloss over with generalizations that attempt to unify them.

This inherent diversity poses a profound and often ignored conceptual muddle. The tendency to presuppose that the mass media represent identifiable sets of shared characteristics plagues much of the analysis of political communication. The problem is one of abstraction. Individual outlets surely do carry recognizable forms of political intelligence. We can describe and study, to cite several instances, a set of specific newspaper editorials—CBS News coverage of the signing of the Camp David agreements between Israel and Egypt, or *Time*'s editorial policy on Vietnam War coverage in the late 1960s. We may even be able to trace patterns evident in the coverage of a presidential election by the national press: for example, in the wire services, the networks, and the *Washington Post*. But the limits of description are distorted by conclusions that attempt to bridge the enormous range of sources of information available to Americans. The tendency to still discuss political communication in terms of this highest of high abstractions may serve a heuristic purpose. But the descriptive force of a claim discussing the media is extremely weak. It makes no sense, for example, to talk about media politics or media candidates. Virtually all but the very smallest of political offices depend upon various forms of mediated public communication. That reality has been with us since the first political tracts accompanied the waves of European settlers to North America in the first half of the seventeenth century. No precision is possible when one attempts to assign an undifferentiated media with certain attributes, causes, and effects. The historical counterpart to the use of this abstraction might be the sixteenth-century admonition of a religious fanatic against the influence of books—all books—on the lives of their readers.

Part of our difficulty is that we have equated the rapid development of radio and television in the interwar years as nothing less than a communications revolution. The assumption was obviously that pre-electric communication affected readers and subjects alike in far different ways. But in actual fact the vigorous print press of prewar America represented a kind of media that differed from its modern electronic counterparts more in degree than in kind. Even in the life of George Washington one finds the public relations problems thought to have been invented with radio and television: press fascination with his personality, a chain of publicity-based pseudoevents leading up to his appointment, news management in the publication of his farewell address, and the kind of elevation to celebrity status that would have made *People* magazine proud.[5]

All of these traps we have identified are ones that we ourselves have stumbled into. To clarify that scope of our own discussion here we will generally deal only with those national print and electronic mass media that service smaller outlets with programs and stories. The most ready examples are the television networks and the newspaper wire services. Since much of the routine political content of the media comes from national sources, the concept of the media is much more focused when it stands for the major corporate entities in the United States which serve clients with material they cannot get themselves. These companies include the three networks and their smaller but growing cable competitors, their radio counterparts, the major wire services such as UPI and AP, the large film production firms, and the major newsweeklies. Together these industry giants account for a huge portion of the output carried by any one local mass media source. Most local newspapers and television or radio stations receive a significant portion of their content from one or more of these national sources. In addition, these important giants tend to establish the patterns of reporting that are followed by other organizations.

## Media and Determinism

For several decades now researchers and analysts have been exploring the intensely complex relationships that exist between news sources and public attitudes. Their conclusions invariably point to the difficulties involved in attributing the flow of public opinion to specific mass media sources. The questions that media researchers ask are intriguing because they imply effects that touch nearly everyone. But questions about so broad a range of society make attributions of causation difficult. Are correlations between public attitudes and intense public communication causally related, or simply two artificially frozen points in a process that involves less apparent forces? How accurate are recall surveys? How accurate are media usage studies? Are the mass media collectively so powerful that they function like a "magic bullet," piercing the consciousness of everyone in its path? Or are they so diffuse that they are analytically impenetrable?[6] The more the research accumulates, the more the last question seems to characterize the difficulties of coming to grips with mass media research. The impression conveyed by the layman or the journalist is often of an all-powerful mass media: a media establishment that relentlessly controls the flow of political information, and thus influences public attitudes.[7]

But specific studies—some of which are cited in this chapter—often reveal complexities that temper such overzealous determinism. The collective weight of both critical and empirical studies on the effects of broadcast and print messages leaves a number of important qualifiers in force. All must be considered before statements implying cause and effect can meaningfully be made. From the early work of Lang and Lang examining political television in the 1950s,[8] to the more recent work of Michael Robinson, Sidney Kraus, Thomas Patterson, and countless others,[9] a number of important antideterministic conclusions reappear. The first being that no single mass media source commands total loyalty and certain credibility. There is little reflexive acceptance of suasive or informative messages, including those of the most important mass media. Second, people are generally selective about what they hear, making the actual effects of a piece of political communication highly unpredictable. Conclusions other than those intended by the sender are sometimes reached. Messages may be considered, momentarily accepted, and then later rejected. And, most humbling of all, messages such as political commercials may produce the reverse of their intended effect: creating greater hostility rather than increasing support. Third, there is a great deal of elasticity in the attitudes of individuals. Attitudes may be stretched and momentarily altered by the appeals contained in a news story, editorial, or political broadcast. But the individual psyche is likely to retain the original contours of belief. Individual events, even whole campaigns, may leave an impression on the resilient exterior of public attitudes. But it is less evident that their impact is lasting. And, finally, because opinions and attitudes are the products of aggregate experiences, the messages of the mass media must be treated as only one of many causes. To imply that the media alone are prime causes in attitude formation is to overlook both other sources of attitudes (i.e., those gained from interpersonal contact). Attitudes are produced interactively rather than unilaterally.

## Media and the Corollary of Mediated Messages

A third caveat deals with the intriguing extension of the simple noun *media*, into the process-centered idea of *mediated communication*. The mass media are frequently understood as organizations with staffs, budgets, constraints, obligations, and self-defined roles. But it is often more useful to focus more on the process of message-construction by media organizations, than on the organizations themselves. The idea of mass mediated communication is not centered on the location of entities, but of communication processes with enormous psychological and social consequences. Mediation is at the core of all forms of communication: representing the internal processes necessary to link audience and writer, or speaker and listener. To talk, to write, to think, is to construct a world from an elaborate pre-existing reservoir of symbols that we think will fit the reality we have experienced. We always must mediate between the world we think we see, and the world inside that we know. The danger in some approaches to the mass media is that it is easy to believe that they impose demands that are unique. This point was elaborated in more depth in Chapter 1. In actual fact, however, the mass media share the same basic processes for communicating. They simply do it for larger numbers, and frequently at the same time. So the impact of the rhetorical decisions made by their workers may have a greater impact on the society as a whole.

## THREE FUNDAMENTAL EFFECTS OF MASS-MEDIATED COMMUNICATION

Politics is mediated for us in three basic ways. That is, there are three dominant processes that routinely intrude on messages as they make their way through the labyrinths of mass media channels. First, outlets which distribute information and entertainment serve collectively to establish a public consciousness on a limited range of community and national concerns. Second, popular forms of media that provide news and entertainment give form and substance to the raw and nearly inexhaustible world of events with potential political significance. And, finally, they normally provide the groundwork that involves reducing abstract and ideological principles to their human or personal components. All three represent important dimensions where the realms of politics, the business of mass communication, and the shifting weight of public opinion interact. The first involves what is often described as the agenda-setting function; the second, the construction of specific political realities (sometimes called the gatekeeping,) and the third, the personalization of ideas. An examination of each effect follows.

### Agenda Setting

There can be little doubt that even in our pluralistic environment the mass media collectively exert a considerable influence in determining the agenda of topics that will be given prominence. "The press," Walter Lippmann has noted, "is like the beam of a searchlight that moves restlessly about, bringing one episode and then another out of darkness into vision."[10] What we conclude about what we see may well be up to us. But the direction to which we are encouraged to look seems largely out of our hands.

The potential number of political events that could be reported by any outlet in a given day will obviously always outstrip its capacity. That outlet must therefore choose what to cover. At the local level, the newspaper must decide how to divide up the available "news hole": leaving space for a limited number of stories that meet the formulaic and journalistic requirements of the paper. Should a story on the mayor be included? How much effort should be given to state legislative business? to political party news? to insurance reform proposals? Should space be used to report on the governor's reelection campaign, or to a third-party presidential candidate touring the city? How much if any space should be used to describe the pending divorce of a member of Congress? The range of choices is nearly limitless, and governed to some extent by the sequence in which items become available for use. It would be naive to assume that what is reported in any medium represents all of the news. The sheer number of human events that could qualify as newsworthy will always outstrip the capacity of any number of channels available at any given time.

The bases for story selection—or for the emergence of an individual or issue into public awareness—are diverse. Some analysts such as Herbert Gans have emphasized the traditional journalistic rules for story suitability. Something has news value if it involves public officials, affects the nation, has an impact on large numbers of people, or says something about where we are going.[11] An event may be deemed worthy of coverage if it contains a degree of novelty, an element of action, the drama of actual or potential conflict, and so on.[12] These are familiar journalistic standards—based in part on pleasing the largest possible audience, and in part on a general set of standards for determining what is important.

Many others have approached the study of news and information content by exploring topic and story selection from a subjective or consensual perspective. From this view, news is what we (or some group) chooses to call it. The informational agenda is a group product: a matter of agreement based on shared attitudes and routines. Author Tim Crouse's study of reporters covering the 1972 presidential campaign, for example, firmly planted the concept of "pack journalism" in the lexicon of public communication studies. Reporters traveling for days with a presidential candidate frequently began to consider the material written by other reporters as a basis for determining their own stories and approaches. For example:

The [*New York*] *Times* team filed a lead saying that [Hubert] Humphrey had apologized for having called [George] McGovern a "fool" earlier in the campaign. Soon after they filed the story, an editor phoned from New York. The AP had gone with a [George] Wallace lead, he said. Why hadn't they?

Marty Nolan eventually decided against the Wallace lead, but NBC and CBS went with it on their news shows. So did many of the men in the room. They wanted to avoid "call-backs"—phone calls from their editors asking them why they had deviated from the AP or UPI. If the editors were going to run a story that differed from the story in the nation's 1,700 other newspapers, they wanted a good reason for it. Most reporters dreaded call-backs. Thus the pack followed the wire service men whenever possible. Nobody made a secret of running with the wires: it was accepted practice. At an event later in the campaign, a *New York Daily News* reporter looked over the shoulder of Norm Kempster, a UPI man, and read his copy. "Stick with that lead, Norm," said the man from the *News.* "You'll save us a lot of trouble." "Don't worry," said Norm. "I don't think you'll have any trouble from mine."[13]

Crouse's study is sometimes taken as a microcosm. Conformity in reporting protects individual reporters as well as entire organizations by extending the illusion of news as something that selects itself. If a lead story or certain issues are standard across a wide range of media, the public has little reason to question the competence or credibility of any one source. The reverse—a highly idiosyncratic and nonstandardized version of the week's top events—might point to the unflattering conclusion that there is an inherent selectivity possible in setting the agenda of newsworthy events.

A variation on the idea of a news consensus notion has been put forth in interesting detail by Edward Epstein.[14] His central argument has been that agenda setting in the information age is covertly affected by the organizational and structural constraints imposed by the *business* of the mass media. In his study of NBC, Epstein found a good deal of variation between the choice of stories covered by the three networks.[15] But he also found that story selection was heavily influenced by political and organizational ground rules that had little to do with the intrinsic newsworthiness of an event. Does it have accompanying pictures? Will the story interest a large group of television viewers? Are we overemphasizing one kind of story? Are the images of the story readily identifiable? (Criminals should look like criminals; the poor should look poor; victims should look victimized.) These were real concerns, and largely independent of substantive considerations. Budget constraints, the need to hold an audience, the tendency to identify news with official action, all represent different kinds of operating constraints that shape the final form of news presentations.

The news agenda may not be manipulated intentionally to exclude any one kind of topic. It may simply be the case that largely routine operational circumstances tend to preselect versions of news. The path to commercial success is guaranteed by the existence of riveting action, official acts, stereotypic images, and dramatic conflict. As Epstein has summarized:

> To maintain themselves in a competitive world, the networks impose a set of prior restraints, rules and conditions on the operations of their news divisions. Budgets are set for the production of news, time is scheduled for its presentation, and general policies are laid down concerning its content. To satisfy these requirements—and keep their jobs —news executives and producers formulate procedures, systems and policies intended to reduce the uncertainties of news to manageable proportions. The timing, length, content and cost of news thereby becomes predictable. Since all of the networks are in essentially the same business and compete for the same or similar advertisers, affiliates and audiences, under a single set of ground rules laid down by the government, the news product at each network is shaped by similar requisites. The basic contours of network news can thus be at least partly explained in terms of the demands which the news organizations must meet in order to continue operating without crises or intervention from network executives.[16]

Yet another source of influence on the information agenda—an ideological requirement—has been proposed by a wide range of observers on both the political right and left. Numerous observers have claimed that the national press in particular has a left-wing, antibusiness, anti-Republican bias. The most systematic attempt to chronicle this bias was perhaps Edith Efron's *The News Twisters*.[17] But few studies support its sweeping claims about liberal dominance. The more accurate view is probably the one argued by Gans: "If journalists are neither quite as liberal, especially on economic issues, as their critics on the Right believe them to be, or as conservative as their critics on the Left think, they are, on the whole, more liberal than their superiors and their colleagues in the business departments, as well as their sponsors and advertisers."[18]

A more sweeping critique, however, comes from the political Left. Where the Right tends to criticize latent attitudes that surface in the reporting of specific stories, the Left tends to focus on fundamental values that shape the general choice of news and informational topics. The primary criticism that is made (and developed more fully at the end of this chapter) is that the news agenda encourages acceptance of the economic and political status quo. News story selection, such critics argue, at best reveals a bias for incremental change as a standard for dealing with serious social problems. Radical political change is not considered, or else is portrayed as threatening and unreasonable. From this viewpoint the great organs of mass communication appear as organizations with deep investments in the society as it is, not as it could be. As businesses with a primary stake in secure and undisrupted markets, their interests are said to lie in a delicate balance. On one hand they must go through the motions of reporting objectively on the urgent, unusual, and problematic. But they seek to do so in a way that will not jeopardize their advertisers: vital sources of revenue with their own interests in a stable acquiescent society. For authors such as Todd Gitlin[19] and Lance Bennett[20] the steady diet of news and fantasy in the American mass media has served to "delegitimate" significant change in unjust American institutions. The ideological core of American television, Gitlin argues, is one of static acceptance —of consideration of social dislocations in terms other than weaknesses inherent in American capitalism. Establishment sources may often get the last word in a story. More deference may be shown to the official than to the outcast. The result is the production of an informational agenda that has been depoliticized. Problems such as poverty, substandard health care, and unemployment may be described in terms of their personal consequences rather than their deeper economic roots. Because it is usually easier to portray the physical dimensions of a problem than its historical or ideological roots, public understanding is limited to a superficial awareness of a problem's most visible elements.

As a case in point, it is now evident that the disorganized antiwar movement in the 1960s failed to produce at an ideological plane what the grim carnage on the nightly news produced at a more visceral level. The news, Gitlin and others have asserted, rarely gave segments of the movement the kind of legitimacy it needed to make its arguments against the war credible. Our eventual withdrawal from the Vietnam struggle was not because there was a groundswell of feeling that we were intruders in a South Vietnamese civil war, but that we were in a militarily unwinnable war. The national debate that slowly built on the war was for some years muted in comparison to the anger and grief over the scenes vividly portrayed in what Michael Arlin aptly called the first "living room war."[21] The television networks, for example, agonized over every minute of Senate hearings they carried that debated the assumptions and principles justifying our involvement.[22] Such hearings involved explorations into the troubling and ambiguous ideological rationales for fighting a land war that had no certain connection with our own national security. But no such similar agony was evident in the decisions to present the vivid and riveting war footage night after night.

### The Construction of Political Realities

In his seminal study of staged news events Daniel Boorstin recalls that "We used to believe there were only so many events in the world. If there were not many intriguing or startling occurrences, it was no fault of the reporter. He could not be expected to report what did not exist."[23] If such a time ever existed, it has long since passed. In Chapter 2 we argued that political events and attitudes are quintessentially symbolic. What we know about the exercise of power is largely derived from verbal and symbolic constructions that give an immediate presence to policies, intentions, and attitudes. News accounts, political campaign commercials, press conferences, and countless other forms of communication are pieces of rhetorical equipment designed for securing the public relations objectives of politicians.

No one can deny the existence of "spot" news that essentially demands coverage, or demands a response from a political figure. The Iranian hostage crisis which dogged the Carter administration was (at the beginning) such an event. But, like Walter Cronkite's decision to end each newscast by noting the number of days the hostages had been held, most political occurrences that are reported are within the control of someone or some group. The rituals of political activity are not spontaneous. They are usually planned for particular effect. Press conferences, speeches, bill-signings, proclamations, heated exchanges in debates, are rhetorical constructions designed to secure the attention and support of an audience, and timed to have the greatest impact. Boorstin was perhaps only half right in calling them "pseudo-events." The term carries the connotation that they are somehow less real or less important than startling occurrences that seem to be more authentic. Without doubt, the start of the Iranian crisis would have been hard to ignore. But there are also countless times when issues of questionable validity acquire an interested audience, and thus the necessity for a serious response. The comments and lifestyle of President Carter's brother, Billy, attracted a good deal of attention, but usually had little relevance to the activities of Carter as president. Because Billy created attention, however, the president was obligated to answer questions about his brother, and to deal with the "Billy problem."

Political life has always involved the rhetorical arts—the construction and expression of states of anger, concern, threat, and reassurance. Just as religion is, in a rhetorical sense, "words about God,"[24] so is politics essentially words about pending and past decisions affecting the community. The events discussed are only partly out there. In basic ways political occurrences start and are reported when individuals feel motivated to make such events happen. They may indeed be complete fabrications: pseudoevents turned into managed and manufactured news. Their acceptance, however, makes their occurrence no less real than the spot news of an assassination attempt or a declaration of war. What makes them real or urgent is their surfacing in the public consciousness. "Events are not events until they get themselves communicated."[25]

Much of this goes without saying. But we often seem reluctant to take the implications of this perspective to their full conclusion, particularly with regard to the reporting of a nation's civil life. Without difficulty we accept the political speech as a manufactured event. But we assume the *reporting* of it is somehow more objective and less creative. We expect that public officials will orchestrate events to serve their own political ends, but we frequently cling to the view that the news media stand apart, reflecting rather than transposing the constructed event. Politicians are easily cast into the role of the rhetorician. They are seen as constructors of rhetorical visions. But journalists are not. The former are thought to engage in artful rhetorical deceits in order to please audiences. The latter are widely seen as observers rather than participants. The mythic reduction of the journalist is to the image of being the neutral eyes and ears of the public.

A more accurate picture of the rhetorical dimensions of reporting requires some revisions of these falsely dichotomized roles. Michael Novak has correctly noted what most good journalists will concede: "All reporting is angular, perspectival, selective."[26] It must be. Both the reporter and the politician are, in key ways, working the same side of the street. Both must attribute motives. Both must explain the nontangible principles that form the honorable rationales for political action. And both must please audiences with reconstructions of attitudes and events which are inexact and diffuse. If the political speaker chooses to talk about the plight of the poor in America, the reporter assigned to cover him must exercise similar rhetorical options to relay the tone and nature of the event to the reader or listener. As Novak notes, the pressures for pleasing a constituency are usually every bit as strong in the journalist as they are in the politician, and equally corrupting:

> The tradition of American journalism demands "news." An "angle." Something "different." Something "fresh." . . . The world isn't made that way—"There's nothing new under the sun," men believed for thousands of years—and good politics is seldom a matter of novelty. But journalism has a voracious appetite for novelty.
>
> Commentators, I think, fail to see how *corrupting* the practices of journalism truly are: the cult of celebrity, the cult of "news," the manipulative skills of "riding the wire," supplying two new daily "leads," "grabbing headlines," manufacturing "events" and "statements." Journalists speak as if *money* were the great corrupter of our times; but the corruption of intelligence and imagination by the demand for "news" is deadly.[27]

Paul Weaver has similarly noted that electronic political reporting is itself a political act, because it is inherently judgmental:

> When television covers politics, it is giving us not only facts, but judgments—judgments that make candidates look good or bad; judgments that are shared by some and rejected by others; judgments in other words, that are essentially political.[28]

The best studies of newsgathering organizations tend to by-pass the epistemologically futile exercise of verifying the empirical accuracy if a story against original events. All seem to note the tendency to reduce the complex to its simplest (and often distorted) elements.[29] But most have focused on the conventions and news-framing routines that serve to normalize discrete events. Gans, Epstein, Robinson, MacNeil, Bennett, Nimmo and Combs have all discussed the formulaic elements of newsgathering, usually in terms of the stylistic and thematic dimensions that make popular news an accessible kind of public communication.[30]

It is impossible here to recount the various schemes that have been proposed. But it is worthwhile to offer a brief sketch of several of the more problematic routines that carry profound political consequences.

1.   Ritual objectivity is given priority over synthesis and analysis: facts add up to something less than understanding.

Nearly every news organization gives priority to some form of fairness or objectivity. Aside from the ostensible goals of letting the reader or viewer decide, an emphasis on fact-gathering removes journalism from the risks that come with sharply critical or analytical rhetoric—the alienation of news service subscribers, readers, advertisers, and news subjects. The code of objectivity renders journalism motive-free. The obligation to report or observe is separated from the political persuader's more obvious persuasive intentions. This has the effect of conserving journalism's credibility and commercial saliency.

2. "Official" voices are the prime beneficiaries of the mass media. Objectivity also serves the interests of political advocates with official positions. Its deeper significance in the political world is that it usually gives an enormous amount of credibility to official sources, more or less by default. Very few critics of a governor, party leader, cabinet official, legislator, or president will be able to make refutations that contain the force that comes with such officials. The reason is obvious. A fact-based system of reporting frequently gives political newsmakers two sources of legitimation: one based on their ongoing role as public officeholder, the other as a compulsory respondent to nearly any story affecting their work. The presidential press conference dramatically illustrates this power. The president is uniquely able to make claims that, by simple journalistic standards, must be reported. He is also invited to comment on other topics of the day. No other source—not the objective journalists present, his critics, or opposing leaders in the other party—are able to match his ability to use legal authority to communicate his attitudes and feelings. As Bennett has noted, "most news stories reserve for official sources the first, the last, and many of the words in between."[31]

The irony in this, of course, is that the news media organizes its work around the perception that it has an adversarial relationship with government officials.[32] But the reality is that access comes much easier, and with less critical scrutiny, to holders of official positions in government and business than to their noninstitutionalized critics. Gitlin makes the point in an extended study of the messages of the radical Students for a Democratic Society (SDS) in 1965.[33] Their arguments against the Vietnam escalation—more reasonable now than they appeared in the sixties—were largely reported as the work of destructive and rebellious youth. The pattern was repeated in press reporting of the Watergate break-in and cover-up. Authors David Paletz and Robert Entman conclude that most of the coverage was at least initially always careful not to undermine the legitimacy of official White House explanations:

> They began by neglecting the scandals, calling them a caper. Then, when events were thrust into prominence by investigations and hearings, the bulk of the press cooperated with Nixon's strategy of laying the blame on associates. . . . Then, as evidence of Nixon's guilt became overt, dramatic, and threatening, the media contributed to his downfall. But they then helped to resolve public disquiet without pursuing the underlying lessons of the corruption.[34]

Based on a number of cases the authors judge that the "powerful should be grateful." The mass media help "prevent [the] erosion of legitimacy"[35] even as they are lauded as watchdogs of the powerful.

The pattern of supporting the status quo by supplying ample access to those with the largest stake in it is obviously far more complex than these two examples suggest. And, indeed, there is no unanimity among press critics and observers on how much support the media give the political mainstream.[36] As noted earlier, some outlets are more supportive than others.

Even so, the long-term effect of news that derives from official sources is enormous. If access itself is not power, it is at least a requisite condition to political control. And access frequently goes to governmental sources who have the most to gain by maintaining a steady stream of positive publicity about their work. Such publicity is made all the more potent when it comes to the receiver in the guise of journalistic neutrality. A general effect of much straight news reporting is thus to make significant social change difficult, and outspoken advocates of reform apparently disrespectful of legitimate authority. All but the most gradual forms of change may be made to seem threatening and unreasonable, foreclosing the kind of public debate that journalism ostensibly encourages.

3. Political action is framed by the conventions of melodrama. No frame of reference has proved more durable in studies of political behavior than the superstructure of terms and concepts associated with drama. Political reporting rarely ignores the elements of theater. Roles, scenes, acts, and audiences are endemic to descriptions of political events.[37] Characterizations of melodramatic images of foolishness, villainy, and heroes are common. The themes used to outline many stories are constant: the triumph of the individual over adversity, justice winning over evil, redemption of the individual through reform, the rewarding of valor or heroism. We say melodrama, because

unlike the treatment of actual or would-be politicians in classical drama—in Hamlet, Coriolanus, or King Lear, for example—the characteristic popular reporting of today emphasizes optimism rather than tragedy; a sense of upbeat predictability rather than of haunting human imperfections. The plot lines of political reporting are modulated to conform to the need for familiar themes and unambiguous conclusions. Stories may not always have happy endings. But the reader or viewer is usually left with the impression of what the ending should be. Along with countless others, Nimmo and Combs have noted that contemporary news reporting is "a literary act, a continuous search for story lines."

> Such story lines may incorporate the metaphors and plots of novels, folk traditions, and myths. . . . The same melodramatic formats available to entertainment programmers are options for producers of TV news: adventure, mystery, romance, pathos, nightmare, comedy. . . . When faced with an event that requires prolonged storytelling—say a presidential campaign, the seizure of hostages in a foreign country, a threat of war, and so on—a variety of melodramatic formats may be adapted to news coverage, thus imposing a thematic unity (a story) on what might otherwise seem unrelated events.[38]

Reflecting the logic that has long dominated the writing style of the newsweeklies such as *Time* and *Newsweek*, former NBC News chief Reuven Frank vividly made the same dramatistic point.[39] In what is now a widely reprinted memo to his staff the executive wrote:

> Every news story should, without any sacrifice of probity or responsibility, display the attributes of fiction, of drama. It should have structure and conflict, problem and denouement, rising action and falling action, a beginning, a middle and an end. These are not only the essentials of drama; they are the essentials of narrative.[40]

Television news in particular, notes Paul Weaver, "is not governed by a political bias, but by a melodramatic one." It is characterized by intensified peril, simplified values, and exaggerated intensity.[41]

Whether this effect is confined largely to electronic journalism is a matter of debate. A good argument can be made that print journalism has been transformed by the success of its newer electronic competitors. There is ample evidence in such print forms as Time-Life's *People* and Gannett's *USA Today* that print forms are developing the pace and personalized style of television news. In general terms, broadcast journalists probably still look to the older respected print forms for professional legitimacy. (The very concept of "journalist" is an anachronism when applied to TV.) But few can doubt today that visibility and credibility of electronic newsgathering give it unprecedented clout with audiences.

4. Political reporting has drifted toward an emphasis on "strategy" rather than ideology.

Perhaps reflecting the pace of television, or the natural interest television places on human motives (all drama requires the discussion or the assignment of motives), political reporting has changed from what it was several generations ago. The reader of a newspaper earlier this century was more likely to find news reports of political activity dominated by long excerpts of speeches and remarks. For a number of years in the 1920s and 1930s even radio was content to carry political addresses with a minimum of commentary. This journalism was not necessarily better, but it was different. The central theme of many contemporary reports—especially those that deal with the actions of particular agents—forces attention on political strategies and tactics. Faced with the choice of recounting to readers or viewers what a particular figure said, or analyzing the motives behind remarks addressed to a specific audience, more and more political journalism seems to emphasize the latter.

This pattern is represented by the now familiar common sight of a network correspondent delivering a "stand up" against the backdrop of a politician voicelessly explaining himself to an unknown audience. The option to let the politician's words speak for themselves is rarely exercised. The reporter feels the need to act as narrator: not simply telling the viewer what has just been said, but assessing the motivations underlying the political scene. Particularly on television politicians frequently end up with less time to talk about their ideas or programs. By serving as a constant presence (or intruder) in a report, the journalist is able to assign unseen motives, and to provide the pacing that is sought for a medium whose content is governed by the adage that time is money. As two recent observers of network campaign coverage have noted, "Hard issue information is the . . . victim of television journalism's preference for pictures. A candidate standing before the camera discussing an important campaign issue, such as unemployment, often cannot compete with Charles Kuralt covering a logrolling contest in Idaho. . . . "[4][2]

A sequence of three reports on a more or less typical CBS newscast illustrates how motive becomes more dominant than idea. The theme of political courtship is carried in campaign stories by correspondents Lesley Stahl, Jerry Bowen, and Bernard Goldberg. They were woven together in this 1980 broadcast by acting anchor Kuralt.

*Kuralt*: Campaigns in this country traditionally start on Labor day. So President Carter went home to the South today. John Anderson went home to Illinois, and Ronald Reagan went to a place where he could make a speech with the Statue of Liberty over his shoulder—each of them trying to appeal to a constituency he will need to win the presidency.

*Stahl*: President Carter chose the heart of George Wallace country for today's traditional campaign kick-off; he chose Alabama because he is concerned that the Wallace vote among Southerners and blue collar workers may be slipping to Ronald Reagan.

*Kuralt*: To win Ronald Reagan will have to make inroads in the big industrial states. So he started out today in a tough one—New Jersey. Jerry Bowen has that story.

*Bowen*: Ronald Reagan seems to have pulled out all of the stops as he brought his campaign to heavily Democratic New Jersey for a rally set against the New York skyline and the Statue of Liberty. . . .

*Kuralt*: Independent John Anderson also bore down heavily on economic issues as he campaigned in Illinois. Bernard Goldberg has our report.

*Goldberg*: It almost rained on John Anderson's parade today, but after a few minutes under the umbrella the sun came out and Anderson began walking the suburbs of Chicago, trying to win some support in Calumet City, where workers wear blue collars and normally vote Democratic.[43]

This pattern of focusing on the logistics of politics at the expense of ideas and issues is most evident in campaigns. But it occurs in all forms of political reporting. David Riesman predicted this pattern in his seminal study, *The Lonely Crowd*. Politics, he said, encouraged a game-player's enthusiasm for technique, and the sharing of the "insider's" superior understanding of how to play the game of politics well. "Inside dopester's" discount for the higher ostensible goals of political discourse, focusing instead on the status that is assured with access to inside knowledge:

There are political newsmen and broadcasters who, after long training, having succeeded in eliminating all emotional response to politics and who pride themselves on achieving the inside-dopester's goal: never to be taken in by any person, cause, or event.[44]

This produces a reporter who talks in the same strategic terms and with the same tactical thinking of a press secretary or campaign consultant. To simply report a public figure's words may seem uncomfortably close to functioning as a "flack" for a certain point of view. The way to demonstrate insights about the realpolitik of American life is to report on its theaterlike manipulations. The credibility of reporters is presumably enhanced because they demonstrate the ability to see through the veneer of public rhetoric to the supposedly different political realities underneath.

Theodore White has cast himself as perhaps the archetypical journalist-insider. His *Making of the President* series legitimized the convention of making the communication and political strategies of major political figures the substance of a report. Tim Crouse notes that some reporters came to see White as a "political groupie" sought out by politicians for the flattering portrayals that he could produce. But many nevertheless considered White's style a good model: "it made sense to them to treat a political campaign as a growing, organic drama and to examine the psychological and sociological causes of political decisions."[4][5]

## The Personalizing of Political Information

The final broad form of mediation that seems evident in many forms of political intelligence is the tendency to link most discussion of public policy to the circumstances and characteristics of particular individuals. This is not simply to say that we focus more today on personalities than on issues. The components of this pattern are more complex than this simple dualism. Fundamentally it means that political intelligence is frequently made comprehensible to vast numbers when it centers on the actors involved: the agents for change, the victims of inaction or social neglect, and the villains responsible for creating social unrest. Except for the most erudite and scholarly of publications, public policy today is described largely in terms of the personalities of proponents, opponents, and affected citizens.

To be sure, this tendency is an inexact one to trace. It has always been the case that the character of the public figure has been a subject of public interest. The politics of ancient Greece enshrined the role of ethos: the personal qualities important to strong leadership.[46] The plays of Shakespeare, for example, and didactic theater in general, have encouraged the exploration of the linkages that connect specific personal qualities to the advocacy of doctrines of the public good. Freud, psychoanalysis, the invention of psychology as a study suitable for undergraduates, and the popularity of biography, are but some of the few influences that have fueled interest in the public personage. Every age has contained its share of mass literature identifying progress and change with the personal strengths and weaknesses of its leaders. As with the Checkers speech, the political agent's vivid personal response is always the more concrete part of the political equation. Motives, values, attitudes, decisions—all of the intangibles affecting work in the public domain—are made evident when reduced to the visible actions of individuals. As Machiavelli has warned: to the casual observer, the apparent character of public figures is a convenient if highly misleading window on the politics that they seem to endorse.[47] Such cautions aside, our fascination is usually unremitting.

The intensification of this trend is to be seen everywhere. In the newsmagazines ideas are not discussed apart from their advocates; they are portrayed as being enacted by them. The popular discussion of ideas makes sense to many only when personalities are entwined with their issues. Social problems are not discussed in general terms, but when the specific effects of the problems are shown at work on specific people. The most thoughtful of political figures know this. They must temper their desire to construct elaborately reasoned speeches. They know that they must pause for the inevitable sidetracks through the vital media/celebrity circuits: TV talk shows, "lifestyle" interviews, and the like. In the realm of television entertainment, countless network television films not only treat a range of social problems that imply political solutions—child custody laws, unemployment, police corruption, etc., they also include docudramas on the final days of the Nixon administration, the Cuban missile crisis, the Jim Jones cult, and toxic wastes at Love Canal. Supermarket tabloids, syndicated newspaper features, and magazine-format television shows explore the personal tastes and attitudes of political celebrities. Hundreds of biographies ranging from those on the Kennedy family to flamboyant governors and mayors, offer glimpses of the human side of major political figures, often with more interest in their personal lives than their political accomplishments.

Richard Sennett has written on what he brilliantly argues is the steady increase in value we assign to the personal attributes of political figures. In *The Fall of Public Man* he notes:

A political leader running for office is spoken of as "credible" or "legitimate" in terms of what kind of man he is, rather than in terms of the actions or programs he espouses. The obsession with persons at the expense of more impersonal social relations is like a filter which discolors our rational understanding of society; it obscures the continuing importance of class in advanced industrial society; it leads us to believe community is an act of mutual self-disclosure and to undervalue the community relations of strangers.[48]

Sennett argues his point at several levels. He claims that we have forgotten the arts of public (formal) communication, where roles are clearly defined, and public rhetoric expresses the obligations of people not simply as "nice people," but as representatives of institutions. The public act has been replaced by behavior that glorifies the self-disclosure and enforced intimacy of private life. The newspapers' gossip columns have always performed this function: printing intimate information that supposedly reveals the true identity of a public personality.

Today it is almost as if the substance of political debate has become so impenetrable that political communicators redeem their credibility with calculated affirmations of character rather than substantive debate. This shift in emphasis trivializes political discourse. It might also salvage the interest of even the least analytical of political consumers. But at what cost? Such personalization may help explain why President Kennedy was widely thought to be more politically progressive than he was. The Kennedy style which received so much press attention contrasted with the "square" and old-fashioned style of the previous Eisenhower-Nixon years. The handsome family looked and sounded like members of the liberal Northeast aristocracy that had given rise to the popular and venerated Roosevelts. The presidencies of Teddy and Franklin Roosevelt contained a revered combination of aristocratic tradition and populist obligation to the exploited and the poor. Kennedy seemed to be in the same mold. In actual fact, however, he was hardly a liberal president. Most of his initiatives—in civil rights, European affairs, in Asia, on military spending, or conciliation with the Soviet Union—could have been (and later were) accommodated by his 1960 opponent, Richard Nixon. Stylistic differences between the two men were enormous: Kennedy was the paragon of grace, self-assurance, and wit; Nixon was awkward, less handsome, and often publicly defensive. These differences turned out to be critical as the attractive Kennedy gained a slight edge as the first series of television debates progressed.

The personalization of twentieth-century politics is frequently laid at the feet of broadcasting. Television is treated as a "compulsively personalistic" medium.[49] It encourages the political communicator to trade in a particularly superficial kind of imagery, rather than in the sustained discussion of ideas. With television the presenter dominates. By contrast, in print forms the presence of the reporter or persuader is comparatively unobtrusive. We focus almost exclusively on the message (unless of course, the message is directly about the writer).

Placing the advocate immediately before us makes television an instrument that invites the careful measurement of intention and motive. What we hear is tempered and often eclipsed by the complementary (or occasionally dissonant) image of what we see. Television campaigning, notes Paul Corcoran, "seems to demonstrate a preference for communication designed to convey images and symbols rather than argument, scenes rather than speech, actions rather than words, emotions rather than thoughts."[50] A prime form of such imagery is a kind of artificial interpersonal milieu (what is sometimes described as "para-social" communication) which has the effect of presenting the performer as a close acquaintance of the viewer, a figure worthy of trust. The inanimate world of ideas that is intrinsic to political discussion is forced into an animate mold. We frequently cannot conceive of the principles governing foreign policy; instead, we see the residents who would be affected. We cannot tolerate extensive discussion of tax law revisions without seeing graphic depictions of the affluence or lack thereof which is at stake. Television reduces news, politics, campaigns, policy debates to their material and personal dimensions. The intimacy of television, notes Sennett,

> connotes warmth, trust, and open expression of feeling. But precisely because we have come to expect these psychological benefits throughout the range of our experience, and precisely because so much social life which does have meaning cannot yield these psychological rewards, the world outside, the impersonal world, seems to fail us, seems to be stale and empty.[51]

Many of the objects and persons depicted in television news have become synecdoches: standing as reductive symbols, reshaping the political world into the familiar dimensions, and making every event representative of something bigger.

In more specific terms, the personalizing nature of the popular mass media has lessened our interest in the old supporting structures of American political life, most notably the party organizations and smaller political jurisdictions.

That the parties have suffered has been chronicled by many observers.[52] They still wield a good deal of influence in the politics of particular states, especially in the Northeast and the South. But their national influence has waned as the media-intensive presidential primaries have taken over the presidential selection process. The quadrennial summer conventions now merely tend to affirm a selection process that is essentially over by mid-spring. Candidates at various levels of government have learned that skillful use of the news media can replace the party machinery that used to have control over the selection of candidates.[53] Local politicians such as state assembly members, mayors, and some members of the U.S. House still cultivate networks of support within local party organizations, particularly where the intermittent spotlights of local news organizations rarely shine. But they often follow a different path than holders of major public offices. National politicians have grown accustomed to building their own media-based bridges to constituencies. The public official with a broad constituency has learned that party support is capriciousness. At many levels of office the party means much less on election day than the availability of mass media exposure. The transition from organizational to personal politics came in full force in the 1970s. By then traditional party loyalists—the Richard J. Daleys, Lyndon Johnsons, and Sam Rayburns—had faced challenges from "the pretty boys" who were using the new politics of the direct mass media appeal. The imagery of this change is vivid, if somewhat overdrawn. The cronies of the old political machines lost ground to well-financed media candidates appealing to large segments of voters, often with only the thinnest veneer of party loyalty. In style and demeanor these new candidates often matched the finesse and rhetorical sophistication of the professional communicators and interviewers they were keeping company with on television—the news anchors, actors, and interviewers who dominate modern television. David Halberstam cites Lyndon Johnson's bitter response to the passing of this old political order:

All you guys in the media. All of politics has changed because of you. You've broken all the [party] machines and the ties between us in Congress and the city machines. You've given us a new kind of people. . . . Teddy [Kennedy]. [John] Tunney. They're your creations, your puppets. No machine could ever create a Teddy Kennedy. Only you guys. They're all yours. Your product.[54]

## THE STRUCTURE OF THE POLITICAL MASS MEDIA

The routine channels of political communication in the United States are well known. Aside from the vital roles played by television and print journalism, significant use is made of direct mail, radio and television advertising, and special-interest publications. In this section we will briefly examine some of the guidelines that govern the use of these forms, as well as some representative attempts to measure their efficiency in reaching citizens.

## Media Usage and Credibility

The most common question asked about political media is whether some forms are more persuasive than others. The simple answer to this question must be a qualified yes: television (in both news and advertising contexts) probably presents the greatest potential for affecting citizen attitudes. But the details of available research also point out many exceptions and qualifications.

Perhaps the most widely followed work on mass media credibility has been conducted by the Roper Organization. Since 1959 it has been asking a cross section of the American public a number of questions about media usage and attitudes toward various media forms. Their polling has generally been synoptic: asking respondents to record attitudes and estimate time spent with television, newspapers, radio, national news on television, and so on. The numbers generated are exact, but the categories naturally deal with media that have wide variations within them.

The key trends are worth noting.[55] In capsule form they include the following (all data that follow are from Roper, unless otherwise identified. Percentages equal more than 100 because Roper has accepted multiple answers):

Since 1959 the number of respondents getting "most" of their news about what's going on in the world today has gone up for television and down for newspapers. In 1982, 65 percent mentioned television and 44 percent mentioned newspapers. Radio trailed behind with 18 percent (see Table 6.1). Newspapers top television as a source of news only when respondents are asked about where they get information about local elections (see Table 6.2).

Since 1961 television has been seen as the "most believable" news source. In 1982, 53 percent rated it the most believable medium, followed by 22 percent for newspapers, and 6 percent and 8 percent each for radio and magazines (see Table 6.3).

When asked to rank the overall quality of television news—both local and national—most respondents (between 80 and 90 percent) thought it was "excellent" or "good."

Given the well-documented evidence of how central a fixture television in the home has become, the results can hardly be surprising. In 50 short years television has grown from its status as a novelty to a household necessity. It has become a major source of information for the vast numbers of Americans who want to experience the sensation of news without the troubling and complex details. Even so, the

**Table 6.1** General Information Sources

*"First, I'd like to ask you where you usually get most of your news about what's going on in the world today—from the news-papers or radio or television or magazines or talking to people or where?"*

| Source of most news (%) | 12/59 | 11/61 | 11/63 | 11/64 | 1/67 | 11/68 | 1/71 | 11/72 | 11/74 | 11/76 | 12/78 | 11/80 | 12/82 |
|---|---|---|---|---|---|---|---|---|---|---|---|---|---|
| Television | 51 | 52 | 55 | 58 | 64 | 59 | 60 | 64 | 65 | 64 | 67 | 64 | 65 |
| Newspapers | 57 | 57 | 53 | 56 | 55 | 49 | 48 | 50 | 47 | 49 | 49 | 44 | 44 |
| Radio | 34 | 34 | 29 | 26 | 28 | 25 | 23 | 21 | 21 | 19 | 20 | 18 | 18 |
| Magazines | 8 | 9 | 6 | 8 | 7 | 7 | 5 | 6 | 4 | 7 | 5 | 5 | 6 |
| People | 4 | 5 | 4 | 5 | 4 | 5 | 4 | 4 | 4 | 5 | 5 | 4 | 4 |
| All mentions | 154 | 157 | 147 | 153 | 158 | 145 | 140 | 145 | 141 | 144 | 146 | 135 | 137 |

*Source:* Television Information Office, 1983, p. 5.

**Table 6.2** Information Sources in Local Elections

*"From what source did you become best acquainted with the candidates running in local elections—like mayor, members of the state legislature, etc.—from the newspapers or radio or television or magazines or talking to people or where?"*

| Local elections (%): | 1/71 | 11/72 | 11/74 | 11/76 | 12/78 | 11/80 | 12/82 |
|---|---|---|---|---|---|---|---|
| Newspapers | 41 | 41 | 41 | 44 | 45 | 36 | 39 |
| Television | 27 | 31 | 30 | 34 | 39 | 44 | 37 |
| Radio | 6 | 7 | 8 | 7 | 10 | 6 | 6 |
| People | 19 | 23 | 14 | 12 | 15 | 11 | 15 |
| Magazines | 1 | 1 | 1 | 2 | 1 | 2 | 1 |
| Other | 5 | 5 | 5 | 6 | 7 | 5 | 7 |
| Total mentions | 99 | 108 | 99 | 105 | 117 | 104 | 105 |

*Source*: Television Information Office, 1983, pp. 10-11.

Roper results (and the widely held views about television dominance among academics and journalists that they reinforce) need additional clarification and comment. Among many possible observations, we offer the following.

The Roper studies might lead one to conclude that these media are competitors, and that television is by far the clear victor. And in some senses these assessments are true. But increasingly detailed analyses of media usage patterns indicate that there is a far more complementary routine of citizen involvement than might first be evident. There are problems in concluding that television is the primary news medium. The difficulty is identifying what it means to say that a particular form is used "most." Thomas Patterson's own study of news media usage among consumers in Erie Pennsylvania and Los Angeles is revealing:

> The problem stems from the evidence on which the judgment is based. To ask people where they get most of their news is to fail to regard distinctions in the amounts of news they receive. . . .
>
> A more precise assessment of the political audience is obtained by asking people how often they see the news on television or in the newspaper. When this is done a much different picture emerges. It is actually the newspaper, not television, which has the larger regular news audience.[56]

As Table 6.4 shows, Patterson has attempted to isolate frequency of use, a refinement of a similar question asked by Roper. In addition,

**Table 6.3** Relative Credibility of Sources

*"If you got conflicting or different reports of the same news story from radio, television, the magazines, and the newspapers, which of the four versions would you be most inclined to believe—the one on radio or television or magazines or newspapers?"*

| Most believable (%): | 12/59 | 11/61 | 11/63 | 11/64 | 1/67 | 11/68 | 1/71 | 11/72 | 11/74 | 11/76 | 12/78 | 11/80 | 12/82 |
|---|---|---|---|---|---|---|---|---|---|---|---|---|---|
| Television | 29 | 39 | 36 | 41 | 41 | 44 | 49 | 48 | 51 | 51 | 47 | 51 | 53 |
| Newspapers | 32 | 24 | 24 | 23 | 24 | 21 | 20 | 21 | 20 | 22 | 23 | 22 | 22 |
| Radio | 12 | 12 | 12 | 8 | 7 | 8 | 10 | 8 | 8 | 7 | 9 | 8 | 6 |
| Magazines | 10 | 10 | 10 | 10 | 8 | 11 | 9 | 10 | 8 | 9 | 9 | 9 | 8 |
| Don't Know/ No Answer (DK/NA) | 17 | 17 | 18 | 18 | 20 | 16 | 12 | 13 | 13 | 11 | 12 | 10 | 11 |

*Source:* Television Information Office, 1983, p. 6.

**Table 6.4** Exposure to Network Evening Newscasts and the Daily Paper's Political News Sections (percent)

| Level of News Exposure | Erie | | Los Angeles | |
|---|---|---|---|---|
| | Newspaper | Network News | Newspaper | Network News |
| Regularly | 48 | 34 | 33 | 24 |
| Somewhat often | 21 | 30 | 15 | 27 |
| Once in a while | 11 | 23 | 10 | 30 |
| Infrequently | 7 | 12 | 15 | 16 |
| Never | 13 | 1 | 27 | 3 |
| Total | 100 | 100 | 100 | 100 |

*Note*: Table percentages are average of respondents' replies for the five interviews. That respondents were questioned as many as five times provides a control on measurement error. To be classified as a regular user, a respondent had consistently to indicate frequent exposure. Typical of the questions asked was the following: "Most people don't have the time or interest to read the entire newspaper. They normally read only certain parts such as the sports, the comics, the news, the business pages, the women's pages, and so on. How often do you read the *news pages* of your daily newspaper? Do you read the news pages regularly, somewhat often, only once in a while, or almost never (infrequently)?" People who did not receive a newspaper or did not have a television set were placed in the never category.

*Source*: Patterson, *Mass Media Elections*, p. 59.

Patterson has noted that, at least from a consumer's viewpoint, journalists from different kinds of media are not necessarily competitors (though they do compete for advertising dollars). News readers, he notes, are also likely to be news viewers. And viewers—all except the least politically interested—also read newspapers.[57]

Michael Robinson and Margaret Sheehan have indicated that the network half-hour newscasts may offer as complete a picture of a political story as their print counterparts at the major wire services. But it is also a slightly different one. At least with regard to campaign news at CBS and UPI, CBS tended to cover more information about the candidate's personal behavior. It also tended to be more analytic about the political motivations and processes, and more critical of politics and politicians in general.[58] On the whole they conclude that CBS gave a different, but not necessarily less complete, version of the day's news.

Though few would argue with the claim that television has expanded the audience for political information, it is still the case that print press still exerts the greatest influence on story selection. For this reason it is dangerous to underestimate the importance of the print media—especially the so-called "prestige press" (the *New York Times, Washington Post, Newsweek, The Wall Street Journal*, and the smaller national political journals). Because their readers often include other journalists, they can play a critical role in focusing attention on a particular story, or a new angle to an existing one. This pattern builds on our earlier discussion of agenda setting. A story printed in the *New York Times*, for example, is likely to be picked up by other reporters and editors as worthy of coverage. The publication of an item in a highly regarded print source has the effect of certifying it as legitimate news. Traditionally, the more thorough print press has provided the lead on stories that involve investigation, long-term research, and trend setting. The *Washington Post*'s persistent coverage of the Watergate break-in, for example, was largely echoed by the networks until the news agenda of the event was firmly embedded in the public's memory.

Finally, a judgmental caveat: although there have been dramatic increases in the sophistication and quality of television news reporting, its increasingly important role as a filter for all kinds of political information must be considered disturbing. The primary reason is obvious. There are tremendous time constraints which operate on the networks that prevent in-depth explorations of a subject. A half-hour network newscast is actually only 22 minutes long. The formula for dividing up that precious space leaves little room for any detailed look at a political candidate, a complex issue, or an explanation of an emerging social problem or trend. Many reporters have become masters at the construction of miniature documentaries that cram a remarkable amount of information and clarity into 90 seconds or two minutes. But a story is still only as information-rich as the rate of carefully spoken words will permit. After all, television is still as much oral as it is visual. The capacity of television news is seriously impaired by the leisurely pace of spoken delivery—a problem that is unlikely to be changed soon.[59] (There is irony in this. We tend to think of television as the new medium that separates our age from archaic oral cultures. But political television is an affirmation of oralism. The burden of explaining most political stories is usually in the oral narration, not in the accompanying pictures.) Even Walter Cronkite, for so long the dominating archetype of the network journalist, has lately earned the in-house nickname of "complainkite" for his recent postretirement speeches on the inadequacies of network news shows.

It is probably easy to overestimate the quality of thoroughness of the average wire service story reprinted in the average American newspaper. But it takes little insight to realize that print remains as the mass medium with the greatest capacity for describing the essential details of a story. A broadcast report might make a story more vivid, but it rarely has the space to develop the depth that comes from an in-depth print story in a good newspaper or newsmagazine. As Cronkite has noted, there is an "inadvertent and perhaps inevitable distortion that results through the hyper-compression we all are forced to exert to fit one hundred pounds of news into the one-pound sack that we are given to fill each night."[60]

## Controlled and Uncontrolled Media

There is no greater threshold in the world of politics than that which separates messages which have been paid for, and those which reach the public via free channels. The former include advertisements and political tracts purchased by their proponents, like Richard Nixon's redemptive Checkers speech. The latter include the much more persuasive conduit of news or information that reaches the reader, viewer, or listener without direct payment from the source receiving the coverage. Much of our discussion thus far has focused on news media which are beyond the direct control of political newsmakers. Our observations here will be on key issues regarding the use of paid messages.

The political campaign is the event that most sharply focuses on the distinctions between free and paid media. Seekers of major offices purchase stunningly expensive blocks of television time to present messages wholly controlled by them. Such presentations are obviously different from the images of the campaign that come across in news reporting. They may attempt to manipulate—but cannot completely control—reports of press conferences, news releases, and speeches. Political consultant John Deardourff sees a "constant tension between our interests and the media's interest. . . . Our difficulty is in transmitting a candidate's views in his own words." The requirement to use paid media, he says, is virtually "forced upon us."[61]

Other types of advocates sometimes face the same threshold, but usually in a less dramatic way. The co-sponsors of a key congressional bill or members of a single issue movement—for example, those against legal abortions, in favor of prayer in public schools, or opposed to a decrease in the minimum wage—will always think in terms of these two routes for reaching the American public. They may decide to pay for newspaper space or broadcast time. And they will often hire direct mail advertising firms to design and send messages intended for families on carefully chosen mailing lists.

But they will also have to plan how to exploit the free media, by finding ways to court bona-fide journalists who will give them publicity in the context of a news story. A kind of implicit exchange is undertaken, based on mutual reciprocity. In return for the coverage newsgatherers give to a press conference, speech, or rally, the publicity seekers make such events conform to standard definitions of news. The political group seeks a way to reach the medium's audience. The medium seeks an event that will interest its audience. The vehicle that satisfies both is one that has the outward signs of a news story: the timely release of information, the refutation of a public official. The currency that is exchanged between newsgatherer and newsmaker is not money, but control. Unlike the advertisement that is constructed and paid for by the advocate, the final context of the theme of a news story is in the hands of the medium rather than the political persuader. From the advocate's point of view successful control of the event may lead to good press, which results when journalists covering the story leave a generally favorable impression with the reading and viewing public. On the other hand, the reporter wants to preserve at least the appearance of journalistic independence.

One of the ironies of American life is that so few groups with political objectives can afford to purchase access to major forms of mass media. We are inundated with slick propaganda urging us to consider individual types of designer jeans. But we are routinely cut off from unfiltered debate that discusses the pros and cons of hundreds of pressing issues. For example, because the merchandizing orientation of television usually precludes selling time in programs that include extended discussion, most policy advocates are left with the need to devise ways to secure free publicity for their causes. They must enter a different kind of market: as we just noted, it falls to them to attract news organizations who will buy their message as a news item. Since the paid propaganda that is advertising is generally accessible only to relatively affluent businesses and corporations, most political advocates are confined to seconds of free publicity in the guise of news.

The vast majority of political candidates, parties, and special interest groups lack the resources to purchase the time or space that is used so freely to sell everything from soft drinks to deodorants. With the exception of the smallest local outlets such as small weekly papers or radio stations, the price for a one-time message must be figured in the thousands of dollars. Thirty seconds of network television time or a full-page ad in a newsmagazine may be sold for more than $100,000. The space in a highly rated local newscast, or in a daily newspaper, often runs between $5,000 and $10,000. And these figures are only the beginning. The chance to have any sustained impact will only increase if such time and space purchases are duplicated many times over.

Advertising is thus relegated largely to the commercial segments of society, not to those in the public sector who are interested in communicating views on matters of national or regional policy. As John Kenneth Galbraith has noted, "Every corner of the public psyche is canvassed by some of the nation's most talented citizens to see if the desire for some merchantable product can be cultivated. No similar process operates in behalf of the nonmerchantable services of the state."[62] When applied to political candidates, the only significant exceptions are those celebrity-politicians who are running for the offices with the biggest constituencies. And even their chances at success are narrowed by the further necessity to start out as plausible winners, because only such viable candidates can attract the necessary campaign contributions that are needed to underwrite advertising costs. They must have enormous potential constituencies—as president, senator from California, mayor of a major city—in order to justify the economies of scale that ultimately make the mass media efficient. It is worth remembering that most of the people who directly participate in the 80,000 governments in the United States fall somewhere outside of these broad parameters.

Advertising has been perhaps the most studied and most debated of all of the controlled media. To some, the advent of the political campaign commercial (in 1952 at the beginning of the Eisenhower presidency) was a setback for the electoral process. "The effect on politics," notes broadcast historian Eric Barnouw, "has been devastating."[63] Case histories of national and regional campaigns are rife with examples of potential problems. In his landmark study of the 1968 presidential campaign, Joe McGinniss claimed that staffers packaged the Nixon persona like a product.[64] Theodore White declared that broadcasting "is subject to manipulation by experts in a way the printed press is not."[65] Reflecting the prevailing view, Robert Spero has noted that political advertising has the "ability to reach from 30 million to 80 million people at once" and has the "unprecedented power to change their minds when it does reach them. . . ."[66]

But the marriage of politics and marketing also has its defenders. As Gary Mauser notes, there are some strategic benefits that a candidate achieves by treating his campaign as a variation on the techniques used to market new products. Whether or not it is accepted as a suitable model for political persuasion, marketing theory has been adapted to communication patterns of the electoral process:

> This procedure enables a political candidate to measure his image, determine how his image compares with those of other candidates, examine alternative positions and postures, and position himself in the contest so as to take maximum advantage of his strengths or his opponent's weaknesses.[67]

Mauser notes that there is nothing inherently evil about treating campaign persuasion in the framework of marketing theory. For example, the marketing concept of positioning—the placement and description of the candidate with conscious attention to how he differs from others —is a useful conceptual tool for deriving campaign strategy. It builds on the notion that the measure of success cannot be absolute, but is related to the available alternatives.

The difficulty with such an approach is that commercial marketing uses major forms of mass media that require budgets which are unthinkable for all but a few of the nation's political candidates. Still, the buying of political advertising goes on because such ads remain as one of the few realistic alternatives for direct communication with constituents and voters.

In addition, several recent studies have pointed out that some long-held views about the superficiality of political advertising need to be rethought. Perhaps the most interesting work challenging the old assumptions has been done by Thomas Patterson and Robert McClure. Using both content analyses and attitude formation studies, they have concluded that television ads may in fact be more informative than the widely respected newscasts of the television networks. The picture of advertising they describe is less bleak and less cynical than the one that is usually painted by the print press. The authors reserve most of their fire for the campaign reporting to which advertising is usually unfavorably compared:

> The only noticeable effect of network campaign news is an increased tendency among voters to view politics in the same trivial terms that the newscast depicts it. Regular viewers of network news are likely to describe an election campaign as a lot of nonsense rather than a choice between fundamental issues.
>
> Although commercials are surely full of their own nonsense, blatant exaggerations, and superficial symbolism, presidential candidates do

make heavy use of hard issue information in their advertising appeals. In fact, during the short period of the general election campaign, presidential ads contain substantially more issue content than network newscasts. This information is particularly valuable to people who pay little attention to the newspaper. Advertising serves to makes these poorly informed people substantially more knowledgeable.[68]

Patterson and McClure also tackled the common belief that advertising is a very powerful, if not irresistible, form of persuasion. Their contrasting judgment was that political commercials are usually not effective in changing voter attitudes or behaviors. "[T] he vast majority of Americans are immune to advertising's propaganda. . . . And the reason is simple: They know too much; their views on politics are too clearly defined."[69] It would be difficult to make such a statement stick in every case. And the authors themselves temper it elsewhere in their study, noting especially that low-interest voters (i.e., people who rarely seek out news about a campaign) and late deciders may be influenced by ads. Their work generally corroborates the work of other researchers who have discovered that the effects of ads by themselves are probably minimal. The reason is probably that there is "broad public awareness of the use of marketing techniques in campaigns . . . [and] as campaigners have sharpened skills in the arts of political advocacy, the voter has kept pace in his appreciation of their craftsmanship."[70]

Television can play a critical role in a small number of voters. If a contest between two candidates is very close, the attitudes of perhaps 3 or 4 percent could be vital, and within the reach of a successful ad blitz pitched to increase the casual voter's recognition of the candidate's name and image. It is felt—probably correctly—that a crucial number of undecided voters can be persuaded to support a candidate if they are reassured that they have seen the politician, and they know something about him. At least this is the logic that drives most modern campaign strategists.[71]

Ads also allow the candidate who can afford them an opportunity to speak directly to the electorate. The ad gets the candidate's message through without subjecting it to the conflicting imperatives of newsgathering described earlier. The journalistic urgency for creating drama in campaign stories, for allowing reporters to have equal billing with the subjects they are ostensibly covering, and for working under tight time restrictions, all point to the inadequacies that make campaign advertising something of a necessity. The seasoned political journalist may, as so many have, criticize the sterile and contrived nature of advertising. But in fact some of the evidence cited above suggests that many who claim a political beat are doing very little themselves to increase the public's competence to master the complex political terrain.[72]

Author Mary Ellen Leary provides evidence for this conclusion in her study of the California gubernatorial campaign of 1974. California is a notoriously difficult location to run for statewide office. It is larger than some European countries. The major population centers are spread out on a long north-to-south axis. And a vague antipathy separates the interests of those living in the arid populous south from the water-rich north. The race produced significant press attention. Within the state it is a given that campaigns must be planned around the needs of the mass media centers. And yet none of the six television stations she monitored allowed the candidates to speak routinely or in any sustained way to the public. The eventual winner, Jerry Brown, accumulated only 57 minutes of speaking time on all of the newscasts over the course of the entire campaign. "With such abbreviated news exposure," she concluded, "advertising time became the critical avenue for getting a message across to television viewers."[73] Even if thoughtful reporting had been available across so large a state . . . candidates would still have needed some opportunity to state their views directly."[74]

Radio and direct mail also play important roles as political advertising vehicles. Radio is perhaps the most practical of the electronic forms. A regional or districtwide campaign carried out on several stations is within the range of almost any political candidate or interest group. The spots are inexpensive to produce and easy to prepare on short notice. And the more specialized formats of radio make it easy to target messages to particular audience segments such as men, young adults, and women at home.

Few radio stations reach the levels of penetration that are possible with other forms of local or national media. And it goes without saying that radio messages usually lack the impact and attention-getting appeal of television. But for many political candidates, our system of decentralized radio (with over 9,000 stations across the United States) remains the most accessible and affordable of media buys.

Perhaps radio's biggest drawback—and one it shares with television—is that those who manage stations and networks are reluctant to carry advertising that does not deal with consumer products or bona-fide political campaigns. What is sometimes called "editorial" or "issue advertising" is discouraged in both media.[75] The most visible form of such political advertising today is confined to the op ed pages of major newspapers. Corporate sponsors such as Mobil, Kaiser, and Rodale Press, for example, regularly pay for ads offering what amount to corporate-sponsored editorials on topics ranging from Senate timidity on votes affecting their businesses, to praise for a president's economic policies.[76] The major networks in particular have been reluctant to grant access to such paid issue-oriented advertising. The ostensible reason is because their legal obligations to fairness would require airing too many differing opinions. (The F.C.C.'s Fairness Doctrine requires outlets to air a variety of viewpoints on controversial topics if they air any one point of view.) A more likely explanation, however, is that the industry prefers to keep its audiences quiescent by serving as a merchandizing vehicle for products rather than ideas.

Direct mail is potentially almost as useful. It ranks just behind newspapers, magazines, and television in total advertising revenues.[77] Adopting the techniques used by bulk mail marketing strategists, politicians and public interest groups now frequently use direct mail appeals distributed to thousands of preselected addresses. A number of firms specialize in the collection and sale of mailing lists thought to list individuals with certain desirable social or political traits. Large numbers of organizations with policy interests utilize elaborate polling and demographic data to match particular types of messages with receptive readers. As is noted in Chapter 9, members of Congress have long used their free mail prerogatives to send newsletters and questionnaires to their constituents. Given the potential to use computer-assisted means to target messages, members can send "personal" letters to specific types of constituents who might be favorably influenced by what they read.[78]

One such targeting scheme described by Vincent Barabba is called the Precinct Index Priority System.[79] It is used for districtwide campaign planning. The objective of this data collection method is to give priority rankings to individual voting precincts in a district, thereby determining which should be targeted for particular direct mail messages and other appeals. The system essentially involves the collection and tabulation of data on a precinct's voter registration status, previous voting patterns, and census data. Census information is especially useful in providing a sharp profile of a community: its relative prosperity, the average income and educational level of its members, and so on. In one campaign, Indiana Republicans collected information ranging from the percent of welfare recipients in a precinct to the percent of homes with daughters as members of the Brownies. Playing on a number of political hunches, they produced rankings of precincts which could be targeted for direct mail messages. Rather than spreading resources haphazardly, this computer-assisted system and many others like it permit the targeting of audiences who might be especially responsive to direct appeals.

## The Saliency of Individual Messages and Campaigns

It is strong testimony for the power of the mass media that in 1973 Georgia's Governor Jimmy Carter could appear on the television game show "What's My Line?" and stump the panelists. The object of the show was to question a guest to determine his or her line of work.[80] Little could the questioners know that the anonymous man whose identity they were trying to determine (unblindfolded) would conquer the presidency just four years later. That Carter could rise from obscurity to prominence in so short a period of time demonstrates the potency of mass media exposure.

By far the most vexing problem facing political advocates is attempting to predict the impact that individual messages or entire campaigns will have on mass media audiences. Our predicament at the end of the twentieth century is still much like that of tobacco magnate George Washington Hill, who believed that half of the money that his company spent on advertising was wasted. The unresolved problem, he said, is to find out which half.[81] We tend to remember the spectacular successes: the effective speech or series of commercials that dramatically transformed a troubled situation into a victorious one. Richard Nixon's Checkers address cited at the outset of this chapter, the 1960 presidential debates between John Kennedy and Richard Nixon, Ronald Reagan's effective 1980 campaign against Jimmy Carter ("Are you better off today than you were four years ago?"), are but a few of the hundreds of catalytic events where attitudes changed in response to an effective marriage of mass media and message. That a dramatic and well-publicized gesture can have a significant effect on public opinion is in little doubt. Like television advertisers, who can dramatically increase the market share that comes to a given product, every public figure with access to mass media audiences is conscious of its suasive benefits.[82]

The problem of assessing the specific relationships that exist between mass media and public opinion has increasingly consumed the work of empirically minded researchers in several disciplines. As we have seen, nearly every observer assumes that mass-produced forms of political communication produce significant effects. But how these effects manifest themselves is less than certain. "Some kinds of communication on some kinds of issues, brought to the attention of some kinds of people under some kinds of conditions, have some kinds of effects."[83] That was Bernard Berelson's 1948 summation of the state of mass media research. And it still seems valid. It is extremely difficult to locate true cause and effect relationships. And it is additionally difficult to come to terms with the fact that any description of what the public thinks is closely tied to the categories and approaches set by those who ask the questions and define the measurement procedures.[84]

Even the assertions that can be made with confidence present their own unique problems. One of the certainties regarding human attitude formation, for example, is that attitudes are highly resistant to short-term appeals. Opinions, beliefs, and attitudes tend to be elastic when confronted with the hard surface of an opposing point of view. They may momentarily give some ground to a persuasive appeal. But they are likely to assume their old shape when the stimulus for change is withdrawn or forgotten.[85] Individual speeches, occasional exposure to advertisements, and similar short-term encounters are unlikely to have much effect on what we think, and even less likely to produce durable changes on attitudes and behaviors. Unfortunately it so happens that short-term exposure is precisely the kind of variable that is most controllable in the experimental setting. When we concede as we must that attitudes are shaped by long-term factors we also are forced to recognize that "neat" experimental or survey research on attitude formation becomes extremely difficult. Microscopic studies which isolate specific effects with particular media and messages are possible but unnatural—given the pluralism of influence that exist in ordinary life. The problem is compounded by the existence of many intervening variables that are both hard to account for and highly variable across the entire population. A corporation introducing a new product on the market may indeed be able to trace the effectiveness of advertising and other marketing strategies, because public knowledge of the new item will have started from a zero base. No similar vacuum of knowledge exists for most presidential candidates, national issues, or pending legislative questions. (In experimental terminology, no control group exists that allows comparison with a group subjected to the experimental variable.) All usually have some public history that reduces the ability of the student of mass media effects to attribute attitudes to isolated message-centered variables.

Another problem is that the word *effect* is much too broad to account for the varied forms of personal influence. The social products of the mass media are multidimensional. Institutions and the whole cultural fabric are altered as well as individuals. An effect may be to provide information, but without any apparent tie to a new attitude. Political attitudes (or related behaviors, such as voting, signing a petition, or speaking in behalf of a position in public) are sometimes formed, but are more likely to be reshaped from a present and largely durable form. This is because the process of *changing* attitudes is much harder for the persuader and the persuadee than the process of *forming* them. The first involves the discarding of an inconsistent or conflicting belief in favor of a new one: a process that is very slow and usually incremental. The latter is psychologically easier: something is simply added rather than replaced. This explains why most changes that occur in individuals subject to political appeals are defined in terms of the *activation* or *crystallization* of attitudes.[86] For most individuals, political activity is likely to translate into levels of interest based on one firm attitude, rather than on changing attitudes. Political persuasion is usually not a matter of painful rethinking of a well-defined view, but more likely the motivation to endorse what is already a relatively fixed attitude.

A further complication arises from the fact that there is often an assumed relationship between how one feels and what one does. But such a relationship does not always hold. Individuals, for example, may hold racist attitudes, as measured by a paper and pencil survey, but act in a nonracist manner when placed in an integrated environment.[87] The reverse is also possible, and perhaps even more likely. The way a person actually votes may be at variance with what they say they will do. Pressures from peers or the desire to please a questioner may well result in a vocalized response that conceals inner feelings.

The saliency of political issues and individuals is thus contingent and conditional. What we can attribute to the work of a medium is always subject to an enormous range of far-reaching but nonstandardized variables. Sources, messages, and mediums can never be completely studied in isolation. The level of knowledge that can be transferred from one context to another is thus limited. At least in the realm of political persuasion precise causal formulas developed in one context have little force when used as predictors for settings that are similar but not identical.

Even so, we are not completely in the dark. There is a long tradition of effect-centered research. Some of it, such as the early Payne Fund studies on children and film viewing, sought to estimate the potential for various forms of influence in a medium.[88] It is not in the scope of the present chapter to attempt a summary of such areas. We can only touch on the growing body of work on the formation of political attitudes. Much of it, when taken collectively, points to several key trends in efforts to assess the effectiveness of mediated political messages.

The following conclusions seem particularly important and universal. First, consumers of all forms of political discourse are selective rather than reflexive. Most are primarily attentive to messages that corroborate rather than challenge existing beliefs. Others are able to read support into information that contradicts their basic view. What these now well-known conclusions lack in novelty they make up for in durability. Psychologists have long known that individuals have the ability to selectively take in information, even when clearly exposed to views that contradict or challenge old beliefs. The mechanism of selective perception works to ensure the stability of the individual's mental landscape. Change of any kind represents risk, work, and the readjustment of related attitudes. It is to be expected, therefore, that in the context of a campaign the most attentive listeners to a candidate's political campaign commercials tend to be solid supporters. Statements recalled after exposure to a candidate's positions tend to be those that fit pre-existing beliefs.[89]

Second, for most consumers there is an enormous gap between the time spent with any mass medium and what one would normally expect in the way of effects. The thoughtful analyst may marvel at the skill and potency of appeals utilized by a side in a political conflict—expecting that skill to yield sharp responses from audiences. Yet in actual fact citizens who have spent enormous amounts of time listening, viewing, or reading tend to have recall levels that are surprisingly low. These attitudes are far more inert than most persuaders, critics, and analysts often assume. The consistent failure to find dramatic changes in the predispositions of audiences is one ironic effect of the information explosion that has engulfed nearly every corner of the Western world. As a form of protection against the constant buffetings created by new information, the typical consumer apparently shuts much of it out. Much of the persuasion to which we are exposed washes over the consciousness with what amounts to surprisingly little recall.

In 1978, for example, an Eagleton Poll researcher at Rutgers University found that only one in three New Jersey residents was able to identify one of their senators, Clifford Case. Case was hardly an obscure politician. He had been in office for 24 years, and had maintained a consistently high level of local visibility.[90] What could account for the low recognition? To the casual observer Case's state would seem to be well served by a diverse and vigorous mass media. The northern part of the state is within the largest media market in the United States (based in New York City). And the southern end is in the fourth largest market (Philadelphia). In the center, Trenton, with a population of less than a half million, supports two daily papers. And the remainder of the state is filled with dailies and weeklies oriented to local news. But revealingly, at the time of the poll the state had no commercial television station within its borders. One can be reasonably sure that the daily press (and some regional television coverage) exposed residents to the activities of the senator.

Three problems perhaps explain the low levels of public awareness. The first is a constant: many citizens have no interest whatsoever in national or local politics. Their ignorance is self-imposed. A second is that New York and Philadelphia television paid far less attention to politics across the Hudson River in the north, and the Delaware river in the south. This occurred even though their transmitters were but a few miles from the state line, and they counted on selling the lucrative New Jersey audience to advertisers. The third problem arose because of the wealth of choices available to residents. Because they had an enormous range of media sources to choose from, including many with little interest in state politics, the presence of such diversity probably made it less likely that a large majority would attend to the relatively specialized activities of one senator. In the midst of such media density a significant information gap still can exist.

John P. Robinson found similarly low levels of awareness among national samples, even on the most elemental forms of political information. For example:

> In 1964, half of a national sample were unaware of the existence of two Chinas with their opposing political loyalties. . . . In 1969, A CBS survey found only a third of the country had heard of the Kerner Commission Report. In a 1970 national survey, less than a third of the

population could provide even rudimentary identification of Ralph Nader, Robert Finch, or Martha Mitchell.[91]

Such evidence serves as a constant reminder of what voting-behavior studies have demonstrated over the last several decades: that the size of the attentive, interested audience for political information and dialogue is extremely small. On most issues and toward most political actors the dominant characteristic is apathy. The familiar lament of most observers of democratic politics is that most Americans live in their own here and now, not in what is for them the ephemeral world of political issues and public policies.

Another set of conclusions can also be partly inferred from the low levels of interest. They grow out of what has become known as the "uses and gratifications" perspective. Simplified, this approach begins with the notion that citizen interest in politics exists when there is some psychological reward or pay-off.[92] Political interest, it is thought, is driven less by duty than by the attraction of vicarious participation in exotic events that provide gratification. In some ways this idea is essentially a recycling of a classical rhetorical model where a message is explained in terms of the satisfaction of audience needs. It implicitly argues that information-seeking may not be the prime reason attention is given to such disparate bits of the political process, such as televised debates or issue-oriented editorials. For example, if a television viewer tunes to C-SPAN, the cable channel devoted to Congress, he may watch a debate not because he wants to be informed, but because the debate is on TV, and TV-watching itself (or the promise of witnessing a heated confrontation) is considered a pleasurable activity. Nimmo states:

> It is possible . . . to argue that the political media have substantial effects on lesser involved citizens even though these citizens do not derive information from the media. The argument rests on the notion that, from the standpoint of an audience member, the function of the media is not to inform but to act as a source of subjective play.[93]

News stories about a national campaign may well have the kind of novelty and entertainment value built into the dramas that occupy prime-time television. The heavy viewer who is sedated by a steady diet of low-demand entertainment is perhaps predisposed to strip away the minimal policy-oriented substance of a report, leaving the dramatistic and emotional elements intact.[94]

Third, political communication needs to be envisioned as occurring in tiers of influence, with the mass media as but one level. The mental reduction that sometimes occurs with intense interest in mass persuasion sometimes mistakenly gives the media sole possession of the power to persuade. But such a simplification obviously distorts what is a far more complex reality. The mass media are acted on by many forces, as well as initiators of their own forms of influence. They exist in the middle of a hierarchy. Networks, stations, and publishers are subject to the influence of many forms of elites—political, business, and educational opinion leaders. It is also the case that other elites are influenced by certain forms of the mass media, essentially acting as relays to larger mass audiences. The effectiveness of mediated messages must therefore be measured with these important intervening steps in mind.

Elite theory is an old concept, but also an undoubtedly vital one. The notion that elites control political discussion has been referred to at the outset of this chapter. To be sure, it is at odds with the traditional watchdog notion of the press. For casual observers of the news industry it is easy to assume that evidence of the adversarial relationship that exists between journalist and governmental official precludes one acting in concert with the other. The nation's belief in the independence of the press is too firmly rooted to be ignored in favor of a simplified view of involving a class-based conspiracy. Like most everything else dealing with politics, there is both truth and romance to the ideal of press independence. But elite theory in its many forms is more panoramic. There is a fundamental similarity of outlook that emerges when news organizations report on the activities of various outposts of political leadership. David Paletz and Robert Entman have boiled down the theory to very concrete dimensions:

> Despite the complications and exceptions, the general impact of the mass media is to socialize people into accepting the legitimacy of their country's political system . . . ; lead them to acquiesce in America's prevailing social values . . . ; direct their opinions in ways which do not undermine and often support the domestic and foreign objectives of elites . . .; and deter them from active, meaningful participation in politics— rendering them quiescent before the powerful.[95]

Doris Graber and others have pointed out the tendency of press reports to sanitize and justify the sometimes marginal performance of elites in government and business, making them appear more efficient and organized than they really are.[96] Several authors note the monitoring of a North Carolina city council, revealing that the disorder and disinterest of politicians attending housing hearings was transformed by local journalists into accounts of orderly decision making.[97] Others have noted that official explanations frequently deserve far more skepticism and scrutiny than they normally receive.[98]

As Graber notes, the press is not automatically immune from the truism that "most institutions within any particular political system go along with it if they wish to prosper."[99] Such a view does not mean that there is anything like a routine desire on the part of working members of the press to make sure that every printed or uttered word supports the powers that be. The tie-ins that develop are less structures, but still pervasive. They are also so common that any consideration of how political discourse is shaped must include the inevitable crossovers between governmental and mass media elites.

A specific case from the presidency of Lyndon Johnson illustrates one such crossover. President Johnson was long aware of his inadequacies as a television spokesman for his own administration. Television captured all too well the turgid defensiveness of his increasingly unhappy presidency. At best he was a slow and stiff public speaker: a style that concealed what others who knew the private Johnson recognized as a more animated and likable man. Johnson sought help from Robert Kintner. He made the former president of NBC Television his special assistant. Although Kintner's duties varied, and his tenure was comparatively short, he sought to help the sagging Johnson image in the years before the 1968 decision not to run for reelection.

A member of the media establishment was now helping the premier member of the nation's political establishment. A sampling of some of the confidential memos Kintner sent to the president just before and after the 1967 State of the Union Address points to the broadcaster's ability to tap the support of former colleagues for political gain. They demonstrate a pattern common to all forms of politics to build bridges between what are supposedly separate power blocks:

> I had a meeting with [Johnson advisers] Harry McPherson, Doug Cater, Joe Califano and Walt Rostow particularly in relation to the meaning of the Civil Rights portion of your State of the Union address, but also in relation to the principal points of the talk. We divided up various key [journalism] people in town to background including . . . [Max] Frankel, . . . [James] Kilpatrick, [Joseph] Kraft, [Tom] Wicker, . . . [Hedley] Donovan, . . . [Charles] Bartlett, Joe Alsop, etc. . . . In addition, I will try to do some work with the news chiefs of ABC, NBC and CBS.[100]

> [In planning for the coverage of the speech] I would guess that they [the networks] would not try to put a one-half hour entertainment show [after the speech] and would run major news reaction programs.

At least that is what I would do if I were running the networks. I have a pretty good idea of NBC's plans.[101]

In talking with *Newsweek* about the Civil Rights section of your speech [columnist] Ken Crawford volunteered that he thought your TV appearance was the best that you had done in a speech, and that you seemed well prepared and at ease.[102]

Another part of the tier of influence is closer to the bottom, at a grass-roots level where media-endorsed views have the power to influence opinion leaders or organizations with their own constituencies. In this view media influence on the general public is not direct, but through leaders who essentially act as relays. Their power derives from their credibility, and from their ability to give a conclusion inherited from a mass media source a local voice. This configuration is called the two-step or multi-step flow model.

In the typical case of the two-step flow, the effectiveness of a particular media outlet is compounded by its ability to enlist agents who will carry its perspectives. An understanding of the importance of this principle has been basic to political campaigners for years: there is no satisfactory substitute for direct interpersonal contact as a way to elicit influence.[103] It has long been known that people vote or acquire opinions based on what sources they respect say. The sources themselves are likely to be heavy news consumers. What matters in the end, given this sequence, is that a message relayed through a medium ends up transposed into vital but microscopic face-to-face encounters.

This process is also evident in newsgathering organizations. There is a definite pecking order that exists within the national news industry, and extends down to local outlets. As was noted earlier, major wire service "budgets," as well as stories, in the *New York Times* and *Washington Post*, are known to affect at least some of the subsequent reporting of the major television networks.[104] And because of what the networks report, local television news organizations may set their own patterns of national coverage. As a result, even though an opinion-leading publication such as the *New York Times* has a circulation that falls far below that of the networks and some other dailies and weeklies, its influence is still a significant force in daily determinations of what national events and trends are newsworthy.

The realities of influence could be compared to the actions of a pinball on its unpredictable path. One cause may precipitate a news event, but thereafter its portrayal frequently becomes a matter of action and reaction as the story drifts through various channels—some of which are mass media-centered, and others more interpersonal.

Fourth and last, in spite of the widespread diffusion of political information via television, the gap between the information rich and the information poor is probably widening. The information rich we define as people who have the means and motivation to use a variety of carefully selected resources to increase their economic, political, and social leverage. Discussion of this point inevitably involves imprecise speculation. But there is reason for concern in the evidence from Roper and others that television—with its synoptic news and advertising—carries more and more of the burden of explaining the complexities of government and policy making to most Americans.[105]

"Politics," notes Murray Edelman, "is for most of us a passing parade of abstract symbols. . . . " It creates "a moving panorama taking place in a world the mass public never quite touches."[106] For many it suggests a world of unreality, at best a spectator pastime featuring individuals, ideas, and activities that are far removed from one's own local roots. Beyond localized issues involving schools, taxes, and city services, political information creates mass ambivalence as much as interest. And yet against the malaise and cynicism that characterizes most public attitudes toward political discussion, there exists a diversity of information that is truly staggering. For the information rich, access to a diversity of media is a source of power. The task is to organize and tame it so that it serves personal needs. They may choose information sources (i.e., special interest magazines, computer-accessed data, and investment data) as tools that provide an edge in coping with the labyrinth of hurdles imposed by modern life. Such data may be in the form of detailed reports on how interest rates for borrowing may be affected by governmental policies, how tax incentives can be exploited to protect high personal earnings, or on upcoming legislative activity that threatens a cherished tax loophole.

The position of the information rich is in sharp contrast to the large stratum of Americans who use the mass media—especially television and the tabloid press—more for escape than for information. What many in this category seek is a series of media-made reprieves from lives dominated by boredom or victimage. Instead of seeking data that increases their involvement in many planes of activity, they seek media as an escape. To be sure, the lines between the two are not distinct. But there is an undeniably large gap between audience-specific media that require effort (and cash) but yield significant returns, and the mass-oriented entertainment media that offer painless escapism. The former builds on and extends the intellectual capacities of its consumers. The latter, because they are "free" and directed to the largest (and, hence, lowest) audience levels, hope to hold audiences by exploiting their capacity to consume aimless diversion. Many Americans seem to consume a media diet that offers the modern counterpart to ancient Rome's promise to citizens of free bread and circuses. The endless distractions of prime-time television and its print counterparts has the effect of draining off the motivation and anger that is necessary to produce political change. To use the term suggested by Lazarfeld and Merton, heavy exposure to less comprehensive forms of mass media can have a "narcotizing" function, substituting what is at best a secondary contact with political reality in the place of a more direct social action.[107]

It is probably no coincidence that television is the dominant medium in America's poorer neighborhoods.[108] In more affluent parts of the nation the viewing of television remains heavy, but it is augmented by other kinds of media that offer a greater diversity of information.[109] The diffused nature of the "massest" of the mass media provides little direction and less incentive for intense political involvement. Aiming at the lowest common denominator as a standard for programming discourages the use of information for all but the most trivial forms of self-help. The television schedule is typically filled with remedies for loneliness or weight loss, but usually not for building a life-long career, or a deeper understanding of the interrelationships that drive our perceptions of American politics. The pattern of presentation for most of the popular media, Marshall McLuhan noted of television, is a "mosaic" of discrete bits—game shows, melodramas, thousands of news headlines, and endless commercials and announcements—all of which have the likely effect of weakening the individual's capacity to concentrate experience and insights in any one area. "Television dependents" are thus thrust into a double bind that is a potential threat to themselves and to the society they can change through the vote. The medium to which they are wed tells them more and more about less and less. It holds the potential of making them vulnerable to persuasive appeals that hang on the thinnest of insights. As Zukin has speculated:

There is clearly a segmentation in the American public in terms of media reliance and learning from the media. The poorer educated rely more and more on a medium that gives them little in the way of a framework in which to understand politics. News stories confined to 60 or 90 seconds cannot provide a context conducive to comprehension. Tele-vision-dependents are less knowledgeable about public affairs and more susceptible to persuasive messages.[110]

The problem is not that people easily succumb to the suasive attempts or incomplete accounts offered by television. As we have noted, they often do not. Rather, it is that if an enormous segment of the society fails to seek out diverse media to help understand complex political realities, the information vacuum that segment inherits creates a world that is likely to be an incomprehensible and threatening place.

## POLITICAL CONTENT IN NONPOLITICAL FORMS

One of Ronald Reagan's biographers has noted that the former film actor only played a villain once, in what was by his own admis-sion a forgettable film called *The Killers.* He preferred to play heroes, as he did in two of his favorites, *Kings Row* and *Knute Rockne, All-American.*[111] That Reagan would have rather enacted such roles cannot come as a surprise. In this politically minded actor's preference there is a lesson about the importance of entertainment as a shaper of political attitudes. More than most presidents, Reagan's rhetoric has always been heavily laced with graphic images of personal courage and selfless sacrifice.[112] Even in a Warner Brothers B-film they were important. Depictions of heroism, on film or in speeches, dramatize an essential premise in Reagan's brand of political conservatism: that the individual is fundamentally responsible for his own circum-stances.[113] Evocations of heroism give weight to the idea that people should do more for themselves and government should do less.

Film, television, and the theater can be effective vehicles in shap-ing political attitudes. It is estimated that only 3 percent of commer-cial television time is devoted to national public issues.[114] The rest of the remaining space cannot help but contribute to political per-ceptions in both planned and accidental ways.

The mainstay of film has always been uncomplicated and mass-oriented entertainment. But the film industry and its television off-spring have never divorced politics from effective storytelling. From the earliest days of film political messages have been explicit. For example, D. W. Griffith's spectacular silent epic, *Birth of a Nation,* has long engendered controversy over the eulogistic treatment given to the Ku Klux Klan.[115] In World War I government use of film as a suasive tool was augmented by all forms of media, including hundreds of popular recordings glorifying American honor and bolstering those with wavering courage. These recordings and the Victrolas to play them on were routinely issued to troops in the field. At the beginning of World War II propaganda techniques had been refined. German films such as *Triumph of the Will*, and American efforts such as Frank Capra's *Why We Fight* series or *Mr. Smith Goes to Washington*, were vivid attempts to meld entertainment and political advocacy. Reagan's own war service was confined to this kind of work. He was assigned to a Hollywood production unit responsible for instructional and propaganda films.[116] Years later, while he was president of the Screen Actor's Guild, his union confronted a nation fearful of the impact that the political left in Hollywood might have.

Even forms of mass media with ostensibly nonpolitical objectives frequently contain at least a political subtext. A film, a play, a television melodrama that may have the manifest goal of simple entertainment may also carry latent messages with policy or political implications. But our purpose here is not to speculate on the deep metalanguages that may lie buried in plays or films. Our more modest goal is to briefly point out some of the ways political values and controversial issues surface in ordinary forms of mass entertainment.

In some ways drama is the perfect vehicle for mass-oriented political discussion. It comes to the receiver in an attractive context (as entertainment) and in a perfect persuasive environment (when the viewer's defenses against persuasion are lessened). The narrative in all of its forms has always served as a medium for political dialogue. Dramatists routinely function as messengers to the society about its successes and failures.[117] In Hugh Dalziel Duncan's apt phrase, drama is "the means by which we become objects to ourselves. . . . "[118] Plays and novels have "historically something of the same importance as journalism has for our own day."[119] Drama allows us to see our counterparts respond to shifting situations, many of which are personal, but many that also describe the extensions of public policy into our worlds. Even seemingly innocuous fare can have direct political connotations. Gershwin's musical *Strike Up the Band*, and the children's story, *The Wizard of Oz* come to mind. The first was a subtle but thorough send-up of presidential corruption and military spending.[120] The second was written (in book form) as a Populist diatribe against the presidential lethargy of William McKinley.[121]

Popular melodramas and comedies (perhaps especially comedies) are suited to conveying the ironies and hypocrisies built into institutions. Like films or plays that unmask the mythical venality and greed of the rich (i.e., *Citizen Kane, My Fair Lady, Grapes of Wrath, Trading*

*Places*) dramatists routinely judge a social order in ways that strike a responsive chord in the audiences they want to reach. In just the area of protection of routine civil rights, recent films such as *To Kill a Mockingbird, Kramer vs. Kramer, Whose Life Is It Anyway?, The Conversation, Absence of Malice,* and *The Front* have all raised challenges to positions at odds with established legal and legislative practices.

The reverse is also possible. A story, a play, or a film may legitimize and vindicate the existing political and social hierarchy in ways far more attractive than would be possible in a straight and unadorned rhetorical defense. That the established institutions of nearly every age have been prime patrons of the arts—from church-sanctioned medieval dramas to military assistance in filming wartime movie epics —points to the value that is implicit in favorable dramatizations of events with policy implications. The steady stream of war pictures that have been made with the assistance of the military suggests that the armed forces believe that these efforts produce audiences that will be sympathetic to their objectives.

## Three Patterns of Analysis of Popular Entertainment

Several lines of thought are evident in much of the analysis that is undertaken on the political content of contemporary film drama. One is that a good deal of what is seen is ahead of its audiences, liberalizing their experiences and increasing their tolerance. A second is that most commercial film and television production is firmly rooted in a defensive legitimizing posture, protecting dominant social values and major institutions. The third is more process-oriented, pointing out that the political implications of most problems presented in films and teleplays are muted; serious social problems are robbed of their full political (and often revolutionary) implications.

### The theory of liberalizing influence

Part of the conventional wisdom that comes with the study of the pluralistic mass media in Western nations is that they create a window on the world that has unprecedented breadth and scope. Mass media within the reach of nearly everyone provide a wealth of new experiences that expand horizons and widen perspectives. When measured against the limited experiences of any one individual, the opportunities made possible by television alone represent a vast increase in a person's awareness of the distant parts of his society. McLuhan's pivotal notion that we now live in a "global village" carries the implication that distance is no longer an impediment in gaining access to a diversity of human actions and attitudes. We can now extend ourselves far beyond the experiences that were possible to those even two generations ago. No one can deny that these experiences come to us second-hand. Nor can it be refuted that the diverse corners of the world that we now can observe come to us through a fine screen of bureaucratic and commercial gatekeepers. But it is an enlarged world that most people see, nonetheless. The 1960 CBS documentary, "Harvest of Shame," for example, showed millions of Americans the exploitation and racism common to American farm labor practices. As with many documentaries on social problems centered in one region, some affiliates fearing the wrath of advertisers or angry viewers would refuse to air them.[122] But those defending this doctrine of liberalizing influence have argued that films and documentaries have always provided widespread access to views and ideas that would otherwise go unvoiced because of local or provincial concerns—on unionism, racism, socialism, religious piety, and political corruption.

The complaint is frequently made that such attempts to treat minorities or significant social issues results in simplified images and watered-down representations.[123] But even given their constant quest for mass audiences, film and television producers will still net millions of consumers whose world will be enlarged by even the simplest recapitulation of progressive social values. Compared to the limited social and political consciousness of the average citizen, some programs may even seem daringly provocative and innovative.

In the entertainment field the individual often credited with putting political issues into prime time is veteran producer Norman Lear. Responsible for programs that frequently treat topical issues—shows such as "All in the Family," "Sanford and Son," "Maude," and "The Jeffersons"—Lear has been clear about his intentions. "The essential strategy" of the programs, according to broadcast historian Eric Barnouw, "was to seize on topics and relationships involving deep tensions, and introduce them in a comedy aura."[124] One of Lear's goals was to ridicule disruptive prejudices and traditions deeply woven into parts of the American fabric. He introduced an element of doubt into issues that have often been discussed with a sense of rigidly moral certainty. "Interracial marriage, a young man's siege of impotence, an older woman's pregnancy and indecision about abortion, were suddenly topics of warm comedy."[125] Whether the innovative producer succeeded in dramatizing the pain of such continuing sources of friction—such as the deeply imbedded racism portrayed in "All in the Family," "Sanford," and "The Jeffersons"—is uncertain. At least one study of audience reactions to the character of Archie Bunker noted a surprising sympathy for the fictitious bigot.[126] But few could deny that Archie provided a perfect case study of the irrationality of ethnic stereotypes.

Even commercial television's strongest critics have found examples of entertainment programming which discuss issues that might otherwise never surface on the consciousness of some. Writing originally in the *Socialist Review*, Douglas Kellner noted:

> Miniseries like "Roots," "Holocaust," "Captains and Kings," "Second Avenue," "The Moneychangers," and "Wheels" have dealt with class conflict, racism and antisemitism, imperialism, and the oppression of the working class and blacks. They have often sympathetically portrayed the oppressed, poor, minorities, and workers, and presented capitalists and right-wingers as oppressors and exploiters. Docudramas like "Tailgunner Joe," "Fear on Trial," and "King" have criticized Joe McCarthy, J. Edgar Hoover, and the FBI, and vindicated Martin Luther King as well as victims of McCarthyism and FBI persecution in the entertainment industry.[127]

### The Theory of Defense of the Establishment

Another important critical judgment is that television programming is especially supportive of the political status quo. The argument generally runs along the following lines. Since the industry depends on gaining its revenues from the mainstays of corporate America (through advertising), it is forced to deal with the values of that essential clientele. Almost all segments of the entertainment industry are supported by advertising which requires the satisfaction of two separate audiences, one in the business community, and one involving the general public. They must attract large segments of this latter group, the mass audience, with their programming. And they must "sell" that public to potential advertisers who want to reach them with their sales messages. The first audience may accept some political content in popular drama. But the history of television indicates that those portions of corporate America which purchase large segments of advertising time have little interest in social criticism as a vehicle for reaching audiences. To broadcasters the ideal selling environment is one that is benign and nonthreatening. It is better to sell cars, toothpaste, beer, deodorant, and thousands of other similar products to a viewer who has been entertained rather than provoked to anger, reassured rather than threatened by what is being shown. As an ABC vice-president put it:

Program makers are supposed to devise and produce shows that will attract mass audiences without unduly offending these audiences or too deeply moving them emotionally. Such ruffling, it is thought, will interfere with their ability to receive, recall, and respond to the commercial message.[128]

The revenue-producing program is thus easier to sell if it presents an image of stability rather than rage.

Since politics involves controversy, and controversy intensifies anxieties and hopes, the most stable television entertainment is ideally seen by the average viewer as apolitical. But apolitical does not mean nonpolitical. Most popular entertainment avoids controversial issues and unpopular political ideas. But this decision itself has political implications. The world of prime time opts for what amounts to a subtle deference to most of the segments of the economic and social order that are already established. This unstated but vital maxim of programming results in depictions of a world where individuals know their place, where order triumphs over disruption and dispute, and "the system" (or major social subsystems such as the police, the courts, and the schools) generally work. Few police shows suggest that murders go unsolved. It would be unusual for a continuing series to trace the grinding effects of poverty on its victims, or the severe life-long traumas of the victims of crashes in unsafe cars, or the unremitting discrimination experienced by an immigrant family living in the hostile environment of a major city. Films and occasional television dramas may present such unpleasant images without the closure of a happy ending. But programs depending on a loyal audience week in and week out generally do not. They may well suggest that a community or a city has problems, or that unemployment among black males is very high. But the roots of such dislocations are rarely traced back to fundamental failures in the society or its governmental institutions. As Paletz and Entman have argued:

> Advertisements and entertainment programs lead viewers away from political awareness. When television characters do exhibit imperfections or experience problems, their misfortunes are linked to bad luck, laziness, ineptitude. The structure of power rarely obtrudes into their lives; economic justice, class, race, or age discrimination, illness caused by the workplace injuries or industrial pollution—these dilemmas are absent.... The implicit lesson is that people are not constrained by the social order.[129]

Thus, Mary Tyler Moore keeps her closet feminism in the closet, rarely using it to lash out at a system that perpetuates her subordination to the crusty Lou Grant. The doctors in medical dramas such as "St. Elsewhere" are shown to have all of the human motivations and impulses of other kinds of workers. But they are practically never incompetent, and always deserve the adulation they get from their devoted patients. "Owen Marshall," "Perry Mason," "Trapper John," and "Marcus Welby" rarely failed to do less than their best. Most of the heroes who populate the prime-time schedule are seen enacting highly eulogistic versions of their roles. In most cases it is as if the scripts were written by the public relations organizations that represent the real professionals the actors are imitating. Thus, while ordinary television entertainment presents a system that may need some refinement, it serves fundamentally as the bearer of positive messages about the existing social order.

## The Theory of Hegemony: Forcing Fantasized Remedies To Intransigent Political Problems

This third theory is an outgrowth of the above analysis, and is generally associated with the work of Todd Gitlin, Herbert Gans, and Gaye Tuchman.[130] They have argued that many popular forms of media reflect fundamental class differences and tensions. Given many exceptions, elites pass their control through the society not just through direct channels, but through indirect ideological controls as well. Gitlin notes that "those who rule the dominant institutions secure their power in large measure directly *and indirectly*, by impressing their definitions of situation upon those they rule. . . ."[131] The power to reinforce existing orders shows up in the routines of journalists, in the kinds of myths, values, and solutions implanted in entertainment programming, and in the range of subjects that are considered appropriate for a given medium.

Gitlin describes a world with circles of power that are sometimes visible and sometimes invisible. It is, in the Marxist sense, a world of ruling classes perpetuating the ruling ideas of their own self-serving ideologies. With regard to news coverage of the political left, as we have previously noted, Gitlin comes close to proving what he asserts: that the establishment media divested the major antiwar groups of the integrity and credibility of their arguments.[132] In looking at entertainment television, Gitlin's assertions advance beyond his evidence. But the conclusions are no less intriguing:

> However grave the problems posed, however rich the imbroglio, the episodes regularly end with the click of a solution: an arrest, a defiant smile, an I-told-you-so click of an explanation. The characters we have been

asked to care about are alive and well, ready for next week. Such a world is not so much fictional as fake. However deeply the problem is located within society, it will be solved among a few persons: the heroes must attain a solution that leaves the rest of society untouched. The self-enclosed world of the TV drama justifies itself, and its exclusions, by "wrapping it all up."[133]

A hegemonic message is one that falls short of advocating the solutions a look at "raw" reality would dictate. The problems befalling many of television's victims are redeemed by personal heroism rather than social activism. The show displaying serious crime may glorify police solutions (tracking down the criminal) rather than confronting the deeper social causes of crime that might reflect basic cultural deficiencies.

But Gitlin's theory leaves some unexplained gaps. What he has perhaps overlooked as a cause of hegemony is the key role that every society assigns to its collective fantasies. Part of our refusal to deal with actual causes of social problems resides not just in commercial motives, but in the desire to preserve key myths. Fantasy themes take on many forms in popular entertainment. A national fantasy is a generalized mixture of our collective wishes and values. The fantasy drama—as in Capra's *Mr. Smith Goes to Washington* or a *Star Wars* adventure—lets us idealize our national character by implanting values in at least semiplausible dramatic events. Jimmy Stewart as Jefferson Smith makes the jaded kingpins of the Senate face up to their idealized public responsibilities. And the fearless young warriors in *Star Wars* overcome incredible odds to turn back a repressive proto-Soviet regime with awesome military strength.

One important aspect of fantasy is that it usually focuses on the individual free agent, rather than on institutions. In popular drama there is a continuous preference for describing problems and obstacles that can be overcome by force of character. This predisposition, in turn, has profound political consequences. The reason is based in the fact that the melodrama of popular culture treats solutions as psychologically rooted. Policies can never compete with characters as dramatic instruments. It is far easier to demonstrate conflict and resolution at the interpersonal level rather than culturewide or at the governmental level. The political or governmental solution to a personal trauma is not the stuff of great art. Audiences would indeed feel cheated if a victim of social injustice was saved by a slow-working agency carrying out the mandates of a new state statute. Melodramatic fantasy calls for something more sweeping and catalytic, for a victim to be transformed into an agent for his own redemption, for a person of no special talent (such as Clark Kent) to be changed into an idealization of heroism.

Films as diverse as *Death Wish* and *The China Syndrome* present problems for which institutional processes are in place (violent crime and nuclear safety, respectively). Yet the pivotal dramatic moments in each involve personal nonbureaucratic solutions: fantasized personal responses that cut through the ambiguity that comes with less cinematic institutional outcomes. In both cases victims became heroes by creating their own personal solutions. Their messages had an implicit political imprint: organizational solutions often don't work, and that coordinated group efforts are often undependable. Remedies to crime that involve investigation and research, or the need to assure nuclear plant safety through laborious oversight, certainly are the only suitable long-term ways to treat such problems. But they are not the kind of solutions that engender excitement or interest. One reason the politician is normally a stock villain in popular entertainment is that he represents the kind of incrementalism and shared responsibility that flies in the face of fantasies of individualism.

Even a popular television show about life during the Great Depression, "The Waltons," minimized the political solutions inherent in the New Deal. For the members of this remarkable family, rural southern poverty was bearable, even nurturing. The power to overcome the dislocations caused by the collapse of the financial house of cards built in the 1920s lay in the collective resources of the family, not in the responsibilities of the state.[134] Members of the clan were idealized. Their individual strong personalities spoke to the average viewer's desire to witness mastery over severe and disrupting circumstances. It would have been totally out of character for a prime-time television series such as "The Waltons" to have taken an overt political stance. Had Grandpa Walton cursed F. D. R. for not doing enough to help, or had John Boy turned into a Socialist and picketed the local bank, the program would have been deemed unsuitable as a series. The hegemonic response is to keep problems manageable, or to make their eventual resolution the task of the individual. Collective guilt for social problems, and the collective redemption offered by political parties and ideological systems, represent judgments that come too close to hard-hitting social criticism. Feature films that make such judgments (i.e., *Taxi Driver, Midnight Cowboy*, and *Missing*) may eventually find what is usually a limited audience. But such potent and socially insightful criticism is still more an exception than a routine occurrence for commercial television.

## A FINAL WORD

Even in our efforts to suggest the complexities involved in understanding the political uses of the mass media, we have been simplistic. The power relationships between the media and political establishments are often so subtle and variable that they cloud the crystal ball of even the most penetrating of analyses. Our goal in this chapter has been to touch on a few of those relationships, and some of the pressures that shape the strategies of each side. We end up with an assessment that permits few certain conclusions, but instead points to the fact that no one single interest holds a decisive edge in the pursuit of approval from the American public.

Perhaps this tenuous state of balance provides some room for optimism about the future of American politics in the age of mass communication. To be sure, the American public is generally apathetic, uninformed, difficult to influence, and prone to exclude the most serious of mass media discussions. Although we have the technical means to provide full and adequate discussion of political affairs, those means are frequently turned to more lucrative commercial goals. And yet it is possible to conclude that these circumstances—short of the democratic ideal though they are—result not so much in a quagmire as a kind of socially redemptive stalemate. We have fallen into a system that performs at far less than what is the capacity of public or the press. But we have at least preserved a balance that disperses control and discourages blind manipulation by any single source. Within governmental systems the diffusion of power, as between a legislature and executive, may produce stalemate and inaction. But the relationship between the political world and the mass communication industries is more varied. In a word, it is pluralistic.

None of the many contributors to mass political communication —press, advertising industry, campaign consultants, film industry, political celebrities, and power blocs—have a complete franchise on the political process. Many citizens seem enraptured with the drama of politics. Others are skeptical or inattentive. Most are resistant to the manipulations of political and mass media rhetoricians. Establishment-power centers are able to significantly influence the news agenda, and the way certain kinds of stories are reported. But such centers have their own dissidents, and their own alternative voices.

All of this is faint praise for a system that could do a far better job of representing local and national politics. But we also realize that at its best the "system" is made up of semiautonomous components. Press, commercial, and political segments need each other, and frequently develop alliances of convenience that ignore the larger public good. But each also remains capable of sustaining goals at odds with the self-serving interests of even the most powerful of national blocs. The society as a whole benefits from such friction, though the heat that is produced is often mistakenly viewed as evidence of our disintegration. In some ways events like the Watergate scandal—with its conflicting White House, congressional, and national press objectives—demonstrated the vibrancy that is possible in a pluralistic state. We should be grateful rather than weary for such moments in our political history. The more routine ties between politics and the mass communication industries give less reason for satisfaction. We should expect much more from a society so well endowed with the means for creating a truly enlightened democracy.

## NOTES

1. Edward R. Murrow quoted in Fred W. Friendly, *Due to Circumstances Beyond Our Control* . . . (London: MacGibbon and Kee, 1967), p. 251.

2. Richard M. Nixon, *Six Crises* (New York: Pyramid, 1968), p. 126.

3. Ibid., p. 125.

4. Walter Lippmann, *Public Opinion* (New York: Macmillan, 1930), p. 29.

5. Forrest McDonald, *The Presidency of George Washington* (New York: W. W. Norton, 1974), pp. 24-26.

6. For an introductory review of several evolving assessments of mass media impact on public opinion see Melvin L. DeFleur and Everette E. Dennis, *Understanding Mass Communication* (Boston: Houghton Mifflin, 1981), pp. 273-98.

7. See, for example, Joe McGinniss, *The Selling of the President, 1968* (New York: Trident Press, 1969); and Robert Cirino, *Don't Blame the People* (New York: Vintage, 1971).

8. Kurt Lang and Gladys Engel Lang, *Politics and Television* (Chicago: Quadrangle Books, 1968).

9. Michael J. Robinson and Margeret A. Sheehan, *Over the Wire and On TV: C.B.S and U.P.I. in Campaign '80* (New York: Russell Sage, 1983); Michael J. Robinson, "Television and American Politics: 1956-1976," in *Readings in Public Opinion and Mass Communication*, 3rd ed., ed. Morris Janowitz and Paul Hirsch (New York: Free Press, 1981), pp. 98-116; Sidney Kraus and Dennis Davis, *The Effects of Mass Communication on Political Behavior* (University Park, Pa.: The Pennsylvania State University, 1976); Thomas E. Patterson, *The Mass Media Election: How Americans Choose Their President* (New York: Praeger, 1980); and Thomas E. Patterson and Robert D. McClure, *The Unseeing Eye: The Myth of Television Power in National Politics* (New York: G.P. Putnam, 1976).

10. Lippmann, *Public Opinion*, p. 364.

11. Herbert J. Gans, *Deciding What's News* (New York: Vintage, 1980), pp. 146-52.

12. Ibid., pp. 167-71.

13. Timothy Crouse, *The Boys on the Bus* (New York: Ballantine, 1972), pp. 22-23.

14. Edward Jay Epstein, *News From Nowhere: Television and the News* (New York: Vintage, 1974), pp. 37-43.

15. Ibid., p. 38.

16. Ibid., pp. 258-59.

17. Edith Efron, *The News Twisters* (New York: Manor Books, 1971).

18. Gans, *Deciding What's News*, p. 212.

19. Todd Gitlin, *The Whole World is Watching: Mass Media in the Making and Unmaking of the New Left* (Berkeley, Calif.: University of California, 1980), pp. 249-82.

20. W. Lance Bennett, *News: The Politics of Illusion* (New York: Longman, 1983), pp. 21-27.

21. Michael J. Arlen, *Living Room War* (New York: Viking, 1969), pp. 6-9.

22. Friendly, *Due to Circumstances*, pp. 213-365.

23. Daniel J. Boorstin, *The Image, or What Happened to the American Dream* (New York: Atheneum, 1962), p. 8.

24. Kenneth Burke, *The Rhetoric of Religion: Studies in Logology* (Berkeley, Calif.: University of California, 1970), pp. v-vi.

25. Robinson and Sheehan, *Over the Wire*, p. 284.

26. Michael Novak, "Notes on the Drama of Politics and the Drama of Journalism," in *The Politics of Broadcasting*, ed. Marvin Barrett (New York: Thomas Crowell, 1973), p. 176.

27. Ibid., p. 174.

28. Paul H. Weaver, "Captives of Melodrama," *New York Times Magazine*, August 29, 1976, p. 6.

29. An example of the older "accuracy of reporting" approach can be seen in Lang and Lang, *Politics and Television*, pp. 36-77.

30. For analyses of the conventions of newsgathering see Robert MacNeil, *The People Machine: The Influence of Television on American Politics* (New York: Harper and Row, 1968), pp. 18-55; Dan Nimmo and James E. Combs, *Mediated Political Realities* (New York: Longman, 1983), pp. 23-46; Gans, *Deciding What's News*, 146-81; and Epstein, *News from Nowhere*, 152-80.

31. Bennett, *News: Politics of Illusion*, p. 21.

32. See our discussion of this relationship in Chapter 9.

33. Gitlin, *Whole World is Watching*, pp. 21-77.

34. David L. Paletz and Robert M. Entman, *Media Power Politics* (New York: The Free Press, 1981), p. 158.

35. Ibid., p. 157.

36. For a view that differs sharply from that of Gans, Gitlin, and Bennett, see Robinson and Sheehan, *Over the Wire*, pp. 296-98.

37. A good example of political analysis spun off from the terms of drama is James E. Combs, *Dimensions of Political Drama* (Santa Monica, Calif.: Goodyear, 1980), pp. 1-17.

38. Nimmo and Combs, *Mediated Political Realities*, p. 28.

39. Robert P. Newman, "The Weekly Fiction Magazines," *Central States Speech Journal* (May 1966): 118-24.

40. Quoted in Epstein, *News from Nowhere*, pp. 4-5.

41. Weaver, "Captives of Melodrama," p. 6.

42. Patterson and McClure, *The Unseeing Eye*, p. 36.

43. Quoted in Robinson and Sheehan, *Over the Wire*, pp. 214-15.

44. David Riesman with Nathan Glazer and Reuel Denney, *The Lonely Crowd*, abridged ed. (New Haven: Yale University, 1961), p. 182.

45. Crouse, *Boys on the Bus*, p. 38.

46. Aristotle discusses character extensively in Book II of *The Rhetoric*.

47. Niccolò Machiavelli, *The Prince*, trans. Christian Gauss (New York: Mentor, 1972), pp. 93-94.

48. Richard Sennett, *The Fall of Public Man: On the Social Psychology of Capitalism* (New York: Vintage Books, 1978), p. 4.

49. The wording is Sennett's, p. 284 in ibid.

50. Paul E. Corcoran, *Political Language and Rhetoric* (Austin, Tex.: University of Texas, 1979), p. 161.

51. Sennett, *Fall of Public Man*, p. 5.

52. See Robert Agranoff, "The New Style of Campaigning: The Decline of Party and the Rise of Candidate-Centered Technology," in *The New Style in Election Campaigns*, 2nd ed., ed. Robert Agranoff (Boston: Holbrook, 1977), pp. 10-23.

53. For a case study describing this pattern see Mary Ellen Leary, *Phantom Politics: Campaigning in California* (Washington, D.C.: Public Affairs, 1977).

54. Quoted in David Halberstam, *The Powers That Be* (New York: Knopf, 1979), p. 6.

55. W. Roper Burns, *Trends in Attitudes Toward Television and Other Media: A Twenty-Four Year Review* (New York: Television Information Office, 1983).

56. Patterson, *Mass Media Election*, p. 59.

57. Ibid., pp. 59-60.

58. Robinson and Sheehan, *Over the Wire*, pp. 208-13.

59. For a discussion of the problems of the 30-minute format see MacNeil, *The People Machine*, pp. 18-55; and Av Westin, *Newswatch: How TV Decides the News* (New York: Simon and Schuster, 1982), pp. 53-95.

60. Walter Cronkite, Remarks to the RTNDA Conference, Miami Beach, December 13, 1976, in *Rich News, Poor News*, ed. Marvin Barrett (New York: Thomas Y. Crowell, 1978), p. 195.

61. Quoted in "Television and Presidential Politics: Brainstorming the Possibilities," *Broadcasting* (February 8, 1982): 92.

62. John Kenneth Galbraith, *The Affluent Society*, 3rd ed. (Boston: Houghton Mifflin, 1976), p. 198.

63. Eric Barnouw, *The Sponsor: Notes on a Modern Potentate* (New York: Oxford University, 1978), p. 96.

64. McGinniss, *Selling of the President*, pp. 33-37.

65. Theodore H. White, *The Making of the President, 1972* (New York: Atheneum, 1973), p. 250.

66. Robert Spero, *The Duping of the American Voter* (New York: Lippincott and Crowell, 1980), p. 5.

67. Gary A. Mauser, *Political Marketing: An Approach to Campaign Strategy* (New York: Praeger, 1983), p. 19.

68. Patterson and McClure, *The Unseeing Eye*, pp. 22-23.

69. Ibid., p. 130.

70. James H. McBath and Walter R. Fisher, "Persuasion in Presidential Campaign Communication," *Quarterly Journal of Speech* (February 1969): 23.

71. See, for example, Joseph Napolitan, *The Election Game and How to Win It* (Garden City, N.Y.: Doubleday, 1972), pp. 64-88.

72. Patterson and McClure, *The Unseeing Eye*, pp. 47-58.

73. Leary, *Phantom Politics*, p. 90.

74. Leary, pp. 90-91.

75. Sydney W. Head and Christopher H. Sterling, *Broadcasting in America*, 4th ed. (Boston: Houghton Mifflin, 1982), pp. 481-84.

76. See, for example, Robert G. Meadow, "The Political Dimensions of Nonproduct Advertising," *Journal of Communication* (Summer 1981): 69-82.

77. "Current Statistics on Mass Media in the United States, 1982," in *Readings in Mass Communication*, 5th ed., ed. Michael Emery and Ted Curtis Smythe (Dubuque, Iowa: Wm. C. Brown, 1983), p. 533.

78. Michael J. Robinson, "Three Faces of Congressional Media," in *The New Congress*, ed. Thomas E. Mann and Norman J. Ornstein (Washington, D.C.: American Enterprise Institute, 1981), pp. 60-61.

79. Vincent P. Barabba, "Basic Information Systems—P.I.P.S.," in *The New Style in Election Campaigns*, 2nd ed., ed. Robert Agranoff (Boston: Holbrook, 1977), pp. 224-36.

80. Betty Glad, *Jimmy Carter: In Search of the Great White House* (New York: W. W. Norton, 1980), p. 216.

81. Andrew Hacker, "Poets of Packaging, Sculptors of Desire," *New York Times Book Review*, June 24, 1984, p. 31.

82. For a dramatic example of an ad campaign that is credited with greatly increased sales see Scott Hume, "Wendy's Aims to Get Better With Its Best," *Advertising Age*, April 30, 1984, pp. 4, 64.

83. Quoted in Cliff Zukin, "Mass Communication and Public Opinion," in *Handbook of Political Communication*, ed. Dan D. Nimmo and Keith R. Sanders (Beverly Hills, Calif.: Sage, 1981), p. 385.

84. Ibid., p. 386.

85. This emphasis on the dominance of attitude reinforcement rather than change was argued most convincingly by Joseph T. Klapper in *The Effects of Mass Communication* (New York: Free Press, 1960). For applications of the minimal effects theory see Dan Nimmo, *The Political Persuaders* (Englewood Cliffs, N.J.: Prentice-Hall, 1970) pp. 167-79 and Doris A. Graber, *Mass Media and American Politics* (Washington, D.C.: Congressional Quarterly, 1980), pp. 183-89.

86. A summary of categories of media-affected attitudes is offered by Nimmo in *Political Persuaders*, pp. 164-67.

87. For a general discussion on differences between behaviors and attitudes, and on basic attempts to deal with these differences, see Philip G. Zimbardo, Ebbe R. Ebbesen, and Christina Maslach, *Influencing Attitudes and Changing Behavior*, 2nd ed. (Boston: Addison-Wesley, 1977), pp. 49-53, 153-68.

88. DeFleur and Dennis, *Understanding Mass Communication*, pp. 278-79.

89. Kurt Lang and Gladys Engel Lang, "The Mass Media and Voting," in *Readings in Public Opinion and Mass Communication*, 3rd ed., ed. Morris Janowitz and Paul Hirsch (New York: Free Press, 1981), pp. 327-39.

90. Zukin, "Mass Communication and Public Opinion," p. 369.

91. John P. Robinson, "Mass Communication and Information Diffusion" in *Readings in Public Opinion and Mass Communication*, 3rd ed., ed. Morris Janowitz and Paul Hirsch (New York: Free Press, 1981), p. 349.

92. See Jack M. McLeod and Lee B. Becker, "The Uses and Gratifications Approach," in *Handbook of Political Communication*, ed. Dan D. Nimmo and Keith Sanders (Beverly Hills, Calif.: Sage, 1981), pp. 67-100.

93. Nimmo, *Political Persuaders*, pp. 183-84.

94. A general discussion of the inability of many citizens to internalize well-presented information is given by Raymond A. Bauer, "The Obstinate Audience: The Influence Process from the Point of View of Social Communication," in *The Process and Effects of Mass Communication*, rev. ed., ed. Wilbur Schramm and Donald F. Roberts (Chicago: University of Chicago, 1971), pp. 326-46.

95. Paletz and Entman, *Media Power Politics*, p. 149.

96. Graber, *Mass Media and American Politics*, pp. 80-81.

97. Ibid., p. 81.

98. For two different views of this pattern see Ben H. Bagdikian, "Journalist Meets Propagandist" in *Media Power and Politics*, ed. Doris A. Graber (Washington, D.C.: Congressional Quarterly, 1984), pp. 331-37; and William Rivers, *The Adversaries: Politics and the Press* (Boston: Beacon, 1970), pp. 68-133.

99. Graber, *Mass Media and American Politics*, p. 80.

100. Memo from Robert Kintner to President Johnson, January 11, 1967, State of the Union Address File, WHCF (White House Central File), LBJ Library.

101. Ibid., January 9, 1967.

102. Ibid., January 11, 1967.

103. See, for example, Lynda Lee Kaid, "The Neglected Candidate: Interpersonal Communication in Political Campaigns," *Western Journal of Communication* (Fall 1977): 245-52.

104. Westin, *Newswatch*, p. 232; Epstein, *News from Nowhere*, p. 37.

105. See, for example, Jarol B. Manheim, "Can Democracy Survive Television? *Journal of Communication* (Spring 1976): 84-90.

106. Murray Edelman, *The Symbolic Uses of Politics* (Urbana, Ill.: University of Illinois, 1967), p. 5.

107. Paul F. Lazerfeld and Robert K. Merton, "Mass Communication, Popular Taste, and Organized Social Action," *The Process and Effects of Mass Communication*, rev. ed., ed. Wilbur Schramm and Donald F. Roberts (Chicago: University of Chicago, 1971), p. 565.

108. Donald F. Roberts and Wilbur Schramm, "Children's Learning From the Mass Media," in *The Process and Effects of Mass Communication*, rev. ed., ed. Wilbur Schramm and Donald F. Roberts (Chicago: University of Chicago, 1971), pp. 598-99.

109. John P. Robinson, "Mass Communication and Information Diffusion," pp. 351-57.

110. Zukin, "Mass Communication and Public Opinion," p. 377.

111. Helene Von Damm, ed., *Sincerely Ronald Reagan* (New York: Berkley Books, 1980), p. 18.

112. Gary Woodward, "Heroic Imagery in the Rhetoric of the Reagan Campaign" (Paper presented at the Eastern Communication Association Annual Meeting, Pittsburgh, Pa., April 26, 1981).

113. See, for example, Reagan's flattering comments to the director of the film, *Patton*, in Von Damm, *Sincerely Ronald Reagan*, pp. 19-20.

114. Paul M. Hirsch, "The Role of Television and Popular Culture in Contemporary Society," in *Television: The Critical View*, 3rd ed., ed. Horace Newcomb (New York: Oxford, 1982), p. 289.

115. Robert Sklar, *Movie-Made America* (New York: Vintage, 1975), pp. 58-61.

116. Ronald Reagan and Richard G. Hubler, *Where's the Rest of Me?* (New York: Karz, 1981), pp. 113-25.

117. Hugh Dalziel Duncan, *Communication and Social Order* (New York: Oxford, 1968), pp. 373-416.

118. Ibid., p. 79.

119. Ibid., p. 80.

120. Deena Rosenberg, "A 'Lost' Musical by Gershwin Makes a Comeback," *New York Times*, June 24, 1984, pp. H4, 13.

121. Dan Nimmo and James E. Combs, *Subliminal Politics: Myths and Mythmakers in America* (Englewood Cliffs, N.J.: Prentice-Hall, 1980), p. 146.

122. Friendly, *Due to Circumstances*, pp. 163-88; Epstein, *News from Nowhere*, pp. 52-53.

123. See the criticisms of Cecil Brown, "Blues for Blacks in Hollywood," in *Readings in Mass Communication*, 5th ed., ed. Michael Emery and Ted Curtis Smythe (Dubuque, Iowa: Wm. C. Brown, 1983), pp. 153-63.

124. Erik Barnouw, *Tube of Plenty: The Evolution of American Television* (New York: Oxford, 1975), p. 434.

125. Ibid.

126. Neil Vidmar and Milton Rokeach, "Archie Bunker's Bigotry: A Study in Selective Perception," *Journal of Communication* (Winter 1974): 36-47.

127. Douglas Kellner, "TV, Ideology, and Emancipatory Popular Culture," in *Television: The Critical View*, 3rd ed., ed. Horace Newcomb (New York: Oxford, 1982), p. 412.

128. Barnouw, *The Sponsor*, p. 114.

129. Paletz and Entman, *Media Power Politics*, p. 182.

130. Gans, *Deciding What's News*; Gitlin, "Prime Time Ideology: The Hegemonic Process in Television Entertainment," in *Television: The Critical View*, 3rd ed., ed. Horace Newcomb (New York: Oxford, 1982), pp. 426-54; Gitlin, *Whole World is Watching*; and Gaye Tuchman, *Making News: A Study in the Construction of Reality* (New York: Free Press, 1978).

131. Gitlin, *Whole World is Watching*, p. 10.

132. Ibid., pp. 146-246.

133. Gitlin, "Prime Time Ideology," p. 447.

134. For the general perspective of our analysis we are indebted to Anne Roiphe's "Ma and Pa and John-Boy in Mythic America: The Waltons," reprinted in *Television: The Critical View*, 3rd ed., ed. Horace Newcomb (New York: Oxford, 1982), pp. 198-205.

# 7

# The Symbolic Nature of the Presidency

Every four years a gong goes off and a new Presidential campaign surges into the national consciousness: new candidates, new issues, a new season of surprises. But underlying the syncopations of change there is a steady, recurrent rhythm from election to election, a pulse of politics that brings up the future, the dominant theme of the same basic themes in order, over and over again.[1]

It is, perhaps, rather obvious that rhetoric is vital to the functioning of a democratic society. We go beyond the assumption and posit that rhetoric, or specifically the nature of the communication activities that comprise the office, best defines the institution of the American presidency. By examining the rhetoric of the office, we can best understand the relationship of the office with the public historically or in contemporary times; discover how individuals in the office govern the nation; and how individuals adapt, adopt, reject, or redefine the presidential role in society. Such examinations are both descriptive and prescriptive. To discover the office is to discover ourselves, our nation, and our history. They address issues of public and private motives, public and private concerns, and public and private actions.

The presidency has become the focal point of our political system. This was not always the case. Early presidents seldom gave public

---

The central argument of this chapter is based on Chapter 3, " 'Mind' and the Emerging of the 'Presidential Self' " and Chapter 5, "The Symbolic Crisis of the American Presidency" in *The Symbolic Dimensions of the American Presidency*, Robert E. Denton, Jr. (Prospect Heights, Ill.: Waveland Press, 1982).

addresses. Written statements served as notice of issue positions. Campaigns were conducted by the parties. Only a handful of people were knowledgeable and aware of public issues. Even fewer actually voted or participated in the electoral process. Today, presidential rhetoric and communication activities are a source of tremendous power: power to define, justify, legitimize, persuade, and inspire. Everything a president does or says has implications and communicates "something." A president surrounds himself with communication specialists. Every act, word, or phrase becomes calculated and measured for a response. Every occasion proclaims a need for utterance.

James Ceaser, with several other colleagues, agrues that three factors have attributed to the rise of the "rhetorical presidency."[2] The first factor is the modern doctrine of presidential leadership. The public expects a president to set goals and provide solutions to national problems. To be a leader of men is a cherished concept and a political expectation and, hence, necessity for our presidents. The second factor giving use to the rhetorical presidency is the development of the mass media. The mass media have increased the size of the audience, provided immediate access to the public, and changed the mode of communicating with the public from primarily the written word to the spoken word delivered in dramatic form. The final factor contributing to the supremacy of the rhetorical presidency is the modern electoral campaign. Contemporary presidential campaigns require national travel, public performances, image creation, issue definition, and the articulation of problem solutions. A "common man" can become known and win an election. Competition for communication opportunities is great.

Thus, the rhetorical presidency refers to more than a collection of speeches delivered by any one president. It refers to the communicative attributes of both the institution and its occupants. The presidency is an office, a role, a persona, constructing a position of power, myth, legend, and persuasion. Although the presidency is indeed a real office with an elected official, space, desks, and staff, it remains elusive and undefined. When consulting the ultimate authority—Article II of the Constitution delineates the functions and duties of the president—one notices how short, sketchy, vague, and almost trivial the description of the office appears. In reality, as Grant McConnell argues, "the presidency is the work of the presidents."[3] Yet, virtually every American, from seven to seventy has a list of criteria of what makes a good president. Expectations are created through presidents' rhetoric, use of symbols, rituals, and sense of history. At home and in schools we are taught that America is the home of freedom, equality, opportunity, and democracy. Within such an environment, as Rossiter notes, the president becomes " . . . the one-man distillation of the American people" reflecting their perceived dignity and majesty.[4] Consequently, elaborate criteria are envisioned for the man who desires the sacred office.

Symbolic leadership is an emergent phenomenon resulting from the interaction of the public and the politician. As political drama begins, according to Orin Klapp, roles are identified, interpreted, and projected upon the politician and no distinction is made between "what a thing 'is' and what the audiences see that it is."[5] The key, therefore, in becoming a symbolic leader is to take advantage of the dramatic elements in any setting. Settings become drama when "things happen to audiences because of parts played by actors; the function of the actor is to transport an audience vicariously out of everyday roles into a new kind of 'reality' that has laws and patterns different from the routines of the ordinary social structure."[6]

The sources of images or preconceptions people have of the qualities of leadership are vast. There are, however, three major influences upon such leadership construction. First, history rather carefully characterizes past national leaders. Washington was a man of integrity (the cherry tree), determination (Valley Forge), and was democratic (refusal to be king). Lincoln was a man of patience (preserve the Union), forgiveness (malice toward none), and a lover of freedom (Emancipation Proclamation). Second, television greatly contributes to the creation of leadership ideals. The open forums give the impression of being able to assess candidate qualities. Finally, leadership qualities are portrayed in dramatic programs and literature. Often voters openly compare the qualities of politicians to those of professional entertainers. Bob Hope, the deceased John Wayne, and Charlton Heston could probably all easily poll a majority of voters. In fact, Walter Cronkite's name occurred in political polls rather favorably as well as being mentioned as a vice-presidential candidate for the 1980 Anderson Independent presidential bid.

Thus, the greatest American mythic endeavor is to find a great man as leader. As a people, Americans find pleasure and comfort in searching as well as in finding heroes. "Two centuries ago," Daniel Boorstin argues, "when a great man appeared, people looked for God's purpose in him; today we look for his press agent."[7] Yet, ironically, hero-worship counters democratic dogma. The heart of hero-worship, however, is not reverence for divine qualities but appreciation for popular virtues. Heroes are admired "not because they reveal God, but because they reveal and elevate ourselves."[8] In addition, Walter Fisher argues, presidential heroes as romantic figures express certain American ideals as individualism, achievement, and success.[9] A true American hero will be visionary, mythic, and a subject for folklore and legend.[10]

In short, the presidency is a national political symbol. And political symbols are the direct link between individuals and the social order as argued in Chapter 2. As elements of a political culture, political symbols function as a stimulus for behavior. They can provide insight into macro- and micro-level behavior. The use of appropriate symbols results in getting people to accept certain policies that may or may not provide tangible rewards, arouse support for various causes, and obedience to governmental authority. Political symbols are actually means to material and social ends rather than ends in themselves.

There is, however, a long process from symbol creation, definition, acceptance, and subsequent behavior. For implicit in the argument thus far is the notion that successful leadership and control is dependent upon the successful manipulation of political symbols. There is a constant competition and struggle for national symbols. At one level, a president attempts to manipulate symbols in order to mobilize support, deactivate opposition, and insulate himself from criticism. On a broader level, national symbols are perpetuated in order to preserve the prevailing culture, beliefs, and values. Thus, the ongoing manipulation of political symbols takes place in the context of an existing set of symbols grounded in the political culture.

In this chapter, we will investigate the symbolic nature of the American presidency by considering the symbolic aspects of the institution as well as individual occupants' attempts to reinforce the symbolic expectations associated with the office.

## INSTITUTIONAL ASPECTS OF THE SYMBOLIC DIMENSIONS OF THE PRESIDENCY

### Presidential Functions

Of all the major clauses in the Constitution, the one governing the presidency is the shortest. The members of the Constitutional Convention simply did not delineate in great detail the powers and responsibilities of the presidency. According to Rossiter, eight key decisions were made at the convention which really created the form and structure of the American presidency.[11]

1. A separate executive office should be established apart from the legislature.

2. The executive office should consist of one man to be called president of the United States.

3. The president should be elected apart from the legislature.

4. The executive office should have a fixed term subject to termination by conviction of impeachment for high crimes or misdemeanors.

5. The president should be eligible for reelection with no limit as to the number of terms.

6. The president should derive power from the Constitution and not simply from Congress.

7. The president should not be encumbered with a specified body to seek approval for nominations, vetos, or other acts.

8. As president, one may not be a member of either house of Congress.

These key decisions created the office, but they contain little information as to what the office entails. Nearly half of Article II simply deals with tenure, qualifications, and election of the president. Section 2 of Article II states that the president "shall be Commander in Chief," "shall have power to grant reprieves and pardons," "make treaties, provided two-thirds of the Senators present concur," "appoint Ambassadors, other public Ministers and Consuls, Judges of the Supreme Court, and all other officers of the United States . . . by and with the advice and consent of the Senate" and "shall have power to fill all vacancies that may happen during the recess of the Senate." Section 3 adds that the president "shall from time to time give to the Congress information of the State of the Union," "convene both Houses . . . on extraordinary occasions," "shall receive Ambassadors and other public Ministers," and "shall take care that the laws be faithfully executed."[1 2] These, then, are the duties as specified in the Constitution. On the surface, they appear rather simple and straightforward. It is the fulfilling of these functions the complicates the office.

Contemporary scholars, when addressing presidential functions, seldom delineate constitutional provisions. Rather, they group presidential tasks into broad, general categories. These categories, of course, differ in number. For Thomas Cronin, the job description of the president involves six major functions.[1 3]

1. Symbolic leadership which must generate hope, confidence, national purpose;

2. setting national priorities and designing programs which will receive public attention and a legislative hearing;

3. crisis management which has become increasingly important since 1940;

4. constant legislative and political coalition building;

5. program implementation and evaluation which has also become increasingly difficult in modern times. And,

6. general oversight of government routines which forces the president to be responsible for governmental performance at all levels.

Somewhat related to Cronin, Bruce Buchanan identifies four "generic" functions of the presidency: national symbol, policy advocate, mediator among national interests, and crisis manager.[14] Reedy believes, however, that what a president must do can be boiled down to two simple fundamentals: "He must resolve the policy questions that will not yield to quantitative, empirical analysis; and he must persuade enough of his countrymen of the rightness of his decisions so that he can carry them out without destroying the fabric of society."[15]

From this brief discussion of presidential functions, the Constitution as a job description is vague and general. A president clearly does more than what is outlined in the Constitution. Even as commander-in-chief, the president may undertake crisis management, legislative and political coalition building, etc. It is how one meets or carries out the functions that provide insight into how the institution influences behavior.

Edward Corwin was the first to mention presidential roles as sources of power.[16] A president's power is based upon five contitutional roles: chief of state, chief executive, chief diplomat, commander-in-chief, and chief legislator. These roles are roughly analogous to the various areas of responsibilities outlined in the Constitution. A president who creates additional roles and hence additional power approaches a dangerous "personalization of the office."

As chief of state, the president functions as the ceremonial head of government not unlike the monarch of England. Some would argue that the majority of presidential activity is ceremonial. Projected upon the president is the symbol of sovereignty, continuity, and grandeur. As chief executive, the president is manager of one of the largest "corporations" in the world. Whether the president likes it or not, he is held responsible for the quality of governmental performance ranging from a simple letter of complaint to military preparedness. In event of war, the president as commander-in-chief must ensure strategic execution and victory. Within modern history, the field of foreign relations has become extremely important. The formulation of foreign policy and the conduct of foreign affairs force the president to serve as the nation's chief diplomat. Finally, by providing domestic leadership, the president must guide Congress by identifying national priorities for legislation. These legitimate, Constitutional roles are obviously interrelated. Yet, the various hats require rather distinct approaches, strategies, and temperament. Even these, however, may be situationally bound.

Clinton Rossiter, building on Corwin's analyses argues that five extra-constitutional roles must be recognized: chief of party, protector of the peace, manager of prosperity, world leader, and voice of the people.[17] Rossiter, as Corwin, believes that the source of presidential power lies in the combination of the various roles. Rossiter, at least, recognizes the expanding nature of the presidency. These extra roles resulted from the growing activities of a president plus the growing expectations of the public. As Myron Hale has succinctly stated, "roles became obligations and duties, as each role became a Presidential responsibility."[18] When speaking of presidential roles, most scholars cite Rossiter's classic *The American Presidency*. Hence, the list of roles is fairly stationary. Yet, as the functions or duties of the presidency grow, so do the roles. As the various tasks become more complex, numerous roles may be required to carry out one function. One should also note that each role may require very different skills and techniques. Roles, then, are more numerous than functions. They are labels or characters that people see and each has a distinct mode usually congruent with public expectations which will be developed later. Finally, if a role set is good or successful, the set may become a model. The model may thus serve as an overall approach to the fulfillment of the functions. The role set, as a model, may be praised, condemned, imitated, or serve as a guide to performance.

### Presidential Roles

Most all political scientists recognize that the presidency is both an institution and a role. As such, the presidency has a great deal of influence upon those who occupy the office as well as upon the general public.

Political roles are not concrete, static entities. Rather, they are ideas about what people expect to do in certain situations as well as what others expect them to do in certain situations. While the concept of role does deal with behavior, it is not the activity of behavior itself. The distinction between what individuals think they should do and what in fact they do should not be ignored. As Norton Long notes:

> The actors in the world of politics are neither the rational calculators of economic man nor the uncultured savages of Hobbes' state of nature but are born into a political culture, albeit frequently an ambiguous one, and are socialized to a range of response patterns that may be invoked by diverse stimuli. With this equipment, they confront a reality that seems to each public, one-dimensional common sense but, in fact, through the differing glasses that it is viewed, presents widely differing perspectives.[19]

Political actors, therefore, possess a repertory of responses or roles. Upon any stimulus, the appropriate role behavior is a product of what the actor perceives the defined role to be which also fulfills the expectations of the public. "The existence of these patterned sets of roles is part of the technology of the political culture and permits the actors to function with the same ease as a ballplayer playing his position."[20]

Thus, roles (political or otherwise) are comprised of internal and external elements.[21] The former consist of the individual's own perception of what a task demands and how to fulfill it; the latter are the expectations and orientations of members of society. However, as Height and Johnston point out,

> the division into roles can be deceptive . . . and one must never forget the fact that one man plays all the parts. The President can never separate his problems and divide them into preconceived categories for decision. Each decision will involve the President as a whole man, and he will need in some manner to accommodate several often conflicting roles in order to determine a course of action.[22]

## Role Expectations

A "role set" is a set of "behavioral relationships that exist between positions."[23] Borden, Gregg, and Grove argue that there are two kinds of role sets: traditional role sets and unique role sets.[24] Traditional role sets refer to institutionalized relationships such as husband and wife, lawyer and client, etc. These role sets provide general guidelines for behavior. Traditional role sets serve primarily task-maintenance functions. Unique role sets refer primarily to person-maintenance functions. Thus, traditional role sets provide already established interaction patterns and set up general expectations of the participants.

Certainly, the American presidency has established a rather clear traditional role set. The title of president implies more than simply a job description. To know that a person is president is to know in a very general way how the individual is likely to behave and how others will behave toward the individual. The title not only provides a means for anticipating a range of behaviors, but also confines the range of behaviors possible. Thus, behavioral expectations and restrictions are attached to all social positions. Richard Rose notes that "empirical investigation usually reveals that leaders are often constrained by the expectations of their followers and in some cases compelled to follow their followers or risk deposition as leader."[25]

Cronin recognizes the basic tendency of Americans to believe in great personages, " . . . that someone, somewhere, can and will cope with the major crises of the present and future."[26] Within our society, the presidency fulfills this need and becomes the symbol of our hopes. Presidents are much more likely, historically, to be placed on a pedestal rather than under a microscope. Although the tendency is acknowledged by political scientists, Cronin insists that political scientists have " . . . usually not read in such meaning, or at least have not infused their view of the Presidency with connotations of a civil religion."[27] Consequently, to simply speak of presidential functions in no way adequately describes what the presidency really is.

Emmet Hughes, in *The Living Presidency*, states that a president faces two constituencies: "the living citizens and the future historians."[28] This certainly is not an easy task. Nearly all scholars agree that any American president inherits a vast, complex set of role expectations. "The fact that there are many roles involved in the most important political office gives a politican the discretion of deciding which to emphasize and which to ignore. He can, at the least, choose what he ignores."[29] But such a choice is not a one-way street. Roles create expectations but societal expectations can create political roles. Murray Edelman perceptively notes that

> expectations also evoke a specific political role and self-conception for those individuals who accept the myth in question: the patriotic soldier whose role it is to sacrifice, fight, and die for his country; the policeman or National Guardsman whose role it is to save the social order from subhuman or radical hordes.[30]

For Edelman, the degree of attachment to a political myth and the role it creates plus the fervor with which the role is acted out depend upon "the degree of anxiety the myth rationalizes, the intensity with which the particular expectation that forms the central premise of the myth is held."[31] When Alfred deGrazia speaks of "the myth of the President," he is referring to "a number of qualities [that] are given to every President that are either quite fictitious or large exaggerations of the real man."[32] He further notes that "the myth is not alone the property of the untutored mind, but of academicians, scientists, newspapermen, and even Congressmen."[33]

Thus, the office of the presidency has grown because of interaction; interaction of the office with the public and the public with the office. As public expectations increase, so does the job. Concurrently, the job is forced to expand to meet public expectations.

As already mentioned, there appears to be a growth in public expectations of the presidency. However, twentieth-century presidents, because of the use of mass media, have encouraged the public to identify with the candidate and potential of the office. Theodore White asserts that especially since 1960, our idea of government consists of promises—promises to take care of people, the cities, the sick, the old, the young. According to White, "by 1980 we had promised ourselves almost to the point of national bankruptcy."[34] Consequently, the public has responded by holding the president accountable for meeting various demands. David Easton has identified two types of expectations that citizens have of political leadership.[35] One focuses on the office and the other focuses on the individual who holds the office. Thus, public expectations are vast and complex. Upon investigating the research on presidential and public expectations, Herzik and Dodson conclude that indeed "a consensus does exist concerning public expectations of the President—a consensus focused around general traits of personality, leadership, and individual virtue."[36]

Disappointment in presidential performance is not the only consequence of false expectations. False expectations also encourage presidents to attempt more than they can accomplish in any term of office. Thus, false expectations invite presidents to overpromise and overextend themselves. This, in turn, creates the need for image-making activities. Such activities, in some cases, become the major task or work function of an administration. Soon, the emphasis, out of necessity, becomes style over substance. "The public-relations apparatus," as Cronin argues, "not only has directly enlarged the Presidential work force but has expanded public-relations expectations about the Presidency at the same time. More disquieting is the fact that, by its very nature, this type of press-agentry, feeds on itself, and the resulting distortions encourage an ever increasing subordination of substance to style."[37]

## Presidential Roles Created

Political roles, although undergoing constant modification, exist prior to any political event. Politicians, however, do not consciously decide each morning during what parts of the day they will act as a statesman, an administrator, or a partisan vote-getter. Yet, as we already argued, public expectations of behavior and performance are rather clearly defined. Such expectations develop over time and consequently are slow in changing. Because political roles are fairly well defined, they are learned by politicians through the process of socialization. New legislators soon learn what roles are appropriate in various situations.

Roletaking, as Edelman notes, is action.[38] It is both behavioral and observable. The process of roletaking by politicians directly influences the behaviors of officeholders by revealing public expectations and hence expected behavior. Edelman succinctly explains the process as follows:

> Through taking the roles of publics whose support they need, public officials achieve and maintain their positions of leadership. The official who correctly gauges the response of publics to his acts, speeches, and gestures makes those behaviors significant symbols, evoking common meanings for his audience and for himself so shaping his future actions as to reassure his public and in this sense "represent" them.[39]

This process of role socialization, argues Rose, is "emotionally intense and highly compressed in time; it is the chief means by which people fit and are fitted into place in established institutions."[40]

One of the major points made in discussing the paradoxical nature of the presidency, is that the expectations and functions of the office are often competing, conflicting, and contradictory. Role conflicts are an essential element in political life. Role conflict occurs "when contradictory types of behavior are expected from a person who holds different positions or when contradictory types of behavior are expected within one role."[41] A successful politician, therefore, is one who can handle role conflicts. Unfortunately, depending upon one's view, when a discrepancy develops between individual preferences and institutional role expectations, it is more often the individual who changes. For Richard Rose, the best measure of a politician's greatness is his ability to create new roles for an established office.[42] In fact, Rose views such an ability as one attribute of charismatic leadership.

Politics is a primarily symbolic activity that touches the lives of a significantly large number of people.[43] Such activity has a unique and often profound meaning because, in the words of Kenneth Burke, man is uniquely "the symbol-making, and symbol-misusing animal."[44] Political reality, whose implications and consequences are felt and observable is conveyed through the creation of significant symbols. Images of politics are largely, therefore, symbolic. The degree to which images of politics are useful and gratifying, according to Nimmo, is related to three factors:

> First, no matter how correct or incorrect, complete or incomplete may be one's knowledge about politics, it gives that person some way of understanding specific political events. . . . Second, the general likes and dislikes in a person's political images offer a basis for evaluating political objects. . . . Third, a person's self-image provides a way of relating one's self to others.[45]

Political images, then, are beneficial in an individual's evaluating and identifying with various political leaders, events, ideas, or causes.

Many attitudes about the presidency stem from messages received in childhood about the virtues of various presidents. Studies continually find that the president is ordinarily the first public official to come to the attention of young children.[46] Long before children are informed about the specific functions of the presidency, they view individual presidents as exceptionally important and benign. David Easton and Robert Hess found that children stressed personal characteristics of the president which include: honesty, wisdom, helpfulness, powerful, good, and benign.[47] Such attitudes probably result from parents omitting negative aspects of the political world from the children plus the general tendency of children to selectively perceive more supportive characteristics of individuals in a wider environment. Generally, by the age of nine, virtually every American child has some detailed awareness of the presidency and can identify the incumbent president. Such cognizance of the American president, according to Fred Greenstein, goes beyond national boundaries. He reports that surveys of children in Austria and Canada reveal that the name of the United States president is better known than the name of the prime ministers of their own country.[48] Even in 1973 at the height of the Watergate episode Greenstein found "numerous idealized references to the President."[49] Thus, esteem and respect for the office independent of the occupant is established at a rather early age.

## Presidential Roles Permeated

Every year since World War II, seven or eight of the ten most admired men and women are involved in national politics. And the president, regardless of performance, is among them.[50] Doris Graber, in a study designed to analyze images of presidential candidates in the press during campaigns, found that citizens tend to selectively extract information about a president's personal image that is beyond the media content which ignores issue elements.[51] Therefore, apparently, citizens perceive and evaluate a president as a person rather than on his policies and skill in office. According to Greenstein, when people are asked to indicate what they like or dislike about a president, they usually cite aspects of personal image.[52]

Another result of childhood socialization is the heavy dependency for leadership on the presidency, especially in times of national crisis. Pious argues that in times of national emergency, we discard skepticism and return to childhood images of the presidency.[53] As adults, we still desire to see the president as a combination of Washington and Lincoln, making wise decisions and working harder than the average citizen to preserve the quality of life.

A presidential campaign emphasizes the childhood visions and qualities of the office. Hence, campaigns themselves perpetuate the mythic and heroic role demands of the office. To mobilize a nation is indeed a somewhat mysterious process. For McConnell, it is the essential dimension of the presidency resulting from becoming a "national symbol" and in so doing, gives substance and purpose to the nation itself.[54] The process of selecting a president is important and vital. Campaigns may best be characterized as noisy, disorderly, contentious, and even absurd. "The gap between the indignity of the process and the grandeur of the end is enormous."[55] Yet, the process allows the opportunity to assess and project presidential qualities upon the candidates.

Media advisers must project appropriate images of the candidates which are always simplified depictions of reality. In a memo to Richard Nixon, Ray Price argued, "It's not what's there that counts, it's what is projected—and carrying it one step further, it's not what he projects but rather what the voter receives."[5][6] James Wooten, in addressing the 1976 Carter campaign, wrote that Carter " . . . believed that the candidate who took clear positions on every issue was not long for the political world. There would be only one issue on which a successful candidate would be judged that year, the amorphous, ethereal concept of integrity, honesty, trustworthiness, credibility."[5][7] Patrick Caddell is quoted as warning Carter during the transition that "too many good people have been beaten because they tried to substitute substance for style."[5][8] Is this ethically, logically, or even morally right? Carter's pollster Gerald Rafshoon believed that there was nothing wrong with a candidate adjusting himself to an ideology or "rhetorical stance" judged to be acceptable by the voters. Rafshoon argued to Wooten, "He was always Jimmy Carter. . . . Hell, you wouldn't expect Sears Roebuck to step into a big multimillion dollar promotion without having the benefit of consumer research on what people are most interested in purchasing."[5][9] Consequently, the image projected by a candidate should meet the expectations and childhood visions of presidential behavior. The best image is one that is vague enough for the voters to complete. In the simplest terms, this means that conservatives should be able to see the candidate as conservative and, likewise, liberals should be able to see the candidate as liberal. Above all, this should be done without seeming contradictory or insincere.

From this perspective an election is seen not simply as a reflection of the preference for one individual over another. Rather, it is a composite of all the individual desires, hopes, frustrations, and anger of citizens encompassing an infinite number of issues or concerns. However chaotic, the process has value. As McConnell notes:

> Purists may well wish for more graceful campaigning, and more incisive and intellectually elevated debates. Quite possibly, however, achieving these desirable conditions might rob the process of much of its vitality and leave the ultimate winner with no accurate sense of the temper of the American people. A Presidential election is, above all, an articulation of the mood of the electorate.[60]

By inauguration day a candidate has emerged as president. A tremendous transformation, at least in the eyes of the public, has occurred. Americans want and even need to believe that the common man they elevated to the presidency is a Lincolnesque bearer of infinite wisdom and benevolence. The perceived qualities are confirmed as soon as the candidate takes the oath of office.

The public's relationship with the presidency is more than a search for the fulfillment of childhood notions of the office. For some time empirical and clinical evidence has shown that the office provides, for a large portion of the population, an outlet for expression of deep, often unconscious personality needs and conflicts. Harold Lasswell, as early as 1930 in his classic *Psychopathology and Politics*, argued that private needs become displaced onto public objects and rationalized in terms of general political principles.[61] Greenstein, a student of Lasswell, continually investigated this phenomena in relation to the presidency.[62] He recognizes six major psychological uses of the presidency for the population.

1. The office serves a cognitive aid by providing a vehicle for the public becoming aware of the functions, impact, and politics of government.

2. The presidency provides an outlet for affect, feelings, and emotions. The office serves as a focal point of pride, despair, hope, as well as frustration. It can easily be responsible, in the eyes of the public, for all that is bad or for all that is good.

3. The office serves as a means of vicarious participation. The president becomes an object of identification and consequently presidential efforts become citizen efforts resulting in a sharing of heightened feelings of potency.

4. Especially in times of crisis or uncertainty, the presidency functions as a symbol of national unity. When a president acts, it is the nation acting as one voice expressing one sentiment.

5. Likewise, the office serves as a symbol of stability and predictability. We assume that the president is knowledgeable and in control of events thus minimizing danger or surprise.

6. Finally, the presidency serves as a lightning rod or an object of displacement. The office is the ultimate receptacle for personal, which becomes national, feelings and attitudes. The president becomes either idealized or the ultimate scapegoat. Truman's cliche, The buck stops here, is true—at least in the minds of the public.

## The Symbolic Nature of the Presidency

On each inauguration day history is being made and another chapter of American history is carefully recorded during the next four years. Every detail of presidential behavior is noted and significance is attached. The nation "joyfully" recalls that Millard Fillmore married his school teacher; that James Buchanan never married; that Grover Cleveland was the only president to be married in the White House; that William Taft was the largest president (6 feet, 3 inches and 300 pounds); that John Tyler had 15 children; that John Adams was the first president to live in the White House; that Millard Fillmore had the first bathtub installed in the White House; that Andrew Jackson was the first president to ride a train; that Abraham Lincoln was the first to make a whistlestop campaign tour; that Woodrow Wilson was the first to use radio to speak to the nation; that Franklin Roosevelt was the first to be on television; that Dwight Eisenhower was the first to travel by jet; and that there have been 24 lawyers, four military men, three teachers, three authors, three farmers, a tailor, a haberdasher, and an actor as presidents. Why are such trivia important to American citizens? Because these men are the leaders of the nation. They are chosen to lead and consequently they are a part of us. "America has provided the landscape and has given us the resources and the opportunity for this feat of national self hypnosis." Daniel Boorstin concludes that "each of us individually provides the market and the demand for the illusions which flood our experience."[63] But such illusions make it difficult to distinguish between what is truly significant and what is merely a matter of curiosity. The overlay of myth and magic on the presidency makes assessment of the institution most difficult. "The fatal need for personification of society, animation of ideals, and worship of heroes introduces continuous disorder into the matter-of-fact problems of running a country."[64]

Of all the political myths of the nation, Theodore White argues that the supreme myth is the ability of the citizens to choose the "best" man to lead the nation.[65] From this belief followed the notion that the office would ennoble anyone who holds the office. "The office would burn the dross from his character; his duties would, by their very weight, make him a superior man, fit to sustain the burden of the law, wise and enduring enough to resist the clash of all selfish interests."[66] Thus, the presidency is a combination of symbol and reality. However, the symbolic dimensions of the office are increasingly becoming more important as the role of mass media has become both "maker and breaker" of presidents. As Edelman notes, "the symbolic component is more crucial to the degree that people lack meaningful social commitments that provide a benchmark for evaluation."[67] In fact, the manipulation of salient symbols clouds issues and blurs situations resulting in emotionally charged but nebulously defined symbols.[68]

The presidency as a symbol or image has six characteristics.[69] The presidency is synthetic, believable, passive, vivid, simplified, and ambiguous. As synthetic, the impression of the office is carefully planned, manipulated, and created to serve a specific purpose. Details of leadership become massive strategies. The institution is believable in that it has prescribed meaning, significance, and expectations attached to the symbol. The office is real and manifests criteria for each occupant. Yet, the office is passive in the sense that the symbol is an ideal, a mixture of hope, myth, and fantasy. In being believable, the office as a symbol is vivid and concrete. As the ideal, whatever its composition, it becomes publicly shared; the office is "real" in its significance and consequences. As is the case with every symbol, however, it is more simple than the object it represents. The intricacies and complexities of the job are reduced to a few broad, general characteristics that are more readily identifiable. Symbols, as simplified, are also ambiguous floating between imagination and reality awaiting people to fill in the gaps and thus to attach personal significance to the symbol. Thus, the presidency, as a symbol, aims at suggestion, comprehensiveness, the texture of experience, and passional intelligence.[70]

Perhaps the forefathers were aware of the fact that the most practical method of unifying people was to give them a symbol that all could identify. When the symbol is manifested in a person, the efficacy and effectiveness are greatly enhanced. Clearly the president of the United States is the focal point of the political system. Every action by the president is symbolic because not only is he merely an executive but also a carrier of meaning. What the individual symbolizes to each person or group depends upon the system of interpretation of the person or group. "Political symbols bring out in concentrated form those particular meanings and emotions which the members of a group created and reinforce in each other."[71] Consequently, "from the beginning to the end of his term in office, his every action is a means by which citizens interpret life in the United States."[72]

Just what are the symbols through which the president communicates to the people? The answer: simply everything. To provide a laundry list of specific artifacts, phrases, or actions is not important. There is no way to gauge the intensity and saliency of every action.

For some, whether the president wears a suit or not is important. Even the flag carries many levels of response in the nation. What is more important to understand is what makes various actions of the president symbolic is the cluster of memories and associations inherent in the actions while recognizing that responses differ for different audiences.[73] It is more beneficial, therefore, to speak of the presidency as a highly symbolic office rather than identifying specific actions or isolated symbolic endeavors of a president.

Such a position, however, should not be viewed as attempting to avoid specifically describing the symbolic nature of the presidency. The epitome of identifying the symbolic nature of the presidency is Taft's often quoted description of the president as "the personal embodiment and representative of (the people's) dignity and majesty."[74] Clinton Rossiter reflects that Taft's statement in proclaiming that the president "is the one-man distillation of the American people just as surely as the Queen is of the British people."[75] The office is the symbol of justice, freedom, equality, continuity, and grandeur. The presidency, more specifically, mirrors all that is best about America as perceived by each citizen. In accordance, Cronin notes: "The Presidency is nearly always a mirror of the fundamental forces in society: the values, the myths, the quest for social control and stability, and the vast, inert, conservative forces that maintain the existing balance of interests."[76]

It is a serious mistake, however, to view such a characterization of the presidency as passive. The very potency of the presidency as a symbol gives the office purpose and pragmatic nature. Americans expect presidents to prod, unite, as well as to provide direction and a sense of purpose. As such, the presidency fulfills the parental functions of supreme leader, guide, and teacher. It is important to note, however, that symbolic power is the precondition of pragmatic power. Much legislation and many programs have failed because they were not symbolically acceptable. The key to success, of course, is presidential leadership. Not surprisingly, the most frequent complaint of the presidency since the Vietnam War is the lack of leadership. But leadership, from an interactionist perspective, is more than effective management and the ability to isolate and derive solutions to problems.

Recognizing the symbolic importance and dimensions of leadership is not to support the old notion that one is born a leader or that leadership is simply a matter of charisma. Rather, true leadership is granted by people comprised of their own unique perceptions, needs, and expectations. Klapp distinguishes three levels of leadership ranging from practical doers within social structures to those whose influence is entirely symbolic.[77]

The first level of leadership consists of those who do things without achieving popular images. This level includes such leaders as football coaches, ministers, or corporation presidents. The second level of leadership Klapp calls "dramatic actor." At this level the leader escapes from the limitations within social structures. Impact on an audience is more important than outcomes or results. The final level of leadership Klapp identifies is the "durable symbol" where the leader is institutionalized. "Finding such a niche means that an image has been consolidated and that a symbolic leader has hit upon a permanent function."[78] Any systematic study of leadership reveals how society finds and serves its needs by choosing leaders who best symbolize something that others desire. They are leaders "in the sense that they initiate feelings, orient multitudes, and are used psychologically so that audiences or followings can move to a state of mind, if not a course of action, that would not be possible without the leader's help."[79]

It is in presidential elections, however, that symbolism is increasingly becoming the most powerful and planned component. A campaign attempts to legitimize the candidate's visions and to demonstrate leadership capabilities. During an election, the nation is not a classroom but a theater; not an event but a saga competing for the symbolic centers of America. Novak describes a presidential campaign as

> a contest for the souls, imaginations, and aspirations of Americans as much as for the nation's levers of power. It is also a contest between national self-images. Not infrequently citizens will vote against their self-interest, coldly and economically defined, for the sake of symbols more important to them.[80]

The symbolic significance of campaigns is interwoven with their pragmatic quest for power.[81] One can recall when a single word or phrase may destroy a candidate's chances (Romney's "brainwashed") or give a candidate serious trouble (Carter's "ethnic purity"). An alarming show of personality may damage a campaign as Muskie's tears in New Hampshire, Nixon's rage in 1962, or George Bush's confrontation in the second candidate forum in 1980. Symbolic violations may inhibit electoral success as Stevenson's marital status and Teddy Kennedy's episode at Chappaquiddick. The rich do not always win (i.e., Lindsay, or Connally) and the underdog may just triumph as McCarthy in 1968, McGovern in 1972, and Carter in 1976. Simply stated, the intangibles are many and the realm of the symbolic is important. In electing a president, "we elect the chief symbol-maker of the land, and empower him in the kingdom of our imaginations as well as in the executive office where he supervises armies, budgets, and appointments."[82]

Perhaps the most often used analog in describing the role of the presidency in America is the link to royalty. As Barber argues, "we elect a politician and insist that he also be a King."[83] But kingly treatment of presidents is one source of trouble resulting in isolation of presidents from reality.[84] Yet, the continual respect, awe, and deference given presidents despite recent failures and disappointments are considerable. For Americans, the president both rules and reigns. To think of the presidency as royalty brings unity and simplicity to the image of government. The role of television contributes greatly to the coronation. "Its cameras need a single actor, seek the symbolic event as the desert hart seeks water."[85]

For Novak, Americans not only elect a king, but also a high priest and prophet.[86] Together, the terms speak to the symbolic importance and influence of the office. For the president is king in the sense of being the symbolic and decisive focal point of national power and destiny. The president is prophet in the sense of being the chief interpreter of national self-understanding and defining future endeavors. He is priest in the sense of incarnating the nation's value, aspirations, and expressing these through his behavior.

Thus, to define the presidency as principally a symbolic institution is not to lessen the significance and importance of the office. Rather, it emphasizes the subtle impact of the institution upon every citizen. To describe the president as priest, prophet, and king is to acknowledge the respect, expectations, hopes, and values of the American people. And the interactionist perspective best reveals the public's response to the institution and their effect upon its nature.

## OCCUPANT ASPECTS OF THE SYMBOLIC DIMENSIONS OF THE PRESIDENCY

Generally, most presidential scholars, although using somewhat different terminology, believe that the American people expect three major aspects of presidential behavior. First, the president is expected to be a competent manager of the vast machinery of government. Second, the American people expect the president to take care of their needs by initiating programs, legislation, and safeguarding the economy. Finally, the people want a sense of legitimacy from the president. The office, while providing symbolic affirmation of the nation's values, should faithfully represent the opinions of the public as well.

What type of person should be president of the United States? What qualities should one have for the job? On the surface, these seem to be legitimate questions. Scholars and citizens alike have confronted the issue. Indeed, judgment is required at least every four years. Simple surveys easily produce a laundry list of desired presidential qualities, a very demanding list to be sure. It is much more difficult, however, to isolate the roots of such qualities. Are desired presidential qualities founded in history, myth, and merely perpetuated through textbooks? The implications of the answer to such a question are important.

Rossiter, in his classic work, identified seven qualities "that a man must have or cultivate if he is to be an effective modern President."[87] First, a president must have bounce; "that extra elasticity, given to few men, which makes it possible for him to thrive on the toughest diet of work and responsibility of the world."[88] In addition, the presidency demands affability, political skill, cunning, a sense of history, the newspaper habit ("must be on guard lest he be cut off from harsh reality"), and a sense of humor. Such qualities are indeed needed. However, they would also be an asset for one contemplating pursuing a Ph.D. degree. And certainly presidents of major corporations should probably likewise be so characterized.

Hughes' *The Living Presidency*, also of a "White Knight" orientation, prefers to address the quality that "shapes and makes an effective Presidential style."[89] Such a style includes:

1. A sense of confidence; " . . . with no harm to his leadership so grave as a show of hesitation."
2. A sense of proportion; "the avoidance of excess and extravagance."
3. A sense of drama; " . . . a truly important presidency has never failed to raise the noise and dust of combat."
4. A sense of timing; " . . . sure instinct for pace and rhythm."
5. A sense of constancy; "With no necessary loss of popular trust, he may vary his methods, but he must not appear to vary or to waiver."
6. A sense of humanity; " . . . humility and humor, and toward the people, with warmth and compassion."
7. A sense of perspective; " . . . no saving quality that a president may lose more swiftly upon entering the White House. . . . "
8. And above all, a sense of history.

Such an approach is more profitable. It provides more of a guideline to presidential performance than a list of specific qualities.

Another way to ascertain the qualities a president should have is to confront those who have worked closely with presidents. They not only know the qualities of specific presidents but also know the demands of the job. Many of their assessments, however, are equally as vague and disappointing.

Sherman Adams, a key figure in the Eisenhower administration, believes that the two qualities vital to the success of any president are "intellectual receptivity and the instinct to recognize his own prejudice or bias."[90] Clark Clifford, counselor to Truman, Kennedy, and secretary of defense for Johnson, cites in order of importance the qualities of "character, intellect, decisiveness, political understanding, and awareness of the potential of the office."[91] Theodore Sorensen, a close aide to John Kennedy, believes that the personal qualities of judgment and leadership are the most important.[92] How does one measure the qualities? What are character and leadership? In terms of intellect, one is reminded of a quip by Homes: "For a President can always hire brains. But there is no way for him to lease fortitude or borrow intuition."[93] Yet, how does one *develop* intuition? More importantly, how does one *measure* intuition during a campaign?

Perhaps a better approach in attempting to view the qualities a president should have is to view the characteristics of specific popular presidents and to view specific behaviors the public would oppose. A Gallup poll conducted in 1980 asked respondents, "Of all the Presidents we've ever had, who do you wish were President today?"[94] The results revealed in order of preference: John Kennedy, Franklin Roosevelt, Harry Truman, Dwight Eisenhower, Abraham Lincoln, Gerald Ford, Richard Nixon, Theodore Roosevelt, Jimmy Carter, and Lyndon Johnson. Even these results are suspect. Are Jimmy Carter and Gerald Ford really better presidents than Washington, Jefferson, or Jackson? Did Kennedy really provide more unity, leadership, and legislation than did Franklin Roosevelt or even Lyndon Johnson? Thus, before these results are useful, one must know the specific qualities possessed that caused individuals to be ranked highly. It appears that one simply needed to be a somewhat recent president and a product of some historical myth building.

Most characteristics or job specifications for the presidency can be grouped in three major categories: "the body," "character and temperament," and "brains or intelligence."[95] First, a president must look like a president—mature, tall, healthy, and athletic. The public was often reminded of Ford's golfing and days of playing football; Carter's jogging and fishing; and Reagan's chopping wood and horseback riding. Second, presidents are judged on qualities of integrity, perseverance, compassion, dignity, courage, and mental stability. Finally, a president must display intelligence and common horse sense by providing a vision of the future, solutions to problems, knowledge of detailed facts of situations, and wisdom in judgments.

The general public is rather clear, however, on what they do not want a president to do. A national survey by Gallup found that:

70 percent oppose a president smoking marijuana;
43 percent object to a president telling racial or ethnic jokes;
38 percent object to a president not belonging to a church;
36 percent object to a president occasionally using tranquilizers;
33 percent object to a president using profanity;
30 percent object to a president having seen a psychiatrist;
21 percent object to a president wearing jeans in the oval office;
17 percent object to a president being divorced;
14 percent object to a president having a cocktail.[96]

Although some of the percentages appear to be rather low, scholars generally agree that if as few as 33 percent of the public objects to any practice, a candidate's chances of election are very slim. The survey also revealed that 74 percent *would not* vote for an atheist. Interestingly, only 58 percent thought a divorced individual could be elected, 40 percent a Jew could be elected, 37 percent a black could be elected, and a mere 33 percent a woman could be elected.

What can be surmised from such diverse lists of desired presidential qualities? First, they are largely useless. The qualities may be characterized as admirable, often contradictory, general, abstract, and even biblical. Many do not have a direct relationship to job or task performance. Second, as a result, the question becomes whether the public imposes these qualities on the president or do presidents create the impressions of meeting these qualities. Clearly, the answer is both. As a result of the interaction, when presidents appear to meet the desired qualities, then the qualities become embedded as part of the public's expectations. Finally, the desired qualities often reflect individual senses of goodness, morality, and ideas of right and wrong. Individuals may occasionally drink but be appalled at such behavior from their ministers. Consequently, it is not surprising that the public desires presidents "not to do as the citizens do, but what they say to do." There is no test that presidential candidates take to reveal true intelligence, integrity, a sense of history, etc. They are simply forced to demonstrate through campaigning that they, in fact, are intelligent, honest, knowledgeable, etc. Hence the qualities are in the mind and largely depend upon perception as to their reality.

## The President as Priest, Prophet, and King

The importance of presidents meeting the expectations of the public cannot be overemphasized. Carter was very successful in rising from obscurity in 1976 to president of the United States. As a presidential candidate, Carter was most successful in presenting himself as a common man and a man of the people. James Wooten noted that Carter "worked hard at establishing himself in the eyes of the public as a common man, just another American hired to do a particular job."[97] Carter also effectively articulated the traditional values of an average American citizen. Carter's campaign rhetoric reflected how Americans wanted to conceive of themselves and the myth they wanted to live by as evident in Carter's slogan of "a government as good as its people." A vote for Carter became a vote for us reaffirming our national values and virtues in the wake of Nixon's disgrace.

But an interesting paradox of the American presidency is that once elected we demand uncommon leadership, great insight, and vast knowledge from our presidents. A president must appear presidential as defined by history, culture, and status of the position. Carter was often criticized for his lack of presidential behavior, dress, and demeanor. Carter wore a blue suit for his inaugural rather than a morning coat and top hat; took the oath of office as Jimmy Carter rather than as James Earl Carter; walked down Pennsylvania Avenue rather than ride in a limousine; prohibited the playing of "Hail to the Chief"; sold the presidential yacht *Sequoia*; sent Amy to a public school; carried his own luggage; and wore blue jeans at the White House.

In July 1977, Carter received a 64 percent positive rating on the question of restoring public confidence in government. Just one year later, however, Carter received a 63 percent negative response to the same question.[98] There is evidence to suggest that the public soon resented and rejected Carter's attempts to reduce the perceived stature and dignity of the presidency. Carter, much too late, realized the fact. In his memoirs he writes:

However, in reducing the imperial Presidency, I overreacted at first. We began to receive many complaints that I had gone too far in cutting back the pomp and ceremony, so after a few months I authorized the band to play "Hail to the Chief" on special occasions. I found it to be impressive and enjoyed it.[99]

Simply stated, the presidency is both our administrative office and our ceremonial office. Our president must meet and entertain other kings and rulers of nations. The office, and hence the individual embodies the hopes, desires, dignity, and wealth of our nation.

Ronald Reagan clearly understood the importance of this notion. Early in his presidency, he significantly increased the parties, dinners, and receptions at the White House. After only three years in the White House, Reagan had personally entertained 222,758 guests and hosted 28 state dinners at a cost of more than $500,000 a year.[100]

Treating the presidency as a royal office is a large task and an expensive one. When Reagan visited Jamaica in 1982 for a few days of rest:

1. 100 workers had to lay communication cable and install 50 phones for his use;
2. 3 cargo planes took 3 armored limousines, 4 armored cars, 4 helicopters, 2 fire engines, and *all* the President's food—even his own water to drink;
3. 150 Air Force personnel attended to fix and guard vehicles and equipment, 50 Secret Service, 2 photographers, and Reagan's personal staff of 30—over 300 people at a cost of over $5 million.[101]

Just to visit his home in California for a few days rest required over 200 people to accompany him.

Of course, personal indulgences are indeed part of the office. Everything and virtually anything the president wants is granted. For example, on the fourth space shuttle mission, the shuttle spent two extra hours circling earth so Reagan could sleep in to 9:15 A.M. rather than getting up at the scheduled 7:30 A.M. landing.[102]

The same expectation of treatment is also afforded ex-presidents. In 1958, Congress provided presidential pensions and other perks because of Truman's financial situation. Truman was not a millionaire. He refused to take any job after leaving the presidency because he feared that the employer would trade upon his past contacts and position. Truman spent most of his time answering correspondence, speaking to public groups, and various other activities that were indeed a financial burden. In two weeks of being home he received over 70,000 letters and spent $30,000 from his private bank account to pay for postage and paper. It was clear that former presidents needed assistance.[103]

Today it costs over $12 million a year to pay for the upkeep of former presidents. Maintaining presidential libraries costs an additional $14 million a year. The lifestyle of former presidents is not much less than that of the current president. Note some of the bills we paid for recent former presidents: $2,826 for periodicals a year for Nixon; $500 to open Nixon file cabinets after he lost the keys; $249,000 office expenses in 1983 for Ford; $34,549 phone bill in 1982 for Ford; $12,000 for an Oriental rug for Carter's office; and $292,800 office expenses in 1983 for Carter. Yet, few Americans complain of the cost to maintain the lifestyles of former presidents; "Somehow it just wouldn't be right to treat former leaders of the most powerful nation in the world as common folks." To do so would violate the very majesty and dignity of our national self-pride.

## CONCLUSION

The American presidency is a center of ever-accumulating functions, roles, obligations, and expectations. It is a universe unto itself which is constantly growing and expanding. From a distance one only notices singular "planets." But closer observation reveals a strong interdependence of the planets. As an individual interacts with the constitutionality of the office, roles develop. These roles not only constrain individual behavior but also help create expectations of specified behavior. As expectations grow so does the job. The public's perceptions of the office are institutionalized into models, myths, history, and textbooks. Unrealistic demands and expectations produce reliance upon style over substance; image over issues. A president must appear active, moral, fair, intelligent, common, etc. But appearances are deceiving and paradoxical. For how can one be both active and passive, common and uncommon, impotent and powerful?

Such ambiguity attests to the symbolic nature of the presidency. As an institution the presidency is synthetic, believable, passive, vivid, simplified, and ambiguous. The office is our symbol of justice, freedom, equality, continuity, and national grandeur. The presidency is itself a significant symbol: comprised of many levels and elements. The institution reflects the beliefs, attitudes, and values of the public already established through socialization. All occupants, therefore, must demonstrate that they possess the perceived qualities of the office. Presidential authority is largely a matter of impression management. Presidential elections, as were discussed in Chapter 4, are also largely a contest for symbolic legitimation.

# NOTES

1. James B. Barber, *The Pulse of Politics* (New York: Norton, 1980), p. 4.

2. James Ceaser, et al., "The Rise of the Rhetorical Presidency," in *Essays in Presidential Rhetoric*, ed. Theodore Windt (Dubuque: Kendall/Hunt, 1983), p. 7.

3. Grant McConnell, *The Modern Presidency* (New York: St. Martin's Press, 1976), p. 9.

4. Clinton Rossiter, *The American Presidency* (New York: Mentor Books, 1962), p. 16.

5. Orin Klapp, *Symbolic Leaders* (Chicago: Aldine, 1964), p. 51.

6. Ibid., p. 24.

7. Daniel Boorstin, *The Image* (New York: Atheneum, 1962), p. 45.

8. Ibid., p. 50.

9. Walter Fisher, "Romantic Democracy, Ronald Reagan, and Presidential Heroes," *The Western Journal of Speech Communication* 46 (Summer 1982): 301.

10. Ibid., pp. 299-310.

11. Rossiter, pp. 72-75. See also Charles C. Thack, *The Creation of the Presidency* (Baltimore: The John Hopkins Press, 1969).

12. For a good discussion of the Constitution see Thomas J. Norton, *The Constitution of the United States: Its Sources and Its Application* (New York: Committee for Constitutional Government, 1965).

13. Thomas Cronin, *The State of the Presidency* (Boston: Little, Brown, 1975), pp. 250-56.

14. Bruce Buchanan, *The Presidential Experience* (Englewood Cliffs, N.J.: Prentice-Hall, 1978), p. 29.

15. George Reedy, *The Twilight of the Presidency* (New York: World, 1970), p. 29.

16. Edward S. Corwin, *The President: Office and Powers*, 3rd ed. (New York: New York University Press, 1948), pp. 20-23.

17. Rossiter, *The American Presidency*, pp. 28-37.

18. Myron Hale, "Presidential Influence, Authority, and Power and Economic Policy," in *Toward A Humanistic Science of Politics*, ed. Dalmas Nelson and Richard Sklar (Lanham, Md.: University Press of America, 1983), p. 404.

19. Norton Long, "The Political Act as an Act of Will," ed. Paul Tillett, *The Political Vocation* (New York: Basic Books, 1965), p. 179.

20. Ibid., p. 179.

21. For a good concise discussion of these two dimensions see Fred Greenstein, "What the President Means to Americans: Presidential 'Choice' Between Elections," in *Choosing the President*, ed. James D. Barber (Englewood Cliffs, N.J.: Prentice-Hall, 1974), pp. 121-47.

22. David Haight and Larry Johnston, *The President: Roles and Powers* (Chicago: Rand McNally, 1965), p. 366.

23. Don Faules and Dennis Alexander, *Communication and Social Behavior: A Symbolic Interaction Perspective* (Mass: Addison-Wesley, 1978), p. 67.

24. As stated in ibid., p. 67.

25. Richard Rose, *People in Politics: Observations Across the Atlantic* (New York: Basic Books, 1965), p. 110.

26. Cronin, *The State of the Presidency*, p. 34.

27. Ibid., p. 34.

28. Emmet J. Hughes, *The Living Presidency* (New York: Penguin Books, 1972), p. 26.

29. Rose, *People in Politics*, p. 111.

30. Murray Edelman, *Politics as Symbolic Action* (Chicago: Markham, 1971), p. 55.

31. Ibid., p. 55.

32. Alfred deGrazia, "The Myth of the President," in *The Presidency*, ed. Aaron Wildavsky (Boston: Little, Brown, 1969), p. 50.

33. Ibid., p. 50.

34. Alvin Sanoff, "A Conversation with Theodore H. White," *U.S. News and World Report*, July 5, 1982, p. 59.

35. David Easton, *A Systems Analysis of Political Life* (New York: Wiley, 1965), pp. 273-74.

36. Erick Herzik and Mary Dodson, "The President and Public Expectations: A Research Note," *Presidential Studies Quarterly* 12 (Spring 1982): 172-73.

37. Thomas Cronin, "The Presidency Public Relations Script," in *The Presidency Reappraised*, ed. Rexford Tugwell and Thomas E. Cronin (New York: Praeger Publishers, 1974), p. 168.

38. For a good discussion of political roletaking see Murray Edelman, *The Symbolic Uses of Politics* (Urbana: University of Illinois Press, 1964), pp. 49-51, 188-94.

39. Ibid., p. 188.

40. Rose, *People in Politics*, p. 99.

41. Faules and Alexander, *Communication and Social Behavior*, p. 71.

42. Rose, *People in Politics*, p. 114.

43. For such an orientation to political behavior see Dan Nimmo, *Political Communication and Public Opinion in America* (California: Goodyear, 1978).

44. Kenneth Burke, *Language as Symbolic Action* (Berkeley: University of California Press, 1966), especially pp. 3-24.

45. Nimmo, *Political Communication*, pp. 227-28.

46. Fred Greenstein, "What the President Means to Americans," pp. 121-47 and Fred Greenstein, "Popular Images of the President," in *The Presidency*, ed. Aaron Wildavsky (Boston: Little, Brown, 1969), pp. 287-95.

47. David Easton and Robert Hess, "The Child's Political World," *Midwest Journal of Political Science*, no. 3 (August 1962): 241-42.

48. Greenstein, "What the President Means to Americans," p. 129.

49. Ibid., p. 134.

50. Bruce Campbell, *The American Electorate* (New York: Holt, Rinehart, and Winston, 1979), p. 78.

51. Doris Graber, "Personal Qualities in Presidential Images: The Contribution of the Press," *Midwest Journal of Political Science* 16 (February 1972): 142.

52. Greenstein, "Popular Images of the President," p. 292.

53. Richard Pious, *The American Presidency* (New York: Basic Books, 1979), p. 6.

54. McConnell, *The Modern Presidency*, p. 19.

55. Ibid., p. 21.

56. As quoted in Pious, *The American Presidency*, p. 90.

57. James Wooten, *Dasher: The Roots and Rising of Jimmy Carter* (New York: Warner Books, 1978), p. 35.

58. As quoted in Pious, *The American Presidency*, p. 91.

59. Wooten, *Dasher*, p. 277.

60. McConnell, *The Modern Presidency*, p. 39.

61. Harold Lasswell, *Psychopathology and Politics* (Chicago: University of Chicago Press, 1930).

62. His findings are usually contained in any book on the presidency. In addition, Greenstein has written many articles on the subject expressing six basic psychological uses of the presidency. For rather concise statements see: Greenstein, "Popular Images of the President" and "What the President Means to Americans."

63. Boorstin, *The Image*, p. 3.

64. Alfred deGrazia, "The Myth of the President" in *The Presidency*, ed. Aaron Wildavsky (Boston: Little, Brown, 1969), p. 50.

65. Theodore H. White, *Breach of Faith* (New York: Atheneum, 1975), pp. 323-24.

66. Ibid., p. 324.

67. Murray Edelman, "The Politics of Persuasion," in *Choosing the Presidents*, ed. James D. Barber (Englewood Cliffs, N.J.: Prentice-Hall, 1974), p. 160.

68. Roger Cobb and Charles Elder, "Individual Orientations in the Study of Political Symbolism," *Social Science Quarterly* 53 (June 1972): 87.

69. These characteristics are provided by Boorstin in discussing an "image." The "presidency" as a symbol clearly has the same characteristics. See *The Image*, pp. 185-93.

70. For an outstanding discussion of the distinction between the functioning of signs and symbols in relation to the presidency, see Michael Novak, *Choosing Our King* (New York: Macmillan, 1974), especially pp. 7-10.

71. Edelman, *The Symbolic Uses of Politics*, p. 11.

72. Novak, *Choosing Our King*, p. 8.

73. For a discussion of specific symbols through which a president communicates to the people see ibid., p. 8.

74. This quote by Taft appears in almost every major textbook on the presidency. See Rossiter, *The American Presidency*, p. 16.

75. Ibid., p. 16.

76. Cronin, *The State of the Presidency*, p. 239.

77. Klapp, *Symbolic Leaders*, pp. 52-58.

78. Ibid., p. 58.

79. Ibid., p. 51.

80. Novak, *Choosing Our King*, p. 46.

81. Novak is good at such analysis; see ibid., Part One, pp. 3-56.

82. Ibid., p. 28.

83. James D. Barber, "Man, Mood, and the Presidency," in *The Presidency Reappraised*, ed. Rexford Tugwell and Thomas Cronin (New York: Praeger, 1974), p. 205.

84. See George Reedy, *The Twilight of the Presidency* (New York: World, 1970).

85. Novak, *Choosing Our King*, p. 20.

86. Ibid., especially pp. 3, 50-52.

87. Rossiter, *The American Presidency*, pp. 172-74.

88. Ibid., p. 172.

89. Hughes, *The Living Presidency*, pp. 107-34.

90. As quoted in ibid., p. 312.

91. Ibid., p. 315.

92. Ibid., p. 364.

93. Ibid., p. 278.

94. *Every Four Years: A Study of the Presidency*, Public Broadcasting Service, 1980, p. 5.

95. This discussion is based upon Hedley Donovan, "Job Specs for the Oval Office," *Time*, December 13, 1982, pp. 20-29.

96. *Every Four Years*, p. 11.

97. Wooten, *Dasher*, p. 361.

98. As reported in Victor Lasky, *Jimmy Carter: The Man and The Myth* (New York: Richard Marek, 1979), p. 16.

99. Jimmy Carter, *Keeping Faith* (New York: Bantam Books, 1982), p. 27.

100. As reported in Patricia Avery, "Reagan White House Steps Up Social Pace," *U.S. News and World Report*, January 23, 1984, pp. 52-54.

101. As reported in "Trapped in the Imperial Presidency," *Time*, April 26, 1982, p. 20.

102. As reported in "Protecting Presidential ZZZZ's," *Chicago Tribune*, June 20, 1982, sec. 12, p. 2, col. 2.

103. "Being Ex-President is Lucrative Business," *Chicago Tribune*, April 10, 1983, sec. 16, p. 5.

# 8

# Ghostwriters, the Presidency, and the Bureaucracy

> It is a pity that modern Presidents have abandoned even the pretense of
> handcrafting their public utterances. Except for waiting to be hanged,
> nothing else so concentrates the mind on truly important matters.[1]

Americans probably hold few illusions about a president's utterances. Most know that a high proportion of the executive's rhetoric originates in the minds of subordinates. Nonetheless, the nation readily succumbs to the partial illusion that what a president says is his own. Few journalists even bother to inquire about the writers who assisted in preparing a particular message.

Ghostwriters have long lived in the shadows of public awareness, at least since a Sicilian named Corax received payment to coach awkward orators over 2,000 years ago. Academics such as Plato might later quarrel about the presumptuous ethics of teachers and writers who would help "the weaker look the stronger." But the existence of republican government has always required coaching in the arts of leadership and rhetoric. It comes as no surprise that politics can put good people into rhetorical roles that must be partially learned. Among many other things, electoral politics especially requires the mastery of scripts that others have a hand in preparing. The propriety of using a collaborator is arguably as acceptable as the relationship between mentor and apprentice, legal counsel and client, or expert and layman.

But there is a thin line that cannot be crossed. While the sharing of a political burden is an accepted political folkway, public figures must not seem to relinquish control over what is issued in their name.

Collaboration cannot be capitulation. With the presumption of author-ship comes the burden of responsibility. When rumors were broadcast that John F. Kennedy's Pulitzer Prize-winning book, *Profiles in Courage*, was actually the handiwork of the senator's aide, that boundary had been crossed. Kennedy angrily denied the charge and started pro-ceedings against ABC Television for allowing columnist Drew Pearson to make it. A retraction by the network and the columnist was ob-tained. But Kennedy did not deny Theodore Sorensen's extensive help in gathering part of the book's materials. Sorensen's collaboration was acceptable; his alleged total responsibility was not.[2]

Among the peculiar characteristics of the presidency is that one of its most personal elements—what a president says and professes—is to a significant extent the work of others. Tom Corcoran, Samuel Rosenman, Emmet Hughes, Ted Sorensen, Bill Moyers, William Safire, Ray Price, Robert Hartmann, James Fallows, and David Gergen are not household names. But all had the significant power to shape a president's words. All served at various times as speechwriters and editors. Along with their own staffs and the enormous executive bureaucracies, they worked mightily to give coherence to the pinnacle of power that most Americans associate with government.[3] As a natural adaptation of their trade as writers, and spurred with perhaps a touch of rebellious vanity, such aides often conclude their period of enforced anonymity with articles and books that document the dependencies that exist between a leader and his assistants. Richard Nixon is said to have once introduced William Safire to a friend with the caution, said half in jest, that discreetness around Safire would be wise: "He's a writer."

This chapter has two purposes. Most obviously, it describes how presidential ghostwriters do their work. Greatest attention is paid to three distinctly different types of presidents: John Kennedy, Gerald Ford, and Lyndon Johnson. A second goal is to outline some of the routine ground rules that affect the flow of information between governmental units. Presidential ghostwriting is—to be sure—a very specialized and prized occupation. But perhaps the most valuable lesson its study teaches us is that it is bound by the same kinds of organizational constraints that affect most political institutions. What we note here about how responsibilities and prerogatives are delegated from the top down ultimately says a good deal about how intragov-ernmental communication works at all levels.

We begin with a reminder of just how critical the speech-writing apparatus has become to the presidency.

## MANUFACTURED PROSE: THE SHIFT FROM ELOQUENT TO EFFICIENT SPEECH

A romantic but incomplete view of the presidency is that its historic form—under Washington, Jefferson, the Adamses, Jackson, and especially Lincoln—was heavily dependent on a grandiloquent rhetorical tradition. What an eighteenth- or nineteenth-century president left for future generations was often represented in legislative landmarks clearly documented in related speeches and addresses. Washington's Inaugural and Farewell Address, Jefferson's First Inaugural, Jackson's popular challenges to Calhoun on the issue of nullification, and Lincoln's wartime and emancipation statements have all become part of America's literary political tradition. The sonorities and spaciousness of eighteenth- and nineteenth-century rhetoric vividly recalls the heyday of the orator, but also what seems at first glance to be an old art in advanced decay. Today's political rhetoric appears to draw less excitement from what remains of the crowds. Its very conciseness often renders it incapable of provoking the range of emotions that a Lincoln-Douglas debate running well over two hours could muster in the mid-1800s. Its metaphors and images are more mundane: with language from the conversation rather than the book. Lincoln drew images from Shakespeare and the Bible; President Reagan found models of strength in figures like George Gipp taken from the simpler world of his Hollywood films. "Few species of composition seem so antiquated, so little available for any practical purpose today," notes Richard Weaver, "as the oratory in which the generation of our grandparents delighted."[4]

But if the style of political discourse has changed, and if the less than monumental scope of contemporary address shows more pragmatism than vision, the immediate political consequences of many current presidential statements remain remarkably awesome. Even the self-conscious prose in an address by Richard Nixon could surpass in immediate impact the profoundest efforts of presidents in power before the age of the microphone. Jefferson's Inaugural, for example, was uttered in a barely audible voice before just several hundred members of Congress in the still uncompleted Capitol building.[5] Nixon, in sharp contrast, easily reached over 70 million Americans via what he called "the big stick" of television in a 1969 address cautioning against a hasty Vietnam "retreat."[6]

The potential for rhetorically improving the climate of opinion has never been greater. With the evolution in the 1920s of mass radio audiences for a single speech, presidential utterance was rendered cautious and tactical rather than spacious and all-encompassing. Franklin Roosevelt addressed the rough equivalent of all of Jefferson's presidential audiences in one 15-minute "fireside chat." Changed most dramatically by radio, oratory that previously had to be suited to only the immediate presidential audience on hand (and a smaller secondary audience of newspaper readers) suddenly had to suit a nation of diverse constituents held together by the invisible thread of a radio network. The temptation to use this medium and to widen the appeal of key speeches made the speechwriter an attractive addition to the White House staff. By allowing a writer to undertake what had been for Woodrow Wilson and Theodore Roosevelt an immensely time-consuming task of speech drafting or dictation, a president not only saved time, but gained the confidence of knowing that someone was available to flag a bad remark.

Broadcasting an address to the farthest concerns of the nation meant that political rhetoric had arrived to a new and wider audience than ever before. Its hearers needed neither literacy nor self-discipline to wade through the fine print of the published speech. The risks of an unintended slur were increased, and meant that others would now intervene in what had been to most presidents the least delegatable tasks. As a public document having the widest possible distribution, it was thought a speech could no longer risk the candor expected by a gathering of limited size. Presidents after Theodore Roosevelt were largely unwilling to jeopardize their careers with their own memories, and especially their possible miscalculations of the public mood. Too much was now at stake.

## GROWTH OF THE WHITE HOUSE STAFF

The enormous growth of the immediate White House staff has been well documented. Under Abraham Lincoln, for instance, there were only two close aides, both young and extremely effective. John Hay would later befriend Theodore Roosevelt, and serve for a time as his secretary of state. The other, John Nicolay, became almost an alter ego to Lincoln through the long war years when the White House and the telegraph office in the War Department were scenes of endless presidential vigils.[7] Over a hundred years later the staff under Jimmy Carter had grown to 600 people, pigeonholed into a complex array of titles and job responsibilities.[8]

A president's aides and counselors may be delegated many shifting duties which fit his patterns of work. Generally, however, they fall into five more or less discrete areas. Some are given responsibility to coordinate White House activities with leaders and members of the Congress. Others—often trained as lawyers—serve as domestic aides, preparing and organizing legislative and policy positions on matters as wide ranging as reclamation policy, to the drafting of counterproposals to the opposing party's legislative plans on Capitol Hill. Some are economists, particularly responsible for coordinating the Council of Economic Advisers and the increasingly powerful Office of Management and Budget. And still others are charged with formulating administrative positions on national security and foreign relations. Among the most influential are those who collectively work as administrative aides. None have been more immortalized than the Nixon administration's supporting cast of villains, H. R. Haldeman and John Ehrlichman. They and others before them shaped the political and administrative organizations of the White House. And, finally, the public relations staff—including press aides, writers, mail answerers, speechwriters, and others—make up the remainder of what is the first line in the sprawling executive bureaucracy that blankets Washington.

Under recent Republican administrations this area has been especially large and stratified. Beyond handling the usual duties of preparing press releases, proclamations, speeches, letters, and "White House messages" (statements written under the president's name but presented in written rather than oral form), influential political lieutenants such as Clay Whitehead under Nixon and David Gergen under Reagan coordinated a separate staff concerned with overall "White House communications policy." In the Nixon years presidential attitudes were expressed on everything from the proper role of public television to long-term policy planning for cable television, much to the consternation of the four national television networks. As the primary conduits of information about Vietnam and Watergate, they were sensitive to the use of potential television regulatory reprisals for what they saw as honest reporting of the Nixon administration. The Reagan White House, at least initially, used this Office of Communications to organize strategies and speakers to combat the Democratic congressional leadership in order to push through budget and tax reduction programs.

But the heart of presidential public relations remains centered not on policy planning, but on the skills of the press and speech staffs. The Ford speech group, for example, was divided into two crews: one for oral remarks, and the other for written messages and research. The writers of major messages were often Robert Hartmann, Robert Orben, and Milton A. Friedman, with help also coming from major agency heads such as Secretary of State Kissinger and Treasury Secretary William Simon. Messages of lesser import were drafted by what Hartman described as "a new editorial team of fresh, enthusiastic, facile writers, including this representative cross section of second-level staffers:

> Pat Butler, a Georgia preacher's son, fluent, fast, ambitious, always eyeing the main chance; David Boorstin, our intellectual would-be playwright, sone of the Librarian of Congress; George Denison, a calm, mellow *Reader's Digest* alumnus; John Mihalec, from a congressional staff, intense, intrigued by politics; and Craig Smith, a bearded University of Virginia speech professor who filled in during the summer trying to disprove that "those who can't, teach."[9]

There was also a separate staff for written messages and research, which rounded out the 41 spots allocated to the writing area.

The size of the total White House staff increased most notably under Republican presidents, reaching unprecedented numbers under Eisenhower in 1959 with 275 employees, and Richard Nixon in 1973 with 510 (a jump of 318 over the Johnson administration).[10] The reasons for the increase under Nixon were probably administratively based. The greatest power during his tenure was reserved for himself and key aides such as Kissinger, George Schultz, Dwight Chapin, and H. R. Haldeman. Cabinet members—even powerful personalities like John Mitchell and John Connally—were kept at arm's length and often circumvented by the use of a strong network of allies, such as Bryce Harlow, with back channels directly to the White House. Even though Nixon had served under Eisenhower for eight years, he adopted a totally different pattern of tight undelegated control. In marked contrast to his mentor, the solitary Californian and only a few lieutenants kept the major decisions for themselves.

The growth in the number of special assistants and aides concerned with public relations and speech-writing tasks—what Thomas Cronin considers "one of the more disquieting aspects of the recent enlargement of the presidential establishment"[11]—has been equally dramatic. The first speechwriter to assist a president is usually thought to have been Judson Welliver. He joined the Harding administration with that designated role in 1920.[12] By any standard Harding needed all the help he could get to defend what became an increasingly troubled and corrupt administration after the Teapot Dome and Justice Department scandals in 1923. Actually, Chester Arthur employed a friend named Daniel Rollins earlier in the 1880s to help draft a number of presidential messages clandestinely from New York. Perhaps, because ghostwriting would have been an unthinkable sharing of the load for a president at the end of the nineteenth century, Rollins went to great pains to keep his help to the ailing Arthur a total secret.[13]

To a large extent speechwriters were to remain a rarity in the White House until the administration of Calvin Coolidge began in 1923. Prior to Coolidge, the White House worked at the president's rather than the office's pace. Theodore Roosevelt not only answered the phone on occasion, but relished the chance to write and deliver speeches on as broad a range of topics as a president has ever claimed to conquer. War, physical fitness, politics, conservation, human rights, corporate control, and natural history were frequent topics heard from his "bully pulpit." For Woodrow Wilson, who followed William Howard Taft in 1912, the importance of speeches remained. Trained by a Scots-Presbyterian minister who placed the highest importance on his son's oratory, Wilson spent hours perfecting what still remains as some of the most thoughtful and coherent of all presidential rhetoric.

Calvin Coolidge managed to vastly increase the number of presidential speeches through the continued aid of Judson Welliver and others, thereby establishing both an important precedent and a harmful liability for an emerging publicity-conscious executive branch. The precedent was that the enlarged staff became a known fixture to the public, and perceptions of the office changed accordingly. It became commonplace to think of presidents in the modern sense: as leaders whose fate was determined by the quality of their staffs, as well as by their own efforts. The liability was that rarely again would the executive's words reflect the undiluted visions and attitudes of just one person. The impact of these changes did not go unnoticed for long. "It is a misfortune," wrote an observer of the Coolidge administration, "that as President he had permitted so many of his formal addresses to be written for him by members of his staff. These have made him seem prolix, jejune, and ordinary to a degree."[14]

"Silent Cal" had managed to double the number of addresses over his eloquent predecessor, but at a heavy cost. No longer would presidents be content to write their own speeches, offer them for review and comment to close friends and advisers, and then deliver them. The emerging pattern was to be a reversal of that process for all except the most important speeches. Others would write early drafts, with varying degrees of presidential guidance, and the editing would be done by the president.

The basic pattern remains today. Though presidents occasionally write sections of important speeches, such as convention acceptance addresses, inaugurals, and portions of state of the union addresses, they now more usually function as final editors of drafts written elsewhere in the bowels of the White House. The highest praise that one usually hears from aides working with a president is not that he is a good co-writer, but a good editor. His ability to quickly rework an aide's manuscript so that it represents an authentic copy of his own prose "signature"—what is characteristic of him in terms of idiom, ideas, and style—tests his editorial skill. The result is the synthetic duplication of a rhetorical style that offers an approximation of what a president would produce, could he have spent the necessary time.

As will become apparent, the demands placed on writers charged with shaping this rhetorical legacy creates a number of opportunities and dangers.

## HOW SPEECHES ARE ASSIGNED

A president looks to a writer not just for nice slogans. A ghostwritten speech must be faithful to the personal history, legislative record, and political philosophy of the speaker. The major flaws and skeletons-in-the-closet of a candidate or an incumbent must be known. An address must show deference to the speaker's carefully constructed public persona, the image that is more familiar to constituents than the favored ideas for reform or change. John Kennedy might be heard quoting Plato or Camus; but it would be an awkward violation of role-type to give those same words to Lyndon Johnson or Gerald Ford. The response the ghostwriter seeks is the speaker's recognition of the tone and feeling of a message as his own. In many ways this fact makes the first submission of a speech draft to the president *the* critical test of a speech. Later, reactions of the audience for whom it was written are a second and not so ominous obstacle. The trick is to strike the right chords in a president that will resonate with his sympathy, understanding, and essential agreement.

Robert Hartmann, for example, had been a member of Vice-President Ford's staff long enough to recognize the essential closeness of Ford to his family, and particularly to his wife Betty. When the former congressman was thrust into the presidency by Nixon's resignation, Hartmann was able to draft the first critical speech with an empathy that assured his position with the new executive. Ford recalled his reactions to a draft calling for a "healing" of the national wound of Watergate: "As I read his draft, tears came to my eyes. 'I am indebted to no man,' he had written, 'and only one woman, my dear wife.' Hartmann understood my feelings perfectly."[15]

Key writers of important speeches usually have had a comparatively long association with the president, often in many capacities other than as speechwriter. Hartmann was a one-time (and unsuccessful) staff coordinator for Ford. As Ford tells it, disorder tended to be the more frequent result.[16] Moyers was a personal assistant, press secretary, and general sounding board to Johnson. Sorensen was one of Senator Kennedy's legislative assistants.

When pondering a major speech, a president will typically seek out whoever has been a reliable writer among his closest aides. Frequently these people have been with him for years. For Franklin Roosevelt it was Judge Samuel Rosenman, an old friend and former member of the New York Supreme Court. For Kennedy the call was inevitably to Sorensen, Schlesinger, or Goodwin. Eisenhower used Hughes and the politically astute Bryce Harlow, but Sherman Adams more regularly assigned first drafts to one of any number of subordinates. In time these men became de facto managers of speech-writing assignments, sometimes initiating first drafts themselves, but often serving as a final editor in what has become an elaborate process of bureaucratic and in-house review of any message.

The White House under every president functions differently. And no less can be said of the speech-writing staffs. Some administrations —such as those guided by Eisenhower, Nixon, and Carter—made a greater show of organizational and management technique. But even the clearest charting of lines of responsibility obscures the way the process of speech preparation actually works. In every recent case it has existed outside of the neat organizational divisions that characterize other related areas, such as the White House Press Office and the Congressional Relations staff. This is because senior writers are usually also counselors to the president on domestic, foreign, or political affairs. They are intended to be floaters, available for a wide range of jobs of limited duration. Also, writers as a group have been concealed from the casual journalist under titles that are nondescript, such as special assistant or counselor. This has been due in part to a certain amount of presidential ego. Johnson reminded one new recruit who devoted nearly all of his time to speeches that "A speech writer is supposed to stay in the background. If somebody asks you about a speech, just say 'I don't know anything about that.' "[17] The limbo a speech writer is in reflects the hazy division between speechwriting as an activity, and a number of sometimes unrelated tasks, such as advancing presidential visits (i.e., making police, hotel, and political arrangements). High-level aides may advise on policy, plan staff reorganizations, negotiate in behalf of the president to members of Congress, and serve as a political adviser in addition to drafting speeches. Bill Moyers and Ted Sorensen clearly had such diverse responsibilities, and the ulcers to go with them.

Reflecting the inevitable tie between policy and the way it is articulated, an organizational chart misses the fact that key policy makers are also often on hand to subvert or intercept major addresses. What better method is available to ensure that a good intention is translated into a firm commitment than to write the script of that commitment in behalf of the president? As a matter of routine, new policy initiatives in foreign or domestic affairs usually are in a sense sponsored by a cabinet or presidential staff person with a deep interest or ideological investment in its success. Secretaries Rusk and McNamara, and especially Clark Clifford and Walt Rostow, regularly guarded their cherished access to Lyndon Johnson in order to shape his Vietnam War statements made on national television.[18] Under Eisenhower, Secretary of State Dulles often submitted entire drafts of speeches prepared at the State Department for presidential use. Dulles hoped he could keep the president's internationalist tendencies in check by providing virulent anti-Communist speeches.

State of the union messages customarily include the advice and solicited inserts of cabinet secretaries representing state, agriculture, what is now health and human services, and other key agencies. For instance, in preparation for his 1967 State of the Union Address, Lyndon Johnson asked Health, Education and Welfare Secretary John Gardner for suggestions during a visit to the L. B. J. ranch. After returning to Washington, Gardner cabled back a general list of suggestions on the tone the message should take. It read, in part, as a kind of recipe for a conventional message of uplift:

> Emphasis on forward movement. The American people always respond to a strong and convincing "Let's move forward!" We don't respond very well to cautious or prudent leadership. That's something Eisenhower never understood. We're not afraid of sacrifice or hardship, but we hate inaction. We need a clear call to act, to pull together, to be true to the best that's in us. We need to believe that this is a time when forward movement is called for, when we can and should put our backs into the struggle, when the future is opening out.
>
> I believe the positive note can be struck despite Vietnam, budget problems, etc.[19]

Since Coolidge speechwriting has rarely been the exclusive province of any one group or individual. The stakes are too large. A president may give as few as 10 or 15 major addresses in one year. To see a personal wish translated into a presidential utterance—with the reflected glory of a film clip on the networks' evening news, or the key passage in the *New York Times*' Quotation of the Day—is enough to make writing for the president a cherished and competitive prerogative.[20]

Lesser speeches usually involve one or two subordinate speech writers serving nominally under a senior aide and writer, or a special assistant assigned to oversee the president's political calendar. If a minor message directly involves a shift or new development in policy, a first draft or an outline of "talking points" is usually requested from the agency responsible for the particular area. Otherwise the speech is given to one of the 10 or so writers who also work on press releases, important mail, reports, and the like. The assignment will usually come with advice on who to contact for background information. See, for instance, Figure 8.1. Only on rare occasions will a president be involved before several drafts have been refined and edited by senior writers. Normally he is given a final draft from a few days to—in Eisenhower's case—two weeks before it is to be delivered. It may be entirely rejected, sending the staff into frantic high gear to produce something new in a short period of time. More commonly, it is edited by the president, sometimes with the order to clean up or alter one or two passages. Few modern presidents (except Ford) have purposely followed Roosevelt's occasional practice of permitting two teams of speechwriters to come up with competing drafts for approval. That can be understandably trying on the morale of those laboring in front of the typewriter. What is somewhat more common is a pattern whereby a formal speech is generated from within the normal White House channels, while at the same time an unsolicited manuscript from a close aide or friend is sent to the president. For instance, John Kennedy received several unsolicited inaugural speech drafts from friends, newsmen, and complete strangers.[21] These speeches are usually not radical counterproposals. Johnson, for example, probably never saw drafts of Vietnam speeches sharply at odds with official policy. Instead, alternate drafts usually carry a slightly different emphasis in one area or another which reflects the sender's attempts to neutralize certain biases in the original writer. In the Nixon White House each of the three top-level writers earned a more or less accurate caricature reflecting what key staff members perceived as their strengths and

October 12, 1962

Dear Kenny:

If the President wants a few sentences that

would be helpful to me, here are some

brief suggestions.

I hope you are along when he comes to

Connecticut.

Best personal regards.

Sincerely,

*Abe*

The Honorable Kenneth O'Donnell
The White House
Washington, D. C.

**Figure 8.1** Suggestions from a Senator to the president for "helpful" remarks during the 1962 campaign.

*Note*: Some of the suggestions were included in the president's written remarks given in Connecticut, but the president at the last moment ad-libbed his comments, and thus deleted the suggestions.

*Source*: John F. Kennedy Library, Boston.

This year the medicare bill was defeated in the United States Senate. One vote would have made the difference. Abe Ribicoff's vote can be that one vote needed to pass this bill.

It is vitally important that Abe Ribicoff be in the Senate of the United States when the medicare bill comes up next year. No man in this country knows more about this great problem than he does. No man is in a better position to supply leadership within the Congress. If we are to pass the medicare bill next year, we will need Abe Ribicoff in the United States Senate to be in the forefront of this fight.

\* \* \* \* \* \* \* \* \* \*

Abe Ribicoff was a source of great strength in my Cabinet. He served with distinction as Secretary of Health, Education and Welfare. I was proud to appoint him, and I would have been proud to appoint him to any position he wanted. But Abe Ribicoff came to me some months ago and told me that he wanted to relinquish his appointed position and seek election to the United States Senate. He told me in the privacy of my office that the type of public service he felt was most useful was elective office and that he wanted to serve in the Senate as long as the people of this state would support him. I respected his decision, and I respect and admire the man for making this decision.

Abe Ribicoff knows Washington. Abe Ribicoff knows Connecticut. His experience as Congressman, Governor and Cabinet officer will enable him to be an outstanding senator for this state. And his sound judgment and independent thinking will be a great asset to the people of Connecticut and the entire nation.

Figure 8.1 (cont.)

weak points. If a speech was to offer heavy doses of compassion, the liberal Ray Price was said to offer the most philosophical and least partisan of prose. Patrick Buchanan, in contrast, could carve up liberals with a sabre of righteous right-wing indignation, as was clearly evident in some of the well-publicized attacks on the press in 1969 which he wrote for Spiro Agnew. Safire, it was thought, could take almost any idea and make it memorable and at least superficially eloquent through the judicious use of alliteration and repetition.[22]

But there is little evidence to suggest that a writer chosen for a routine speech is selected because of his expertise or natural affinity for a topic. The mundane dynamics of office work, such as the pragmatic problem of finding someone free to take on the three or four days it may take to draft a speech, seem to be more important. If writers have completed one task they are given another. What emerges from various memoirs and accounts is that anybody from as many as five or six writers could usually be assigned to produce a first draft. The speech-writing task becomes critical in the editing phase, where an early draft may serve as a vehicle for determining the direction that a major rewrite should take.

There is also little support for what would seem to be the natural conclusion that a president at least oversees the assigning and outlining of a speech in its early development. The memoirs of most presidents contribute to this false impression. They frequently speak of "the need for a speech" to the National Association of Broadcasters, the V.F.W., the National Press Club, or thousands of other potential groups. There is often talk of a decision to address such groups to urge their support. But the implication that the president initiates where he will speak and what he will say is partially illusory. In fact the decision to give a speech—and the secondary step of assigning a specific writer—may well fall to one of several of the president's chief political advisers. With so many preoccupations available to a president, he may follow the lead of Eisenhower, Johnson, Carter, and Reagan in delegating the entire evolutionary process to subordinates. What is left to the president by choice is usually the reserving of two essential prerogatives: one is to decide whether or not to speak at a preselected occasion, and the other is to rework a refined draft of a message so that the final ideas and style are characteristic of the president's self-image.

Sherman Adams cites what seems to be a more or less routine chain of events preceding a 1953 address by Eisenhower to the Future Farmers of America in Kansas City:

The invitation came to the White House through Ezra Taft Benson, whose policies even in that first year of the Administration were already under fire. . . . Leonard Hall, then the Republican National Chairman, came in to ask me to help him. "Can't we get the President out there to make a speech?" Hall said to me. "They'll listen to him but they are getting down on Benson." I told Hall that I would see what I could do, and immediately summoned the indispensable [Gabriel] Hauge and a few experts from the department of Agriculture to see if we could work out a plan for a speech. In this instance we agreed to steer clear of any partisan approach and work on a world peace theme stressing the contribution of the American farmer. A few days later we met again to study the first draft of the writing and decided that the slant was right but it needed better brushwork and stronger treatment. So it was agreed that I would call a farm expert in Des Moines and ask him to come and help.

In preparations like this, Eisenhower would not know about the plans in progress. Instead, until an acceptable working draft had been prepared and tentative plans drawn up by myself and the staff, he would not want to know. . . . The preparation usually meant days, sometimes weeks, of staff work. . . . Then Hall and I, probably with [Jerry] Parsons and Hauge, would tell Tom Stephens that we wanted fifteen uninterrupted minutes with the President.

A few days later, the President would call Hauge or myself into his office. The speech would be on his desk. "This moves along pretty well," he would say, handing back the draft, "but it seems to labor too much in trying to meet a lot of picayune criticism. . . . " That would mean more hours of brain-racking and writing by Hauge. Finally Eisenhower would sit down at his desk alone, marking up the revised draft himself.[23]

Eisenhower was willing to delegate most of the writing chores to others. His time and patience for the task were limited. With a combination of genuine interest and a certain amount of facesaving self-respect, like probably every other modern president, he would go through the ritual of editing and rewriting speeches.

Lyndon Johnson had always relished the opportunity if not the specific task of speaking to a large audience. He treated it as one of his most solemn public duties. But he also came to the realization that the presidency would place heavy limitations on his freedom to fashion his own rhetoric. In his long, successful congressional career the former Senate majority leader had been a nonstop ad-libber, a politician who genuinely enjoyed the euphonious "corn" so much a part of speeches given from the steps of the local Johnson City courthouse. He remembered trips with his father through wide-streeted central Texas towns, where the long-winded but animated "speak'n" would fill the air at the late fall political rallies.[24] His ascendency to the presidency took some of the pleasure out of this part of his political life, perhaps because his audiences had grown too large and too diverse to be stroked by the rich hill-country idioms that he loved to use. Ad libs became more risky, for the leader of the Western world. Speaking to an audience offered rewards diminished by the burden of defending the failing attempts to prop up South Vietnam after 1966.

In recalling a happier cause, Johnson briefly sketched the evolution of his perfectly timed March 15, 1965 address to Congress on civil rights, which led the way for the Voting Rights Act four months later:

> I assembled some of my key staff men to help prepare the message. A Presidential speech is rarely a private product. The pressures of the office do not afford the luxury of such personal handicraft. But this time, as much as humanly possible, I wanted to reach the American people in my own words.
>
> I sat with my staff for several hours. I described the general outline of what I wanted to say. I wanted to use every ounce of moral persuasion the Presidency held. . . . And I wanted to talk from my own heart, from my own experience. Between midnight and dawn these loose thoughts were translated into sentences for the first draft of the speech. I received that draft shortly after awakening. I penciled in changes and rewrote sections. The draft went back to the speechwriters. Several hours later a new draft came back. I made additional changes. And so it went, back and forth, right up to the final moments.[25]

In this instance the writers were subordinates to the will of a president sitting in on the crucial formative stages of a nationally televised key address. The extent of the president's intervention was immediately evident to those who heard the personal allusions that no writer could "ghost" for someone else.

For lesser occasions Johnson depended on the first drafts coming from the scribes, no doubt a challenging obligation to those writers put in the position of charting a path of ideas that virtually included a wilderness of other possible alternatives. "What he was doing, of course," recalls one of his writers, "was reposing great trust, great responsibility, and ultimately great confidence in the individuals he deputized to act as his alter ego in the middle stages of the speech process."[26]

An even less interventionist pattern of speech development is recalled by a writer for Gerald Ford in the middle of 1976. Ford, it seemed, had infinite faith in a routine of speech clearance that involved very little of his personal time. A recognizable sequence was observed:

> 1. The President and his advisor decided that he would speak on a given occasion. 2. One of the five speechwriters working under Presidential counselor Robert Hartmann was assigned the task of producing a draft. He was given background information, and an assessment by the "advance team." 3. The draft was examined for errors by an editor, Robert Orben, and the research staff. 4. The speech was "staffed." That is, appropriate members of the administration studied the draft to see whether it was consistent with White House policy. 5. The speech was then returned to the original writer for correction. 6. Next, a final draft was typed for the President on large cards in large script. 7. The President then rehearsed the speech, meeting with the writer to suggest changes. 8. The speech was delivered. 9. Finally, at an "evaluation session" press review of the speech, along with staff comments, were [sic] taken into consideration.[27]

One can only estimate the ease with which individual presidents could delegate authority for the construction of their most public moments: Eisenhower, with relief perhaps that the details had passed to a clearly designated lieutenant; Kennedy, holding the prerogatives of the podium to himself by using his cool sense of style and ability to ad-lib as a way to make immediate detours around carelessly written paragraphs; and Johnson, alternately using and ignoring his large but disorganized corps of writers in a vain attempt to find the pied piper's illusive tune of obedience. Each in slightly different ways was forced by the circumstances of incumbency to a higher degree of dependence on others.

Organizationally, this continuing dependence on writers produces the somewhat surprising observation that a president is usually at the end, not the beginning, of the whole speech-preparation process. As Figure 8.2 indicates, for all but a few special occasions, a president's self-chosen role is to revise or edit someone else's drafts. If he wishes, he may choose to do a first draft himself, as Theodore Roosevelt and Woodrow Wilson would do. Or an aide can be brought in for a joint attempt at a first draft, which Johnson attempted on some occasions. Usually one of the president's chief political aides will make suggestions to a senior speechwriter based on anticipated travel plans. And then a more or less circular pattern develops. A senior writer assigns a first draft to a staff writer (most likely without anything more concrete than a general sense of what would be "right" for the setting and audience). The first draft is usually reviewed by several top aides, improved in a rewritten draft, and then submitted to the president and perhaps some cabinet officers and aides. The sequence depends to some extent on how willing a president is to contribute to a final polishing of a draft. Typically he is the recipient of what amounts to an ad hoc committee's combined efforts at producing the highest of public documents: a memorable presidential speech.

But for major addresses the pattern is generally reversed. The president and a senior writer are often at the center of preparations, as was the case with Johnson's civil rights address.

The size of the group that may be involved in even the early stages of routine addresses can be sensed from Figure 8.3, a memo from Johnson's one-time speech coordinator and former president of NBC, Robert Kintner, to Marvin Watson. It shows the initial assignments of four speeches for a 1968 trip to the Midwest. Each of the listed stops includes a location, a theme, the writers responsible for development of a draft, and the intended length of the speech. Figure 8.4 is a clearance form for such routine speeches.

1. *Assignment*

   (After tentative decision
   to give an address, a
   senior speechwriter
   assigns speech and alerts
   relevant agencies.)

2. *Writing*

   (Research from within
   White House, and/or
   agency submits draft.)

   (Junior-level writer
   prepares 1st and 2nd
   drafts.)

C
L
E
A
R
A
N
C
E

5. *The President*

   ("Staffed" draft goes to
   president for approval,
   editing, or suggestions
   for a new draft.)

4. *Inner-Circle Editing*

   (Senior political
   aides edit speech.)

3. *Cabinet-Level Depts.*

   (Departments "clear"
   or "staff" speech for
   consistency, accuracy,
   timing, etc.)

**Figure 8.2**  Preparation Stages for Routine Speeches
*Source*: Compiled by authors.

MEMORANDUM

# THE WHITE HOUSE

WASHINGTON

July 19, 1966
10:55 a.m. Tuesday

PERSONAL AND CONFIDENTIAL

MEMORANDUM FOR MARVIN WATSON

SUBJECT:        Possible Presidential Trip

I held a meeting this morning attended by Messrs. Rostow,
Hardesty, Sparks, and Jim Moyers. I also talked with Bill
Moyers and Harry McPherson. Perhaps you might like to
indicate to the President the themes that are being developed
(they will be ready in all cases but McPherson by noon
Thursday) on the possible speeches:

1.      AMVETS - theme of how the U.S. military organization
        is meshed with civilian government to obtain Presidential
        objectives.

        Rostow-Hardesty-Sparks                6 minutes

2.      Fort Campbell - a continuation of the same thing, with
        stress on contributions of the units in Vietnam and around
        the world with special emphasis on the 101st Airborne.

        Rostow-Hardesty-Sparks                15 minutes

3.      Vincennes - This would be one of two talks on the responsi-
        bility of American citizens - this one in connection with civil
        rights, civil disorders, etc. which seem to be what Harry
        McPherson wants to write about.              20 minutes

4.      Indianapolis -   the theme of responsibility of citizens,
        business, and labor and the consumer would be continued -
        with discussion of the domestic economy, individual prosperity,
        necessities for restraint, and our objectives throughout the
        world.
        James Moyers    -
        Hardesty-Sparks - with background to be supplied by Fowler,
        Ackley, Califano without disclosure of the occasion.

                                    20 minutes

---

**Figure 8.3** Memo making staff assignments for future speeches for Lyndon
Johnson, July 1966.
        *Source*: Lyndon Baines Johnson Library, Austin, Texas.

2.

Both the Vincennes and Indianapolis speeches would tie
in the Vietnam operation and foreign aid policy as part
of the responsibility theme.

Robert E. Kintner

CC: Bill Moyers

**Figure 8.3 (cont.)**

REMARKS/~~STATEMENT~~ BY THE PRESIDENT

EVENT: Fund-Raising Dinner in Chicago, Ill.

DATE: May 17, 1966

PLACE:

WRITTEN BY: Sparks/Hardesty - 5/16/66

DRAFT NUMBER & TIME: 1st - 11:30 PM

Edit/Re-write:

Bob Kintner okay? _REK - 5/16/66._

WORDS: 1679

FOR THE PRESIDENT:

APPROVE:

DISAPPROVE:

**Figure 8.4** Standardized clearance form for speeches given by Lyndon Johnson.
*Source*: Lyndon Baines Johnson Library, Austin, Texas.

## MULTIPLE DRAFTS AND THE PROBLEM OF CLEARANCE

In many ways the life of an American chief executive has been made more difficult since the advent of the Xerox machine. Twenty years ago the number of people who could receive a draft copy of a proposed speech was limited by the good will of the secretary facing the tedious task of retyping copies, and the finite pieces of carbon paper a typewriter would ingest. As few as two copies of any one presidential speech draft were produced in the Lincoln, Taft, or Theodore Roosevelt years. But today the copier makes it possible to virtually publish a draft copy of a speech by making hundreds of offspring. Circulating them to any or all of the mandarins on the White House staff can be achieved with the least amount of effort. In the past, when a president wrote his own drafts he was perhaps less compelled to permit the speech to circulate. But with delegated speechwriting a fact of life, widespread editing of a speech is at least a guarantee to a busy president that a foolish mistake by a politically insensitive writer will be caught.

In practical terms this has meant that in White House operations which tend to feature many "kitchen cabinet" aides who have routine access to the president, there is likely to be an enormous amount of "gatekeeping" and editing that can ultimately dilute rather than enhance a speech. As a type, state of the union messages have been especially prone to the advice of too many cooks who want to have their name on the menu. Gerald Ford recalled, for example, that the delivery of his message in 1976 was preceded by the chaos of two teams (a total of ten people) working on two different messages. A key aide, Dick Cheney, had disliked a first draft prepared by Robert Hartmann and his staff. When a round-table discussion among all the participants predictably failed to produce a final compromise, Ford recalls a rare loss of temper: " 'Damn it,' I said, slamming down my hand on the table, 'we've got to stop bickering over these details. I want a final draft by noon tomorrow.' "[28] It was the second time in as many years that Ford had faced a deadline for the annual message with two teams working independently. Ford's habit of making redundant assignments regularly created this awkward arrangement.

Those working for Johnson also remember occasions when it seemed as if no one was in charge. Interviewed just after he had helped the president draft his 1969 State of the Union Message, the normally durable Harry McPherson recalled that its preparation was a total fiasco:

Every state of the union speech has been a trauma for President Johnson. He gets into an incredible mood, horrible mood, and things start flying out. Other people get brought in, everybody but the cook gets brought in to make it more personal or human or whatever. I gave up in the last two days. I just couldn't bear it anymore. I fought some a little the last couple of days, but not as much, as things were further added to it.[29]

Of the previous attempts in 1968 McPherson lamented that "it had been sent to God knows how many people."[30]

Under similar pressures Hartmann likewise mourned "the curse of universal literacy" that led nearly every person in the White House to the conclusion that they were "Shakespeare, or at least a Bacon."[31]

It is tempting to dismiss such complaints from disgruntled speechwriters. After all, it is a natural vanity to have a president use what one has agonizingly prepared, especially in a city that gives its highest prestige to those who are able to husband the prerogatives of power. Presidential speechwriters are the proudest when pointing out their contributions to the public record of an administration. It is not uncommon to find two or more writers claiming to have written the same remarks. Shared responsibility for a message produces other problems as well. One of the most apparent has been documented in a more general sense by Soloman Asch,[32] and by Irving Janis as the "groupthink" phenomenon.[33] Laymen might recognize it as a loss of courage in the face of pressure from a group to conform with its norms. Stated in the simplest way, this principle of organizational life states that when facing a problem that must be solved, groups may impose more conformity on new ideas than might otherwise be the case for individuals working alone. In the decision-making process (and, by implication, in the decisions governing the final contours of an address) the conventional view is that groups tend to be cautious and conservative. On abstract questions this may not be true: there is evidence to suggest that sometimes a large number will engage in wholesale risk-taking on hypothetical questions which surpass what a single individual might accept.[34]

But where there are multiple interests that must be served, not the least of which is the protection of the president's credibility and prestige, the motive for change may indeed be muted. In addition, as Janis has noted, and as George Reedy has documented with regard to the Johnson administration, the deviant edges of individual opinion are frequently eliminated in a group as the risk of holding them in the potentially hostile presence of others becomes greater.[35] Speeches prepared by committee, therefore, put a premium on conformity to old conventions and norms. They penalize pluralism within the group. Such rhetoric can emerge from the process as a kind of mellow jelly that offers offense to no one, but is digested quickly and forgotten.

This kind of pattern could be seen during the first Eisenhower campaign in 1952. One speech in particular had been so clearly sanitized that eventually the calculated blandness itself became a news story. Emmet Hughes had written a campaign address for a stop in Milwaukee which included a modest but courageous defense of Eisenhower's long-time friend, General George C. Marshall. Marshall had recently been attacked by Wisconsin's rabid anti-Communist senator, Joseph McCarthy. One paragraph specifically rebuked the senator, for his baseless charges of disloyalty against Marshall, an attack initially sanctioned by the candidate himself. Nonetheless, the remarks were deleted from the address at the last moment, though printed in press copies distributed in advance. According to Hughes, the culprit was aide Jerry Parsons who inserted himself between the speechwriter and the candidate in an effort to avoid what was seen as a needless political snub to the Wisconsin local audience. The speech was defanged of its bite, but contributed to what became the longstanding notion in the American press that Eisenhower lacked political courage. As Hughes wryly noted, "The scent of irresolution in politics is never pleasant, and this time was no exception."[36]

The number of people or agencies that may be asked to clear a speech prior to its delivery is obviously subject to a number of variables. Theodore Roosevelt used to invite Oval Office visitors with completely unrelated business to read over a pending address, a habit sometimes practiced by his later namesake.[37] Lyndon Johnson, with much of his ambitious legislative program in the hands of what was then H.E.W., kept Secretary Anthony Celebrezze and domestic policy coordinator Joseph Califano well posted on speech themes. Nixon consulted with a relatively small group of trusted aides, and a few cabinet secretaries, particularly those running the Departments of Commerce, Treasury, and Agriculture. Carter, in contrast, often worked with so many suggestions for speeches that the staff sometimes succumbed to the fatal expedient of putting incompatible elements together in one unwieldy whole. Efforts to overreach the natural limits of compromise were evident to both insiders and the press in an address to the Naval Academy in June of 1978. It was an incompatible mixture of the anti-Soviet militance of National Security

Adviser Zbigniew Brzezinski, and the more conciliatory ideas of Secretary of State Cyrus Vance.[38]

Perhaps Carter was tempted to use the draft speech as a kind of soothing reminder to neglected staffers that their advice still mattered. The ploy of asking for suggestions is a common bureaucratic maneuver to buy peace from jealous members of an organization. But such collective responsibility asks for trouble.

Oral communication demands a singular personal point of view. There is simply no good mechanism available in oral address for the faceless anonymity that can exist in print. Written prose can be understood with or without personal pronouns. But speech is a more personal medium. In all but the most trivial sense it always implies the existence of a specific personality. Unlike the faceless writer giving directions or information *en vacuo*, the speaker necessarily stands with his words. Speech needs the context of the author's background: his *persona*. One cannot be separate from the other. What a person says has meaning only when wedded to his or her presence in a particular time and place.[39] It can come as no surprise that a speech that labors under the weight of 14 or so different contributors, and perhaps nine or ten drafts, ceases to be an extension of anyone. It simply becomes some thing, an organizational rather than personal document. The fixed perspective that one writer initially brings to the enterprise can, under the scrutiny of many, yield to a formless mass that dilutes and sometimes contradicts the essence of oral communication as speaker-centered. We measure the importance of a message not primarily by what was said, but by who said it. Had Edward Everett delivered Lincoln's rather than his own address at Gettysburg, the president's words would probably be consigned to oblivion today.[40] What mattered was that the president—the war leader—displayed his humanity and compassion. Coming from others, the speech would have meant less.

In response to this need for a single voice behind a message, writers may go to elaborate lengths to protect their work from unwanted contributions from other writers and assistants. Robert Hardesty, for example, complained that while Johnson himself was a good editor of speeches, too many others (presumably Jack Valenti, Robert Kintner, Bill Moyers, and others) could supersede a second-level writer and substitute a part or a complete draft for one of their own design. "I don't know that anybody did it deliberately, but your tendency was to not turn them (the drafts) in until the last minute so that you could preserve what you thought ought to be preserved."[41]

## MARCH 31, 1968: A CASE STUDY IN DELEGATION AND CLEARANCE

In what was perhaps the most dramatic and pivotal presidential address in the entire decade of the sixties, a tired and relieved Lyndon Johnson went on national television in the middle of the Vietnam-clouded 1968 political primary season to announce a partial bombing halt. He also closed his address with the statement of his decision to not seek reelection for a second term. Not since Coolidge's decision to bow out in 1928 had a first-term incumbent made such a move.[42]

In retrospect, the events of 1968 seemed to require Lyndon Johnson's withdrawal from politics. Johnson's arch political enemy, Robert Kennedy, had been cruelly martyred by an assassin in the dingy back hallway of a California hotel. Senator Eugene McCarthy had emerged as the elder flower-child of the antiwar movement, and made national headlines with a second-place finish against Johnson in New Hampshire which was widely interpreted as a win. But at the time, the news of the president's decision still came as a shock to the nation. It was an unmistakable confirmation of America's failure in Vietnam, and a reflection of a break in the nation's normally endemic spirit of optimism.[43]

The events leading up to the speech—which attempted to elicit some face-saving concessions from North Vietnam's Ho Chi Minh—required a prolonged White House effort. In this case some 16 separate drafts, and the suggestions of at least 17 top-level aides, cabinet secretaries, and political sages from previous administrations were involved.

Beginning with a critical series of meetings in mid-March, Johnson consulted with his informal Vietnam Advisory Group, including Dean Acheson, former secretary of state under Truman, Douglas Dillon, ambassador to France under Eisenhower and secretary of the treasury under Kennedy, as well as Cyrus Vance, McGeorge Bundy, General Omar Bradley, Abe Fortas, General Matthew Ridgeway, and others. During these meetings a decisive battle was waged for the future course of Vietnam policy. Some, such as Omar Bradley and Walt Rostow, wanted to maintain or increase the current levels of bombing and military involvement in the war. But an emerging larger group was counseling the president that his policy had reached a deadlock. The domestic battlefield was fast becoming as hotly contested as the airstrips and villages near the Demilitarized Zone.[44] And a proposed presidential speech to the nation was to be the prize most coveted by the victors.

Work on the address actually began in February. Harry McPherson had gone through five drafts of a tentative message to the nation asking for patience in the face of the renewed determination of the North Vietnamese after their successful Tet offensive against the South. But a new series of drafts was begun when the speech date was moved back to the end of March.

The first of a second round of attempts was written by McPherson in longhand on a simple tablet. When completed, it was typed and submitted to the president, Bundy, Clifford, Rusk, Rostow, William Jordan, Juanita Kreps, and Arthur Okun.[45]

Johnson had many reasons for giving the speech. There was the continuing need to appear presidential at a time when urban riots in the nation's inner cities had created a sense of national unease. It was also the political season. Increasingly bitter attacks against the president reflexively led him to seek a forum he could dominate in order to shore up an Asian policy that seemed to be coming apart at the seams. But the major factor was the highly criticized bombing of North Vietnam. In Johnson's words:

> I wanted to put the enemy's Tet offensive in proper perspective, and now that the offensive had been blunted and there was a chance that the enemy might respond favorably, I wanted to announce our new initiative for peace. If we were going to take the risk of a bombing pause, I felt I would make it clear that my decision has been made without political considerations. . . . The most persuasive way to get this across, I believed, would be to couple my announcement of a bombing halt with the statement that I would not be a candidate for reelection.
>
> I also hoped that the combined announcement would accomplish something else. The issue of Vietnam had created divisions and hostilities among Americans, as I had feared. I wanted to heal some of those wounds and restore unity to the nation. This speech might help do that.[46]

In fact, Johnson was also under extreme political pressure to back away from his bombing and troop commitments. Insiders close to him, most notably Clifford, Bundy, Dillon, and Vance, had begun to challenge Johnson's assumptions about the war.[47] As an accurate barometer of the partially hidden attitudes of his aides, he had started to register the lack of ease that was building under their outward expressions of support.

The speech went through six drafts between March 20 and 27. McPherson feverishly wrote and rewrote various sections as well as a new ending, submitting revisions to the president, Bundy, Rostow, and others. So many drafts came and went so quickly that on at least several occasions some of the president's own contributions were cut as they lost the identity of their author.

As the speech evolved it changed in what seemed to be more or less predictable ways. All heavily revised speeches are somewhat like a bellows: alternately puffed up and bloated, and then compressed as the alternate whims of amplifying and simplifying points are acted on. At one point it was almost 5,000 words long. In final form it emerged at slightly under 4,000 words. At its earliest stages it had a more cohesive theme to it, reflecting McPherson's original intention to develop a defensive rather than conciliatory stance on Vietnam. Later it would sound more eclectic, as the compulsion to maintain a consistent policy front was tempered by the desire to appear less war-like. Through various revisions the long and sometimes complex sentences of the original draft grew shorter as various editors corrected what were for them ambiguous and unclear references.

Working in secret during this period was another aide and writer, Horace Busby, who was preparing the final bombshell lines of the speech announcing the decision not to run for reelection in 1968. Shaping the terms that would announce the president's retirement was an important task. Johnson wanted to sound brave and unequivocal. But no doubt his greatest desire was to leave with whatever tattered remnants of his image as a statesman that he could salvage.[48] Busby's words would mark a monumental transition for Johnson and the nation. They had to strike a tone of courage rather than defeat.

March 27, just four days before its delivery, the speech took a major turn. Reflecting the debate within the White House on the future course of the no-win war, the address itself became an instrument in the intense high-level policy struggle over the possibility of winning by military means. Clues to the conflict in Washington are reflected in a memo by Bundy noting that "Harry's present draft does just what was decided yesterday, but I think as it stands it will be profoundly discouraging to the American people."[49] Clifford also strongly objected to the tone of the speech, noted that "What the President needs is not a war speech, but a peace speech."[50] As a result of the dissatisfactions, McPherson started a third round of drafts on March 28 emphasizing a limited bombing halt over most of North Vietnam. And for the first time these alternate drafts showed elements of what would be delivered on March 31. Doodles in the margins of the manuscript indicate that McPherson had been reading Irwin Ross's book, *The Loneliest Campaign*, which prophetically documents the low popularity and uphill battle facing Harry Truman before the 1948 elections.[51]

Succeeding drafts were distributed, and among those observing the evolution of the speech was Mrs. Johnson, though her office returned copies that were read but unmarked. Clifford, in contrast, saw himself as one who was thrust into the middle of a great silent war over access to the delicate terrain of the president's agreement. He raised a number of points in attempts to soften the speech's hawkish tones. One particularly troublesome line was in reference to the dangers of pulling completely out of Vietnam. The speech contained the warning: "God help us if we do" pull out. The soft-spoken but eloquent Clifford objected. "The speech still locks us into a war that is pictured as being essential to our security but is not proven as being essential to our security."[52] In the continual give-and-take that followed, the drafting of the speech and the reshaping of a key policy occurred at the same time.

A speech draft is often an instrument for the articulation and resolution of conflicts among high-level policy makers. Such was the case in the decision-making process that was underway during the national trauma of the Cuban missile crisis. After numerous deadlocks Sorensen used speeches as "a means of focusing on specifics" and moving the discussions forward.[53] What seems as a way to streamline the president's workload not infrequently functions as a vehicle for the resolution of conflict between various centers of power within the White House.

On March 30 McPherson was still working on a new draft of what was clearly emerging as a peace overture speech. He added new lines in the middle to assure Americans that the South Vietnamese would do more of the actual fighting, incorporating comments from Rusk and others. His draft at this point, labeled as "alternate draft no. 4," was actually the fifteenth attempt since early February. In a memo to the president he indicated that he was working on another more conciliatory closing in order to avoid "lighting up the sky with rockets." The speechwriter was anxious to have the president appear to be the guardian of peace. If the closing were too harsh, he noted, people will say, "ah—now here comes the real Johnson, old blood and thunder. . . ."[54]

After final revisions and editing by Johnson, the speech was typed in large-sized letters on 8½-by-11-inch sheets of paper. This was to be his back-up delivery copy of the address, bound in a looseleaf folder, marked for emphasis, and ready to use should the Teleprompter fail.

The networks had been notified several days earlier, and agreed to carry the speech without the complaints and suspicions which had accompanied some of their previous reluctant approvals for air time. Preparations were made for CBS to offer "pool" coverage of the speech with a single camera in the Oval Office. It was scheduled for 9 P.M. in the east. The networks hoped that it would be limited to a half hour so the remainder of their lucrative prime-time schedule would be intact. Johnson's address put the impatient audiences for "Bonanza" and the "Smothers Brothers Comedy Hour" on temporary hold.

On the day of the address Johnson rehearsed before a small television camera attached to a video tape recorder. Both were gifts to the White House by a Japanese electronics firm. The run-through was planned primarily to smooth out the Teleprompter reading copy of the speech. The Teleprompter device was mounted to the CBS camera, and contained a rolling manuscript of one-inch high words that were projected onto a transparent mirror located directly in front of the camera. This enabled Johnson to appear to be talking directly to the nation's television viewers while actually reading the manuscript from in front of the camera lens. At one point he stopped his rapid read-through of the remarks to correct an awkward phrase. "Gosh, if that's not State Department language, I never saw it," he remarked to no one in particular.[55] But final corrections were noted and changed before the evening telecast.

Perhaps reflecting his own unconscious attempt to transform the difficult political decisions of the last two weeks into a performance that would exude a style of confidence and resoluteness, Johnson matter-of-factly now referred to the carefully constructed speech as a "script."

In many ways the address given to the battle-weary nation on that Sunday evening was a reflection of those who helped shape it. From Acheson, Clifford, and others counseling peace came as much a concession as Johnson could tolerate: "Tonight, I renew the offer I made last August—to stop bombardment of North Vietnam. We ask that talks begin promptly, that they be serious talks on the substance of peace. . . . And we are doing so unilaterally, and at once."[56] But the voices of his military advisers were also to be heard. Johnson committed more U.S. troops to the struggle in order "to reequip the South Vietnamese forces, [and] to meet our responsibilities in Korea, as well as our responsibilities in Vietnam." And for the allied hard-liners unchanged by the deteriorating climate of opinion at home, the address fell back on the harsh eloquence of lines spoken by John Kennedy in more idealistic times:

> Of those to whom much is given much is asked. I cannot say and no man could say that no more will be asked of us. Yet I believe that now, no less than when the decade began, this generation of Americans is willing to pay any price, bear any burden, meet any hardship, support any friend, oppose any foe, to assure the survival and the success of liberty.

And then came the end. Johnson consigned himself to a humiliating and premature political retirement, knowing that the specter of defeat later in the fall elections was a very real possibility. Horace Busby's clandestinely prepared words were to become the most widely reported of any in the speech:

> With America's sons in the fields far away, with America's future under challenge right here at home, with our hopes and the world's hopes for peace in the balance every day, I do not believe that I should devote a hour or a day of my time to any personal partisan causes or to any duties other than the awesome duties of this office—the Presidency of your country. Accordingly, I shall not seek, and I will not accept, the nomination of my party for another term as your President.

Charged with the overtones of political drama ending in fatal tragic flaws, the speech was a magnified example of the eclecticism of most presidential rhetoric. No one author except the president could technically claim ownership of it. Containing both ritual platitudes and specific statements of policy, it was a highly complex guide to the era and its changing climate of opinion. The careful reader finds within its well-edited statements ample evidence of a battle for the mind of the president which was waged in the drafting process itself.

## WHOSE MESSAGE IS IT? GHOSTWRITING AND ACCOUNTABILITY

Every serious observer of politics must sooner or later address the question: Who really authors presidents' speeches? Few illusions are as transparent as that which conceals the publicist and writer behind the politician. To be sure, no one is particularly naive about this. Most people know that a president's messages are the result of shared effort. What troubles many professional observers is the question of whether there is any sense in holding presidents and others using ghostwriters accountable for speeches that are largely the work of other hands.

Many would readily agree with Ernest Bormann that if an audience is to truly "know" a speaker by what he says,

> then he must be honest with them and present himself as he really is. When he reads a speech that reveals to his audience a quiet humor, an urbane worldliness, subtle and incisive intellectual equipment, then he should be that kind of man. If his collaborators . . . are responsible for the "image" revealed in the speech, and if the speaker has different qualities and intellectual fiber, the speech is a deceit and it can be labeled as ghostwritten and condemned as unethical.[57]

But Bormann asks for information that is very difficult to get. What if accountability cannot be assured? By what logic can the importance of presidential speaking be defended in the absence of precise knowledge about whose speech is really being heard? None of these questions are easily answered. Studying the labyrinth through which even the simplest speech travels leads to the conclusion reached by Harry Truman that "almost every presidential message is a complicated business."[58]

The equating of who we fundamentally *are* with what we *say* is normally a simple and straightforward article of faith in human relations. Oral language, in a basic sense, is thought to be "a fingerprint of the man,"[59] that is, a clear representation of the inner person, with many of his dreams, fears, biases, assumptions, and judgments lingering under the transparent surface of speech. But political language is not ordinary or conventional. It is more carefully constructed, and it offers few chances for the assessment of character based on the normal spontaneities of unplanned conversation.

The suspicions inherent to any discussion of ghostwriting seem to rise out of two common assumptions that may no longer be applicable to modern presidents. One is that the president—like other public figures in politics, religion, and social reform—is still primarily engaged in a form of communication that aspires to be a set of aesthetic norms. His rhetoric must not only provide information and points of view; it is expected to provide a visceral feeling of pleasure, stateliness, and grace as well. The problem, of course, is that a committee consisting of a group of writers cannot usually write momuments of English prose. The more pens on the paper, the more "cramped" the style. The impulse to transmit an eloquent perspective requires one dominant writer, and the freedom to pursue familiar paths of personal thought. The entire process of clearing or staffing a speech has the effect of breaking down the unity and style of an address written from a single perspective. Whatever their value as documents of state, today's remarks are usually pale imitations of better attempts written by great presidential orators such as Lincoln, Wilson, and Theodore Roosevelt. Anything that has the pretense of conveying more than basic information must have the dominant vision of only one creator. "Style may be the man," notes Bormann, "but when that style is five men, it ceases to be any style at all."[60]

But the aesthetic pretense in current presidential rhetoric is paper thin. Presidents now only honor the faintest outline and scale of grand oratory. Since the end of World War II their rhetoric has been almost continually homogenized. John Kennedy perhaps rekindled some of the nearly burnt-out remains of what used to be called "the grand style" in his campaign and inaugural addresses, but arguably more for the fleeting drama of the moment than as a sustained expression of personal style. For example, the inaugural's most famous Kennedy-Sorensen phrase, "ask not what your country can do for you, ask what you can do for your country," has at least the superficial lilt of eloquence.[61] But that famous line actually was at odds with the new administration's brand of activist federalism. Kennedy wanted to do more for individuals, not less.

Today, style is an after-the-fact consideration for those who prepare what is often a rhetoric concerned primarily with the documentation of administrative policy. What was once a common form of ceremonial oratory has become scarce, and has been deferred in favor of occasions that invite more technical presidential defenses. Where Lincoln could construct what was essentially a poem to the dead at Gettysburg—noting the anguish and human sacrifice necessary to preserve the Union—a modern president more regularly lives by his wits as a tactician manipulating public opinion on specific policy goals. As one reads such crisis addresses as Truman's March 1947 speech to Congress outlining the Truman Doctrine,[62] or Kennedy's remarks to the American people in October and November of 1962 on the Cuban missile crisis,[63] the old flourishes of nineteenth-century grace seem to have been torn away to expose the hard political and legal dimensions of the issues under question. Facing the stony realities of postwar world politics, Truman and Kennedy gave up all but the simplest aesthetic pretenses in order to document or make official the studied decisions of their foreign policy technicians. A rhetoric that once traded heavily in appeals that would evoke feeling and emotion has increasingly become a rhetoric of exposition.

The elements of celebration, euology, and effusive hyperbole have not disappeared from the presidency, but they have been regularly eclipsed by more press attention and public interest in the strategic foreign and domestic commitments of the executive. In comparison to the Jackson, Lincoln, or Teddy Roosevelt eras, little of what is said today will remain alive for future children to quote in school declamations. The ideas of a great national *administrator* have gradually but clearly lost ground to the policy defenses of an *administration*. What remains is discourse of a different type that must be assessed for what it is: no longer a form of literature in service to politics, with obligations to the standards of each discipline. Now it is a hybrid form of political action itself. And as such it positively invites the contributions and involvement of alliances and groups—represented by ghostwriters—in the process of authorship. A pluralism of viewpoints *in* means a pluralism of viewpoints *out*, and results in a rhetoric that guarantees a wider net in which the capture the allegiances of supporters.

This is not to say that presidential speeches are devoid of style. The very necessity to make choices about what a speech will include and exclude implies that style is inherent to all discourse. Rather, the dominant private initiatives of old oratory have increasingly given way to a more austere corporate form. A president today speaks not only for himself and his party, but for an enormous bureaucracy with diverse constituencies and obligations.

Ironically, presidential speech which in reality speaks for the entire executive establishment still attempts to mimic the intimacy of a more personal style of politics. Where someone like Woodrow Wilson personally developed private thoughts that would be heard by thousands crowded together, presidents today have used batteries of writers to produce illusory "personal" dialogues. Wilson distributed the collective efforts of speechwriters; current presidents depend on them. He gladly armed himself with his own shorthand drafts and handtyped speeches for appearances in crowded halls and arenas; presidents today usually use the words of others to address Americans gathered separately and alone in front of private television sets. The significance of these changes lies in the fact that a personally developed and sumptuous rhetoric of larger-than-life images (still evident in most inaugurals, and much of the campaign speaking of presidential contenders such as Al Smith, Adlai Stevenson, and Hubert Humphrey as recently as 1968) at least had a pretense of timeless eloquence. Hubert Humphrey's "politics of joy," for example, was intended as much to produce feelings of goodwill between himself and his audience as to promote programs and issues. He gave "stemwinder" speeches in the nineteenth-century mold. They were meant to be quoted and recalled as permanent testimony to the greatness of the nation's citizens and principles.[64] And for the most part they read well in the once dominant political medium of newsprint.

Radio, by contrast, forced politicians into a simpler style. In place of an oratory attempting to use the conventions of hyperbole and grandeur for long-term permanence and effect, public figures came to realize that the new electronic forum offered unprecedented opportunities to repeatedly reach constituents. Words reprinted in newspapers and anthologies, and even chiseled on the marble walls of a national monument, might have been the measure of the effectiveness of preradio oratory. But in no sense could they match the immediate impact of a "fireside chat" or "conversation with the president" broadcast simultaneously to millions. After the first stations went on the air in the early 1920s, the casual ease of a Will Rogers began to replace the hall-filling thunder of a William Jennings Bryan. Oratory became the servant of the skillful political operator in a new way. It was increasingly less fashionable to fall back on the old, timeless homilies spoken as if from a pulpit. As a form of theater, it supplied the illusion of spontaneity and intimacy, but within the bounds of what was essentially a performance scripted by writers with an ear for dialogue.

Franklin Roosevelt was especially attuned to radio's potential. To the surprise of many of his listeners, he read his fireside chats. Such was the illusion of his and his ghostwriter's craft that these radio addresses presented a seamless thread of exposition made from the ideas and catchphrases of many, including Roosevelt, Grace Tully, Raymond Moley, and Samuel Rosenman. He introduced and nearly perfected a dialogue within a monologue—the scripted conversation—as a means of political persuasion.[65]

But if ghostwriting contributed to the demise of single dominant visions, it has also provided an accidental gain as well. It has at least helped to remove some of the extreme obfuscation that is possible in the more predictable forms of the set political speech. Rhetoric that passes by the critical ear on the hot air of glittering generalities and threadbare clichés is no longer quite so available to the speaker. The disillusionment of World War II, Korea, Vietnam, and Watergate were among the problems that would not go away even when concealed under the veil of ineffable Americanisms that were so prominently featured in their early stages. In the summer of 1973, when finally compelled to defend himself against the Watergate revelations coming from the White House, future defendants, and the press, Richard Nixon's inelegant response was that he was "not a crook." With that response, one could both lament the passing of a more dignified idiom for the leader of the Western world, and find pleasure in the evolution of political address to a level of unambiguous meaning. Nixon's addresses in April and August of 1973 were prepared by Ray Price and others with the specificity of a legal brief.[66] These, followed by several more before his resignation in August 1974, raised the general public's consciousness of the nature of the crisis to new heights. Contrary to the widespread belief that these were among the darkest days in the history of the nation, probably in no recent time had so many understood the legitimate struggles for power which were taking place in Washington. The Congress, the courts, the president, and the press were engaged in a fight for privilege and position that made the constitutional provisions delimiting their prerogatives at least meaningful, if not totally clear.

A second assumption also leads to perhaps a misplaced suspicion about the influence and acceptability of ghostwriters. It is that if a president is not the author of his remarks, he is in some way not as likely to be committed to them. And in such a state a president could be rendered useless as a leader. In an obvious sense it is easy to see why it might be believed that ghostwritten statements inherently carry less personal weight for a president than those he utters under the power of his own creativity. Michael Medved, once a speechwriter for a U.S. Senate candidate, recalled his own feeling of awe in writing words someone else would ultimately have to be responsible for:

> I had been given the authority to issue statements in his name through our press office even if he had never seen the material before its release. It was an eerie feeling to read in the newspapers "the candidate said today . . . " and to know that all the press was really reporting were words that a totally obscure . . . aide had put into the candidate's mouth.[67]

How committed could any politician be under a similar situation, if asked to defend positions put forth by an inexperienced subordinate? Surely common sense tells us that ghostwritten remarks carry a broken and dangerously obscured line of responsibility.

But what would seem to be the case often isn't. National politicians are in fact very loyal to both their staffs and staff decisions taken in their name. None of the numerous memoirs cited in this study, for example, give any space to the complaint that writers misdirected the intention of a president in any significant way. To the contrary, most presidents have been somewhat reluctant to give full credit to their writers, not only for the best of their efforts, but for their worst rhetorical moments as well. Whatever doubts exist prior to a decision, and the speech announcing it, once a decision is consummated by a public remark, presidents at least outwardly assume Harry Truman's dictum that "the buck stops here."

The key to this readiness to accept responsibility lies, I think, in the fact that ghostwriters are really *subordinate* collaborators, rather than authentic independent authors. It is easy to forget this and, as a result, assume that presidents are unduly beholden to their writers. But a president is always the senior partner in every effort, even if his contribution is simply to agree to give the speech as written. What matters most is that he is uniquely a free agent, fully able to decide what he will and will not say. The decision to choose to utter remarks prepared largely by someone else carries with it the full obligations of authorship. In various ways every president has signaled his adherence to this commitment. Eisenhower, for example, in a barely veiled attempt to say that every speech was at least partially his own, reminded the readers of his memoirs that "I have never been able to accept a draft of a suggested talk from anyone else and deliver it intact as my own."[68] Even if the imprint of the president was minor and largely cosmetic, the superficial changes essentially made the speeches his alone. Truman was also sensitive to this burden, noting that, regardless of who wrote the drafts of a speech, "The final version . . . is the final word of the President himself, expressing his own convictions and his own policy. These he cannot delegate to any man if he would be President in his own right."[69]

Whether the result of a corporate psychology involving the chivalry of a one for all logic, or a desire to seem to be at the center of all White House activities, it seems evident that claiming responsibility for speeches turns out to be not a presidential liability, but a source of personal pride. A clearly weak speech will be rejected, an occurrence frequently known to writers for Kennedy, Johnson, and Nixon. They and several other presidents were particularly skillful in improvising from the podium. What is used, therefore, is the product of a screening process that suggests full commitment, at least as far as the public record is concerned. "When the President walks to the podium with that black ring-binder notebook," noted L. B. J. aide Ben Wattenberg, "it doesn't make a damn bit of difference who wrote what paragraph —it's his speech. The speechwriter is a creature of the President, not the other way around."[70]

Ghostwriting is thus a peculiar activity. To a substantial degree its existence requires a president to accept more viewpoints, and a less monumental style of speaking in his rhetoric. Functioning as editors rather than true writers of their own prose, presidents have been forced to treat speeches as documents: more reflective of the joint decisions of an administration, and less revealing of the inner man.

But it is equally apparent that presidential rhetoric has not been rendered meaningless by the fact of ghostwriting. Writers are an adjunct to an executive, not a replacement for him. The personal vanity, and the political savvy of one who has traveled so far and so successfully down the political path all point to a reasonable presumption in behalf of full presidential accountability. What a president chooses to utter is, indeed, "the President's rhetoric." As Emmet Hughes notes,

> the only politically meaningful fact is not what the aide writes, but what the President says. The former may give important inflections to the latter. But the only decision of political moment belongs, wholly and unqualifiedly, to the President. Whatever he publicly declares is profoundly his.[71]

## NOTES

1. Robert T. Hartmann, *Palace Politics* (New York: McGraw-Hill, 1980), p. 404.

2. Theodore Sorensen, *Kennedy* (New York: Harper and Row, 1965), pp. 68-70.

3. This chapter, for example, draws upon the published recollections of many speechwriters including: Hartmann, *Palace Politics*; Raymond Price, *With Nixon* (New York: Viking, 1977); Emmet John Hughes, *The Ordeal of Power* (New York: Atheneum, 1963); William Safire, *Before the Fall: An Inside View of the Pre-Watergate White House* (New York: Doubleday, 1975); and Samuel I. Rosenman, *Working with Roosevelt* (New York: Harper, 1952).

4. Richard Weaver, *The Ethics of Rhetoric* (Chicago: Henry Regnery, 1953), p. 164. The author also discusses the style of "spacious" old rhetoric (pp. 164-85).

5. Page Smith, *Jefferson: A Revealing Biography* (New York: American Heritage, 1976), p. 258.

6. Newton Minow, John B. Martin, and L. M. Mitchell, *Presidential Television* (New York: Basic Books, 1973), p. 60.

7. Michael Medved, *The Shadow Presidents* (New York: Times Books, 1979), pp. 15-28.

8. Ibid., p. 6.

9. Hartmann, *Palace Politics*, p. 387.

10. Thomas E. Cronin, *The State of the Presidency* (Boston: Little, Brown, 1975), p. 119.

11. Ibid., p. 137.

12. Elmer E. Cornwell, Jr., *Presidential Leadership of Public Opinion* (Bloomington, Ind.: Indiana University, 1965), p. 70.

13. Medved, *The Shadow Presidents*, p. 73.

14. Cornwell, *Presidential Leadership*, p. 95.

15. Gerald R. Ford, *A Time to Heal* (New York: Harper and Row/Reader's Digest, 1979), p. 26.

16. Ibid., pp. 184-85.

17. Transcript, Robert Hardesty Oral History Interview, August 2, 1971, by Joe B. Frantz, p. 29, LBJ Library.

18. Townsend Hoopes, *The Limits of Intervention* (New York: David McKay, 1969), pp. 57-61, 119-34.

19. Memo from John Gardner, sent by Douglass Cater to the president in Texas, December 30, 1966, Speech File, White House Central Files (WHCF), LBJ Library.

20. Transcript, Charles M. Macquire Oral History Interview, July 29, 1969, by Dorothy Pierce McSweeny, p. 39, LBJ Library.

21. Sorensen, *Kennedy*, p. 240.

22. These are, in part, Henry Kissinger's characterizations from the *White House Years* (Boston: Little, Brown, 1974), pp. 77-78.

23. Sherman Adams, *Firsthand Report, The Story of the Eisenhower Administration* (New York: Harper, 1961), pp. 81-82.

24. See Doris Kearns, *Lyndon Johnson and the American Dream* (New York: Signet Books, 1976) pp. 36-39, 72-73.

25. Lyndon B. Johnson, *The Vantage Point* (New York: Holt, Rinehart and Winston, 1971), p. 164.

26. Transcript, Charles Macquire Interview, p. 14.

27. Craig R. Smith, "Addendum to 'Contemporary Political Speech Writing,' " *Southern Speech Communication Journal* (Winter 1977): 191-92.

28. Ford, *A Time to Heal*, p. 350. For a different version of the same event see Hartmann, *Palace Politics*, pp. 287-97. Hartmann suggests that the president had the habit of making unclear dual assignments.

29. Transcript, Harry McPherson Oral History Interview, tape 4, January 16, 1969, by T. H. Baker, pp. 10-11, LBJ Library.

30. Ibid., p. 12.

31. Hartmann, *Palace Politics*, pp. 382-83.

32. Soloman E. Asch, *Social Psychology* (Englewood Cliffs, N.J.: Prentice-Hall, 1952), chap. 16.

33. Irving Janis, *Victims of Groupthink* (Boston: Houghton Mifflin, 1972) chap. 1.

34. W. T. Edwards, *Social Psychology: Theories and Discussions* (London: Longman, 1974), pp. 181-82.

35. George E. Reedy, *The Twilight of the Presidency* (New York: World, 1970), pp. 96-98.

36. Hughes, *Ordeal of Power*, p. 43.

37. Richard Murphy, "Theodore Roosevelt," in *A History and Criticism of American Public Address*, vol. 3, ed. Marie Kathryn Hochmuth (New York: Russell and Russell, 1965), pp. 333-34.

38. James Fallows, "The Passionless Presidency" *The Atlantic Monthly* (August 1977): 43.

39. For a theoretical discussion of this concept see Lloyd Bitzer, "The Rhetorical Situation," *Philosophy and Rhetoric* 1 (January 1968): 1-14.

40. Everett—a former secretary of state, Senator, minister to Great Britain, and Harvard president—was actually the major speaker at the battlefield's dedication. He spoke for nearly two hours, arguing the Union cause, and the evils of an enlarged doctrine of states' rights.

41. Transcript, Robert Hardesty interview, p. 11.

42. Lyndon B. Johnson, Address to the Nation Announcing Steps to Limit the War in Vietnam . . . and Not to Seek Reelection, March 31, 1968, *Public Papers of the Presidents, Book 1, 1968* (Washington, D.C.: U.S. Government Printing Office, 1970), pp. 469-76.

43. For a review of the political and social problems that contributed to perhaps the worst year in the civil life of the nation since the onset of the Civil War, see Bruce Page, Lewis Chester, and Godfrey Hodgson, *An American Melodrama: The Presidential campaign of 1968* (New York: Viking, 1969), especially chapters 1, 2, 7, and 10.

44. Hoopes, *Limits of Intervention*, pp. 214-17.

45. Much of the narrative that follows is based on a review of memoranda surrounding the preparation of the speech from the White House Central File, Statements of Lyndon Johnson, March 20 to March 31, LBJ Library.

46. Johnson, *The Vantage Point*, p. 427.

47. Hoopes, *Limits of Intervention*, p. 224.

48. Johnson, *The Vantage Point*, pp. 427-30.

49. Memo, McGeorge Bundy to the president, March 21, 1968, Speech File, WHCF, LBJ Library.

50. Hoopes, *Limits of Intervention*, p. 219.

51. Harry McPherson, "Alternate Draft," March 28, 1968, Statements of Lyndon Johnson, WHCF, LBJ Library.

52. Memo from Clark to Harry McPherson, March 28, 1968, Alternate Draft No. 2, Statements of Lyndon Johnson, WHCF, LBJ Library.

53. Sorensen, *Kennedy*, p. 692.

54. Memo from Harry McPherson to the president, March 30, 1968, Alternate Draft No. 5, Statements of Lyndon Johnson, WHCF, LBJ Library.

55. Videotape of President Johnson's rehearsal of the March 31 speech, March 31, 1968, LBJ Library.

56. Johnson, Address to the Nation Announcing Steps to Limit War . . . , pp. 469-76. All remaining quotes in this section are from this speech.

57. Ernest G. Bormann, "Ethics of Ghostwritten Speeches," *Quarterly Journal of Speech* 47 (October 1961): 267.

58. Harry S. Truman, *Memoirs: Years of Decisions* (Garden City, N.Y.: Doubleday, 1955), p. 36.

59. Weaver, *Ethics of Rhetoric*, p. 9.

60. Ernest G. Bormann, "Ghostwriting and the Rhetorical Critic," *Quarterly Journal of Speech* 46 (October 1960): 288.

61. John F. Kennedy, Inaugural Address, January 20, 1961, *Public Papers of the Presidents, 1961* (Washington, D.C.: U.S. Government Printing Office, 1962), p. 3.

62. Harry S. Truman, Special Message to the Congress on Greece and Turkey: The Truman Doctrine, March 13, 1947, *Public Papers of the Presidents: 1947* (Washington, D.C.: U.S. Government Printing Office, 1963), pp. 176-80.

63. John F. Kennedy, Radio and Television Report on Cuba, October 22, 1962, pp. 806-9; and Radio and Television Remarks on the Dismantling of Soviet Missile Bases in Cuba, November 2, 1962 (Washington, D.C.: U.S. Government Printing Office, 1963), p. 821.

64. See Albert Eisele, *Almost to the Presidency* (Blue Earth, Minn.: Piper, 1972), pp. 243-49.

65. See Cornwell, *Presidential Leadership of Public Opinion*, pp. 253-69.

66. Richard M. Nixon, Address to the Nation about Watergate Investigations, April 30, 1973, pp. 328-33; and Address to the Nation About Watergate Investigations, August 15, 1973, *Public Papers of the Presidents, 1973* (Washington, D.C.: U.S. Government Printing Office, 1975), pp. 691-98.

67. Medved, *Shadow Presidents*, p. 4.

68. Dwight D. Eisenhower, *Mandate for Change, 1953-1956* (New York: Doubleday, 1963), p. 60.

69. Truman, *Memoirs*, p. 36.

70. Wattenberg quoted in L. Patrick Devlin, *Contemporary Political Speaking* (Belmont, Calif.: Wadsworth, 1971), p. 9.

71. Hughes, *Ordeal of Power*, p. 25.

# 9

# Political
# Communication in the
# Congress

Congress is a verbal culture.[1]

Nowhere else in Washington does one more keenly sense the cyclical movement of policy and publicity.[2]

Congress and the men and women who serve it function in what is in some ways a perfect cross section of American political communication. At the confluence of the nation's political life, the 535 members of the House of Representatives and the Senate must attempt to master the full range of political arts. In a given day a member may engage in forms of political discourse that run across the entire spectrum of possible encounters. A senator or representative may meet with ordinary constituents in the morning, lunch with a lobbyist at noontime, question expert witnesses in an afternoon meeting of a House or Senate committee, and receive an evening phone call from the president soliciting support on a close forthcoming vote. In between these major events he or she may consult with a dozen colleagues, plan strategy on the introduction of a piece of legislation, tape a radio report to constituents back home, and edit a speech for a busy upcoming weekend of campaigning. The member's cramped offices a block or so away from the Capitol building will buzz with the noise of a staff involved in an enormous range of activities: including everything from tracking down a lost Social Security check, to preparing remarks for delivery on the House floor explaining why it is impossible to support the party's leadership on a pending bill. With an eye on reelection, and the demands of an approaching campaign a thousand miles away, the member of Congress must still concentrate on cherished committee assignments, on the need to court interests with powerful friends back home, and the need to work with colleagues who have favors to be repaid, or wish to collect on political debts still owed them.

The prime activity of Congress is not speechmaking, and not single-minded attention of office work, but *lobbying*. Lobbying is the exchange of views—one-on-one or in small groups—for the purpose of winning the support of the listeners. Its diverse characteristics are at the heart of many of the points we wish to raise. The member is both the object and practitioner of much of it: to and from colleagues, constituents, organized interests, other governmental agencies, and even the press. In countless different ways the process of legislating involves an endless series of exchanges in which support for legislation is sought from others, or solicited by them. This chapter examines some of the major relationships and patterns that explain how power is communicated and how legislative support is won.

## EXTERNAL AND INTERNAL AUDIENCES: AN OVERVIEW

Members of Congress serve two broad types of audiences in their work. They must maintain visibility at home, while at the same time work to gain access to a structure in Washington that at least initially makes their single voice relatively insignificant. To some extent most are forced to give one of the two worlds a higher priority. But neither can be totally ignored.

As with all elective politics, the home constituency provides the member's ticket to Washington. A member of the House, for example, can never really afford to think of the District of Columbia as home in the way it is for other high-level government employees. The home state or congressional district is a source of a large chunk of the member's workload, particularly in the first one or two terms of service, when the skillful exploitation of incumbency can pave the way for easier reelection. The cynical aphorism that the first job of the congressman is to get reelected points to the necessity to think and act in terms of the constituency. Even if the member's attentions and interests turn increasingly to national issues, few of the 535 representatives and senators in Congress feel secure enough to neglect constituents back home. Everything else they undertake depends upon the building and mending of bridges to the local community. As is expected, the methods for doing this involve the prime tools of electoral politics: speeches, letters, press interviews, questionnaires, and appearances at countless meetings. Combined with the use of at least one local office, these tools serve to nurture sufficient local support. In an age when many local party organizations have atrophied, the role of maintaining strong local ties has taken on even new importance.[3]

For many House members and more than a few senators the local constituency is their reason for being in politics. But it is only half of the story, and perhaps the simpler half. Congress is an enormously complex institution. It always contains a wonderful variety of individuals. If its members got there by retailing their politics to the average voter, success on Capitol Hill depends upon mastering an institution that trades on equal parts of endless tenacity and skillful rhetorical ingratiation. Very few go about achieving these needs in the same way. For most, getting elected was only the beginning. There is also the equally important need to master the crusty and entrenched congressional establishment. Constituents may be one important audience to address, but those who are potential allies and opponents within the Congress itself are also vital.

Congress has two primary functions: to pass laws, and to provide oversight in the administration of the government. The two objectives are naturally related. The oversight of governmental operations—which today takes in nearly every facet of American life—leads to the revision, repeal, or enactment of laws designed to remedy evident problems. The textbook model for such processes is fairly straightforward. Various standing committees regularly (and frequently with great fanfare) review the enforcement of laws, and the agencies responsible for enforcement. Such hearings frequently serve an educational function, providing the committee or its leadership with the opportunity to orchestrate public opinion as a prerequisite to the introduction of new legislation. On many occasions oversight of particular agencies, cabinet officials, and even the Congress itself consumes the time of the entire body. Such oversight may involve a simple venting of anger in a floor speech over mismanagement of an agency, or may entail the more sensitive consideration of a proposal to expel a member accused of a felony.

The legislative function is equally complex, although the basic procedures and traditions are well known. Bills are introduced by members, usually because they have a special interest in it, or a special constituency they represent. In what is usually a proposal's first critical test, it is routed to an appropriate committee according to what are sometimes unclear jurisdictional lines, and equally unclear political alliances. The committee holds hearings, "marks up" the bill, votes it out to the floor of the House or Senate, votes it down, or simply lets it die (as most do). The bill lucky enough to be reported out of committee is considered by the whole body, amended, if necessary, and voted on. It, or one similar to it, is considered by the other house, and likewise voted on. Then differences between the two passed versions are then worked out in a House-Senate conference committee. But few bills actually move through the Congress in such a straight sequence. Most are tabled, defeated, and amended in what is often a multi-year process. Final passage often comes only after repeated attempts over several sessions. When a bill is passed, it is usually far different from what its initial sponsors had in mind. Its adoption occurs only after a good deal of private bargaining has made it possible to approve it on a suspension of the rules.

In all of this process a vigorous floor debate, airing the great issues of the question before well-attended sessions, may have never occurred. But that is not to say that the legislative cycle did not involve a good deal of communication. It is far more typical that the most vocal and reported debate was constructed by members of the press out of the variegated fabric of press conferences promoted by interested parties, hearing testimony in committees, television interviews prepared and distributed by the member, and presession publicity distributed by all of those with a financial or ideological stake in the proposal.

What emerges as central to the heart of the modern Congress is the vital role played by the standing committees and subcommittees of the House and Senate. Most of the 800 or so bills that are introduced in a session will never be passed, for example, but many still get an initial hearing in a committee concerned with hunger, airline safety, industry regulation, water distribution, taxes, drugs, medical insurance, trade restrictions, land management issues, or other substantive issues. Both houses must approve all bills that become law, although measures that raise funds must originate in the House. The task of passing on high-level non-civil service presidential appointees goes to committees in the Senate.

In both houses the committees are a primary source of rhetorical and legislative work. Chosen to reflect party strengths, and promoted in accordance to overall seniority, House and Senate members generally hope to serve on several major committees and subcommittees, using their gatekeeping role as centerpieces of their own legislative activity and bargaining clout. The specialization that a member develops usually is based on committee work, and the knowledge with years of service on a committee. The Senate, for example, has 18 regular standing committees, with almost 150 subcommittees. The number is similar for the House. As a member of the Senate's prestigious Foreign Relations Committee, or the House's Appropriations Committee, a member gets an opportunity to become one of a limited number of voices in the discussion of vital national interests.[4]

## THE BUILT-IN DILEMMAS OF CONGRESSIONAL COMMUNICATION

By most standards, a member of Congress is given a tremendous opportunity to influence public discussion on a number of issues. Members are a part of a small and exclusive legislative elite. They also have free mailing privileges, full access to radio and television studios paid for in large part by the tax-paying public, sufficient staff research to explore the intricacies of nearly any issue, a wealth of standing invitations to speak, and the opportunity to cross-examine the leaders of countless agencies, businesses, and institutions doing business with or for the government.

In addition to these considerable advantages, members of the more exclusive Senate have ready access to the national press, and to the prestigious forums (i.e., national news shows, and the nation's best Op Ed pages) which reach millions at one time. Running for re-election every six years rather than every two, they also enjoy at least a partial immunity from the representative's constant concern with how every decision affects the chances of renewing the two-year electoral contract.

But from a communications standpoint Congress is full of contradictions. The built-in paradoxes of congressional communication are especially noticeable in light of the effects stemming from television's increasing dominance of the public discussion of issues. In comparison to the president, members are—at best—cast into the role of subordinate players. Even the most eloquent and forceful communicator is only one of hundreds inside and outside of Congress seeking to influence the course of government.

A review of these and other communication-centered dilemmas need to be considered in more depth.

Except for a few select leaders in the House and Senate—notably the Speaker, the minority leader, and a handful of committee leaders in the House and Senate—the individual's personal political clout is severely limited. Every member does retain an important place in the state or district constituency, but the power to be a voice on national issues ranges from minimal to nonexistent. There are two primary reasons for this. One is simply a result of the sheer numbers involved. Any topic of general public interest creates heavy competition on Capitol Hill for the chance to be heard by a wider public. In the search for an elusive (and illusory) Senate opinion or "the feeling of the House," a key leader with an institutional role is perhaps consulted and interviewed for a nationally distributed response. Most are left to seek attention for their views in the local press within their districts. Representatives complain that they are overlooked, sometimes receiving practically no requests for responses from even the mass media in their home regions.[5] And even high-ranking senators have expressed frustration at having to engage in sensational stunts to get an opportunity to express a view.[6]

A psychological factor is also involved. Public communication is inherently viewed as a personal act, even when the communication itself flows from organizational needs. A corporate president speaks for the corporation; the union leader speaks for the membership. Even the president of the United States is accepted in the essentially untenable role of speaking for the nation as a whole, in spite of the fact that the diversity of the population makes a national view a highly dubious concept. Such reductions are psychologically satisfying because they assign human motives to complex organizations. They give unseen and frequently incomprehensible institutions a personal voice and a human dimension. But who does the member of Congress represent? What formal and official structure is symbolized in his communication? There is no simple answer. No one-to-one reduction is possible because congressional roles are so varied, and because Congress was set up to make representation deliberately diffuse. One may be a mouthpiece for a party, for a set of interests, for a regional caucus, or for a home constituency. The problem is that the member usually can claim no permanent and reliable connection with any one institution as the basis for extending the significance of his public rhetoric. Every new legislative and oversight demand may force a realignment of internal and external alliances. The party that is abandoned on one vote may be defended on another. A bipartisan coalition urging a particular tax package in one session may be hopelessly split on a question regarding defense spending.

The price the member pays for being a part of an institution with ever-shifting coalitions is heavy. The fickle nature of alliances in the modern Congress cuts against the grain of a news media conditioned to think of advocates as constant representatives for one point of view. In contrast, the organized defenses of institutions like the presidency seem hierarchical and orderly. An administration attempts to speak with one voice, an impossibility in the organized anarchy of a diverse legislative body. As several recent observers of press coverage of Congress note, "Searching for a single voice beggars the media. Covering all the conflicting subcommittees' and committees' mark up sessions, overlapping hearings, the floor deliberations, is an expensive proposition."[7] Most don't do it, or simply graft a reference to congressional debate onto a report centered on the more personalized White House.

A second dilemma is related to the first, but has been far more thoroughly documented. It is that party influence has declined in spite of the fact that congressional politics really seem to require some sense of party discipline. There is a general but unmistakable trend— at least since World War II—away from the member's sense of party identification. The pattern is evident from top to bottom. In contrast to F. D. R.'s assured party support in the first two terms of the New Deal, for example, Jimmy Carter found that neither the Democratic leadership nor individual Democratic members could be lined up and counted on for a consistent party-based legislative approach. As he noted in his memoirs, he began to "commiserate" with the Speaker Tip O'Neill "about the almost anarchic independence of the House."[8]

In the age of the well-bankrolled candidate, the professional political consultant, and the heavy dependency on television campaigning, there is less and less dependency on party organization. Members of Congress are not inclined to wait to be selected as official advocates for a point of view representing the party or the caucus. They are more apt to take advantage of communication opportunities on an ad hoc basis. "People get elected right off the street," laments a Massachusetts congressman. "They don't have any political loyalties or I.O.U.'s"[9] The tendency is to view one's own political fortunes less in terms of the general successes of the party, and more in terms of the more ambitious objective of making a personal reputation that will sustain a career. Among countless members in the House there is a sense of near desperation to find a way to make a lasting imprint on the voter's consciousness in order to win reelection. The fluid politics brought on by an independence of party places increased emphasis on the member's ability to communicate his own abilities. In the ninety-fifth Congress in 1978, for example, even though the Democrats had a two-to-one edge over Republicans, the leadership lost several key votes because of defections by many primarily young nonteam players. "At one time you'd blow a whistle and say this is what the party wants and the members would line up and say, Yes sir . . . ," a Democratic Whip recalled. "Today they get elected on Monday and they are giving a [floor] speech on Tuesday."[10]

An additional problem facing the Congress as a whole is that it casts its members largely into a reactive role. Against the more positive image of the problem-solving presidency, the impressions left by the frequently divided Congress are colored by the fact that it must *respond* to a legislative agenda set by the executive. In the popular aphorism, the president proposes, and the Congress disposes. Presidential leadership in the setting of major legislative objectives became commonplace during the New Deal, although many bills still originate from individual members.[11]

There is an inherent communication problem built into the reactive role of a legislature, and one that no doubt contributes to the general ambivalence Americans feel when questioned on the effectiveness of Congress.[12] Unless it contains a high degree of support, a reactive response in politics is almost automatically perceived as negative. The presidency provides an endless range of opportunities for its occupants to take bold initiatives, propose necessary actions, and generate what appear to be innovative new forms of legislation. A member of Congress may be equally bold in proposing solutions, but his efforts will occur in what is, comparatively speaking, an information vacuum. Ultimately, the member is left with the necessity to deal with the initiatives of the White House. And, if he is one of the independents we have taken note of, or a member of the opposite party, the odds are large that he will be cast as naysayer against the president. That fact itself is not the basis of a serious problem. After all, parliamentary democracies are supposed to examine and weigh the consequences of proposed legislation. But three factors work against earning the sympathy of the electorate in a reactive communication role.

One is that Americans generally expect that the Congress will cooperate with the president: that it will not use partisan differences as bases from which to fight a powerful and popular president. The public generally expects members to go along with major parts of an executive's program.[13] Presidents exploit this presumption repeatedly, as Truman did in his famous diatribes against the "do-nothing" Congress in 1948. Another is that members of Congress are handicapped generally by the fact that they must be more cautious and more deferential to the president than he must be to them. The symbolism of the presidency works against those who attack it. It is one of the ironies of our political life that a skillful president may be able to take away the credibility of those who would exercise their constitutional functions of challenging his initiatives. Woodrow Wilson's analysis still seems valid today:

> His is the only national voice in affairs. Let him once win the admiration and confidence of the country, and no other single force can withstand him, no combination of forces will easily overpower him. . . . If he rightly interprets the national thought and body insist upon it, he is irresistible; and the country never feels the zest of action so much as when its President is of such insight and caliber. Its instinct is for unified action, and it craves a single leader. It is for this reason that we often prefer to choose a man rather than a party.[14]

Perhaps the most entrenched problem, however, is one that is not so easily quantified, but still easily identified. It is that reactive (and frequently critical) communication is a role that is the dramatic stance of the villain or the pessimist. All things being equal, it is easier to take an affirmative position then to hold back and deny the affirmations of someone else. It is more socially useful to seem to be reaching for new solutions and new ideas than to be attacking the proposals of others. The pattern is readily identifiable at all levels of communication activity. In face-to-face encounters, in small groups, in small assemblies, the same general attitude prevails.

What occurs in national politics is often revealing in this regard. The president, of course, is as much a dissenter as anyone else. The key difference is that *he* has the power to privately alter the legislative agenda by shaping the public discussion of his proposals. His surrogates within the Congress can usually be successful in tabling or killing a bill proposed by others, all without the need to make a sharp public attack on it. But, indeed, the public criticism of a White House proposal may be the only significant way a member of Congress can deal with an item of legislation. A member may rightly judge that his vote may make little difference. Only his criticism may make some impact. One of the few congressional paths into the heady world of the Op Ed page or 30 seconds of network news time may come with a concerted attack on the executive Goliath. The audacity of a far weaker congressional David may be enough to give the conflict a certain notoriety. Part of the art of the presidency is to maintain a grace and equilibrium (done so well by President Reagan) that makes would-be attackers appear all the more insensitive. Likewise, the attacker must weigh the heavy risks to the home district that can come from the momentary news value of a break with a popular president.

Finally, it should be noted that some facets of legislative life are simply out of fashion today. So much of what goes on in legislative deliberation seems either troublesome to the average citizen, or at odds with the needs of modern technology. Except for private constituency service there is no general public admiration for *good* congressional work: for attention to the detail of legislation, for the ability to master the complex procedures needed for passage of laws, for the skill involved in making the necessary compromises and committee "mark ups" that improve a bill, for the mastery of the politics of interparty and intraparty factions. All require a level of political knowledge that is unlikely to be favorably portrayed in most forms of contemporary journalism. By personalizing the presidency we have also personalized much of the rest of our politics. That office can be understood superficially in television terms: it is a place occupied by a personality with at least generally understood managerial responsibilities. The Congress, in contrast, is more a place of arguments, political negotiation, and compromise. It is working as a forum when it speaks with many conflicting voices, and by producing the troubling but necessary sense that our decisions are contingent rather than certain. It takes little insight to realize that the mediation that represents the essential work of law-making will never fire the ordinary imagination in the same way that the popular visionary presidency does. The latter dramatizes the affirmation of universal goals; the former carries on the essential task of getting past easily stated ideals to the hard work of finding pragmatic bases for making actual decisions.

## CONGRESSIONAL ANONYMITY AND STARDOM: LOW AND HIGH PROFILES

In recounting his own unique political odyssey as an aide and counsel in the Congress, Harry McPherson recalls one occasion when he was sitting next to then Vice-President Lyndon Johnson as the future president presided over the Senate. The Kennedy administration was encountering heavy opposition to its legislative program, and Johnson remained grim even as two senators rose to speak in behalf of an administration proposal. "I asked Johnson what was wrong. 'We've got all the minnows,' he said. 'We've got none of the whales.' "[15] The former majority leader (himself a "whale") was characteristically direct in his constant effort to locate the centers of political power. Not all members of Congress are equal. Senators get far more attention from the White House, the press, and each other than members of the House. Many chair important committees, thus having the power to report out or "kill" legislation. Others in the House have the persuasive skills and knowledge of parliamentary procedure to salvage or block bills. For Johnson the whales were those in a position to make things happen. They were able to get votes. For us these people represent a special and small substrata in both houses, because their communication activities are most likely to yield results affecting the course of legislation, and perhaps the fortunes of a president in need of solid legislative accomplishments. Leaving Johnson's prosaic metaphor, we prefer to identify legislative power in parallel parliamentary terms: "backbenchers" and "national" members of Congress.

Every parliamentary democracy can be thought of as having two general types of members. Backbenchers are generally loyal to their party, but to various degrees removed from the government and the center of parliamentary power. Their votes are sought by the legislative leadership and usually won. They are rarely consulted by the national press, and frequently do not wish to be. They enjoy the security and prestige of their surroundings, and are usually proud of the casework load they carry on behalf of their local constituents. To various degrees most members of Congress fall into this general category. Shunted to the less important committees, infrequently consulted by the leadership, and content to let others play the trump cards in the intense game of legislative politics, these members seek to pursue limited personal or political objectives. Primary concerns may include attracting home-based media attention for their work, and concentrating on how votes will affect their districts. In Britain and other party-government systems their loyalty to government "front-benchers" is rarely in doubt. In the United States, which separates the executive from the legislative, the member is more independent. Essential priorities include service to the district and state, and deep interest in federal policy that directly affects that home base. If Washington reminds them of their limits, the local constituency offers a sense of accomplishment. As one member of the House told Richard Fenno:

> My lack of confidence is still a pressure which brings me home. This is my political base. Washington is not my political base. I feel I have to come home to get nourished, to see for myself what's going on. It's my security blanket—coming home.[16]

Backbenchers also suffer from a lack of attention from the press. In a town where egos are measured in column inches of newsprint, prestige is closely tied to the importance the press attaches to your career. There are exceptions, of course. Members of Congress who are unlikely to be defeated may welcome the freedom that a low profile gives them. Or they may seek only to secure coverage in local media within their home district. But for many others the lack of mass media interest translates into a lack of power, or into potential reelection problems. A recent survey of House members, for example, indicated that about 75 percent felt that the national mass media—the television networks, newsweeklies, and prestige press—paid no attention to them.[17] As researcher Michael Robinson has noted, "The fact is the nationals ignore members and pick on the institution—unless there is a scandal to cover."[18]

The pattern is only slightly different for the congressman's local home district media. Many papers are willing to run brief stories based on a steady flow of press releases from a Congress member's Washington offices. But the reporting is usually distinctly second-rate, with many papers and broadcasters contributing little time or thought to the issues and questions that may be intensely important to the legislator. As a new member of the House once noted:

> The role of the newspaper is usually passive, and occasionally hostile. Their news staffs are overworked and understaffed, have very limited budgets, and receive a never-ending flood of materials from all sides. The congressman gets his due along with a thousand other competing interests.
>
> Newspapers at home usually see no need to check with their congressmen on facts or on his position. The number of times that I have been contacted by *any* newspaper in my district in two years can be counted on the fingers of one hand.[19]

A far smaller group in both houses can be truly called national politicians. They differ from backbenchers in that they usually have an opinion-leading function both within the chamber in which they serve, and to special interest constituents who extend beyond the borders of their own state or district. Publicity powers sufficient to influence national debate on a question are sometimes within their grasp.

The political muscle of the national figure is usually based on a formal party or leadership role: as a chairman, subcommittee chairman, whip, minority or majority leader. And, although the lines of power in the Congress are made extremely complex by a system of committee and subcommittee jurisdictions, it is evident that committee leadership provides a gatekeeping role that commands at least grudging respect. In the recent history of the Senate, for example, the names of Howard Baker, Robert C. Byrd, Frank Church, Russell B. Long, Hubert Humphrey, J. William Fulbright, and Lyndon Johnson have become synonymous with congressional party leadership. Johnson proved to be a master negotiator in the late 1950s as Senate minority leader, managing an uneasy coalition of Southern and liberal Democrats, while maintaining good relations with the popular Eisenhower regime at the other end of Pennsylvania Avenue.[20] As chairman of the powerful Senate Finance Committee, Russell Long controlled an enormous range of taxing and revenue-raising proposals, with the equal respect of Republicans and members of his own party.[21] And as majority leader, Republican Howard Baker salvaged a number of crucial Carter administration programs, including the landmark treaty setting in motion the return of the Panama Canal. Their counterparts in the House—reflected in the recent leadership of Robert Michael, Gerald Ford, Jim Wright, and Wilbur Mills—have played equally vital roles in forming well-publicized positions with or in opposition to the president.

In addition, a smaller number of House and Senate members are able to stake out prominent positions for themselves by virtue of externally derived sources of power. A small number of members have always been able to build on a previous reputation, or a special relationship with a national clientele. They command rhetorical if not formal power. Aside from his considerable talents as a senator, for example, Edward Kennedy carefully nurtured the Kennedy ethos to build himself into the role as a major spokesman for the liberal political agenda. Oregon's Wayne Morse did much the same in the late 1960s, using his sharp tongue and celebrated independence as a basis for challenging the power of several presidents. More recently, the ideologically conservative Jesse Helms has done much the same. By vocally criticizing Ronald Reagan in his first term for lapses in completing the conservative agenda on school prayer, abortion, and federally mandated school desegregation plans, Helms achieved a visibility and importance that made him a political force equal to that of whole committees.[22]

Overall, the logistics of news reporting work against the Congress. There is frequent contact with party leaders, House and Senate officialdom, and committee chairs. There is also some interest in members with an independent base of support. Collectively these figures are the human reference points for a complex institution that is largely ignored. The 30-second television news story or the three-paragraph summary of House activity leaves little space for an outline of the ideas of thoughtful members who do not also have the clout of a pivotal position. The mass media focus instead on the formal leadership who may at times have little to say. But their presence provides certain legitimation to a news story.

## VITAL CHANNELS: COMMUNICATION NETWORKS IN CONGRESS

Two major dimensions shape our understanding of congressional communication. One involves the communication networks within the internal structure of Congress and the executive agencies beyond Capitol Hill. The other involves more public information channels. The former might be symbolized by the private lobbying that might take place in a Senate cloakroom between a bill's sponsor and an undecided colleague. The latter is typified by the more familiar responses given to the press by the House Speaker near the White House gate after a bargaining session with the president. In all, we think that there are four primary routes of private communication within the structure of official and unofficial Washington, and four public channels that are intended to reach well beyond.

### Internal Channels

#### Member to Staff

Packed into a few rooms in one of the enormous office buildings that ring the Capitol, the congressional staff labors to make a member of the House or Senate not just a representative, but a source of local or even national power. There really is no typical staff. Every office reflects the priorities of its member. Some put their personal staff allowances into nonpersonal items, such as computing. Others in the House find ways to go over the 18-person ceiling by utilizing part-time or "intern" help. Currently in the Senate, for example, staffs average about 30, but can range as high as 70.[2][3]

Personal staffs are occupied with the usual range of functions within an office, ranging from standard secretarial duties such as typing letters, to far more specialized work such as preparing legislation. There can be no doubt about the importance of the staffs. They perform the vital functions of communicating with the rest of the bureaucracy within the Congress (especially the committee staffs), and the well-oiled executive-branch agencies spread out over the rest of

Washington. Like the representative's staff, the "senator's personal office staffs are important," notes Donald R. Matthews. Indeed, "on routine matters they *are* the senators."[24]

The most common division which is made in the office is between the political side of congressional business, and the legislative side. Every member has several counterparts to the AA, or administrative assistant, and the LA, or legislative assistant. At various times a number of people may take up part of the work in these two broad areas. The first is responsible for the enormous logistical job of making the office responsive to the routine obligations of answering constituent requests and questions (perhaps 2,000 to 3,000 per week), scheduling the member's time, coordinating the member's efforts in various committees, and running the office.[25] The legislative assistant is involved in coordinating office work that involves specific items of legislation. It may be legislation the member plans to introduce or cosponsor. More often the job requires research on upcoming votes, or on bills in one of the member's committees.[26]

Like the staffs in many different types of offices, much of the work to be done is bureaucratized, involving little close contact with the member. Routine handling of constituent requests, correspondence, scheduling, and office management functions involve little need for close consultation. In classifying staff roles, Harrison Fox and Susan Hammond have found many duties that are essentially self-contained office tasks, for example: "writing letters of congratulations," "handling opinion ballots," "mailing government publications," "visiting with constituents in Washington." A much smaller range of responsibilities implicitly involves close interpersonal communication with the member. These tasks involve direct support of the member in a public setting—for example, "accompanying the Senator in committee"—or preparation of important messages that require the full knowledge and understanding of the member: "writing floor remarks and speeches," "bill drafting," and "writing magazine articles, books, and speeches other than those for Senate floor use."[27]

The member's relationship with the staff can vary greatly. Some in the House and Senate prefer to work alone without close ties to those in their offices. Others are just the reverse, looking to the staff for good intelligence, thoughtful advice, and emotional support. Theodore Sorensen's recollection of the Senate office of John F. Kennedy is probably representative of the middle ground.

> The Senator was not always satisfied with his staff's work. He disliked complainers and procrastinators. He wanted the thought and both sides

of an argument, but he had a special distaste for those who brought him only bad news.

The employer, like the man, was patient with his employees, but impatient with any inefficiency or incompetence. He was always accessible and ready to listen, quick to grasp a recommendation and disappointed only when there was none. He never raised his voice when expressing disagreement with our work. Indeed, he was rarely and then only briefly angry at any staff member.[28]

As Fox and Hammond note, staffs "may have positive, neutral, negative, symmetrical or asymmetrical relationships with their boss."[29] There are few guidelines. The only apparent certainty is that there is little room for independence from the thinking and actions of the member. Individuals of course do have private attitudes that differ markedly from the member's. But every staffer must learn that their relationships with the member are governed by an invariant hierarchical relationship.

For the ambitious professionals sought out by members perhaps the hardest adjustment required of life on Capitol Hill is the knowledge that the relationship with the member is never fully reciprocal. It is possible to argue a point of view, or to dissent in private. But on important matters the subordinate nature of the staff job is always evident. Michael Malbin believes that the strongest reason for the bright staff member to move on is the knowledge that he will always be in someone else's shadow. The frustration

> that ultimately starts to grate on so many staff people, is the knowledge that however powerful they may appear, or however often they may have turned their own opinions into laws, they will never be anything other than surrogates for someone else. One successful young staffer who was in the middle of looking for another job captured this in a comment that could have been echoed by hundreds of his colleagues: "I just don't want to spend the rest of my life carrying someone else's water."[30]

## Member to Member

A brief *Congressional Quarterly* description of the moments surrounding a routine budget vote readily points to the key nature of colleague-to-colleague contact in the legislative process. The occasion was a budget vote in the ninety-fifth Congress. The ostensible issue was whether an amendment cutting money from the president's budget would be approved. The hidden issue was the prestige of the Democratic leadership in the House, and the Democratic president. The Democrats had a two-to-one edge on the Republicans.

Freshman Rep. Leon E. Panetta, D-Calif., was having a tough time finishing his phone call in the House cloakroom.

First, Majority Leader Jim Wright, D-Texas, interrupted. Wright was followed by several other Democrats, who took turns breaking in. Then a page brought Panetta a note saying that Speaker Thomas P. O'Neill, Jr., D-Mass., wanted to see him. Panetta found no escape on the House floor. As he left the cloakroom and strode down the aisle into the crowded chamber, Jim Mooney, chief aide to Majority Whip John Brademas, D-Ind., spotted him. Mooney grabbed Norman Y. Mineta, D-Calif., and steered him toward Panetta.

"Can you give us a vote on this?" asked Mineta. Panetta said no, resisting his friend's pleas to change the vote he had just cast in favor of an amendment by Joseph L. Fisher, D-Va., to cut about $7 billion from the first fiscal 1979 budget resolution.

Undaunted by the rejection, Mineta turned to court other Democrats who had voted for the amendment—and against the wishes of the Democratic leadership.

Meanwhile, Wright wove his way through a crowd of younger members in the well of the chamber, urging them to switch their votes by signing little red cards stacked on a nearby table. O'Neill and Brademas stalked up the aisle, looking like hunters in search of prey. They, too, sought vote switchers. By the time the leaders stopped stalking—10 minutes after the House scoreboard showed that time had elapsed on the roll-call vote—16 Democrats had trooped down to the well to change their votes. The amendment, which had been a sure winner when time ran out, instead was defeated, 195-203.[31]

It is probably not an accident that all of the renovations of the Capitol building have left unchanged the many private and quiet places out of public view. A deliberative body always functions with both private and public levels of discussion. No talk of opening up the legislative process will ever reduce the need for private talk among colleagues. The House and Senate floors are theaters to *demonstrate* commitment. The committees and cloakrooms are backstage places to bargain for it. The vital process of educating oneself in preparation for a vote or a floor debate must go on in the many anterooms, offices, and meeting rooms off of the floor. Only private discussion can create an atmosphere that preserves the possibility of a personal change of heart. Some 60 unmarked hideaway offices are scattered within the labyrinth of the Capitol—off limits to the press and the public, but vital to the private communication that oils the public legislative machinery.[32]

Communication among colleagues in the Senate and House has many permutations. The most obvious deals with the decision to vote for or against an item of legislation. The member sponsoring legislation may spend an enormous amount of time seeking co-sponsors, votes from colleagues to get his bill out of committee, or a supporting vote in an upcoming close vote. Caucuses, committee meetings, votes on highly contested bills, disputes over legislative or party leadership, are but a few of the events that spur the member to consult with colleagues. The importance of such contact is obvious. A member of the House may have to vote his district on a bill, meaning he must represent what have perhaps been their vocal interests. He may also vote out of a deep conviction or a well-defined principle. A bill may correspond with his sense of justice, or violate it. But on many floor votes the attitudes of colleagues matter most. Even a member who has been heavily lobbied by a variety of special interests may finally satisfy himself by seeking out the opinions of colleagues. "I try, and I think most other senators try to read the report on a bill before voting on it," notes a member, "but I must admit that I have voted on many hundreds of bills solely on the basis of what other senators told me about them."[33] Another long-time observer of the Congress comes to the same conclusion:

> [D]espite all the high-powered lobbyists, the constituent mail, and the briefs, brochures, and broadsides that might engulf Capitol Hill over a particularly controversial issue, the most important influence on an undecided Senator is usually the personal appeal of another Senator . . . most members of the U.S. Senate are more likely to listen to their peers on the inside than to an outsider, no matter how imposing his or her credentials.[34]

There is another important social dimension to the one-to-one interactions that occur in the Congress. Members are a part of the same institution. They come to share the same general patriotic feelings toward the institution, and frequently against its loudest critics. It is not unusual for members to feel closer to colleagues in the other party across the aisle than to their own party leader downtown at the White House.

This emphasis on cooperation has strong task-oriented objectives. First and foremost is the fact that, in an institution that requires *formal* opposition, interpersonal contact reduces disruptive conflict. There are, in Donald Matthew's phrase, "folkways" that require courtesy and tolerance for conflict.[35] The gulf that separates opposing forces on a pending bill is not expected to extend to future debates. Not only is there an obvious need to keep the door open for future alignments, but talking privately reduces tension by redefining a potentially disruptive relationship. A willingness to talk, to bargain, reminds all participants that the public posturing common to debate on the House or Senate floor is to be viewed as policy-centered, not as an extension of destructive personal animosities.

Additionally, there is obviously a strategic need to build as broad a network of allies and contacts within the House or Senate as is possible (though rarely between them). The rule of reciprocity is one of the oldest and best known of political life. There may be simple vote swapping (for example, support for a public works project in Alabama in exchange for a new military installation in Georgia). But it is more likely that the member simply seeks to keep as many lines of communication open to colleagues as possible. A reservoir of goodwill can thus be tapped as needed.

There are two rhetorical/interpersonal dimensions of legislative life that require a strong network of interpersonal contacts beyond the glare of publicity. The most important is that private discussion provides an opportunity to use an entire range of appeals that would be taboo if spoken in a public forum. Obviously, votes cannot be exchanged in a public assembly. But the effect may involve more subtle changes than that. An advocate seeking a convert can explain his or her own reservations on a bill—caveats that perhaps could never be expressed in the defensive environment of the House or Senate floor. In private it is also possible for a reticent to explain his reasons without needlessly alienating other members, or to express regrets for having to vote his district. It is evident that in the combative environment of debate total candor is impossible. It almost goes without saying that the personal *private* contact is one that minimizes the need to muster some political courage.

A second vital element in this private form of communication is the fact that comments made to one other person are far easier to alter than those made on the official record. Members who are ambivalent on a particular piece of legislation are not likely to give speeches, thereby revealing their own uncertainties. They are likely instead to seek the private counsel of members whose judgment they respect, usually retaining the option to switch positions if pressures from any one of a wide range of sources become significant.

For example, countless acquaintances of Lyndon Johnson have contrasted the formal and somewhat awkward public persuasion of the Senate majority leader with their memory of the private master tactician. The notorious "Johnson treatment" was far more aggressive and sensitive to the political needs of the victim than was ever apparent from the public Johnson. In public he found most of his ideals in the rhetorical images of the New Deal. In private, he was far more inclined to strike all of the notes of personal interest to mobilize a legislative hold-out. Performing the role he played best, as manager of the Senate in a competitive but cooperative environment, Johnson knew how to utilize persuasive arguments that could never be touched in a Senate speech, and how to reassure another senator looking for some indication that a vote of support would not go unforgotten.[36] Johnson never lost the power of one-to-one persuasion as president. It was simply that he couldn't use it as effectively in a public role that required far greater use of benign public appeals.

## Member to Reporter: Off the Record

Normally, the Washington press is viewed as the advocate of the people. It is often said that the ideal relationship between a politician and those covering his activities is a courteous but distinctly wary relationship. And it often is. But one of the results of the professionalizing of political reporting, and of the increased dependency of congressmen on favorable press for reelection, is what can be a special interdependence that is cultivated between key reporters and those they are covering. William Rivers has called this a "sweetheart" relationship.[37] More bluntly, television commentator Harry Reasoner has called these ties "incestuous."[38]

This pattern does not hold for every member of Congress. To many in the Congress, members of the press appear to be either overworked or uninterested. But many others share the belief that the cultivation of the press is necessary to gain local and national recognition.

Reporters representing regional papers may seek to establish friendships with members from the same geographical area. Such contacts help justify the considerable expense of placing a reporter in Washington on a full-time basis. The arrangement gives the paper the best of both worlds: It has an additional source of national news, but it is presented with a local angle. By contrast, contacts with the national press are generally confined to the congressional leadership, or to senior members of the House or Senate with national reputations.

Most members of Congress are friendly to reporters, but also wary of their work. The press represents a vital link to their essential political base back home. But most are also aware of the fact that their greatest problem is not bad press from aggressive home media, but no press coverage at all. The typical member of the House, for example, regrets that little coverage of his work will develop, or that the often ill-prepared local press will lack sufficient knowledge to tell a story with the depth and accuracy that it may need.[39]

The relationship is somewhat different for major figures in the House, and most of the Senate. They are in more demand, and may have a greater stake in attempting the more skeptical national press. The chairperson of a House subcommittee, for example, might realize that an important chance to win eventual floor approval for a favored bill may be to attract the editorial support of key newsweeklies or newspapers. The enthusiasm of a Washington-based columnist who is read nationally may help as well. The relationship that a member establishes with an important member of the press actually turns out to be beneficial to both. The journalist gains inside information which can give his reporting a special perspective. The politican, of course, gains a national forum that translates into an opportunity to alter public opinion. These mutual benefits are so attractive that, as Rivers notes, "the news business in Washington has developed an exceedingly high percentage of 'ins'—and far from enough 'outs.' "[40] With regard to Capitol Hill in particular:

> The tendency of reporters who regularly cover the Senate, for example, is—naturally enough—to make friends with the Senate's ruling group, the primary sources of important news. By itself this is certainly understandable. But over a period of time there seems to be a marked tendency to report the activities of the ruling group in a favorable light and to make challengers to that group appear as though they are social misfits.[41]

Stewart Alsop recalls a fairly typical example of this pattern under Senator Lyndon Johnson:

> In his Senate days, most of the reporters who covered Johnson were personal friends or at least friendly acquaintances. Most of them liked him, and even those who didn't were heavily dependent on the Majority Leader for news. . . . Several days a week, after the Senate adjourned, eight or ten reporters would crowd into Johnson's small, impressive, Brumidi-decorated office suite off the Senate floor, or later, into the vast unimpressive Texas-decorated office suite off the Senate floor, known as "the Taj Mahal," which Johnson co-opted for himself in 1959. Drink would flow generously, courtesy of the Majority Leader . . . amidst much talk. Almost all of it Johnson's.[42]

"Internal" communication between members of the press and members of Congress serves several useful functions beyond the obvious goal of establishing sources for news stories. One of the most important is that this form of hybrid friendship serves as a kind of mutual protection for both parties. The politician views his friendship with an influential columnist or correspondent as a possible guarantee against an unwelcome story. The journalist gains the assurance that a story that should have been covered will not show up first in a competitor's paper. The information that flows between them includes an enormous amount of intelligence gathered in two great parallel information networks. The press, with sources in many executive agencies, for example, may be in a position to pass on intelligence that a member's informal congressional network might miss. Conversely, a member with knowledge about a pending deal between two factions within the Congress may be able to fill in details vital to a journalist's efforts to piece together an elaborate political puzzle.

There is also a tangible lure to the power that is implicit in the friendship that a reporter may be able to cultivate with a key figure on Capitol Hill. The urge to be more than a spectator to the shaping of national laws would appeal to almost anyone's vanity. Reporters are not immune from the lure of influencing the course of American legislative life, even in some small way. Serving as a source of information, as an ad hoc adviser, or even as a supporter of legislation under consideration has its psychological rewards. Columnist Drew Pearson, for example, took an active interest in the Senate leadership of Lyndon Johnson, and the presidential candidacy of Hubert Humphrey in 1959. Jack Anderson was likewise predisposed to the candidacy of Senator John Kennedy.[43] Bert Andrews, a reporter for the *New York Herald Tribune*, won a Pulitzer Prize in part for his work with Senator Richard Nixon in prosecuting alleged spying by Alger Hiss.[44] As Donald Matthews has noted with regard to the Senate:

> Both senators and reporters have it in their power to build each other up. A senator, by giving a reporter preferential treatment, can enhance [a] newsman's prestige among the press corps, his standing with his employers and readers, and his earning power. A reporter, by giving the senator a good break, can contribute substantially to the success of the senator's career. This kind of "back scratching" is far more profitable to both sides than conflict.[45]

## Member to Lobbyists, and Agency Officials

Members of Congress create many communication liaisons for convenience. Two channels of special interest are those that flow from Capitol Hill to various agencies in the executive branch, and from various special interests represented by active lobbyists to the member. In the first case the flow is primarily from the Hill to the agencies:

for general information, for help in solving a constituent's specific problems, and sometimes for mutual support against the intransigence of the White House or the Congress. In the latter case the arrows are reversed. It is obviously the lobbyist who seeks support from the member. But as we shall see, even in exchanges with lobbyists, the member gains something in the transaction.

The men and women in Congress obviously have a profound interest in the work of bureaucracies under nominal presidential control. Ranging from housing, transportation, education, military affairs, land management, and hundreds of similar concerns, the thick blanket of agencies spread over Washington collectively have the power to affect the member's political fortunes. The agencies are responsible for executing policy, and are subject to the oversight of Congress and its specialist committees. These formal structural ties are well known, and create an obvious need for executive-legislative communication.

Taken as a whole, members of federal agencies are responsive to the Congress because the legislative branch has a power that at times even surpasses that of the White House. Congress controls spending, and thus can exert enormous control over an agency. A department that is unresponsive to requests for help from a senior senator, for example, may find that it has lost a crucial ally on future appropriations or tax issue votes. For this reason most executive departments have a legislative liaison staff oriented to giving quick responses to members in need of information or help. The data that is supplied may include straightforward help in behalf of a member's constituent, or information that satisfies his own legislative research or committee needs. Many such staffers are former congressional employees, and are chosen for their ability to forge alliances with members and their staffs on Capitol Hill.[46]

From the agency's perspective the inherent pluralism of the Congress makes the fence-mending process difficult. Keeping a key member of Congress happy can tax the political skill of even a veteran administrator. To cite one instance, the complaints of former Health, Education and Welfare Secretary Joseph Califano are revealing. He recalls the conflicting signals he received from the Congress as the cabinet official responsible for enforcing some of the nation's civil rights laws:

> The Congress has too often been hypocritical—there is no more kind or accurate word for it—in proclaiming glorious rights through authorizing statutes, and subverting the ability to enforce those rights through the

appropriations process. . . . I cannot remember a call from a member of Congress to step up civil rights enforcement action in the racial area; I recall scores of pleas to slow down or blunt such enforcement.[47]

The fact that an administrator must cope with congressional control of annual appropriations in such basic areas as the space program, defense, welfare grants, and public works creates a bind.[48] The burden is obviously placed on the agencies to keep channels of communication open.

In addition, in an age of congressional specialization there is a natural tendency for members to become advocates for phases of administrative action for which they have special interests. Members of Congress lobby each other in behalf of agencies they have come to identify with. For some it is the affluent Pentagon; for others the favored fields may be programs or agencies tied to veterans' affairs, environmental protection, education, banking, small businesses, the fishing industry, health care, foreign aid to a particular nation, or countless other concerns. Specialization encourages the member to become an agency advocate. Far fewer members are critical of the bureaucracies that work in areas of their own concern. In either case the job facing the government department is evident. It must attempt to enhance its surrogate's support on Capitol Hill, with the hope that the favor will someday be repaid.

Lobbyists also represent an important link to persons serving terms in Congress, although the role that special interests play is at least partially misunderstood.

Virtually every organized group with a large financial or social stake in legislation has full-time lobbyists in Washington. Their primary goal is obvious: to make their feelings known on any legislative or direct oversight activity within the Congress. Much of their work is essentially indirect, encouraging supporters to communicate via mail to representatives and senators. Only part of their time involves actual visits to congressional offices to lobby legislative assistants or members.[49]

Most lobbyists concentrate their efforts on members who they believe are already sympathetic to their viewpoints. Their goal is frequently to backstop a member by providing information that can be used to persuade fellow colleagues. This support can come in the form of prepared speech inserts, fact sheets, information on how a bill will effect a local area, and "head-counting" to help determine a bill's prospects.[50] Some of the discussion occurs during arranged meetings with a representative or senator. At other times lobbyists will seek the help of an intermediary who has the respect of a representative.[51] A great deal of lobbying involves communication with a member of the representative's or senator's staff. The problem of how to gain access to a member in the course of his busy day is an ever-present one.

The best solution, many special interests have found, is to hire former members who can utilize their insider status. An interesting use of such channels of friendship was evident to Senator Pete Domenici during his protracted effort to legislate user fees for river barge operators in 1977. The legislation was designed to make the users of America's navigable rivers partially liable for the enormous maintenance costs involved. The barge owners lobbied intensively against the issue. The barge competitors, the railroads, lobbied for it. As T. R. Reid reconstructs it, the barge operators recruited former Florida Senator George Smathers for their fight against the fees. He had formerly worked for the railroads, but switched, and became a powerful force in behalf of the barge companies. "As a former Senator, he was allowed to prowl the Senate floor and the cloakrooms just off it, where Senators congregate and where most outsiders are not admitted."[52] Lobbyists working for Domenici's bill could not produce the same effective personal kind of persuasion. By necessity they took a different approach:

> The railroads and their allies, lacking a prominent individual lobbyist who had personal connections with Senators, concentrated, on the whole, on the Senators' staffs. . . . This staff strategy was a proven winner; one of the great victories in lobbying lore—the civil rights lobby's defeat of the nomination of G. Harrold Carswell to the Supreme Court —had been won by convincing staff members, who in turn convinced their Senators, that Carswell was unfit for the Court. Since Senators were even more likely to rely on staff advice on a relatively unfamiliar issue like the waterway bill, the railroad tactic seemed eminently sensible.[53]

Overall, we probably overestimate the effect that lobbying has on the legislative process. From a communications perspective Congress is preeminently a place for persuasion. As we have already argued, in an extended sense lobbying occurs all of the time. It is not confined to just a few, but to an enormous range of "registered" and unofficial interests, including both groups and individuals. What is often overlooked is that lobbying is often a protective rather than an offensive activity. Like television advertisers who advertise essentially to hold their share of a market, the sheer amount of persuasion that occurs no doubt weakens the effect of any one source. Members spend a good deal of time persuading each other. Constituents offer their own assessments. Friendly reporters—in their unofficial roles as friends —may give their advice as well. The balance of interests may in fact be so close that it is not unreasonable to assume that they often cancel each other out. When that occurs, it may be surprisingly easy for a member to render a good decision on how to vote. Like former Iowa Senator John C. Culver, the member may see a no-win situation as one that frees him to vote on a bill's merits: "if it makes a lot of people unhappy in the process, so be it."[54]

## External Communication

Up to this point we have discussed basic communication patterns within the Washington community: patterns that only indirectly affect the general public. Obviously, however, members seek to exercise influence well beyond the highly politicized world in the District of Columbia. Whether they are communicating with individuals or groups, they seek to reach external publics for whom politics is not a profession, but a process of resolving problems and distributing resources. We start with one of the most basic forms of external contact.

### Member to Constituents

A major portion of a member's time is spent essentially serving as a clearing house between residents in the member's district or state and the enormous federal bureaucracy. The percent of time for the average member seems to vary, but may average to about 18 percent of the typical work week, and about 65 percent of the personal staff's time.[55] As a percent of the member's total effort, constituency work can range from one of many equally important roles (i.e., particularly for a senior senator or a major party or legislative leader) to *the* single most important activity. Indeed, given the imperative for gaining reelection, probably no function is so certain to gain supporters than casework. Particularly for House members it is a form of insurance that enhances a member's electability in the district.

Most constituency contact is relatively impersonal, involving mail or phone correspondence handled primarily by a member's staff. Lost Social Security or civil service checks, disputes over veteran's benefits, and requests for information regarding federal policy rank high on the list of topics.

Many members maintain two or three offices in the home districts, visiting them regularly and providing opportunities for constituents to meet them personally, or consult with the staff. This kind of activity has a special attraction for a number of backbenchers. Compared with the snail's pace of activity in Congress, casework offers the possibility of gaining relatively fast results. In addition, a relatively weak backbencher may regain a sense of importance and mission in face-to-face encounters with constituents who are genuinely impressed with his ability to "get something done."[5 6]

Members also meet constituents for other reasons than casework. Some may try to routinely greet visitors to Washington from the home district. And most plan regular trips to their districts or states for appearances and town meetings before constituents. It is not unheard of for a congressman to attempt to keep a dozen appointments and make a half dozen speeches in a one-day trip back to the district.[5 7] Quite a few seem to believe that no form of activity is as certain to produce support as the contact that comes in a personal appearance before constituents. As one representative with an upcoming campaign on his mind told Richard Fenno, "The best way to win a vote is to shake hands with someone. You don't win votes by the thousands with a speech. You win votes by looking individuals in the eye, one at a time, and asking them [for their vote]."[5 8]

By general consent, a less efficient way to reach ordinary citizens is by using direct mail. Congressional newsletters and opinion polls cascade out of the Senate and House office buildings every year, paid for by the generous postal frank available to every member. Some of the newsletters take advantage of increasingly sophisticated computer technology that can target mail to specific groups. Cross-referenced lists of addresses can produce mailings for minorities, the elderly, veterans, or countless other groups who may be interested in particular pieces of legislation, or the member's latest statement on a specialized area. At least one senator won reelection in 1972 by using such a cross-referenced system to target an antibusing message to white middle-class voters in Michigan. His message deliberately excluded blacks, and eventually resulted in the imposition of tighter standards on selective public-financed mailings.[5 9]

But few members believe that such mail does much more than remind the readers of their representative's name. While recognizing it as a basic tool for remaining in the consciousness of voters, most seem reluctant to depend too heavily on such mailings as a way to communicate with constituents. One aide to a New Jersey senator notes that his boss believes that "once they get the newsletter, they read it between the mailbox and the living room."[6 0]

*Member to the Press (For Attribution)*

In the late 1950s Douglass Cater called the Congress "a happy hunting ground of journalistic enterprise."[61] In some ways it still is. But it is also a troubled preserve, and one in which it is not entirely clear who is the hunter and who is the prey. In the 1970s a number of political writers advanced the theory that the balance of power had significantly shifted: that it was now the press that determined the fortunes and set the agenda of key political institutions such as the Congress. Conservative thinker Kevin Phillips asserted that we now had a national "mediacracy," a liberal, press "affluentsia with substantial control over the knowledge and information functions" of the society.[62] Others saw different trends. Press critic Ben Bagdikian described members of Congress who were attempting to maintain their political power by using print and television stories "to propagandize their constituents at the constituents' expense with the cooperation of the local news media."[63] Edward Epstein examined network television's incomplete definition of political news, shaped as he saw it by the industry's self-imposed constraints of time and entertainment.[64] There is no shortage of judgments that can be made about who maintains the upper hand in the give and take of congressional-press relations.

No questions in this area raise more interesting answers than those which address the relationships between newsgatherers and newsmakers. It can be said with some certainty that it is too simple to depend too heavily on the model of the press as adversary, or even the more enlightened model of the press as involved in a relationship based solely on mutual benefits.[65] Dan Nimmo's extensive 1964 study of the relationships between public information officers and the press in Washington leads to conclusions one would expect to find. The press and those being covered have goals in common, but they also have divergent goals. Neither publicists nor press have a decisive upper hand:

> The attitudes uncovered in the present study do not indicate either a willingness or an ability on the part of either the information establishment or the news media to exert leadership in the opinion process. Both the newsman and the [public information] officer defer to the political official as the primary articulator of issues for public debate. To information officers, conflict was inherently an evil to be avoided in favor of agreement. To publicize agreement is good; to publicize controversy is bad. The newsman views the whole process differently. The publicizing

of agreement, although not bad, is also not news. To publicize controversy is the essence of news.[66]

There are slightly more than 400 domestic reporters who regularly
cover the Congress.[67] Only a relatively few have the luxury of covering it full time, becoming important fixtures in the House or Senate
press galleries. Most reporters writing about the people on Capitol Hill
work for news syndicates or papers that stretch their time and resources to the limits. A Washington correspondent for a midwestern
city, for example, may cover his state's congressional delegation. But
he may be additionally responsible for covering committees and other
executive agencies all over town. They are likely to include those that
are traditionally important to the cornbelt—such as the Departments
of Agriculture or Interior.

The range of stories can be vast. Committee hearings, votes, news
of trips by members, scandals, veto override votes, House-Senate conferences, oversight hearings, interviews of presidential nominees, presidential messages, and campaign news are all fair game for comment
and reporting. Newspapers and television stations from the distant
provinces report these events in capsule form, sometimes with information from their own stringers or correspondents. More often than
not they receive such stories from the wire services or one of the
broadcast networks. A paper with modest means may be almost totally
dependent on such reports for most Washington news. They will also
receive a steady flow of press releases identifying a local member's
contributions to decision making with a local dimension.

There is a significant gap between local and national coverage.
Most members of Congress feel that they must seek out the press in
order to gain publicity for their work. The large majority of the 435
members of the House have faced the fact that if they are sought out
at all, it is by a representative of their own district's press. The major
national networks and the prestige dailies have so many compelling
news sources, that it is a fact of life that they need any one congressional source less than the source needs them. David Paletz and Robert
Entman have succinctly summarized the problem:

> Unfortunately for the legislators, the national press needs any single
> member of Congress less than members desire the press. The opportunity
> to broadcast unmediated speeches and invitations to participate in tele-
> vision panel discussions rarely accrue to ordinary members of Congress.
> In practice, Congressmen and -women court the press as the press courts
> the president. Their problem is the relative lack of interest of the mass

media in most of their activities and the reporters' belief that the information released by legislators is even more self-interested than that coming from the White House.[68]

The tone of press coverage also differs markedly between national and local mass media. Although they have pointed out many exceptions, a number of analysts have noted that local broadcast and print coverage of individual members is far more sympathetic than the reporting that comes from national sources. Magazines such as *Time* and *Newsweek*, dailies such as the *New York Times* or the *Los Angeles Times*, all tend to focus on the collective nature of the institution, or the House and Senate leadership. The networks act similarly. In contrast, local papers and broadcasts tend to emphasize the activities of specific members.

It comes as no surprise that Congress fares poorly when coverage is reduced to its characteristics as a collection of diverse interests. Very little empathy is aroused for any organization described in terms of its decision-making processes. Compared to the simplicity and clarity of an individual's actions, a group's work will always appear more sluggish and less coordinated. The broadcast commentary of NBC's David Brinkley that "it would take Congress thirty days to make instant coffee" is typical of the public frustration which is commonly expressed about Congress as a body.[69] The remarks of former ABC commentator Howard K. Smith are even more revealing—and probably unfair—in their explicit comparison of the deliberative branch with the less ambiguous leadership found in the presidency:

> When Congress dominates, it's a mess, as after the Civil War when it created regional hatreds that are dying only now. The past year the Congress has been mostly in the saddle and among the results—a tax reform that didn't reform, an energy act that in no way meets the fuel crisis.
> Granted, recent presidents have abused power and have had to be checked. Still, we shan't see effective government again till the pendulum swings back to give the executive more leverage.[70]

The national media themselves have an institutional problem in covering Congress. Because they address the nation as a whole, they seem reluctant to focus on the work of typical members. Their vantage points tend to be on the committees, the leadership, and relations with other segments of the Washington establishment. Michael Robinson and Kevin Appel have looked at these and other instances, concluding that—especially with regard to television—Congress is in "a uniquely vulnerable position."

> [L] egislatures in liberal secular societies abound in philosophical con-
> tradictions, intense political bargaining, and what some might call the
> amorality of democracy. This makes for "bad" news, which is, of course,
> "good" copy.

In addition:

> In most circumstances the president is covered too personally, too direct-
> ly, to be maligned by the networks day to day. The networks need the
> president, and *generally* they need him. Congress is less personal and
> hence more subject to attack.[71]

The absence of any single official voice for Congress thus fights the
tide of many journalistic currents, particularly as they are now con-
stituted by television reporting. To be sure, the luxury of space in a
few nationally read journals may guarantee a reasonably accurate portrayal of the legislative process, and the impact of individuals who are
affecting it. But television network news coverage is more typical,
and its superficial coverage provides no such basis for understanding.

Ironically, it is at the local level that readers may see congressional
activity from the vantage point of the individual member. Part of the
member's role is to cultivate contacts with reporters tied to the home
districts.[72] As we noted above, papers want to emphasize the local
angle of a congressional story, and members are more than happy to
oblige, sometimes explaining how a bill will impact on their district,
and occasionally getting the opportunity to release information that
has been routed through them by a sympathetic committee or agency.
From the average member's standpoint, such contacts are too infre-
quent, but satisfying, because they help to maintain the goodwill at
home needed to gain reelection. In journalistic terms, such reporting
is usually inadequate. "Some of the congressmen and staff I interviewed," Robinson recalls, "rejected the premise that the local press
is softer than the national press, but most saw a fairly clear split between the two worlds of news."[73] There is a general feeling that many
members of the local media—because of time constraints, and perhaps
because of less of an adversarial edge—are more willing to be spoon fed.

Sympathetic treatment by the local press is often cited as a reason
for the puzzling differences of opinion Americans express between
Congress as an institution, and *their* own congressman. Studies of
public attitudes point out a general "nationwide contempt for Congress" on one hand, "and district-wide esteem for its members" on
the other.[74] As Robinson indicates, this paradox is at least partially
attributable to the combined effect of the more hostile national media
and the more sympathetic local press.[75]

The publicity machinery that is available to the Congress includes a number of physical and staff resources. A press gallery is set aside in both houses, and is available to credentialed reporters. In addition, reporters have access to some of the anterooms, eating areas, and elevators that are closed to the rest of the general public. They may also enjoy the comfort and prestige that comes with invitations to socialize with leaders in their private offices. Broadcasters may make use of audio and video studios located in the basements of the Capitol and the House Office Building, as long as the object of their attention is a representative or senator. The interviews taped in such locations usually feature a local television or radio reporter, but the true producer is actually the member being interviewed.[76]

The most important press resource, however, is usually the member's staff. Any number of individuals may be variously involved in press-related work, the most common of which is the preparation of "news" releases for distribution in Washington and back home. Press relations specialists are responsible for translating a member's activities into stories that have at least a semblance of news. Their job is essentially to find a way to meet the publicity goals of the member. Those goals may range from simply keeping the local media at home informed so that the ground is laid for an easy reelection, to the more elaborate objective of gaining national recognition for a member's interests. But they must also sell their favorable releases as something that can be taken as serious (and not totally self-serving) information. Because these staff specialists are so common, and because congressional reporting is left to so few, these staffs gain a kind of bogus journalistic responsibility by default. They write "news" items about their employers which are often used uncritically by many home district newspapers and broadcasters. As press critic Ben Bagdikian notes:

> Hundreds of press releases, paid for by the taxpayers, are sent to the media by members of Congress, and hundreds are run verbatim or with insignificant changes, most often in medium-sized and small papers, with only rare calls to check facts and ask questions that probe beyond the pleasant propaganda.[77]

Press releases remain the key piece of press-member communication in the Congress. Among the 14 members of the New Jersey congressional delegation in 1983 there was an average of 86 news releases per member, with a low of 10 from one, and a high of 175 from another.[78]

Other staff members may arrange for private interviews with members of the press, and for scheduling of the television studios to record a broadcast interview. The latter may have much the same quality of a press release, but it is an important adaptation to an age that is increasingly dependent on television. As a representative from North Carolina has observed, "television and radio communication is the 20th-century version of the postal frank."[79]

The attitudes of individual members vary significantly on the importance of such contacts. At one extreme are members who view the press with a good degree of suspicion, and often act on the dictum that a low profile is the safest course. The attitude of a representative from the Northeast is representative:

> I'm not going to look for anyone to talk to. We talk to reporters, but they have responsibilities to check out what is going on. I don't chase reporters and I haven't for 21 years. If they don't know what I'm doing, they're not doing their jobs.[80]

The other extreme is represented by members who have often come to power outside of the traditional party structure, and who are more conscious of the need to maintain public approval with a high visibility public profile. Because of its size and eclectic politics, California is often thought to be the prime state for this philosophy. And, indeed, there can be no doubt that members of the Senate from such a large state must be willing to build press contacts to compensate for the difficulties in communicating with the voters in more traditional ways. But this view is probably national in scope. "I think the public should know where you stand on issues," notes a representative. "You use the mail, press contacts, any way you can get visibility."[81]

### Member to Press and Public: Hearings and Investigations

From a rhetorical standpoint perhaps the most important forum in Washington outside of the White House is the congressional committee. Numerous observers have pointed out that more and more of the substantive work of the Congress is carried out in the standing committees, the subcommittees, and in special investigations.[82] Almost every item of legislation, every high-level executive appointee, and most problems of general national concern will at some point be the subject of public hearings on Capitol Hill.

The propensity for Congress to divide itself into small committees has both a social and constitutional base. By constitutional right members are charged with the responsibility to oversee the functioning government and—when necessary—to investigate areas where government has failed to perform properly. Between 1941 and 1944, few example, Harry Truman chaired the Senate Special Committee to Investigate the National Defense Program. As the name suggests, it was asked to certify that defense contracts were economically and fairly made. By most accounts, it did a good job in the course of its work with 1,798 witnesses and 432 public hearings.[83] More typically, individual House and Senate committees regularly meet to consider new bills, and testimony relating to new or needed legislation. Routine hearings by a committee may run for several hours over a number of days. Very few sessions are closed. But public and press attendance may be low anyway, depending on the gravity of the issues under consideration.

The flavor of a hearing is conveyed in T. R. Reid's detailed study of the Senate's consideration of a user's fee for river barges. The bill brought out 50 witnesses, including other members of the Senate, and advocates from the Carter White House.

> Although the formats of congressional hearings are as varied as their subject matter, it is usually easy to predict the types of witnesses that will show up at any particular session. There will almost always be a few members of Congress who want to testify, either because of a sincere interest in the topic or because of a political need to appear interested. There will be witnesses representing commercial and political causes that will have a direct stake in the measure; just as in a trial, the clash of opposing views from these advocates is supposed to clarify the issues for the decision makers. And there will usually be testimony from some objective observers—a scholar sometimes, or a government official who is supposed to take a disinterested view of the problem and the proposed solutions. Since these objective witnesses frequently have the most credibility with committee members, their testimony is particularly important in shaping the legislation the committee eventually recommends.[84]

Few observers doubt the worth of routine hearings for the purpose of seeking out information about new legislative proposals or presidential decisions. William Keefe and Morris Ogul note that "The Committee is the principal agency of the legislature for gathering information and the principal instrument by which the legislature can defend and maintain itself in struggles with the chief executive and the bureaucracy."[85]

On the other hand, hearings designed primarily to attract attention for a proposal, or investigations intended to shed light on a national problem, suggest their own problems and advantages. Many believe, with Arthur Schlesinger, Jr., that the power to investigate is often well used by the Congress. He notes that "while the conventional assumption is that the strength of legislative bodies lies in the power to legislate, a respectable tradition has long argued that it lies as much or more in the power to investigate."[86] But nearly every study of hearings and investigations also cites Walter Lippmann's searing judgment that the average congressional investigation is a "legalized atrocity . . . in which Congressmen, starved of their legitimate food for thought, go on a wild and feverish manhunt, and do not stop at cannibalism."[87] Lippmann had little faith in the motives or the expertise of the average legislator. Others, such as evidence analyst Robert Newman, find that the truth is frequently abused at the hands of politically motivated committee chairs and members. Newman lists a veritable catalogue of abuses which regularly occur in committee settings:

> Hostile witnesses can be grilled, friendly ones babied. Third-rate authorities can be called, first-rate ones neglected. What matters, from a political standpoint, is headlines of the moment. Few will pore over the record to register a judgment of truth or falsehood, and even if they do, events have moved past the moment of relevance.[88]

Even granting that the quality of individual sessions varies greatly, there is little doubt that the committees of Congress serve several key groups in extremely important ways. From the member's point of view the committee is a way to stand out and apart from the larger body. The specialist committee system encourages the member to develop two or three fields of expertise. Ideally, his knowledge grows as seniority within a particular committee increases. This pattern has several important effects. For the nation it produces legislative experts equal to, and in some cases better than those who work in the executive agencies. The specialist also approaches national problems with a greater understanding of the political consequences of governmental solutions. He may have a better sense of the workability of a bill than other experts who are beyond the reach of public opinion. Representatives and senators may become shrewd students of federal tax laws, farm subsidy programs, the banking or broadcasting industries, rural medical facilities, military procurement procedures, and many other narrow but important areas. Their expertise makes them able to offer effective public cases that can challenge the natural rhetorical supremacy of the executive.

In addition, for the member/specialist there is the advantage of being able to at least momentarily seize attention as an individual rather than as just a small part of the heterogeneous legislature. Harry Truman, J. William Fulbright, Sam Ervin, Jr., William Proxmire, John

Pastore, Henry Jackson, Edward Kennedy, and Howard Baker, Jr. are but a few senators in the nation's recent past who have gained national recognition for their roles in hearings and investigations. With their counterparts in the House they were able to carve out loyal constituencies with altruistic and at times selfish interests in their special areas of competence. Dealing with subjects as diverse as the effects of television violence on children, Korean government influence peddling, the Watergate affair, and countless other similar events in the endless cycle of national concerns, each was able to command a few seconds of precious air time or a few columns of print on a number of consecutive days. Hearings gave them the opportunity to compete with the executive on his own terms: as personal and committed advocates rather than merely faceless members in a body known more for its unromantic political brokerage than its heroism.

Another rhetorically attractive feature of hearings is that they offer a refreshingly different set of roles to the member. Normally, the work of Congress is associated with the need for a member to grasp detail and the fine points of legislative compromise. However, in the committee setting members are not only able to demonstrate their expertise, but they can use it in a way that ingratiates themselves to the general public. In examining the objections that a professional lobbyist may have to a new bill, for example, the member may represent himself as the champion of the public interest, counterpoised against the "special pleaders." His committee role allows him to enact a more heroic public interest-centered approach to politics than might be reflected alone in an examination of recent voting patterns. The "representative" is literally able to enact the very essence of his or her title. By performing as a public trustee, by protecting the federal coffers against those who would unfairly drain them, the representative is able to shake off some of the role-related liabilities that go with the incremental and pragmatic nature of legislative politics.

Reporters love such moments of drama. In an investigation or hearing, members of Congress can be far more direct and accusatory than most other public officials. They can create the legislative conflict that is deemed newsworthy. Just such conflict was produced in the early 1970s when Rhode Island's feisty John Pastore challenged the executives of the three television networks. Pastore used his membership on the Senate's Subcommittee on Communications to press for less televised violence. The patient lecturing that Pastore gave the media moguls was something that could have come from a Frank Capra film. They were in his territory. And he was enacting the role of a man on a crusade. The fatherly senator with simple wire-framed glasses was appalled by the slickness and violence of Saturday morning cartoons, and other television fare directed to children. The politics of the moment were perfect: the decent "everyman" challenging the six-figure-salary executives to be less concerned about profits and more concerned about the welfare of the nation's children.[8 9]

It was similarly said that the Watergate hearings did much the same for the chairman of the House Judiciary Committee, Representative Peter Rodino. A quiet man, Rodino had languished in public obscurity for years. Coming from the tough and often corrupt politics of Newark, New Jersey, no one expected much beyond the stereotype of a backslapping ethnic-Italian politician. To those who knew only his name and his district he was perhaps stereotyped as the kind of politician who was only useful to like-minded folks in Newark's Democratic working class wards. The Rodino persona presented in the widely televised hearings was quite different: seemingly fair-minded, cautious, serious, and genuinely saddened by the prospect of overseeing the impeachment of Richard Nixon.[9 0]

Another important element in the hearings process is what has been called the safety-valve function. Hearings and investigations are a way to let off steam harmlessly, but with some symbolic effect.[9 1] In what might be a nearly complete symbolic gesture, groups may testify, members may offer bills, and social and governmental problems may be discussed without legislative action ever being taken or seriously considered. The resulting hearings may have publicity value, and may provide comfort to its participants by laying the groundwork for future action. Such hearings permit members of the Congress to give what amounts to symbolic service to those for whom legislative action is all but impossible. They also permit the statements and tracts of dissidents to find their way into the *Congressional Record*. Constituents important to a committee member can be given the legitimacy of a congressional forum for their ideas. In the late 1970s, for example, all of these functions were performed by Edward Kennedy, who frequently held hearings in the Senate Labor and Public Welfare Committee urging the passage of a national health insurance plan. Even as the political divide between Jimmy Carter and Kennedy widened, and even though it became obvious that there was little or no chance of producing a bill the Congress could accept, Kennedy pressed ahead. Hearings became an important rhetorical exercise. His purpose, of course, was to keep the health care issue alive, to reassure political allies, and to put pressure on the Carter administration to accept his plan.[9 2]

From a public relations perspective, nothing quite equals the effectiveness of hearings to attract press attention. Because they are conducted in a semijudicial manner, with testifiers, examination, and cross-examination, they provide an ideal mix of personalities and issues. In some ways congressional hearings come the closest to producing real debate on Capitol Hill. Indeed, as was the case in 1966 when J. William Fulbright used the Senate Foreign Relations Committee to examine Vietnam policy, hearings may be designed to create a dialogue in what is otherwise a stillborn public debate. Fulbright's hearings gained national attention. They also created severe pangs of conscience within the networks, forcing one of them to decide between reruns of "I Love Lucy" and the televised discussions of America's escalating commitment in Southeast Asia.[93] Fulbright called the hearings "an experiment in public education," noting that "by bringing before the American people a variety of opinions and disagreements pertaining to the war and perhaps by helping to restore a degree of balance between the Executive and the Congress, [they] strengthened the country rather than weakened it."[94]

Press coverage of hearings is also aided by the fact that the rules on electronic audio and video coverage are more lenient than in any other formal congressional settings. Many committee chairmen will go to great lengths to accommodate the equipment and personnel necessary for live or recorded reporting of statements, questions, and answers.

Robinson and Appel's recent study of network news coverage of Congress shows that the member's emphasis on committees is not misplaced. In 1976 by far the largest single type of news story from the networks was on committee work. Other kinds of stories, such as those dealing with constituent work, scandals, or travel junkets, were infrequently aired. Almost half of all of the reports dealt with committee reports, committee action, and hearings. It is particularly the latter, they note, that "are the *sine qua non* of network news coverage of Congress."[95] "So struck were we with the emphasis on committees, we recorded all committee action stories to get some insight into what was actually going on."[96] What they found was that hearings can be placed in a dramatic context that is well suited to the needs of television:

A substantial proportion of those committee stories with testimony (20 percent) were "fights," fights between congressmen and bureaucrats or between congressmen and corporate executives. But the most "representative" network news story takes place on film, in a Senate committee hearing room, where senators and testifiers talked back and forth on some policy issue.[97]

## Member to Public, via the Set Speech

No survey of the forms of congressional communication would be complete without at least a brief note on the enduring importance of the formal addresses by senators and representatives. Two settings for planned speeches are normal. One is on the floor of the House or Senate. The other is back in the member's district or state.

There is no precise way to assess the impact of floor speeches, although it is safe to say that they can retain considerable importance. They obviously allow the member the opportunity to clarify a position before a key vote. They also provide the means to establish a durable printed record of a position, a record that becomes part of the political legacy of the member.

In spite of our emphasis on private lobbying, committee sessions, and dependence on staff advice, critical legislative alliances are still subject to the verbal give and take on the floors of the Senate and House. A revealing instance is cited by Reid on Senator Pete Domenici's waterway user's fee:

> A few days before the waterway bill came up, Domenici had delivered a strong floor speech criticizing one of [Senator] Mike Gravel's pet legislative projects. Gravel was livid: "You just lost me on that user charge, Pete," he snapped, and Domenici was powerless to win him back.[98]

Few would argue with Barry Goldwater when he states that "speaking in the Senate has degenerated to such a point that it is almost impossible to get anyone to listen."[99] But floor speeches in the House and Senate are important, at least for what they potentially signify. An eloquent floor defense of a bill a member has co-sponsored, for example, has the effect of reassuring colleagues that the speaker has character, can be trusted, and is articulate enough to represent the party or a caucus. A member does not have to be an excellent orator to rise to a leadership position, but it is unlikely that an inarticulate person will be selected for major leadership roles, such as Speaker of the House, a committee chair, or as majority or minority leader. Speaking in the Senate and House has the same symbolic objective that it has for other organizations. It signals an ability to handle public pressure, to comprehend the flow of arguments and refutations. Even the least likely member of the House of Representatives will need to use a speech not only to defend a position, but to demonstrate sensitivity and mental agility to colleagues who may be paying more attention than they appear to be.

The other major venue for speeches is in the district, particularly during reelection campaigns. As Richard Fenno has pointed out, there are many rhetorical objectives that can be met in meetings with constituents outside of Washington.[100] They may range from defending their votes on great national issues, to the more mundane but vital task of relating specific congressional or executive action to local community needs and problems. Most members seem to enjoy local appearances. Their status in the community is larger than it is in Washington. Groups (and the local press) are generally more deferential. Many audiences are flattered simply to be the recipients of the member's attention, paying less attention to the possible contradictions or justifications of particular floor votes.

In an ironic way set floor speeches have taken on new importance for members of the House of Representatives. Legislative action is now covered by House television, and transmitted to cable television systems nationwide. The effect this has had on the member's participation in floor debate is interesting, and takes us to the final subject of this chapter.

## BROADCASTING FROM CONGRESS: THE CONTINUING DEBATE

Television has recently come to the House of Representatives for at least some of the same reasons that microphones have come to Britain's House of Commons, and cameras to Canada's and Australia's parliaments. Legislators worldwide sense the need to compete with other national institutions for access to the airwaves. It is impossible to overstate the importance such broadcasts could have.

In many countries and most U.S. states the legislatures have reacted cautiously to shifts in the existing publicity powers of the executive and legislative branches. But the shifts have been notable. Congress has long recognized the role of television in dramatizing key hearings and investigations, though the widely reported 1954 Army-McCarthy hearings hardly instilled faith in the future of extensive televised coverage.[101] For their part, broadcasters recognized the superiority of print reporters in covering the less public areas of a legislature. But they were also aware of the fact that television could produce a vital national service, as well as a fascinating form of political drama.

Members of legislatures who have been raised in the television age have also realized that the personalizing nature of broadcasting can restore the imbalance in access that has favored presidents and party leaders. "Television," writes Michael Novak, "fixes on the President and makes him the main symbolic representative of the government. Symbolically it dwarfs the Congress and the courts. There may be a balance of powers in the government, but no such balance exists on television."[102]

Currently the national political assemblies of most nations permit some form of broadcast of proceedings. Radio is by far the more common medium, with many countries such as France, Germany, India, and Italy providing full coverage or excerpts.[103] Television's presence is predictably on the increase, with Canada, Israel, Italy, and Australia offering many important debates to the public. Some nations seem to have consciously modeled their systems after the United Nations', where cameras record proceedings which are made available to interested news organizations.

The pattern is much the same in most U.S. state legislatures. Very few states completely prohibit radio or television.[104] Florida and Connecticut have offered elaborate coverage of deliberations, particularly on budget debates. Connecticut's proceedings were broadcast over the state's public television channels in the early 1970s, with estimated audiences as large as 150,000 a week.[105]

Obviously, most broadcasters want full access to congressional floor debate, and to hearings. But they are also conscious of the fact that congressional coverage poses problems. Television in particular is not a natural companion for a legislature. In fundamental ways each cuts against the grain of the other. The nature of legislative debate seems fundamentally antithetical to the pace and diversity of the entertainment-oriented networks. While debate can be lively and theatrical, the norm is usually quite different. Long, pedantic, and extended arguments are more typical. Full coverage of floor debates would not only be difficult to justify as complete commercial network broadcasts, but are arguably difficult to edit for quick summarizing. Debate is a linear event which unfolds (if at all) only over a significant amount of time. Few viewers have the patience to follow such unedited coverage.

Another problem is that television has emerged in this decade as the undisputed merchant of effortless leisure. Its commercial outlets have made themselves less suitable to almost all but the most superficial forms of politics. There is a sense, particularly among politicians and newsgatherers generally, that serious political debate is best represented in the print media, and often only exploited for superficial effects by commercial television. It grates on members of the House, for example, that one of the few times the networks led their newscasts with House television pictures was when a member was formally expelled for corruption.[106]

### Broadcast Coverage in the House of Representatives and the House of Commons

Video coverage of the House of Representatives began in 1979, after a great deal of heated debate about its possible effects. Just a few years earlier Britain's House of Commons took a different position: it permitted radio coverage of its debates. To the present the United States Senate has resisted either form of electronic coverage. With the recent exceptions of the debates on the Strategic Arms Limitation Treaty and the Panama Canal Treaty, the upper House has resisted pleas from Senator Howard Baker and others to permit television coverage.

As noted above, both the Senate and the House permit extensive coverage of hearings, although individual chairmen may impose their own limitations. In most cases cameras are welcome, and usually thought to be beneficial to both individual committee members and to the Congress as a whole.[107]

The House of Representatives system provides an unusual mixture of public access and internal control. The cameras themselves are in control of the House. But broadcasters are free to use whatever they wish. The only channel making extensive use of coverage is C-SPAN, a cable service reaching about 1,200 cable systems nationwide. It is estimated that it reached 16 million homes in 1983. In that year it covered every minute of the proceedings on the House floor, and over 237 hours of hearings held by various Senate and House committees.[108] In sharp contrast the major networks confined their coverage to occasional brief excerpts.

The House totally controls the choice of camera shots. Those shots are confined to the "well" of the House containing the podium from which members speak. The House cameras never include reactions of members, or pictures of the remainder of the House floor. A member may thus read the paper, leave the floor, or even sleep with impunity.

After extensive study and several temporary experiments, the House of Commons chose to prohibit television coverage, but to allow radio broadcasts of proceedings. This was a decision of considerable importance for Britain because—as in all parliaments—executive members of the government continue to sit as members of parliament as well. This fact has great significance because it means that cabinet members and the prime minister must at times face questioning from the opposition—and the opposition party's out of office "shadow government." "Question Time" is a moment of high drama in the House of Commons. Many times it is the single biggest political news story of the week, comparable in some ways to a presidential press conference with members of the political opposition asking the tough questions. The prime minister and her or his cabinet face the toughest of questions, with an almost continual rumble of chants and jeers that would intimidate even the coolest of presidents. The BBC began weekly broadcasts of "Prime Minister's Questions," providing a kind of running play-by-play of who was yelling at whom. But public reaction was dramatic and negative. Britons were genuinely shocked at what they heard from the "mother of parliaments" along the Thames. After several weeks of broadcasts a correspondent for *The Guardian* noted that "The novelty for us and the listener has well and truly worn off. It's too frivolous, too noisy, and it isn't a fair reflection of the working of Parliament."[109] The negative response was not totally unexpected, but few anticipated the discredit brought on by "the faithful transmission of the jeers, insults, cat-calls, impromptu witticisms, interruptions, baying, howling, ranting, point-scoring and general nonsense which characterize PMQs ['Prime Minister's Questions']."[110] Most citizens now hear only excerpts chosen for selected summaries or newscasts.

The results in Congress have been more muted, perhaps because there is less direct debate in the House than in parliament. C-SPAN has gained a loyal audience. In one area on the East coast 8 percent of C-SPAN's households viewed the channel for more than 30 minutes per week.[111] More importantly, most members feel like they have offered up at least a small amount of publicity to compete with all of the other available Washington sources clamoring for network attention. Robinson reports that well over half of the members he surveyed judged the system a success. The exception seemed to be among older members, some of whom felt that discipline and control had been sacrificed.[112]

A partially unanticipated effect was the use to which members would make of House television in their offices. The system has made it possible for a member to keep an eye on floor debate while attending to other House-related business back in his office.[113] It has also made it easier for staffers to see what they had often previously missed because of a need to be in the office. This closed circuit use has been much praised.

## Long-Range Effects of Increased Radio and Television Coverage of Congress

As yet we have incomplete information about the effects the introduction of radio and television can have on legislators. But it is instructive to sift through the pro and con arguments that have been raised prior to key votes on whether to admit microphones and cameras. The arguments, among other things, tell us how observers and participants view the publicity needs of individual House and Senate members. The brief summary here is culled from a number of recent studies on legislative broadcasting. It represents the staggering range of concerns that have been expressed about the effects that twentieth-century technology can have on institutions that were generally products of the eighteenth century.[114]

### Arguments for Broadcasting Floor Action

1. Public figures should be seen doing the public's business. Open societies must have open debates on public policy. Rule by "consent of the governed" necessarily means that the public must be informed about the legislative process as well as its product.

2. Legislative broadcasts are informational. The merits and weaknesses of legislation are exposed before they are codified, when the chance of constituent input is the greatest. Viewers have come to learn the complexities of law-making, giving up some cherished but simple views about legislative life. Seeing floor debate, for example, shows that "good" people can honestly disagree.

3. Present press coverage of Congress is inadequate. In many states newspapers are devoting increasingly less space to legislative news. The longstanding trend of a declining national readership makes it imperative that broadcasting address the need for other ways to reach audiences.

4. A bigger audience for legislative proceedings decreases the time legislators spend on trivia, long adjournments, and unproductive debates. The exposure will improve their efficiency because there is a natural desire to please constituents who might be viewing or listening.

5. More direct coverage of floor debate redresses the imbalance that exists in modern politics between powerful executives and less single-minded deliberative bodies.

6. Television and radio are well suited to any political activity involving conflict, because confrontation is inherently dramatic. The Congress is a good theater for the display of competing ideas; broadcasting exploits the explicitly theatrical aspects of deliberations, producing an informed public in the process.

7. Printed reports of the proceedings are unreliable, and fail to record the emotional climate that exists in a deliberative body. A complete video record is a more accurate document of the body's work, and its emotional intensity.

8. Broadcasts help to equalize access among legislators to the public as a whole. Presently junior members of Congress—like their back-bencher colleagues in Britain—are deprived of a voice in shaping public opinion.

9. Broadcasting of debates encourages better speaking, because of the awareness that a larger audience is watching.

## Arguments Against Broadcasts of Floor Action

1. Legislatures are workshops, not centers for the performing arts. People will not understand parliamentary procedure, though they can and should judge the final results. Too much observation has an inhibiting effect on those who must shape public policy.

2. Full unedited coverage is impossible; and editing itself cannot be impartial. There is no equitable way to select segments for broadcasts.

3. If editing does occur, the tendency is away from the dull and toward the spectacular. This has the effect of publicizing the least representative of the Congress's work, sacrificing political wisdom for political showmanship.

4. The public is not particularly interested; the burden to expand broadcasts rests with those who can demonstrate a significant public need.

5. Legislative traditions are worth honoring. Reforms should proceed only after careful consideration of all the consequences. Since broadcasting may be more of a cosmetic than substantive reform, the risks may not be justified.

6. Celebrities and skillful phonies are likely to dominate broadcasts. While their presence is not a major problem, no move ought to be undertaken which would give them higher visibility.

7. The business of deliberative bodies is serious, but sometimes appears otherwise to the uninformed observer. Broadcasts needlessly alarm citizens who do not understand the complex patterns of the legislative process.

8. The decision to begin or expand broadcasts—given the fact that press freedoms cannot easily be revoked—is probably irreversible.

9. Broadcasting increases the pressure for members to be seen and heard, reducing the percentage of time they spend on committee, constituent, and other business.

10. Broadcasting destroys the intimate nature of a deliberative body because it profoundly alters the relative importance of the various audiences to be addressed. Presently members speak first to their colleagues, and second to general public opinion. Broadcasting changes this. The actual persuasion intended to affect colleagues can become secondary to the use of debate for public consumption. In such an atmosphere debate involving vigorous give and take is not possible. Broadcasting turns legislatures into places for unproductive rhetorical posturing.

11. Television in particular cannot adequately handle the invisible products of legislative toil: ideas and solutions.

12. Any intense public airing of conflict, combined with the glare of publicity given to it, makes it extremely hard to produce compromises. To some extent a legislature should make attitude change possible without forcing the member into potentially humiliating displays of inconsistency.

Many thoughtful observers will ponder these and other issues as the various forms of electronic journalism become more pervasive. The fact is that different people will react in different ways as circumstances change. No one effect will be permanent or constant. The variable range of effects is reflected in the observations of a producer of programs for the Connecticut legislature:

> Legislative leaders sometimes wince at the prospect of a televised session, but nonetheless, they will go ahead and assist us, or even schedule debate themselves on critical issues so as to maximize coverage. . . . On balance the additional time, in my opinion, is neither excessive nor uncontrollable. . . . Closely related to the foregoing point is the often expressed fear that some lawmakers may . . . play to the cameras, or try to deceive their constituents. Others allegedly will enjoy a special advantage because they are more photogenic, more articulate, more flamboyant, or more colorful. These fears are sometimes realized, but it cuts both ways.

Compensating mechanisms come into play with comments during debates, and from peer pressure or leadership pressure. Besides the viewers are not easily fooled.[115]

One conclusion seems certain. Congress will continue to compete with the proliferation of broadcast coverage given to political conventions, the courts, state legislatures, the presidency, and even school board meetings carried by local cable companies. Many may dislike the new demands that it superimposes over the traditional political structure. But there is little chance that the House will reverse itself, and every chance that the Senate will someday make the same change.

As we have seen, Congress remains as the archetypal model of the varieties of political discourse. No Washington institution has as large or as varied a need for constant publicity about its work. Television has, and will continue to become, but one part in a matrix of communication networks that radiate from Capitol Hill. Just as L'Enfant's city plan placed the Capitol at the center of the District of Columbia's road network, so too the Congress will continue to act as a source of influence in almost every other phase of American political communication.

## NOTES

1. Harrison W. Fox, Jr. and Susan Webb Hammond, *Congressional Staffs: The Invisible Force in American Lawmaking* (New York: Free Press, 1977), p. 103.

2. Douglass Cater, *The Fourth Branch of Government* (New York: Vintage Books, 1959), p. 51.

3. See, for example, Donald G. Tacheron and Morris Udall, "Keeping in Touch with the People, Getting Along with the Press . . ." in *Congress and the News Media*, ed. Robert O. Blanchard (New York: Hastings House, 1974), pp. 370-83.

4. Douglass Cater, *Power in Washington* (New York: Vintage Books, 1964), pp. 144-60; Abner J. Mikva and Patti B. Harris, *The American Congress, The First Branch* (New York: Franklin Watts, 1983), pp. 123-54.

5. Clem Miller, "A Newcomer's View of the Press," in *Congress and the News Media*, ed. Robert O. Blanchard (New York: Hastings House, 1974), p. 160.

6. Newton N. Minow, John Bartlow Martin, and Lee M. Mitchell, *Presidential Television* (New York: Basic Books, 1973), pp. 115-16.

7. David L. Paletz and Robert M. Entman, *Media Power Politics* (New York: Free Press, 1981), p. 80.

8. Jimmy Carter, *Keeping Faith: Memoirs of a President* (New York: Bantam, 1982), p. 73.

9. Steven V. Roberts, "Slow Pace of Congress," *New York Times*, October 5, 1979, p. A20.

10. Congressional Quarterly, "House Democratic Whips: Massing Support" in *Inside Congress*, 2nd ed. (Washington, D.C.: Congressional Quarterly, 1979), pp. 29-30.

11. John S. Saloma, 3rd, *Congress and the New Politics* (Boston: Little, Brown, 1969), pp. 94-96.

12. Ibid., p. 5.

13. Ibid., p. 6.

14. Wilson quoted in Sidney Warren, ed., *The American President* (Englewood Cliffs, N.J.: Prentice-Hall, 1967), p. 29.

15. Harry McPherson, *A Political Education* (Boston: Atlantic-Little, Brown, 1972), p. 48.

16. Richard F. Fenno, Jr., *Home Style: House Members in Their Districts* (Boston: Little, Brown, 1978), pp. 217-18.

17. Michael J. Robinson, "Three Faces of Congressional Media" in *The New Congress*, ed. Thomas E. Mann and Norman J. Ornstein (Washington, D.C.: American Enterprise Institute, 1981), p. 87.

18. Ibid.

19. Miller, "Newcomer's View," p. 160.

20. Merle Miller, *Lyndon: An Oral Biography* (New York: Ballantine, 1980), pp. 247-48.

21. Cong. Quarterly, "House Democratic Whips," p. 74.

22. See, for example, R. Ajemian, "Ideologue with Influence," *Time*, May 4, 1982, pp. 20-21; and "Helms Plays Hardball," *Newsweek*, January 3, 1983, p. 11.

23. Fox and Hammond, *Congressional Staffs*, p. 157.

24. Donald R. Matthews, *U.S. Senators and Their World* (Chapel Hill, N.C.: University of North Carolina, 1960), p. 85.

25. Fox and Hammond, *Congressional Staffs*, p. 89.

26. Ibid., p. 90.

27. Ibid., pp. 93-94.

28. Theodore Sorensen, *Kennedy* (New York: Harper and Row, 1965), p. 56.

29. Fox and Hammond, *Congressional Staffs*, p. 149.

30. Michael J. Malbin, "Delegation, Deliberation, and the New Role of Congressional Staff," in *The New Congress*, ed. Thomas E. Mann and Norman J. Ornstein (Washington, D.C.: American Enterprise Institute, 1981), p. 150.

31. Cong. Quarterly, "House Democratic Whips," p. 29.

32. Warren Weaver, Jr., *Both Your Houses: The Truth About Congress* (New York: Praeger, 1972), p. 39.

33. Matthews, *U.S. Senators*, p. 251.

34. T. R. Reid, *Congressional Odyssey: The Saga of a Senate Bill* (San Francisco: W. H. Freeman, 1980), p. 60.

35. Matthews, *U.S. Senators*, pp. 97-101.

36. Miller, *Lyndon*, pp. 212-18.

37. William Rivers, *The Adversaries: Politics and the Press* (Boston: Beacon Press, 1970), pp. 91-133.

38. Quoted in Herbert J. Gans, *Deciding What's News* (New York: Vintage Books, 1980), p. 136.

39. Robinson, "Three Faces," p. 84.

40. Rivers, *The Adversaries*, p. 77.

41. Ibid., p. 75.

42. Stewart Alsop, "Senator Lyndon Johnson: A Correspondent's View" in *Congress and the News Media*, ed. Robert O. Blanchard (New York: Hastings House, 1974), p. 285.

43. Jack Anderson and James Boyd, *Confessions of a Muckraker* (New York: Random House, 1979), pp. 313-15.

44. Bert Andrews, "Correspondents as Participants: Case I," in *Congress and the News Media*, ed. Robert O. Blanchard (New York: Hastings House, 1974), pp. 300-8.

45. Matthews, *U.S. Senators*, p. 214.

46. Fox and Hammond, *Congressional Staffs*, pp. 117-18.

47. Joseph A. Califano, Jr., *Governing America: An Insider's Report From the White House and the Cabinet* (New York: Simon and Schuster, 1981), p. 267.

48. Saloma, *Congress and New Politics*, pp. 145-52.

49. Lester W. Milbrath, *The Washington Lobbyists* (Westport, Conn.: Greenwood Press, 1963), pp. 214-27.

50. Matthews, *U.S. Senators*, pp. 176-83.

51. Milbrath, *Washington Lobbyists*, pp. 241-44.

52. Reid, *Congressional Odyssey*, p. 55.

53. Ibid., p. 54.

54. Quoted in Elizabeth Drew, *Senator* (New York: Touchstone, 1979), p. 89-90.

55. Saloma, *Congress and New Politics*, p. 185.

56. Fenno, *Home Style*, pp. 217-18.

57. Associated Press, "Jersey Pols Differ in Approach to Reaching Voters," *Trenton Times*, January 30, 1984, p. A8.

58. Fenno, *Home Style*, p. 85.

59. Robinson, "Three Faces," p. 61.

60. "Jersey Pols," p. A8.

61. Cater, *Fourth Branch of Government*, p. 52.

62. Kevin P. Phillips, *Mediacracy: American Parties and Politics in the Communication Age* (Garden City, N.Y.: Doubleday, 1975), p. 29.

63. Ben H. Bagdikian, "Congress and the Media: Partners in Propaganda" in *Congress and the News Media*, ed. Robert O. Blanchard (New York: Hastings House, 1974), p. 398.

64. Edward Jay Epstein, *News from Nowhere: Television and the News* (New York: Vintage, 1973), part I.

65. See, for example, Jay G. Blumer and Michael Gurevitch, "Politicians and the Press: An Essay on Role Relationships" in *Handbook of Political Communication*, ed. Dan D. Nimmo and Keith R. Sanders (Beverly Hills, Calif.: Sage, 1981), pp. 467-89.

66. Dan Nimmo, *Newsgathering in Washington* (New York: Atherton Press, 1964), p. 225.

67. Paletz and Entman, *Media Power Politics*, p. 80.

68. Ibid., p. 84.

69. Michael J. Robinson and Kevin R. Appel, "Network News Coverage of Congress," *Political Science Quarterly* 94 (Fall 1979): 413.

70. Quoted in ibid., p. 414.

71. Ibid., p. 415.

72. Tacheron and Udall, "Keeping in Touch," pp. 370-83.

73. Robinson, "Three Faces," p. 77.

74. Ibid., p. 88.

75. Ibid.

76. Martin Tolchin, "TV Studio Serves Congress," *New York Times*, March 7, 1984, p. C22.

77. Bagdikian, "Congress and the Media," p. 390.

78. "Jersey Pols," p. A8.

79. Tolchin, "TV Studio," p. C22.

80. "Jersey Pols," p. A8.

81. Ibid.

82. Roger H. Davidson, "Subcommittee Government: New Channels for Policy Making" in *The New Congress*, ed. Thomas E. Mann and Norman J. Ornstein (Washington, D.C.: American Enterprise Institute, 1981), pp. 99-107.

83. See Theodore Wilson, "The Truman Committee," in *Congress Investigates: 1792-1974*, ed. Arthur M. Schlesinger, Jr. and Roger Bruns (New York: Chelsea House, 1975), p. 336.

84. Reid, *Congressional Odyssey*, p. 24.

85. William J. Keefe and Morris S. Ogul, *The American Legislative Process: Congress and the States* 2nd ed. (Englewood Cliffs, N.J.: Prentice-Hall, 1968), p. 206.

86. Arthur M. Schlesinger, Jr., Introduction, in *Congress Investigates: 1792-1974*, ed. Arthur M. Schlesinger and Robert Bruns (New York: Chelsea House, 1975), p. xxi.

87. Ibid., p. xiv.

88. Robert P. Newman and Dale R. Newman, *Evidence* (Boston: Houghton Mifflin, 1969), p. 97.

89. For a brief summary of these hearings see Harry J. Skornia, "The Great American Teaching Machine—of Violence," in *Mass Media Issues: Analysis and Debate*, ed. George Rodman (Chicago: S.R.A., 1977), pp. 153-54.

90. For a survey of the participants in the Watergate congressional investigations see Elizabeth Drew, *Washington Journal and Events of 1973-1974* (New York: Vintage, 1976).

91. Keefe and Ogul, *American Legislative Process*, p. 207.

92. For one view of Kennedy's motives see Califano, *Governing America*, pp. 88-119.

93. Fred W. Friendly, *Due to Circumstances Beyond Our Control* (London: MacGibbon and Kee, 1967), pp. 213-35.

94. J. William Fulbright, *The Arrogance of Power* (New York: Random House, 1966), p. 56.

95. Robinson and Appel, "Network News," p. 415.

96. Ibid., p. 411.

97. Ibid., p. 412.

98. Reid, *Congressional Odyssey*, p. 102.

99. Quoted in Dudley D. Cahn, Edward J. Pappas, and Ladene Schoen, "Speech in the Senate: 1978," *Communication Quarterly* (Summer 1979): 52.

100. Fenno, *Home Style*, pp. 136-58.

101. For a different view see Sig Mickelson, *The Electric Mirror: Politics in an Age of Television* (New York: Dodd and Mead, 1972), p. 13.

102. Michael Novak, *Choosing Our King* (New York: Macmillan, 1974), p. 259.

103. Valentine Herman, *Parliaments of the World* (London: Macmillan, 1976), pp. 546-65.

104. Congressional Research Service, "Broadcast Coverage of State Legislatures," in *Congress and Mass Communications*, an Appendix to Hearings before the Joint Committee on Congressional Operations, Ninety-third Congress (Washington, D.C.: U.S. Government Printing Office, 1974), pp. 949-50.

105. Frank V. Donovan, "Accountability for the Legislature: The Impact of Extended Television Coverage," in *Congress and Mass Communications*, (Washington, D.C.: U.S.GPO, 1974), p. 752.

106. Robinson, "Three Faces," p. 68.

107. See, for example, Minow, Martin, and Mitchell, *Presidential Television*, pp. 107-108; and Paletz and Entman, *Media Power Politics*, pp. 84-86.

108. David Burnham, "A Channel that Focuses on Government," *New York Times*, February 8, 1984, p. C21.

109. Simon Hoggart, "Broadcast Scrapped," *The Guardian*, January 23, 1979, p. 2.

110. David Leigh, "MPs Worried About Radio Image," *The Guardian*, May 30, 1978, p. 2.

111. Burnham, "Channel that Focuses on Government," p. C21.

112. Robinson, "Three Faces," pp. 67-68.

113. Ibid., p. 69.

114. These studies include: Colin Seymour-Ure, "An Examination of the Proposal to Televise Parliament," *Parliamentary Affairs* (Spring 1964): 172-81; Colin Seymour-Ure, *The Political Impact of Mass Media* (London: Constable, 1974); J. Vernon Jensen, "Attempts to Televise Parliament," *Journal of Broadcasting* (Fall 1962): 461-73; Allen Segal, "The Case for not Televising Parliament," in *The Reform of Parliament*, 2nd ed., ed. Bernard Crick (London: Weidenfeld and Nicolson, 1968), pp. 296-306; and Donovan, *Congress and Mass Communications*, pp. 748-52.

115. Donovan, "Accountability for the Legislature," pp. 748-49.

# III

# Epilogue

# 10

# Politics, Communication, and Public Trust

All intelligent political criticism is comparative. It deals not with all-or-none situations, but with practical alternatives; an absolutistic indiscriminate attitude, whether in praise or blame, testifies to the heat of feeling rather than the light of thought.[1]

*Q.* Well, what do you make, General [Maxwell D. Taylor], of the principle of the people's right to know . . . ?
*A.* I don't believe in that as a general principle.[2]

## ETHICS AND COMMUNICATION: THE PROBLEM OF STANDARDS

No study of political discourse can escape its considerable ethical dilemmas. We started this book by noting that for many Americans politics is nearly synonymous with deception and obfuscation. The popular image of the political figure is of someone who uses grand rhetorical gestures to gain public approval: empty gestures which promise more than is delivered, ultimately coming at the public's expense. The low esteem in which political address is held flows from the belief that its practitioners routinely corrupt the relationships that should exist between thought and action, promise and performance. The assumption carried in this view seems to be that most other forms of communication are immune from similar lapses.

Our approach in this study has been different. We believe that this kind of discourse has often been misunderstood: criticized for what it cannot be, overburdened by criticism that precedes rather than

327

follows sound analysis. Kenneth Burke's caution to critics ready to condemn the evil rhetoric in Hitler's *Mein Kampf* is still a useful reminder that moral superiority is an inadequate basis for understanding.

> If the reviewer but knocks off a few adverse attitudinizings and calls it a day, with a guaranty in advance that his article will have a favorable reception among the decent members of our population, he is contributing more to our gratification than to our enlightenment.[3]

Understanding must precede criticism. But understanding comes from discovering how such rhetoric works. It must inform criticism rather than replace it.

Even so, politics naturally invites negative and positive judgments. The civil life of a nation cannot help but bridge the gap between explanation and judgment. Because the exercise of power involves the distribution of rewards, money, and sanctions, and because we must necessarily consider the motives of political agents (are they representing a position for us or for their own allies?), informed criticism is to be expected and encouraged. To talk about value-free or nonpartisan politics is as futile as searching the calendar for weekends with two Saturdays. The subject requires the insertion of value-laden judgments. To be sure, there is a psychology and sociology of politics. It is clearly possible to find relatively value-free ways to observe political behavior. But there can really be no such thing as an all-encompassing and nonjudgmental "political science." The language and subject matter of politics prohibits that. Because politics is inherently about positions and attitudes it requires the assessment of the stuff of eternal debate: individual motives, priorities, and values. "The essence of a political . . . situation," argues John Bunzel, "is that someone is trying to do something about which there is no agreement."[4] We may find a neutral way to study politics as sheer activity. But we can never come to terms with the political world until we plunge into its inherently pluralistic content.

But if the imposition of values and norms comes with the territory, it still remains difficult to locate the appropriate standards that can be invoked in the name of reasonableness. For example, if a president abuses the language by calling a rocket armed with a nuclear warhead a "peacekeeper" (as the Reagan administration renamed the controversial MX missile), is there a basis other than *personal* judgment for calling the decency of that discourse into question?[5] Does such rhetoric violate some universal code of reasonableness? Is the public interest served by describing destructive weapons as tools for peace?

Are there firm standards by which people of different political per-
suasions could agree on this as a proper or improper form of political
discourse?

Obviously, there can be few unequivocal answers to questions involving the moral or ethical responsibilities of communicators. Because
political communication is an audience-centered activity, universal
rules of conduct are illusive. Any standards that we articulate are subject to exceptions imposed by different kinds of audiences. No system of a-priori standards—including lists of logical fallacies and violations of conventional argumentation—can be imposed on political
discourse with anything more than the hope for widespread assent.
Guidelines for assessing how issues should be presented can be asserted
and argued. But they cannot be rendered unchallengeable.[6]

It may be possible to gain nearly universal agreement on what
constitutes a bribe, illegal payoff, or some other form of corrupt
political *act*. But we think it is far more difficult to judge the ethics
of what someone *says*. A bribe to a legislator from a special interest
group, for example, clearly violates a widely understood code governing the conduct of public officials. To secretly take money in exchange
for political favors is an undeniable abuse of a public trusteeship supported with public funds. But there are few precise rhetorical equiv-
alents. Even pandering and excessive promise making made to the
same special interest involves less clear-cut ethics. The conventions of
rhetorical practice allow a much broader range of appeals. Short of
deliberate lying, we expect that communication permits a greater
diversity of rhetorical means to achieve political ends. This is because
all communication involves the construction of realities. Language
usage is always selective. Just as no group of individuals would describe
the same scene in exactly the same way, so are political realities open
to a diversity of interpretations. Communication requires fabrication.
Realities are not discovered by political advocates; they are constructed. Such constructions may be widely shared, but not universally
accepted.

This is perhaps one reason Ronald Reagan's penchant for providing examples and anecdotes of suspect validity did not harm his credibility with vast numbers of Americans in his first term. In his 1980
campaign, for example, he regularly referred to a Chicago "welfare
queen" who had supposedly become rich through the abuse of state
and federal "handouts."[7] Apparently no such person existed. But
the failure of the example to tally with the facts probably did not
matter. For his strongest supporters, and even for some of his critics,

it was recognized that such rhetoric had an expressive rather than instrumental role. Accuracy of communication is important. But even bowdlerized examples can have their own internal-validity. There is little novelty but still much truth to the observation that political discussion has more in common with the fabrications of drama than with the objective descriptions of the hard sciences.

## THE RECIPROCAL OBLIGATIONS OF POLITICAL DISCOURSE

It has become so customary to focus on the obligations of political communicators that we often fail to give due notice that democratic life carries responsibilities for audiences as well. Electoral politics in particular links the fortunes of advocates to the competencies of audiences. The advocate can never be very far out in front of his audience. What he says must strike chords of recognition if his audiences are going to continue to provide support. While the rhetor may seem to be the active participant in a communication transaction, he is essentially using materials that are provided by the audience he seeks to influence. In a real sense audiences are co-creators of the messages they hear. Walt Whitman's observation that "to have great poets there must be great audiences, too" is as fitting for politics as for poetry. To the extent a speaker is successful in addressing the interests of an audience, the audience must also share the praise or blame that may be forthcoming.

It is a common routine in the course of a political campaign, for example, for the press to lament of the low quality of discourse that has come from competing candidates and parties. The implication is usually that the candidates are too inept or devious to address the tough issues facing the electorate. But the reciprocal nature of communication should force us to reverse the direction of the arrows as well. A public that tolerates mediocre discourse gets not only what it probably deserves, but also what it no doubt *requires* of the candidate. One cannot review film footage from the 1952 or 1956 presidential campaigns without sensing the agony of Dwight Eisenhower and his challenger, Adlai Stevenson, as they tried to reduce their campaign themes to 30-second television commercials. Like so many before and after them, they were forced to take the voters where they found them. And in the 1950s the electorate was increasingly in front of the television set, learning to tolerate interruptions of programming that did not exceed 60 seconds.

The paradox in all of this is that accusations about political incompetence are almost always directed to the wrong audience: to political professionals rather than to their indifferent audiences. Complaints about the low state of integrity among political activists tend to mask deeper indictments of the whole polity. Popular discussions of the venality of political life deflect criticism *away* from the vast segments of the electorate whose marginal political interests make it possible. Any equation that attempts to account for the rise to power of politicians who violate the public trust must include references to the quiescent groups that often let it happen. We wish more discussions of demagoguery—for example, of notorious figures such as Boston's James Curley, Louisiana's Huey Long, or New Jersey's Frank Hague—included consideration of the failures in public competence that the successes of demagogues collectively imply.[8]

Our point is ultimately not to affix blame to any particular side of this equation. Instead, it is to indicate that "the people" have largely been removed from too many popular discussions of political morality.[9] To cite but one discomforting case: Richard Nixon was reelected by a landslide in 1972 *after* substantial information about the Watergate break-in was before the public. That fact should give us pause for what it implies about the reciprocity of political transactions. It is widely thought that the Watergate affair and its aftermath demonstrated the strengths of our political institutions. There was a sense of collective relief when Nixon eventually resigned prior to probable impeachment. Outwardly it appeared that the system had worked. But few observers publicly questioned the lack of wisdom in an electorate that gave the Nixon administration its ill-fated second term.[10]

## POLITICS, TRUST, AND THE CRISIS OF AUTHORITY

It is an old story to note that the severest test facing any political system is how well it can communicate its right to exercise legitimate control. A government that has lost the respect of the citizens faces its toughest communication challenge. As Claus Mueller has noted, "There is no political system that does not need to legitimate itself. . . . "[11] The perception that policies are unjust or failed, that corruption is common, or that levels of government have lost touch with popular sentiments, are all common conditions in industrialized nations. When such feelings increase there is a corresponding sense that the state faces the severest kind of social malady. Such periods have routinely cycled through the history of the United States. The Civil War, Reconstruction, the beginnings of twentieth-century Progressivism, the Great Depression, the Watergate affair, and the last year of the Carter administration are only a few of the most obvious benchmarks indicating various levels of decay in the legitimacy of major political institutions. After Watergate in 1973, for example, over 65 percent of a cross section of Americans agreed with the negative conclusions that "Government is for the benefit of a few" and "You cannot trust government to do right." By contrast, only about 25 percent agreed with these statements in the relatively benign year of 1958.[12] More recently, nearly every evocation of the last year of the Carter administration stands as a symbol for the idea of governmental powerlessness. The humiliating capture of Americans in the Teheran embassy, and the Carter administration's inability to do anything about it, left Americans bitter about the legitimacy of what was regarded as the most powerful office in the free world.[13]

But there is yet a deeper paradox in assessing how political institutions maintain the support of those they both control and serve. It is that democracies which nurture at least the appearance of public involvement are also constructed on the premise that distrust is an essential fact of life. The open society, party politics, a critical press, and electoral politics all work on the assumption that governing is—at best—a shared process. Legal authority may reside with officials, legislatures, and public agencies. But that authority has its limits in the requirement for some measure of public consent. As John Dewey has written, "the events that finally culminated in democratic political forms were deeply tinged by fear of government, and were actuated by a desire to reduce it to a minimum so as to limit the evil it could do."[14]

Pluralistic open societies thus function within a framework of skepticism. Dissent is tolerated, even encouraged. But dissent cannot be allowed to erode faith in basic institutions. The total loss in respect for political leadership is obviously tantamount to social disintegration. Some constituencies may not accept the legitimacy of official administrative acts taken by leaders with different partisan objectives. But factions usually see their redemption in other sectors of the political framework where their interests are represented: most notably with legislative groups, interest groups, or other like-minded partisans who have access to sympathetic members of the press. A true crisis of authority in a democracy is when even these avenues are closed or suppressed. It occurs when large segments of society see no representation for their interests, or experience a sense of betrayal at the hands of those whom they have previously supported. As Theodore White recounted, the idea of betrayal was at the heart of Richard Nixon's breach of faith. It was not just that the Nixon administration had fallen short of its obligations to the entire nation, but that it had violated a much smaller constituency of adamant supporters. As White notes, Nixon's ideological allies were the kind to "fear and hate the imagined conspiracies of men in government. What Richard Nixon did was to convince them they were right in their suspicion."[15] Nixon resigned not because he was about to be impeached, though in all probability he eventually would have been. He resigned because he had lost his credibility with the American public. Given the unfolding of events, he could no longer talk himself out of the tangle of cover-up revelations. The heart of his power was his credibility: the public's sense that he was worthy of belief.

Distrust of the political world—as demonstrated so effectively in the recent "big government" themes of Ronald Reagan—represents what is for many an authentic and positive public attitude. A Jeffersonian suspicion of centralized government is still embedded in the American ethos (at least among those for whom government is seen as taker rather than giver). Yet there clearly is a level beyond which loss of credibility becomes lethal to the state. Vietnam policy and the deaths of Martin Luther King, Jr. and Robert Kennedy produced such disintegration in 1968. Thousands of alienated Americans became the perpetrators or victims of random urban violence. Millions more became vocal in their expressions of bitterness, much of it directed to the eroding legitimacy of the Johnson administration, the Congress, and social institutions in general. Whatever mending of the social fabric that took place slowly after that tumultuous year fell largely to the only national institution to come through the period with its credibility more or less intact: the press. The major networks and wire services grudgingly mediated the disorder by giving slightly greater access to alienated and unofficial voices. Skepticism about war objectives filtered into war reporting. Documentaries elevated Martin Luther King, Jr. from the level of political dissident to the higher realm of political idealist. Johnson, however, felt obliged to leave the scene, thereby avoiding the monumental rhetorical task of rebuilding his credibility as the engineer of the Great Society.[16]

## TELEVISION AND COMMUNICATION ETHICS

As we noted in Chapter 6, assessments of the quality of politics in American life are routinely linked to the effects of the mass media. A commonplace belief is that the advent of television has distorted the roles and objectives of political institutions. Political television is thought to have placed another layer of bureaucracy between rulers and the ruled. Television seems to have supplanted the political parties as the primary network for public communication. It has extended the power of executive offices such as the presidency and governorships. It has obscured the Congress and the legislatures, forced the scripting of political conventions and legislative hearings. And it has emphasized the role of affect in politics; the joining of advocates with issues changes the ways we think about politics. Personalities, for example, are usually secondary in print to the reporting of legislative debates. With television they can easily become primary. No single change in American political life has provoked more discussion than the role of television.[17]

Our discussion here is limited only to a final look at some general trends in the uses of television, trends that seem to have a direct bearing on the general quality of public discussion. In some cases these patterns provide grounds for optimism; in other cases, for pessimism.

## Distaste for a Public Fight: Television and the Search for the Political Middle

The televising of debates, speeches, press conferences, and the like carries the implication that a nonspecific and nonpolitical audience will be taking them in. An address or televised debate may provide the opportunity to sharpen partisan differences. But the very structure of commercial television in particular gives no such incentives. The audiences for most kinds of programs are heterogeneous. The skillful user of television realizes that little can be gained by faithfully serving as an advocate for a sharply defined point of view. There are potentially more benefits to an approach that mimics the logic of prime-time television: namely to find the safe ideological center, and to broaden appeals to include as many in the audience as possible. The very massiveness of the television audience suggests that there is more to be gained by substituting agreement in place of argumentation, by identifying the broadest possible clientele instead of a more limited number of ideological compatriots. Television is not the only force working against the nondelineation of positions. But as the "massest" of the mass media it most clearly suggests the risks inherent in doctrinal purity. By depriving the communicator of an audience with discernible political tendencies, discussion directed to an enormously broad mass audience can result in a strange kind of nonpartisan partisanship. The audience is too big and inert to be instructed. Disagreement with the weight of public opinion carries too many risks. Genuine clarification of hard choices is thus frequently replaced by an enforced recital of noncontroversial pseudo-political doctrines. We often witness heated debates about differences that are contrived for their expressive rather than instrumental values.

Nowhere has this trend been more evident than in the conduct of recent political conventions. The conventions of 1976, 1980, and 1984 were notable for an almost complete absence of convention debate on platform planks, the seating of delegations, and the merits of opposing candidates. To be sure, part of the change is not due to television. The presidential primary system has irrevocably replaced the convention as the basis for selecting presidential standard-bearers. What is less acceptable is the shifting of natural intraparty differences away from the televised convention and into less public venues. The parties now recognize that the conventions provide the possibility of presenting the imagery of unity. Television debates that might lessen such highly contrived images are not given prominence, or are relegated to hours when many Americans are no longer viewing.[18] Convention time is increasingly taken up with patriotic ceremonies and filmed eulogies on carefully selected party icons (with lights out in the convention hall, thus encouraging the networks to relent on their floor coverage in favor of the film). These quadrennial displays have been reduced to demonstrations of an enforced unity without accompanying public discussion. What are now euphemistically called the "streamlined" rules of the conventions largely prohibit floor debate on issues that divide the membership within the parties.

Television exposure places public relations objectives and democratic values at odds. The nation would probably benefit from the debate that is the inevitable result of the two parties' ideological diversity.

### Consistency and the Mass Audience

National distribution of political messages—especially speeches and press conferences—has placed a greater premium on consistency, even as specific audiences change from one location to another. Obviously, television creates a permanent national audience. It dramatizes political continuity, or the lack of it, in ways that are more vivid than are possible with print. Remarks and addresses now routinely travel statewide or nationwide—well beyond their original audience. What is said must be rectified for two audiences. The immediate audience for a political address seeks some recognition of its status and importance to the politician. The larger electronic audience must be assured that policy has not shifted, that previous alliances and commitments are not violated. At best, the existence of twin audiences lessens the opportunity for capricious changes for short-term gain. At worst, the advocate may seek refuge in the vaguest forms of discourse, or may be bound in by an ill-planned promise.

Richard Nixon faced the problem of rectifying the values of two audiences in 1959. During a tour of the Soviet Union as vice-president he was invited to give a national television address to the Soviet citizens. In *Six Crises* he claims that he approached the task "solely with the Russian people in mind."[19] But the future presidential candidate was undoubtedly conscious of the Americans back home who would later wonder what he had told the Soviets. His address had to be conciliatory to the Soviets, but essentially consistent with his reputation as a determined anti-Communist.[20] Just over a year later John Kennedy faced a similar reality. He knew that his Inaugural Address would cross the Atlantic with the same electronic speed that it went into millions of American homes. Kennedy and aide Theodore Sorensen wrote the address with the conscious intention to direct a tone of firmness to Soviet as well as American listeners. As Sorensen notes, Kennedy did not want "any weasel words that [Soviet Premier] Khrushchev might misinterpret."[21]

The passing of time also makes its own requirement for consistency. Presidents, candidates, and legislators are not free to arbitrarily abandon commitments and attitudes that have been publicly asserted. It is commonplace to assume that political promises are routinely ignored. As we noted in Chapter 8, utterance of even the most tangential of statements carries burdens that are not easily shed. In spite of the degradation of political rhetoric as "mere talk," promises carry heavy obligations. History has no shortage of examples. Promises made by F. D. R., Jimmy Carter, and Ronald Reagan to balance the federal budget are obvious cases. Scores of national politicians have been confronted with television news accounts that dramatically juxtapose statements made years ago with newer utterances that are in sharp variance. The split-second "jump cut" which diminishes time by mixing old and new footage has the effect of heightening the viewer's distaste for political hypocrisy. More than ever it is a fact of political life that commitments made in face-to-face televised encounters may lay down tracks of obligations that can seem irreversible.

## Consultants, Speechwriters, and the Distancing of Messages from Their "Sources"

Speechwriters, consultants, staff assistants, and researchers compose an important stratum within the political hierarchy. While the source of the most important statements is still usually the politician, much of the routine preparation of the vast remainder of messages is often relegated to this extensive support system. The more powerful the official or institution, the more likely the burden for routine message preparation will fall to one or more people within a specialized support staff. The tasks of communications experts are not just limited to the forming and wording of ideas. They are also increasingly used to make sense of the vagaries of polling, locate appropriate audiences for messages, schedule appearances, and even oversee television lighting and make-up.

The intervention of so many of these specialists between audiences and communicators naturally raises questions about the speaker's autonomy and authenticity. When does such a person cease being an independent agent? Is there a point at which the best politician is the one who is most malleable?

The image problem facing Ronald Reagan during his entry into both state and national politics involved just such issues. The pundits bombarded the nation with questions implying the inauthentic nature of a politician trained to be a mouthpiece for others. Would an actor be able to play the public role of chief executive better than he could actually perform its administrative duties? Was he—like others before him—essentially the product of the marketing expertise of others? Throughout his career Reagan was a spokesman for a number of groups with either political or commercial objectives. He worked in a radio station, perhaps the ultimate case of serving as a mouthpiece for others. He represented the Screen Actor's Guild in Hollywood. After he left films he represented a soap company (Borax) on television and an electrical conglomerate (General Electric) in hundreds of personal appearances. In short, he had acquired the facility to assume the attitudes of those he served. Politics involves more than the public presentation of ideas—though how much more is debatable. Was Reagan prepared to be an administrator and legislative engineer in addition to assuming the role of advocate? Or was he the product of his theatrical "play any role" background? Among his close advisers early in his administration were advertising consultant Stuart Roberts, pollster Robert Teeter, market researcher Richard Wirthlin, television consultant Mark Goode, and writer David Gergen. But many felt that Reagan would be more comfortable as the articulator of their visions.[22] How much of the Reagan Americans saw in his first term was *their* construction? And how much was the "real" Reagan?

The president's dependence on consultants was obviously not unique. Aides wise in the arts of presentational cosmetics have been around at least since the Eisenhower years. Every administration has had its counterparts to the Reagan public relations team. And the lessons they have imparted have not been lost on officeholders in major cities, the states, the Congress, and the cabinet. There can be little doubt that the rise of the consultant has changed politics, especially video politics. The unresolved issue is whether or not teams of mass media specialists have intervened in a way that is detrimental to the political process. More and more, presidential politics seems to come to the public with a marketing objective of eliciting a feeling of reassurance rather than a mastery of the arguments.[23] The public relations mentality rarely allows hard public policy choices to be described as they are: difficult decisions with personal costs to be weighed against public benefits. Woodrow Wilson and Theodore Roosevelt reveled in presenting elaborate and detailed arguments in defense of policy, often to audiences less intellectually prepared for such discussions than their better-educated contemporary counterparts. With many exceptions the approach to issues today seems far more personalistic, represented most concretely in the 1980 Reagan campaign strategy of focusing almost exclusively on personal prosperity and happiness than on policy.[24]

## Television and the Dominance of the Executive

When the print press was the prime source of political information for most Americans it was possible to communicate intragovernmental tensions in a way that would give proportion to the various factions. Congress and the legislatures could be described with almost the same force and detail given to descriptions of presidents. Well into the twentieth century the Senate, for example, was more than just an equal match for the presidency. Its titans admired by John Kennedy in *Profiles in Courage* were on a more equal public relations level with the president. Various papers had their favorites among the Vandenburgs, Bryans, and LaFollettes. No one national source dominated public attention. Many factors have since tipped the scales in favor of the executive. The balance began to change under F. D. R.: because of the desire for strong leadership after the presidency of Herbert Hoover, because more quasi-legislative decisions were seized by presidents, and because Roosevelt was willing to exploit newer means of communication. Both newsreels and radio were better able to focus issues onto a single person rather than a collectivity. With the advent of television, the need for conciseness frequently made the president a ready spokesman for one side in a dispute. Where Presidents Truman and Eisenhower viewed intense television exposure as a mixed blessing, later presidents—notably Johnson and Nixon—saw it as a source of new power.

The old tensions between Congress and the president, between the political press and the executive, even between the major parties, certainly have not been reduced by television's fascination with a single leader. But they have been muted. At least since the Nixon years, the dominant strategy of the consultant-oriented communication offices of the White House has been to *contain* rather than *engage* disputes. The executive byword today is "crisis management": a strategy that involves treating major political exigencies as exercises in the management and containment of negative public opinion. Straight public debate is frequently avoided in favor of direct televised appeals to the nation. The goal is usually to minimize the negative impressions raised by a controversy. High-level disputes (i.e., between the Speaker of the House and the president) are minimized, thus denying a forum for debate that could put an executive on the defensive. The end result is to use television to deflect public criticism onto political institutions, such as the Congress, which are unable to muster any kind of decisive collective response.

## FOUR CORRUPTIONS OF POLITICAL DISCOURSE

As noted at the outset of this chapter, our interests lie more in explaining the functions and forms of political discourse than in pointing out some of it that fails to meet the rigorous demands of rationalism. Most discourse is not intended to serve as a form of ironclad argumentation. Political communication involves many legitimate expressive functions that have little to do with precise standards of logic. Preaching to the converted, evoking shared values, and providing a basis for official legitimacy are only the most common. Political communication with such objectives must be studied on its own terms, not with a-priori standards imposed from outside.

However there are limits. While the enormous range of objectives of audiences described elsewhere in this book make any kind of moralizing difficult, we are not unmindful of the range of corruptions to which political language is prone. We think it is possible to mark out several thresholds beyond which the public trust is violated. Our emphasis here is on a four-part summary of "bad-faith" objectives based on the distortion of language. They include coercion, deception, mystification, and redefinition. Together they represent at least a taxonomy of rhetorical corruptions in politics.

## Coercion

Coercion is the application of force instead of argument to change the behavior of someone else. It differs from persuasion in several important ways. The individual's freedom to decide (i.e., to form an opinion) is taken away because of threats which directly or indirectly imply that his safety and well-being are at stake. Although coercion may connote impending harm, it is often enough to suggest the *possibility* of harm as the result of noncompliance.

It is a cliché to note that political discourse in a democratic society should not be used to cross the line that separates legitimate persuasion from coercion. But the distinction can be a difficult one to locate. It is one thing for a speaker to imply that the passage of a particular law or the election of a person may have negative effects. In a free society political discourse must consider costs and consequences, positive as well as negative. It is quite another when the arguer extends the discussion of costs to a point where the hearer is given reason to ignore the merits of a question in favor of the dire personal consequences that seem at least implicit. "You better believe this or I'll punch you in the nose" is obviously a case of coercion. The hearer may feel that he has no choice but to outwardly conform to the speaker's request.

But political arguments implying force are usually much more subtle. They often involve intimidating statements that focus on probable harm that must be considered prior to the ideas and appeals that are also present. In the more formal wording of the logician, in coercion

> an arguer wants a respondent . . . to assent to a conclusion. To obtain R's assent, A presents him with premises which do not imply this conclusion, but which, by somehow threatening him, are designed to seem to R as if they did imply it.[25]

For example, if the head of a city agency tells his staffers that "You are free to work for whichever mayoral candidate you like, but you ought to remember the incumbent has been pretty good to us," the freedom that is implied in the first clause is effectively negated by the second. Even the least political of workers would realize that any campaigning done for the incumbent opponent might jeopardize his job. The possibility of making a decision based on the merits of the candidates and their proposals is foreclosed by the implied threat to the subordinate's livelihood.

The television networks and their staffs believed they faced the problem after Vice-President Spiro Agnew gave two speeches in November of 1969 that were sharply critical of television and print press coverage. Among other things, Agnew criticized the three networks for basing their reporting too extensively on the coasts, and not enough in America's "middle America." He also strongly criticized the "instant analysis" that followed the Nixon administration's explanations of Vietnam policy.[26] The most threatening comments, however, were those directed to the nation's networks. The regulation-sensitive broadcast industry professed shock that a spokesman for the president[27] would argue that control of the industry was falling into "fewer and fewer hands."[28]

Taken by themselves, the speeches contained some fair criticism. Indeed, a wide spectrum of journalistic and academic critics had made many of the same points for years. But the vehemence of the comments had hit a raw nerve. The key assets of any news source are its public credibility and institutional independence. The administration had been uncharacteristically bold in implying that both were in jeopardy. To broadcasters the speeches suggested that the lucrative federal licenses that television stations need in order to function were at stake. The threats were made even more ominous by the fact that others close to the administration—such as Office of Telecommunications Chairman Clay Whitehead and Supreme Court Associate Justice Lewis Powell—were voicing similar complaints to receptive audiences. In concert with Agnew, each advocated stronger monitoring of their content.[29] Many within the broadcasting field felt these combined attempts demonstrated that the administration was attempting to force the curtailment of unflattering news. Were these speeches about "fair play" and "letting viewers decide for themselves" simply the airing of complaints by a frustrated administration? Or were darker coercive motives at work? No less a figure than Walter Cronkite noted that " . . . this Administration . . . has conceived, planned, orchestrated and is now conducting a program to reduce the effectiveness of a free press, and its prime target is television."[30]

In fact, soon after Agnew's remarks CBS did end its policy of "instant analysis" of presidential speeches. If goading the networks to back off from their criticism was a goal of the administration, it had partially succeeded.

This example indicates how difficult it can be to separate coercive from noncoercive communication. As we noted at the beginning of this study, political power is inherently about the control of rewards and punishments. It is difficult to conceive of any extended piece of political discourse that does not include appeals to the hearer's sense of jeopardy. Such appeals may be considered an essential form of leverage. In intragovernmental communication these kinds of coercive power plays are common and expected. A Senate or House committee may seek information from a president under the threat of a subpoena to a cabinet member or agency head for noncompliance. Journalists may be "convinced" that it is in their best interests to give up a planned investigative article, if it becomes obvious that a "freeze out" brought on by noncooperative sources will make their work impossible. Legislators may find that their sponsorship and advocacy of one bill requires an exchange of support with colleagues who have different legislative priorities. In each case the grounds for defeat and triumph can be measured in personal as well as ideological terms.

## Deception

The idea of deception is so basic to the discussion of political persuasion that it is useful to approach it first by describing what it is not.

There can be little doubt that the intentional misrepresentation of information is unethical (although advocates of covert government activity may justify official lies, or defend a campaign of disinformation that is intended to confuse an enemy). But the threshold that separates the legitimate rhetorical construction of a reality from the falsification of it is no easier to locate than that which separates coercion from legitimate argument. Discussion of deception in politics is also further clouded by our uneasy awareness that politics operates on the same one-sided premise that governs the presentation of messages in fields such as advertising, public relations, and law. A common presumption that goes with advocacy is that one's obligations extend to providing the best possible case for only one side in a dispute. It is difficult to know when argumentation represents a legitimate delineation of roles, and when it involves deception based on the withholding of information. Most Americans are probably less certain than Kenneth Burke that such selective representation is not hypocritical:

> Imagine that you, as President, were about to put through Congress some measure that would strongly alienate some highly influential class. What would be the most natural way for you to present this matter to the public? Would you try, as far as is stylistically possible, to soften the effects of the blow? You would try to be as reassuring as possible.
>
> Imagine, on the other hand, that the public had been clamoring for such a measure, but you as President did not want to be so drastic. . . . In this case, you would try to put through a more moderate measure— but you would make up the difference stylistically by thundering about its startling scope. One could hardly call this hypocrisy; it is the normally prayerful use of language, to sharpen up the pointless and blunt the too sharply pointed.[31]

Language, notes Burke, is a "corrective" instrument. Its users cannot be condemned *ipso facto* for using it "artfully" to guide thought. In his view it is unrealistic to expect that language can be used to exactly correspond to a singular reality. Because man is an interactor, not a recorder, advocacy that is selective and idiomatic is to be expected. It is part of the human condition rather than indisputable evidence of deception.

In general, we think there are cases when rhetorical deception can be recognized, and when it should be condemned. But we also think that political lying is less common than is widely perceived.

There is one case we touched on at the beginning of this chapter, namely: that ordinary manifestations of pluralistic thought (i.e., as divides those for and those against prayer in public schools) are mistakenly forced into dualistic categories suggesting that only one side holds the truth. The corollary that follows from this view is that the other side is naive, or engaged in a bad faith deception. But the deeper reality is probably that the analyst has misperceived that nature of the controversy. It is axiomatic to politics that disputes cannot be invariably tied to the expectation that there must be true and false sides. Policy questions which deal with issues of merits, costs, and benefits necessarily provide for a plurality of conclusions. There may be a certain degree of psychological satisfaction to assert that one side in a dispute is bankrupt of good reasons, and that advocates representing it are engaged in a colossal form of deception. But in fact the more accurate view may well be that one's own individual investment precludes the empathy necessary to "see" the other side. Ralph K. White's study of North Vietnamese and American perceptions toward the Vietnamese struggle, for example, notes that both sides enhanced their own self-image: a fact that inhibited examining the conflict from each other's point of view. The construction of a "diabolical enemy-image," a "virile self-image," and "a moral self-image" was enough to build up an impenetrable facade of moral and rational certainty on each side.[32]

Another problematic concept in the labeling of deception resides in the very idea of political propaganda. Ominous connotations cling to this overworked phrase. It carries an enormous amount of negative weight. At times it is used as a synonym with lying and hypocrisy in politics: a convenient "put-down" label. It is common to describe one's political enemies as masters of deceptive and manipulative propaganda, and one's own discourse as far more fair and open. "The Russians propagandize, but we simply inform" represents a common but unreflective use of the term. What it ignores is the presence of highly refined forms of political and commercial propaganda (i.e., political and product advertising) which fuel virtually every nation's political and commercial life.

Part of the problem is that the very term connotes more than it denotes. The company that the term keeps, teaches us to dislike it. More often than not, *propaganda* is little more than a convenient net into which we can place all of our anxieties about the nature of political discourse. It stands for the vague sense of betrayal that comes with our sense that we have been victims of untruths and manipulation.

Carl Friedrich gets closer to its essence when he describes it in terms of the intentions of its users. The propagandist is "a person who hands out information in order to gain benefits, material or nonmaterial advantages, for himself or more typically for the group he is acting for."[33] The message involves an advocate with a financial or ideological interest in the success of the message—hardly an ominous or unique trait. Moreover, as Friedrich notes, it is too simple to prejudge propaganda as merely a collection of lies. "While lying may at times be a method of propagandists, it often is not."[34] Our point here is not to define so evocative a term as propaganda, but to point out that it is not unreasonable to conclude that propaganda may just be another form of advocacy, neither better nor worse than past forms of public persuasion.[35]

Are we left, therefore, to declare that we have no basis for assessing (and condemning) deceptive political discourse? Indeed no. The fact that many people mistakenly confuse pluralism in argument as evidence of callous lying should not lead us to the claim that there are no standards from which to assess deception. Political advocates do lie: less often, perhaps, than the conventional wisdom about political morality would lead us to believe. But often enough.

One kind of deception is that which is arguably sanctioned by national interests. The Eisenhower administration's denial that a spy plane had been shot down over the Soviet Union in 1960 was a bold but obvious attempt at deception. The president knew of the missions, since he had personally approved the use of the high-altitude plane. And he could hardly continue to deny the event in light of the fact that the captured pilot and wreckage were displayed for all to see on Soviet television.[36] John Kennedy's similar protests that no attempts were underway to overthrow Cuban leader Fidel Castro were also equally evident as deceptions. Eisenhower and Kennedy had the knowledge to tell the truth or give accurate information, but chose not to. In both cases no doubt each felt that their initial denials served a national security objective.

Similar claims by former Central Intelligence Agency Director Richard Helms, however, proved less convincing. In 1974 a variety of congressional and press studies made it increasingly evident that Helms had misled the Congress in explaining covert CIA actions. Members of Congress and reporters Seymour Hersh and Daniel Schorr received leaked information from former CIA operatives that left little doubt that Helms had deceived members of Congress engaged in oversight hearings. There was hard evidence that the organization had encouraged the overthrow and assassination of Chile's President Salvador Allende, had organized surveillance of members of the antiwar movement within the United States, and had ties to some of the Watergate burglars. Helms's earlier testimony before the Senate Foreign Relations Committee included a number of false denials. On America's role in overthrowing Chile's Allende, for example, Helms was explicit when asked questions by Senator Stuart Symington:

> Symington: Did you try in the Central Intelligence Agency to overthrow the government of Chile?
> Helms: No, sir.
> Symington: Did you have any money passed to the opponents of Allende?
> Helms: No, sir.[37]

The CIA's own information painted a different picture. In Schorr's words:

> He had denied passing money to Allende's opponents in Chile. He had denied any domestic spying. He had denied any pre-Watergate involvement with Howard Hunt. Now he blamed "misunderstood questions for previous contradictions," saying that he "had no intention of lying."[38]

Could Helms have *not* known what his agency was doing? It seems unlikely. Could he have felt that—by definition—covert acts cannot be communicated? Indeed. But members of Congress have security clearances for such information. A claim of exclusive rights to privacy on these actions could not stand against the Congress's preeminent right to oversight.

A larger problem represented by all of these examples is that a secret intelligence service is, by definition, a paradox in an open society. Lies are automatically a part of a clandestine organization's business. But they are lies nonetheless. One of the less savory dilemmas faced by governments in open societies is how the executive's penchant for covert activity against foreign powers can be squared with democratic ideals. If open societies have secrets, when does the public's alleged right to know end and the secrecy begin? What if the secrecy label is used to cover-up mistakes? If a public office is a trusteeship for the interests of the citizenry, when is it not in their interests to have access to information about government activities or administrative failures? The complexity of these questions defies glib and simple answers. The consideration of secrecy as a guise for deception must usually be considered on a case-by-case basis. What is apparent is that abuse of "national security" and "executive privilege" claims on information have left a residue of public cynicism.[39]

Another kind of deception goes beyond the rationale for the need for official secrets. These involve what can be called "bad faith" statements.[40] What makes this a broader concept in our view is that it implies a basic disregard or contempt for the integrity of the audience. A bad faith act violates the trust and respect that is implicit in most kinds of communication. The speaker engages in such communication cynically. Excessive promise-keeping, exaggerated appeals to fear, oversimplification of complex issues, the raising of false two-sided dichotomies, are forms of bad faith. All reflect a failure of the speaker to enter into dialogue with an audience on equal terms: to hear as well as assert, to risk at least as much as is asked of the audience, and to imply no more than is justified by arguments and evidence.

There are a number of bad faith ploys that not only deceive an audience, but also signal the speaker's fundamental contempt. One involves the stereotypical political art of appearing to be all things to all people. The speaker who wears attitudes and values in accordance to the sense of fashion that a particular audience has is engaging in an age-old form of deception. For him values and attitudes can be exploited for their convenience as strategic tools helpful in winning over audiences. "The hypocrite," notes Chaim Perelman, "gives the appearance of adopting a rule of conduct in agreement with that of others in order to avoid having to justify some action which he prefers and which he adopts in reality." In this way, he notes, "hypocrisy is the homage that vice pays to virtue. . . . "[41] The speaker's vice is his bad faith desire to win over an audience fraudulently by passing himself off as one of their own. Hearers are given false grounds for trust, and are asked to give more than they get in return.

Such were the origins of the downfall of Spiro Agnew in 1972. As vice-president, the former governor represented himself in the eulogistic image of the self-made man. Agnew made his vice-presidential career by preaching the silent majority's gospel of hard work, common decency, and law and order. As the son of Greek immigrants, he was the enactment of the American dream. But his plea of no contest to charges that years earlier he accepted illegal kickbacks proved to be too much. This defender of hard work and respect for the law was suddenly accused of illegal graft. His fall was at least partially attributable to what many perceived to be a gross misrepresentation of his values.

### Mystification

Another form of corruption to which political communication is vulnerable involves a different kind of deception. Mystification is more than omission or denial. It denotes the camouflaging of motives in language, sometimes cynically and sometimes naively. In our discussion of administrative rhetoric (see Chapter 5), we used the term in a broad sense. For Marx, and Carlyle, as Kenneth Burke has brilliantly pointed out, mystification was elucidated as a prime basis for the protection of class distinctions. Threads of status-protecting values that have been subtly woven into the fabric of the language provide a basis for mystification. Ideas that seem natural actually work to the benefit of the privileged and to the detriment of the poor. Religion as the "opium of the masses" was Marx's most infamous statement of the idea. Burke has noted that the German scholar and many others provide useful critiques of status-affirming justifications that treat ideas "as primary where they should have been treated as derivative."[42] Religion, in Marx's view, drained off the motive for social change by promising a better life in the hereafter.

In their most insidious political forms, mystifications appeal to eulogized values or ideas that essentially contradict the speaker's private beliefs. Such appeals are laid out in a thin veneer which barely covers private interests that would be unpalatable if known. We use the term here in this narrower sense. As a particular kind of deception, mystifying rhetoric involves the evoking of images and impressions that give listeners some basis for believing that they should defer to the superior wisdom or judgment of someone else. Mystification is not simply deception, but the manipulation of appeals in a respectable language that implies no self-gain. The political communicator exercises his own form of bad faith by couching private objectives in a rhetoric of high-minded public good. Even so abhorrent a policy as nineteenth-century American slavery could be successfully represented to slaves and slave owners alike as an institution of enlightenment:

> Taught by the master's efforts, by his care
> Fed, Clothed, protected many a patent year
> From trivial number now to millions grown
> With the white man's useful arts their own
> Industrious, docile, skilled in wood and field,
> To guide the plow, the sturdy axe to wield,
> The Negroes schooled by slavery embrace
> The highest portion of the Negro race. . .[43]

The very mystery and impenetrability of some forms of technical rhetoric may also establish dubious grounds for assent. Even simple numbers can have such an effect. Darrell Huff analyzes the potential impact of a campaign statement from the 1948 Dewey campaign (against Harry Truman) which seems to offer the illusion of precision —hence undeniability—but which in actuality signifies nothing. Part of the campaign statement said that "when Dewey was elected Governor in 1942, the minimum teacher's salary in some districts was as low as $900 a year. Today the school teachers in New York State enjoy the highest salaries in the world." After noting that Dewey appropriated $32 million for salaries, the statement concludes "As a result, the minimum salaries of teachers in New York City range from $2,500 to $5,325."[44] Huff notes what the casual listener might well miss:

Here you have a "before" of $900 and an "after" of $2,500 to $5,325, which sounds like an improvement indeed. But the small figure is the lowest salary in any rural district of the state, and the big one is the range in New York City alone.[45]

The use of these numbers represents more than a failure of reasoning. They supply the illusion of authenticity and expertise. Their subtle effect is to turn back the impulse to challenge, masking authority in an impressive display of precise mathematical comparisons.

Mystification does *not* depend on exact understanding of what is said, but on a more generalized impression that the listener has no grounds from which to challenge the speaker. In the techno-jargon common to medicine, physics, and other specialized areas there is the implicit suggestion that decisions that affect us might be best left to others (as when a doctor uses a Latinate word to describe his diagnosis of an ailment, and prescribes a drug with an equally impressive name for its treatment). Power and authority are communicated by impressions rather than full understanding.

Political mystifications play upon the credulity of audiences. Appeals used cannot seem to deny what a politician essentially is. But they frequently do. In his study of political demagogues in the early part of this century, Reinhard Luthin notes that most were hypocritical cultivating public personas that were fundamentally in conflict with private attitudes or activities. For example:

The demagogues, while preaching and posing as "men of the people," are not averse to "doing business" with the "interests" whom they blisteringly assail on the stump. While they make dramatic displays of distributing milk to the poor, they all too often in a sense—skim the cream off for themselves.[46]

To be sure, no public official is ever quite as simple as the cultivated imagery that is routinely offered to the public. The threshold that defines the corruption of the political process is when the public imagery conceals individual attitudes and investments that are at odds with public statements. It is perhaps a harmless charade for a member of Congress to misrepresent himself as a lover of music in the presence of an audience of musicians. But it is quite another matter when the same figure presents himself as an altruistic advocate for legislation from which he or close friends will receive financial gain. Such advocacy is dishonest because motives are misrepresented in what may well be important ideas and principles. Like deadly weapons concealed in a child's doll, the mystification uses a legitimate vehicle for illegitimate gain, eventually making even the most honored of objects suspect. Such deception erodes the whole idea of political discussion. Couched in the terms of religion, exploiting the sacred to do what is profane leaves a legacy of suspicion that is deep and lasting.

## Mystification by Redefinition

General semanticists have noted for decades that there is little to be gained by complaining about the "misuse" of language.[47] Language is a dynamic rather than static form of exchange. Dictionaries and grammarians notwithstanding, words and meanings change in nonuniform ways: not by plan or prescription, but by happenstance. Such changes can create new perspectives from which to look down on old topics. Because words and meanings are plastic, their everyday use as instruments of public discussion cannot be frozen in time.

And yet having said it, we still recognize that there are constructions which do impair our abilities to grasp the essentials of situations. It is one thing to extend an audience's understanding of an idea by evoking a term or a phrase in an insightfully new way. It is quite another to place the description of events in a fog of misused terms. Consider two examples. In a radio "fireside chat" in 1940 Franklin Roosevelt called on America to be the "arsenal for democracy."[48] The phrase was one of a number of suasive tools used by Roosevelt to prime American public opinion for entry into the European war as an ally to Britain and France. As an image it bridged two political necessities. One was to shape opinion on the importance of arms production (and the consumer sacrifices that would be necessary). The other necessity was to create a linkage between what was happening in Europe and American values. Far more pragmatic reasons could have been cited by Roosevelt. But it was not hypocritical to claim that the protection of Western European democracies was an honorable goal. Our arsenal could and did save those countries from permanent Nazi domination. In contrast, the similar military example we cited earlier—Ronald Reagan's 1983 radio address urging support for the MX "peacekeeper" missile—seems to involve a fundamental corruption of terms.[49] President Carter had also favored the program, but referred to it by its basic designation: the MX missile. President Reagan routinely added "peacekeeper" to its name. Though it can hardly be classified as a serious form of political malfeasance, the term stretches an idea beyond its reasonable limits. One can perhaps credibly argue that a strong military helps keep the peace or makes the world safe for democracy—two common phrases in the presidential lexicon. But there is a fundamental corruption to the essence of peace when it becomes part of the name of a nuclear missile. A missile is designed to destroy. It may be true that a *policy* of assured mutual destruction and general equity of arms may help discourage aggression. But a single type of missile can hardly qualify as an agency of peace.

George Orwell's *1984* is undoubtedly best known for its study of mystification by redefinition. Orwell's book was both a warning and a prophesy. The concentration of power and communication in modern states, he felt, could be easily misused, much to the detriment of the ordinary citizen's freedom. The fictitious "Oceania" not only centralized government, but the control and the wording of information as well. His description of "Vocabulary B" of the official "Newspeak" language suggests the most oppressive kind of mind control. The goal of the language was not only "to make all other forms of thought impossible," but to use euphemisms to cover up the fundamental venality of the state.[50] The book opens with its famous description of three slogans put forth by the "Ministry of Truth":

WAR IS PEACE
FREEDOM IS SLAVERY
IGNORANCE IS STRENGTH[51]

What Orwell described in 1948 had already come to pass with perverse efficiency in the Third Reich. Claus Mueller cites a number of Orwellian language regulations that were handed down to the German press from Hitler's government in the late 1930s. The following guidelines from the Office of the Press subverted thought by turning meaning on its ear. In the words of the office:

July 27, 1937: According to the new government, the term "propaganda" is a legally protected one, so to speak, and cannot be used in a derogatory sense. . . . In short, "propaganda" only if it serves us; "agitation" for those who are against us.

December 13, 1937: The urgent directive has been given that the term "League of Nations" can no longer be used by the German press as of today. This word no longer exists.

September 1, 1939: The word "war" has to be avoided in all news coverage and editorials. Germany is repulsing a Polish attack.

September 11, 1939: The word "courageous" can only be used for German soldiers.[52]

To conclude that Orwell's predictions about the rhetorical manipulation of attitudes has come true today is too simplistic. No era has had a monopoly on the corruption of meaning. Patterns of redefinition are as old as politics itself. What is apparent is that redefinition continues to be a form of rhetorical abuse, particularly when agencies and bureaucracies rank their public relations requirements higher than their public information objectives.

Military press briefings during the Vietnam War provide a modern case study. To some extent the entire enterprise was plagued with misinformation (i.e., regarding the ground war in Laos between 1964 and 1968, and later, the bombing over Cambodia). But it was primarily near the end of the Johnson administration that calculated disinformation—purposeful deception—became transparent. The credibility of the administration, the Pentagon, and field staff eroded in the face of what seemed like systematic attempts to cover up deaths, troop movements, and ARVN-American military objectives. A conscious strategy of redefinition emerged in briefings. Catchwords were wrenched loose from their usual contexts and given bizarre new meanings. Ordinary descriptive language was shunned. Technical terms were favored over more discursive forms. In routine press briefings napalm became "selective ordinance," bombing became "interdiction" or a "protective reaction strike," jails became "pacification centers," killing became "termination," and off-target bombs became "incontinent ordinance."[5 3] Irate over the vocal objections of the press at such constant attempts at redefinition, one military press officer lashed back, "You always write it's bombing, bombing, bombing. It's *not* bombing! It's air support."[5 4]

No amount of etymological juggling could establish a tradition of usage for such terms. They were used because of what they did *not* imply. By giving clinical operational meanings to events involving human misery of staggering proportions, they built up a facade of respectability that finally could not conceal the costly stalemate.

All jargons are prone to similar misuse. They may originate as specialized languages intended to lend precision to a narrowly focused subject area. But special terms may slowly become more expressive than instrumental, useful more for the image of competence that they suggest than what they specifically communicate. Such language frequently ends its useful life by functioning in what is essentially a prostituted role: serving the suasive interests of the user better than the informational needs of the audience.

## A FINAL THOUGHT

All of what has been said here may seem to confirm the view that politics is a lowly calling. We think it is not. The abuses we have cited are replicated in every form of structured setting: in the politics of business, law, the arts, and probably even among two authors sharing the burden of writing a book. Compared to the relative anonymity of most forms of organizational life, the exposure that normally comes with public service makes it likely that politicians will be among the *most* deserving of the public's trust. It is common for citizens to assume that their disagreement with a politician is a sign of the politician's moral weakness. As long as pluralism exerts contradictory demands, we must accept the fact that no one official can possibly assent to one "correct" position. Political leadership imposes the nearly impossible task of coaxing consensus out of conflict.

It is a gift to be able to function at the center of institutions which must serve diverse constituencies. Attempting to do it requires a search for common denominators that tax both the mind and soul. Those who honorably undertake public office deserve the forebearance of the rest of us. One doubts if many of even the strongest critics of American political life could begin to produce the energy and empathy required for public service. Most of us intuitively know that it is a far easier life to serve the interests of a comparatively small group of company stockholders, professional colleagues, clients, or readers, than to serve a diverse constituency whose individual members identify with specialized rather than unitary goals. It is fairly common to hear reporters, campaign consultants, and constituents express their admiration for individual political leaders. No one says much that is positive about them in the aggregate. This fact should be a clue to us that our political attitudes are often better reflections of our particular circumstances than our collective ideals.

There is nothing new in this. The nation's political institutions are deliberately structured so that many who hold elective office are serving interests other than our own. The intention that the designers of the Constitution had in mind was to take the efficiency out of government, while at the same time protecting the rights of a multitude of conflicting factions. George Washington was to be no king in the European model. He was to have less power than is presently the case for his modern predecessors. His limited formal role was proof of the willingness of the nation's inventors to let debate within Congress and between the branches of state mediate conflict. The diffusion of power that defines nearly every form of government, from Washington, D.C. down to the local town council—at its best—still requires the same respect for shared power and the opportunity of public debate. The structure, in short, replaces preemptory rule with rule that flows from agreements.

If there are risks to this system today, we think that the most serious is that many citizens no longer equate the sound of political talk with the sound of a machine at work. In our time the inherently discordant nature of public dispute is often mistaken as a sign of the corruption or failure in politics. Today political conflict falls too painfully on the ear. In truth, the more ominous sign of a state in trouble is when governance occurs in silence, when rhetoric is preempted by an enforced or manipulated consensus. The greatest threat to an open society is not from the friction of dispute, but from neglect of the public forum. Our concern is that audiences and rhetors will find shorter and more surreptitious routes to their own objectives. In the long run a nation is well served when its civil life is sustained by contentious advocates. It is endangered when they have found means to power that are more efficient than those based on public communication.

## NOTES

1. John Dewey, *The Public and Its Problems* (Chicago: Swallow Press, 1954), p. 110.

2. Taylor quoted in David Wise, *The Politics of Lying: Government Deception, Secrecy, and Power* (New York: Random House, 1973), p. 53.

3. Kenneth Burke, *The Philosophy of Literary Form*, 3rd ed. (Berkeley, Calif.: University of California, 1973), p. 191.

4. John Bunzel, *Anti-Politics in America* (New York: Vintage, 1970), p. 7.

5. Ronald Reagan, Radio Address to the Nation, July 16, 1983, in *Weekly Compilation of Presidential Documents*, vol. 19, July 25, 1983, p. 1,008.

6. See Stephen Toulmin, *The Uses of Argument* (Cambridge, Eng.: Cambridge University, 1964), pp. 146-69.

7. For similar examples see Howell Raines, "Reagan, in Speeches, Doesn't Let the Truth Spoil a Good Anecdote or Effective Symbol," *New York Times*, October 19, 1980, p. 38.

8. For a slightly dated but complete study of demagogues see Reinhard Luthin, *American Demagogues* (Boston: Beacon, 1954).

9. John Dewey and Walter Lippmann remain as two important exceptions. See Dewey, *The Public and Its Problems*, and Lippmann, *The Good Society* (New York: Grosset and Dunlap, 1943) and *The Public Philosophy* (Boston: Little, Brown, 1955).

10. For a discussion of the relationship between the Watergate break-in and the 1972 elections see Theodore H. White, *The Making of the President 1972* (New York: Atheneum, 1973), pp. 297-98.

11. Claus Mueller, *The Politics of Communication* (New York: Oxford, 1973), p. 179.

12. Norman H. Nie, Sidney Verba, and John R. Petrocik, *The Changing American Voter*, enlarged ed. (Cambridge, Mass.: Harvard University, 1979), p. 278.

13. A telling account of the administration's dilemma is given by Hamilton Jordan in *Crisis: The Last Year of the Carter Presidency* (New York: Putnam, 1982).

14. Dewey, *The Public and Its Problems*, p. 86.

15. Theodore H. White, *Breach of Faith: The Fall of Richard Nixon* (New York: Dell, 1975), p. 426.

16. Doris Kearns, *Lyndon Johnson and the American Dream* (New York: Signet, 1976), pp. 324-50.

17. Classic studies on television and politics include Newton N. Minow, John Bartlow Martin, and Lee M. Mitchell, *Presidential Television* (New York: Basic, 1973); Sig Mickelson, *The Electric Mirror: Politics in an Age of Television* (New York: Dodd and Mead, 1972); Kurt and Gladys Lang, *Politics and Television* (New York: Quadrangle, 1968); and Edwin Diamond, *The Tin Kazoo: Television, Politics and the News* (Cambridge, Mass.: MIT Press, 1975).

18. The extent to which conventions are scripted is revealed in Tim Crouse, *The Boys on the Bus* (New York: Ballantine, 1972), pp. 176-77.

19. Richard Nixon, *Six Crises* (New York: Pyramid, 1968), p. 301.

20. Ibid., pp. 472-80.

21. Theodore Sorensen, *Kennedy* (New York: Harper and Row, 1965), p. 240.

22. Sidney Blumenthal, "Marketing the President," *New York Times Magazine*, September 13, 1981, pp. 43, 110, 112, 114.

23. This is a central point in the scholarship of Murray Edelman. See, for example, his *Politics as Symbolic Action* (Chicago: Markham, 1971), pp. 31-52, and *The Symbolic Uses of Politics* (Urbana, Ill.: University of Illinois, 1967), pp. 22-43.

24. Transcript of the presidential debate between Jimmy Carter and Ronald Reagan in Cleveland, Ohio, October 28, 1980, *New York Times*, October 30, 1980, p. B19.

25. Dwight Van de Vate, Jr., "The Appeal to Force," *Philosophy and Rhetoric* 8 (Winter 1975): 43.

26. Spiro T. Agnew, *Frankly Speaking* (Washington, D.C.: Public Affairs Press, 1970), pp. 62-85.

27. Presidential assistant Patrick Buchanan wrote Agnew's speeches with the president's full knowledge. See William Safire, *Before the Fall* (New York: Doubleday, 1975), p. 352.

28. Agnew, *Frankly Speaking*, p. 79.

29. Marvin Barrett, ed., *The Politics of Broadcasting, 1971-1972* (New York: Thomas Crowell, 1973), pp. 39-48.

30. Cronkite quoted in ibid., p. 49.

31. Kenneth Burke, *A Grammar of Motives* (New York: Prentice-Hall, 1954), p. 393.

32. Ralph K. White, "Misperception and the Vietnam War," *The Journal of Social Issues* 22 (July 1966): 1-156.

33. Carl J. Friedrich, *The Pathology of Politics* (New York: Harper and Row, 1972), p. 193.

34. Ibid., p. 176.

35. For a broader and more disturbing description of propaganda see Jacques Ellul, *Propaganda: The Formation of Men's Attitudes*, trans. Konrad Kellen and Jean Lerner (New York: Vintage, 1973), pp. 3-32.

36. Wise, *Politics of Lying*, p. 34.

37. John M. Orman, *Presidential Secrecy and Deception: Beyond the Power to Persuade* (Westport, Conn.: Greenwood Press, 1980), p. 138.

38. Daniel Schorr, *Clearing the Air* (New York: Berkley, 1978), p. 143.

39. This problem is common in many Western nations where there is a presumption in favor of "free flow of information." For a study of British government deception, and the misuse of Britain's Official Secrets Act, see James Margach, *The Abuse of Power* (London: W. H. Allen, 1978), pp. 115-84.

40. The term is Chaim Perelman's and L. Olbrechts-Tyteca's in *The New Rhetoric: A Treatise on Argumentation*, trans. John Wilkinson and Purcell Weaver (Notre Dame, Ind.: University of Notre Dame, 1969), pp. 200-1.

41. Ibid., p. 199.

42. Kenneth Burke, *A Rhetoric of Motives* (New York: Prentice-Hall, 1953), p. 104.

43. William J. Grayson, "The Hireling and the Slave," in *Slavery Defended: the Views of the Old South*, ed. Eric L. McKitrick (Englewood Cliffs, N.J.: Spectrum, 1963), pp. 66-67.

44. Darrell Huff, *How to Lie with Statistics* (New York: Norton, 1954), p. 85.

45. Ibid., p. 85.

46. Luthin, *American Demagogues*, p. 308.

47. For a summary of this view see John C. Condon, Jr., *Semantics and Communication*, 2nd ed. (New York: Macmillan, 1975), pp. 33-53.

48. Franklin D. Roosevelt, Radio Address, Washington, D.C., December 29, 1940, in *Contemporary Forum: American Speeches on Twentieth-Century Issues*, ed. Ernest J. Wrage and Barnet Baskerville (New York: Harper and Brothers, 1962), 246-54.

49. Reagan, Radio Address to the Nation, July 16, 1983, p. 1008; and Reagan, Remarks to the 65th Annual Convention of the American Legion, Seattle, Washington, August 23, 1983, in *Weekly Compilation of Presidential Documents*, vol. 19, August 26; 1983, pp. 1,160-61.

50. George Orwell, *1984* (New York: Signet, 1961), pp. 246-56.

51. Ibid., p. 7.

52. Quoted in Mueller, *Politics of Communication*, pp. 31-32.

53. Quoted in Howard Kahane, *Logic and Contemporary Rhetoric*, 3rd ed. (Belmont, Calif.: Wadsworth, 1980), p. 127.

54. Ibid., p. 128. See also David L. Altheide and John M. Johnson, *Bureaucratic Propaganda* (Boston: Allyn and Bacon, 1980), pp. 210-27.

# Index

# About the Authors

**Robert Denton** has degrees in political science and communication from Wake Forest University and Purdue University. He teaches and writes in the areas of political science, mass media, advertising, and contemporary rhetorical theory. Denton is the author of a book on the presidency and co-author of a book on persuasion and social movements. In addition, he has published articles in the fields of political science, advertising, and communication. Denton is currently an assistant professor in the Department of Communication Studies at Northern Illinois University.

**Gary Woodward** has degrees in communication and rhetorical theory from California State University at Sacramento and the University of Pittsburgh. He has taught in England as well as in the United States. He teaches and writes in the areas of politics, the mass media, and contemporary issues. In addition, he has published articles in the areas of communication and rhetorical theory. Woodward is currently an associate professor in the Department of Speech Communication and Theatre Arts at Trenton State College.